FIRERAISERS, FREAKS, AND FIENDS

Obsessive Arsonists in
the California Foothills

Ed Nordskog

Copyright © 2013 by Ed Nordskog

All rights reserved.

ISBN: 1482327791
ISBN-13: 9781482327793
Library of Congress Control Number: 2013902223
CreateSpace Independent Publishing Platform,
North Charleston, South Carolina

ED NORDSKOG

Cover Art for "Fireraisers, Freaks and Fiends"

Readers will note the dramatic cover art of this book. It was created by the duo Glen Orbik and Laurel Blechman, artists from the Los Angeles area. Their work can be found at www.orbikart.com

I discovered their work in an old bookshop in West Los Angeles in 2011 where I spotted an early '60s detective noir print on the wall. Below it was a trashy looking crime novel bearing the same design. I loved the look and feel of the art, and knew it was what I was seeking for my own book. The bookshop owner directed me to the artists of the print, Glen and Laurel, and said that among other things; they create book covers with that old-school late '50s, early '60s look and feel. I had written my first book by then and was looking for the right kind of cover art to represent my stories.

I contacted Glen and Laurel, and after much pleading, they agreed to do my cover. I gave them a synopsis of my book *'Torchered' Minds: Case histories of notorious serial arsonists* and told them what I envisioned my serial arsonist to look like. Most serial arsonists are lone offenders who wander the streets and alleys at night and have serious mental health issues. I didn't want the traditional sneering, evil arsonist for this cover as it wasn't a true representation of the most common subtype of serial arsonist. Glen and Laurel gave me a sketch and nailed the idea on their first attempt. They chose the color scheme, and I was blown away with the results. I have had dozens of compliments on the "firebug" depicted on the cover art for '*Torchered' Minds*."

For the *Fireraisers* cover, I was a bit more particular as the arsonists depicted in this book are in fact the evil, sneering, diabolical, obsessive, maniacal stalkers and fiends who have often been portrayed in arson lore. These are the real maniacs and madmen who steal people's lives, homes, and senses of security. They haunt and torment their victims for years after their dastardly attacks—they are true boogeymen.

The cover art for this book is a composite of several victims and players who are described in these true stories. The Gypsy shop setting fits perfectly, as there are similar crimes in this book and the sinister image reflected in the crystal ball, along with the alarmed Gypsy, are the only warnings to an impending firebomb attack. The intended victim, a vibrant beautiful woman, is also a composite of many of the victims. She is simply an innocent person trying to leave a troubled past, who happens upon a fortune-teller. As she is peering intently into the crystal ball, she looks for better days and a happier life ahead. She is so absorbed in her yearning and hopefulness that she is oblivious to the shadowy past that has stalked her to this place and time.

Evil incendiary acts exactly like this brought me into contact with all of the victims, suspects, and detectives in this book. This dramatic cover art is exactly as dramatic as the events described in this book.

Reviews of "Torchered Minds" by Ed Nordskog

"TORCHERED MINDS is the definitive work on the crime of arson. Not only does it reveal encyclopedic knowledge of the subject, this book also reveals the Investigator's mind and "thinking like a cop." Crime writers seeking case histories, statistics, and a way into the criminal mind can start and end here. TORCHERED MINDS delivers much more than it promises, it takes you to the smoking scene of the crime, wearing the shoes of the Investigator."

(rated 5 stars out of 5)

– **Elaine Ash,** *Crime Editor*

"The title and cover-a throbbing orange illustration of an old-fashioned fire bug…the text, while popping with lurid details, consists of sober case histories"

– **Gale Holland,** *Los Angeles Times*

"I've just finished reading THE book. You did a remarkable job"

– **Investigator Chris Vallerga,** *Cal Fire, Retired.*

"I thought this was a first class book on the subject...this reflects the actuality of the fire scene and my thoughts on the reality on the motivations and the techniques used...

(rated 5 stars out of 5)

– **SaxonX,** *reviewer on www.librarything.com*

"I've read it and I'm quite impressed with your cogent and thoughtful treatment of the subject."

– **Professor Steve Edwards,** *Phd.; Oklahoma State University; Certified Fire/Explosion Investigator*

"I started reading it, and had a hard time putting it down. A well-written study on a fascinating subject"

– **Deputy District Attorney Susan Schwartz,** *Los Angeles District Attorney*

"A thorough and comprehensive examination of an area of crime that has not received the attention it deserves. Detective Nordskog provides a wonderfully-written master class into this insidious offence"

– **Detective Senior Constable Jeff Stinton,** *New South Wales Police, Australia*

"What an awesome book"

– **Detective Michael Digby;** *Los Angeles Sheriff's Arson/Explosives Detail*

Reviews Of "Torchered Minds" By Ed Nordskog

"For any serious arson investigator this book is a must-read. This is not just a recitation of war stories; each case has an "investigator's analysis" that makes the book such an exceptional resource. Ed carefully dissects each case to examine what worked and what didn't work in the investigation. He then provides a comprehensive examination of the known facts and evidence in the cases, exposing and refuting the gross inaccuracy of long-held assumptions about serial arsonists. Anyone who investigates or prosecutes arson cases should have this book in their library."

– **Deputy District Attorney Sue Wilson,** *Sacramento County; Past President of Sac-Sierra Regional Arson Task Force*

"Vivid portraits of famous cases as well as invaluable observations from the author's own case files"

– ashedit.wordpress.com

"I really enjoyed it. You did a great job of putting it together. As far as accuracy, you covered it correctly.

– **Detective Rich Edwards,** *L.A. Sheriffs, Retired. One of the lead investigators in the John Orr serial arson investigation.*

"By all sources, Detective Nordskog employs just the facts, and only the facts in Torchered Minds. In the past, information on the events pushing so-called serial arsonists to light fires has been incomplete, if not erroneous, based on myths and undocumented accounts. Nordskog dives into the who, the what, and how serial arsonists behave like they do. From the prolific serial arsonists such as John Orr, Paul Keller, and Thomas Sweatt, to those who have the "hero syndrome", and to the female arsonists, there is no fiction in the actions of these people or in Torchered Minds. From being responsible for multiple fires and even in some incidents, multiple deaths the world of the serial arsonist is explored here, like no other. Documented in this book are arsonists from around the globe, from this century and the past, and with so many different motivational factors, but also with common threads. Nordskog has the unique ability to blend his investigative experiences with other arson investigators' experiences, to present his analysis in a well written, factual document. Anyone who has any responsibility for the investigation and/or the prosecution of fires has to have <u>Torchered Minds</u> in their reference library. This book is an excellent added tool in the investigator's tool box. In the end, Nordskog provides a candid look into what investigators should be doing to solve cases involving serial arsonists: thorough documentation of every fire; good old fashion police work (knocking on doors and questioning people); supplemented with forensic evidence. <u>Torchered Minds</u> is a must read for anyone associated with a fire or any other type of a criminal investigation."

– Supervising Arson and Bomb Investigator Joe Konefal,
California State Fire Marshal, Retired.

"Torchered" Minds by Ed Nordskog is a refreshingly frank and candid study of a class of particularly dangerous criminals – the serial arsonists. In the unvarnished language of a tremendously experienced arson detective ... a wide variety of cases are examined (via case studies) and then analyzed. The cases include many in which Det. Nordskog participated, not as an armchair critic, but in the streets pursuing clues and hunting the perpetrators down. In doing so, he punches some well-deserved holes in common conceptions about serial fire-setters and their motives, profiles (and profilers) and statistics.

Nordskog pulls no punches when it comes to assessing the failures of detecting arson, administering "justice" (to both juvenile and adult offenders), reliance on self-proclaimed experts offering profiles and advice based on limited data and experience,

Reviews Of "Torchered Minds" By Ed Nordskog

statistics of fire and arson occurrences, and management of investigations. He offers some very sound advice on improving the detection and solution of arson – be it serial or "one-offs".

This is a book that should be read by every fire/arson investigator – whether from the police or fire "side", by every fire or police chief (and all those making command or management decisions), and by every prosecutor and "social worker" making decisions about suspected fire-setters."

– **Dr. John DeHaan,** *author "Kirk's Fire Investigation"*
as reviewed in the "California Association of Criminalists News;
Second Quarter 2013"

Find a complete list of reviews of the book "Torchered Minds" on www.torcheredminds.com

Dedication Page

This book is dedicated to my family, who for the past twenty-five years put up with my bizarre work hours, missed family events, the constant buzz of the pager or phone in the middle of the night, and the heavy smell of smoke and sometimes death on my clothes as I returned from work each day. I would not have survived without your love and support. I love you all.

This book is also dedicated to Albert Artsvelyan. Albert immigrated to this country with his wife Anahit, raised two beautiful daughters, and built a career, a life, and a home. His only fault was in happening to move into a home next to the most evil man I have ever met, who for no reason whatsoever repeatedly poisoned their dog and tried to murder them all by fire in the dead of night as they slept. Albert was able to save his family from a horrific death, only to have his home burned that night and again three months later by the same monster. For the next four years, Albert and his family were victimized and vilified over and over again by an inept legal system and despicable attorneys. Four years after their neighbor attempted to murder them, the Artsvelyans finally got justice. Throughout this ordeal, Albert continued to place his trust in the detectives and prosecutors helping him. He also continued to embrace his new country and pursue the American dream by rebuilding his family and life while fighting for his justice. Albert, you are a true hero and have my lasting respect, sir.

Finally, this book is dedicated to those who mentored me during my years in law enforcement. These gifted people took the time out of their lives to impart their wisdom, experience, friendship, knowledge, and work ethics to an up-and-coming, eager detective. A personal thanks to Erle Steigauf and Dr. Richard Shigley who kept me on the right path in college. Many thanks to Det. Bob Papini, Sgt. Jack Ferguson, and Lt. Jack Ewell who were my patrol mentors; Sgt. Mike Forst, and Sgt. Joe Holmes who trained me to be a detective; Sgt. Ed Huffman, Lt. Martin Rodriguez, and Det. Tony Shapiro who introduced me to the dope world and the murky skills of undercover work; Senior Special Agent Ron Michel (NICB) who showed me the insurance fraud game; and finally Inv. Joe Konefal, Det. Don Powell, Det. Rich Edwards, and Sgt. John Ament who taught me the black art of arson investigation.

Acknowledgements:

The following detectives, investigators, special agents, analysts, and forensic experts provided their stories, cases, insights, experiences, and assistance to this author in amassing these case histories. I have worked with many as partners, processed crime scenes with some, stood alongside several in courtroom battles, and shared a beverage or two with others who only wanted their stories told. These people have put their lives into their case work, and I appreciate their dedication and professionalism.

Det. Mike Digby, Det. Mike Cofield, Det. Rob Harris, Det. Cindy Valencia, Det. Rick Velazquez, Det. Dana Duncan, Det. Marcus Friedemann, Det. Mike Staley, Det. Rich Edwards, Det. Ron Ablott, Det. Sgt. Don Shively, Det. Sgt. Mike Costleigh, Det. Sgt. Derek Yoshino, Det. Sgt. Craig Anderson, Det. Sgt. Joe Acevedo, Det. Sgt. Gene Leslie, Lt. Julio Salcido, Det. Sgt. John Ament, Det. Sgt. Pat Tapia, Det. Sgt. Henry Saucedo, Captain Chuck Antuna, Det. Todd Anderson, Det. Mike Valento, Det. Mark Lillienfeld, Det. Ty Labbe, Det. George Elwell, Senior Criminalist Phil Teramoto, Senior Criminalist Bob Keil, Senior Criminalist Joseph Cavaleri, Senior Criminalist Steve Phillips, Senior Criminalist Vickie Clawson, Senior Criminalist Eric Wahoske, Senior Photographer Mike Havstad, Chief Photographer John Shaw, Dr. John DeHaan, Dr. Dian Williams, Special Agent Dan Heenan, Supervising Investigator Joe Konefal, Supervising Investigator Greg Smith, Supervising Investigator

Jim Allen, Investigator Tom Fee, Investigator Chris Vallerga, Investigator Brice Trask, Deputy Chief Alan Carlson, Investigator John Madden, Investigator Scott Hall, Investigator Christine Saqui, Investigator Alan Campbell, Chief Keith Mashburn, Captain Tom Oldag, Chief John Graham, Chief John Kabala, Chief Louis Ford, Det. Ken Schiffner, Investigator David Liske, Investigator Tim Crass, Investigator Dan Gaytan, Investigator Ron Huxman, Lt. Randy Litchfield, Crime Analyst Elva Outlaw, and Historical Researcher Mike Fratantoni.

The following prosecutors have impacted many of the difficult cases in this book and have dedicated their lives to seeing that the victims get their well-deserved justice: Deputy District Attorney Sean Carney, Deputy District Attorney Phil Stirling, Deputy District Attorney Darren Levine, Deputy District Attorney Emily Chang, Deputy District Attorney Renee Rose, Deputy District Attorney Sue Wilson, Deputy District Attorney Susan Schwartz, Deputy District Attorney Marion Thompson, Deputy District Attorney Beth Silverman, Deputy District Attorney Valerie Aellene-Rocha, Deputy District Attorney Michael Blake, Deputy District Attorney Ron Smalstig, and Supervising Deputy District Attorney Bill Hodgman. These people are truly courtroom warriors and consummate professionals.

I also want to acknowledge my various unit commanders in the Los Angeles Sheriff's Arson/Bomb Squad who have allowed me the resources, training, backing, and freedom to pursue my cases on my terms. Many thanks to Commander Tom Spencer, Commander Bob Olmsted, Captain John Stedman, Lieutenant Bill Dunn, Lieutenant Mike Connolly, Lieutenant Larry Lincoln, and Sgt. Gary Morgan.

THE LASD ARSON BOMB SQUAD

Since 1985 I've been with the Los Angeles Sheriff's Department. It is the largest sheriff's department in the world and the fourth largest local law enforcement agency in the world, employing over nine thousand sworn deputy sheriffs. They patrol over 80 cities and county areas in the sprawling neighborhoods that surround the city of Los Angeles. Over six million people live in the sheriff's jurisdiction, an area that encompasses pleasant suburbia, gritty urban neighborhoods, beach cities including Malibu and Marina Del Rey, entertainment hot spots including West Hollywood and Universal Studios, and the numerous wealthy enclaves scattered throughout the hills. The sheriffs also patrol massive deserts, a vast foothill region, a thick ring of coastal mountains, and even islands off the coast.

Like all LASD deputies, I started with a stint in the sprawling jail system before moving to a patrol station in the Watts-Compton area. I made Detective in 1990 and moved through a variety of jobs, including plainclothes and undercover work investigating auto theft, property crimes, robbery and assaults, gangs, major crimes, and major fraud-related cases. During this time I worked on every type of criminal case there is, from a simple car burglar to vice, bank robberies, organized crime, sexual assaults, murder-for-hire stings, and homicide. I was promoted to the narcotics bureau where, among other things, I learned that drugs (legal and illegal) were to be the common underlying factor of every single crime I would ever investigate during my career. The narcotics bureau was an ongoing head rush of street buys, reverses, rip-offs, sting operations, surveillances, buy-bust operations, and even getting into military gear and combing the nearby mountains all summer with Green Berets and Navy Seals, looking for heavily-armed marijuana growers. The most intense cops I ever met were the Narcs.

In 1997 I was promoted to one of the senior detective units in the department, the Arson-Explosives Detail (Bomb Squad). This unit consists of twenty-two full-time arson and bomb detectives and is one of the highest paid and trained units in the agency. On a yearly basis, each of us investigates between 90 and 110 fire scenes, and as a unit we respond to about 400 bomb calls. We are one of the largest and busiest arson/bomb units in the world. We supply arson and bomb support to all the cities in the Los Angeles basin and have assisted agencies up and down the state and across state lines. We are involved actively with the FBI and ATF with bomb and explosive training, operational support, and major event support. Due to our high profile and unique duties, the unit is staffed with some of the most intelligent and skilled detectives in the world.

The greatest gift our department gives all of its investigators is the autonomy to conduct investigations at our own discretion. The investigator has full control of his case, and he lives and dies with it. It is one of the few agencies left in the world where the bosses pay us, train us to be experts, and then turn us loose without dictating how to run a case. It is probably why we enjoy a very strong reputation in the courts and law enforcement world and maintain one of the higher solve-rates in the arson business. I thank the LASD command staff for allowing us to operate in this manner.

The Bad Guys

Study carefully the bad guys in this book. I am giving you an inside look at very unique and weird investigations that the average cop doesn't often get to see and most civilians (unless they are victims) can't even contemplate.

Please note the incredible similarities between the suspects described here, even though their cases are years and half a state apart from each other. All of the arsonist subtypes are represented and discussed through these case histories. A few other bizarre associates will be thrown in for good measure. You will be astounded by how many of these bad guys share similar backgrounds, family issues, medical histories, and deviant behaviors. Note how many of these bad guys are paranoid schizophrenics; see how many have trouble sleeping, are addicted to any number of prescription medications, have frequent migraines, or are battling with unseen demons or voices in their heads. Marvel at how many are voyeurs, creepers, prowlers, burglars, and thieves. See how many have pulled fire alarms, abused animals, called in false emergencies, and committed untold numbers of window smashes, tire slashings, and other acts of vandalism before they began committing arsons.

Notice how many of the really colorful bad guys have built completely fake personas, portraying themselves as heroes, secret agents, undercover operators, or cops and firemen—each one a lie.

See how many of these men are cowards and wimps, most often attacking the elderly, the sick, the very young, women, and even small animals. If you do all of this, you will be doing what any good detective is doing—behavior analysis, or more popularly, criminal profiling. I am a strong proponent of profiling events, actions, and crime scenes with the sole purpose of learning all I can about a particular offender.

We in the detective/investigation profession really enjoy our bad guys. Our professional lives and reputations are made on the quality and quantity of the bad guys we catch. Without them we would be nothing. We don't enjoy their crimes, and we are outraged by their actions, but if the truth be told, we need them. We love to chase them, catch them, and hold them responsible for every dirty deed they have ever done. And if ever comes a day when we are too tired or a little too busy with other business, we just have to look into the faces of our victims to be reinvigorated, to get our blood boiling, and to get back on the trail of the bad guys.

Definitions

Fireraiser – the British term for Arson; somebody who deliberately starts fires – *Macmillan Dictionary*

In the early summer of 2004, I was sitting at a bar in Glynco, Georgia, just off the campus of the Federal Law Enforcement Training Center (FLETC) which, among other courses, housed the Alcohol, Tobacco and Firearms (ATF) Advanced Arson Investigation Course. All of the students were long-time arson investigators from around the nation and the world, and each had at least a hundred fire investigations under his or her belt. One of my fellow students in the course was a Divisional Officer from the esteemed London Fire Brigade. As is the case in any sort of school like this, the students were sharing stories of their cases and investigations over a few cocktails. I had just recounted a serial arson case I was in the midst of in Los Angeles when the Divisional Officer turned to me, raised his glass of gin, and said, "Congratulations mate. You've got yourself a fireraiser." I later figured out that the term was a bit of slang—the British/Scottish equivalent of firebug, pyro, or torch. I hadn't heard that one before…I kinda liked it.

Freak – a seemingly capricious action or event; one that is markedly unusual or abnormal; a person who is obsessed with something – *Merriam-Webster Dictionary*

Fiend – devil, demon-person of great wickedness or maliciousness – *Merriam-Webster Dictionary*

Contents:

Foreword *by Detective Michael Digby*	xxiii
Chasing Fireraisers, Freaks and Fiends	xxvii
Prologue	xxix
1. Mission Men	**1**
JPL	2
Burbank Studios	14
Secret Agent Man	25
Rosemead High School	47
2. Serial Psychos	**57**
Doc Hallman	58
Norman Ralph Henderson	71
A Secret Life	79
Sunset Strip-Gypsies, Marijuana, and the Hollywood Fire Devil	94
The Lion that Roared	98
El Dorado County Arsonist	108
Aljuboori	131

3. Whackjobs and Wildmen	**137**
Pro Me Thius- Greek God of Fire	137
Tevin the Demon	142
James Patti	150
Justice for a Buddy	162
Nate the Nut	173
The Devil Next Door	198
Weather Watchers	210
4. Wannabes and Weirdos	**233**
(Nordskog Syndrome)	235
McNeil	237
Sparky the Fire Dog	262
Brock	270
Johnny on the Spot	273
The Poser	308
Alien Head Guy	314
5. Mad Men	**321**
Woodwardia Fire	321
Chang Chinglan	325
Gary Glazier	333
Grail Perkins	387
Patrick Wilson	401
Kevin Patten	417
6. Isolated Idiots	**427**
Jason's dead	427
Carrie and Big Ray	434
Stalking the Badge	443
Strange but True: Zombie Man	462
Selected Bibliography	**473**

Foreword

The sun had yet to rise as I switched on the morning news. The weather forecast called for afternoon temperatures to reach the mid-90s, which meant that even for a summer day in Los Angeles, it'd be a scorcher. But it was a news story briefly mentioned between tales of Hollywood celebrity nonsense that caught my attention. An apartment fire had occurred and a small child had died. The significance of this event would mark the beginning of my new career.

I had prepared myself for this, my first day as an arson detective for the Los Angeles County Sheriff's Department Arson-Explosives Detail, with the understanding that it would be months, if not years, before I would achieve any semblance of expertise. To get there, I would work alongside detectives with years of experience and thousands of fire investigations under their collective belt. The mere four weeks of fire investigation training that I had completed qualified me for nothing more than observation—and learning. And so, on that first day, I would do just that. I was teamed up with more seasoned and experienced arson detectives, one of whom was Ed Nordskog.

I would come to spend hours in the hot and filthy ruins of fire scenes; sifting through debris, smelling for accelerants, searching for evidence, and learning how to "read" fire patterns, find evidence of incendiarism, and gather the evidence necessary to prosecute arsonists. Like my colleagues, I would attend

Firaisers, Freaks, And Fiends

several training courses, watch surveillance videos of arsonists in action, and examine more than a thousand fire scenes. As my arson-investigative experience grew, I would even spend many hours speaking with arsonists themselves, learning their behavior, understanding their motivations, and privately wondering how or where it all went so terribly wrong for them. But that's how I really learned the job—comparing my fire scene observations with the arsonists own words. One thing I learned quickly, interviewing an arsonist is unlike any other interview. Nothing, no training course and no level of experience, can adequately prepare you for a conversation with someone who is equal parts intelligent, articulate, diabolical, scheming, and absolutely crazy. But all of this would come months and even years in my future.

On that day, my first task in my newly-chosen career would be to assist homicide detectives, coroner's investigators, and arson-explosives detectives as they examined the scene of a deliberately-set fire in a two-story home that resulted in the death of an infant sleeping in his upstairs bedroom. The same news story I'd heard a few hours earlier on the TV. Whoever had committed this crime had done so knowing that the only escape route from the child's room would be covered in a wall of flames within minutes. As I was to learn, this fire scene was fairly straightforward—there was evidence of a poured accelerant, fire patterns that led from the point of origin, and the burned remains of an infant male.

I didn't know it at the time, but my day was just beginning. Within hours, Nordskog and I would be assigned to another fire death scene, an hour north of Los Angeles. A mother had set fire to her home with the intention of asphyxiating her five children. The resulting fire killed four of her children in yet another cowardly and evil act. The mother survived and would later be rewarded with a trip to California's Death Row for her efforts.

As tragic as these events were, soon enough they would become the norm for me. Just another soon-to-be-forgotten case reduced to a thick binder labeled "Big Pines," "Edwards Grocery," or "Larsen Fire." These casebooks fill cabinets and shelves, covering almost any flat surface, and giving most squad rooms all the charm and appeal of a hoarder's garage—except with the added heady stench of smoke-stained fire jackets, weathered gasoline, and coffee. But every now and then, a case develops that you *never* stop thinking about. Not even after the arsonist is locked up. It is these casebooks that are never far from the investigator's reach.

While there are well-documented motives for fire-setting behavior—revenge, arson-for-profit, extremism, vanity, crime concealment, and others—with volumes of research material devoted to the very topic, an arson investigator worth his/her salt knows that determining motive is just one aspect of the investigation. Establishing that motive becomes more difficult when it is absolutely irrational and completely beyond belief. These are the storylines that even fiction writers couldn't make up.

As any experienced detective will tell you, there are moments when the hairs stand up on the back of your neck to alert you that danger is near. It's the moment that comes when sifting through an arson scene only to suddenly realize that the scene may still contain undiscovered explosive or incendiary hazards, or that creepy feeling one gets when listening to an arsonist explain in vile detail the commission of a bizarre "torch job" undertaken simply to satisfy some disgusting fantasy. It's the moment of unadulterated revulsion you experience as some nutjob arsonist tries to justify his fiendish behavior as "performance art" during the interview.

The arson cases that you mentally inherit for life, that defy any sort of humanity, the ones that keep you on edge, are the "torch jobs" committed by a unique sub-culture of arsonist—the whack jobs, weirdos, and wannabes. These include the bloodthirsty arsonist who stalks his prey for months or years before striking; the demented fire-setter who taunts her intended victim before and after a fire; the arsonist who serves as a policeman, firefighter, or security guard by day while setting fires at night; the crazed madman who stalk the streets as a real-life arsonist-boogeyman; or the maniac with an insatiable urge to light fires every waking moment of every single day. Spend a few hours talking with this lunatic fringe, listen to them describe the voices in their heads, or see the look in their eyes as they recount in dramatic detail their fascination with fire, and only then will you come to understand what crazy and evil really is. It is these disturbing, true-life cases that are the subject of this book.

The bizarre and fiendish world of arson investigation is one the author knows all too well. He has devoted his investigative career to analyzing not only the actual fire scenes and modus operandi of the arsonist, but studying this strange genre of criminal from "the fire ground" to the courtroom as only an experienced arson detective can. This is not an examination of arsons and arsonists based on an armchair review of reports or the conduct of clinical interviews within sterile institutional settings. Rather, this is a look into a criminal underworld from the perspective of an arson detective *extraordinaire* who has conducted thousands of fire scene investigations, interviewed hundreds of arsonists and, quite literally, stared crazy and evil in the face.

This book is an insider's account of what it's like to investigate some of the most bizarre arson cases committed by arsonists who are wicked and evil to their core. Wherever your interest lies in the field of criminal behavior or arson investigation, prepare to be amazed. Welcome to the fascinating world of arson investigation.

– **Detective Michael Digby**

Chasing Fireraisers, Freaks, and Fiends

My first book, *"Torchered" Minds: Case Histories of Notorious Serial Arsonists,"* was more about the bad guys than the people chasing them. The stories and characters themselves were so compelling that I wanted to talk about as many of them as possible. Because I included so many different cases in the book, I simply didn't have the room to get into the deep, secret details of each case. I have found over the years that people crave the "inside story" of unique or high-profile investigations. It is true that many of the really damning evidence or juicy back stories never make it into the official police reports or courtroom. After an investigation, only the bad guy and the detectives truly know what happened and how things came to pass. Sometimes the detectives employ such unique and creative methods of extracting information or manipulating the suspect into an arrest or admission that the suspect himself is not even sure how he got caught. They are left to wallow in prison and paranoia for years trying to figure out how they screwed up, who snitched, or what bad luck befell them. By the way, this scenario is very soul-satisfying for the investigators.

I've always been a storyteller. I've worked on cases with many people who only see a small slice of the investigation. These people included supervisors, criminalists, photographers, patrol officers, firefighters, prosecutors, the victims themselves, and even other investigators. When the case was finally adjudicated many months or years later, they always hit me up with questions like, "Hey, what did the suspect say when you showed him—?" or, "What happened in court when the judge brought you into chambers?" Like every other person with a heartbeat and a sense of curiosity, they had a need for closure. I usually told them a story that included the specifics of the case, how we identified and caught the guy, how we were able to "break" him during an interview, and how the case was presented in court. I found that all of these people really enjoyed the back story. They were constantly amazed at how much work it took and how much luck (good and bad) was involved to bring the case to a successful conclusion. A very complimentary remark that I often heard went something like, "Gee, I'd hate to have a guy like you chasing me if I was doing something illegal."

This book is about the freaks and the fiends, but it is also about the investigators who chase these villains. I have included more cases in this book in which I was the lead or co lead investigator, and offer many of the intimate details or the flavor of the case. I have also added a few cases from other investigators who I have found to be incredibly talented and determined. They are all colleagues and friends of mine. I hope I am able to do their stories justice.

All of these cases are true and have been taken from actual police reports, court records, news accounts, the lips of investigators, and sometimes the freaks and fiends themselves. This collection is but a small sampling taken from my files and the files of my friends, the other investigators. Enjoy.

– **Detective Ed Nordskog**, *2013*

Prologue

THE FOOTHILLS

"The Foothills" is a generic name given to any region of California that sits in the shadow of the predominant mountain ranges. The state is defined into several unique geographic areas; the deserts, coastline, northern forests, the sprawling, almost infinite Central Valley, two large bay areas (San Francisco and San Diego), and the Los Angeles basin. All of these geographic areas have been formed by earthquakes and are outlined by distinct sets of mountains or looming fault lines. Of the over thirty-five million people living in the state, nearly two thirds live in the foothill regions surrounding these mountains and fault lines. While the vast majority of these numbers live in the endless tract neighborhoods surrounding the dozens of major urban areas, an increasing number have built custom homes and ranches in the wooded and rural foothill areas.

The expansion into the foothills has given emergency response professionals, specifically fire chiefs, a good deal to worry about. The foothills in southern and coastal California are notoriously covered in grasses, thick brush, and ancient stands of oaks. Further north and a bit more inland, these same vegetation patterns lead to higher altitudes and thicker forests. For about three-fourths of the year, there is little to no rain anywhere in California, and by mid to late fall, the threat of catastrophic

FIRERAISERS, FREAKS, AND FIENDS

brushfires weigh heavily on emergency planners up and down the entire state.

Just the volume of people in this area, dubbed the "rural-urban interface" by emergency planners, is bound to lead to many accidental fires. In truth, human activity is the number one cause of wildland fires everywhere, with the bulk of them being accidental or possibly negligent acts. In some areas God has a hand, as many forest fires are the result of lightning strikes. Besides lightning, most wildland fires are started by some form of machinery use, with the automobile being the primary offender. Any Labor Day driver proceeding north from Los Angeles along Interstate 5 through the four-hundred-mile-long Central Valley will note no fewer than fifty different fire patterns in the dry grasses along the sides of the freeway. These patterns range from a few dozen feet in diameter to hundreds of acres. The only thing that prevents them from spreading is the tilled cropland that rolls on forever in this area. Most likely all of these fires, which can be seen any year around this time, are caused by hot items coming off of vehicles. While cigarettes were blamed as the primary causal factor for these fires in decades past, scientific research has shown that cigarettes are extremely unlikely to ignite vegetation. The more likely culprits are over-worked vehicles that have caught fire, disintegrating brake and transmission parts, flaming exhaust particles, malfunctioning catalytic converters, molten lug bolts, and burning rubber items such as flat tires and torn fan belts that are expelled from laboring trucks, cars, and motor homes during hundred-plus degree Central Valley days.

These same vehicle problems cause the majority of the fires in the deep coastal and mountain canyons prevalent up and down the state. Augmenting these ignition factors is the use of industrial machinery in the brush areas. Farming, ranching, mining, and industrial operations have caused dozens of fires to spread to nearby brush. Power lines felled during violent windstorms are another common ignition factor. Even fire mitigation efforts to burn, mow, or cut the brush have led to inadvertent wildfires. Lastly, the tract homes that abut the wildlands hold another major ignition factor—the juvenile fire starter. All of these factors cause over 95 percent of the wildland fires that ravage the California foothills. As an arson investigator, I have to be keenly aware of these fires, examine the start of each one as carefully as possible, and file that information away. Of course I take particular interest in the fires begun by juveniles and examine each young firestarter to assess his danger level and the odds of him reoffending. This all takes up a lot of my work day.

But truly, none of these are the factors that arson investigators are interested in. We take note of them, document them, and then file the information away. We really spend most of our time and energy on the other 5 percent of cases, those with suspicious ignition scenarios—the true arsonists! These are the people we spend large amounts of energy identifying, locating, and catching.

Since the inception of "modern" California in the 1840s, the foothills have held a special place in the culture of crime. Desperadoes, banditos, marauding renegades, highwaymen, claim jumpers, stage robbers, rustlers, and their ilk have always used the dark canyons and thick brush to hide in before emerging and waylaying their hapless victims. The term "bushwhacker" comes directly from these denizens of the hills, lying in wait amidst the forbidding brush only to leap out and molest unsuspecting travelers.

By the 1920s these same canyons were filled with stills for making bootleg booze. About that same time, organized crime gangsters who had migrated west to operate their "rackets" had discovered that the foothill region was a fantastic place to dump the bodies of their rivals. By the 1960s the foothills surrounding Los Angeles, San Diego, and San Francisco were coveted destinations for any group seeking to hide its activities from the general public and local police. Numerous cult groups including devil worshippers and extremist sects such as the Manson Family discovered that the hidden foothills were excellent places to conduct their bizarre rituals. Shortly after this era, with the burgeoning use and escalating price of marijuana, heavily armed pot growers also found the foothill canyons convenient locales to cultivate their crops.

Finally, the gang and drug wars that have rocked the major cities of California since the early 1980s have produced yet another enclave of criminal activity in the hidden areas of the foothills. The desolate canyons or brush areas within or near urban areas have become convenient dumping grounds for the multitudes of murder victims that have arisen out of urban violence. It is not uncommon for a California homicide investigator to find a duct-taped, beaten, stabbed, and shot gang member or drug dealer in the first dark canyon outside of any urban area.

The reason that these areas have long been and continue to be hotbeds of criminal activity is simple; these areas are some of the few places in a large and populous state where there are no prying eyes to spot a criminal carrying out their heinous activity. The foothills provide hidden areas not found in cities, and are places where, quite literally, no one can hear you scream. Any number of rapists, kidnappers, and torture-murderers has carried a live victim out to these hidden areas in order to fulfill their depraved and deadly fetishes without fear of being seen or heard.

While there are significant wildland areas throughout the nation, the California climate and topography has provided the arsonist a very unique workshop. Wildland fires hold a particular allure to an excitement-based arsonist. There is no other crime in the world for which a criminal can get as much excitement, attention, activity, and media coverage out of such a limited amount of work. A simple match placed in a secret, brush-filled canyon during the right weather conditions can have the same impact as the detonation of a nuclear device. One match can cause a wildfire of such massive scale that it can burn hundreds of thousands of acres, hundreds of homes and businesses, and threaten thousands of lives. The resulting response of hundreds of fire engines, thousands of firefighters, and the evacuation of thousands of people along with their pets and livestock, can create chaos on a near biblical scale. The financial costs of a single match can easily reach into the hundreds of millions, if not billions, of dollars.

California Fires

From the earliest days of statehood, California has had a close relationship with fire. Modern California was born out of the gold and silver bonanzas that occurred periodically from 1848 until 1880. The mines were dug in the most inhospitable locations in the state, on the slopes of the Sierra Nevada Mountains and the edges of the burning deserts. Following each gold strike, an army of miners and lumberjacks descended upon the area and denuded the local forests of timber to be used in the mines and to hastily erect towns to support the operations. The lumber was always dry and unfinished, and the towns were built with shelter in mind, not public safety. Because the use of open flames in all aspects of life and work were common in those days, the danger of accidental fire was ever present. Not surprisingly, dozens of mining towns burned to the ground, only to be rebuilt within just a couple weeks.

Major western cities of the era were not spared the flames. Again because of poor building codes and the use of open flames in the form of fireplaces, candles, wood stoves, and oil or kerosene lamps, accidental fires were a common occurrence. Because of the dry western winds and the lack of space between buildings, a small errant flame could easily result in a catastrophic fire. In his historical masterpiece of the Far West, *Men to Match*

Fireraisers, Freaks, And Fiends

My Mountains, historian Irving Stone documents the role that wildfires played in the history of California. He mentions that virtually every single gold mining camp town had a devastating fire in its first few years of existence. He calls San Francisco "the most frequently burned down city in the world." Stone describes that in 1850 alone San Francisco suffered five major fires, two of which completely burned the city to the ground. Only the millions of dollars flowing from the nearby gold fields enabled the city to be rebuilt over and over again. Stone describes similar massive fires in the cities of Sacramento, Bakersfield, Tulare, and Virginia City, Nevada.

A natural by-product of these fires was the formation of the first volunteer and semi-professional fire companies in the West. Each city, and sometimes each mine or railroad, sponsored its own fire company. Stone's historical research notes some very unique firefighting techniques that were employed in those days when these small fire companies attempted to take on a full, wind-driven conflagration. Water, as always in the West, was a true scarcity. In lieu of water or the equipment to employ it against a large fire, some fire companies used drastic methods to deprive the fire of fuel. In some western towns, the firefighters opted to "back burn" some buildings toward the large fires, in hopes of depriving the large fire of fuel. This method is still the preferred tactic today when wildland firefighters conduct "back burns" of vegetation around large wildfires. An even more drastic method of fire suppression used on occasion was the employment of explosives, usually dynamite, in an attempt to destroy fuel in the path of the flames. Sometimes this sort of technique backfired and actually added to the problem.

The turn of the twentieth century did not abate the fire problems in California. One event was so catastrophic that it literally changed the fortunes of two major cities. The San Francisco earthquake of 1906 damaged thousands of buildings and caused the rupture of gas mains. This resulted in a double catastrophe for the city as the fires that followed were some of the most devastating in world history. In that event, three thousand people died and three-hundred thousand were displaced. Over twenty-five thousand buildings were destroyed as thirty separate fires eventually merged into one massive firestorm. The army and fire department were so desperate to stop this conflagration that they resorted to the most drastic of methods. They employed tons of explosives and even artillery fire to form a firebreak by destroying the buildings that were feeding the fire. This method appeared to only make the fire larger. This fire was so damaging that San Francisco ceased being the hub of California commerce and industry. Almost immediately, so much commerce was diverted to sleepy Los Angeles that, virtually overnight, it became the most important city in California.

Since WWI, California has been cursed with dozens of massive brushfires that only get more devastating each season. As more and more homes are built into the brush land, the fires become more costly, and the threat to humans becomes more real.

The Devil Winds

The normal wind pattern in the California coastal mountain region is something called a "diurnal mountain slope" wind. This is when, because of heating and cooling during the day, the winds generally run upslope during daylight hours and then reverse and run downslope during the cooler nighttime.

The near-annual California wildfire season makes national and sometimes international headlines. The coastal fog and sea influence pushes moist air inland for 95 percent of the year, which makes the brush grow tall and thick during the California winters. The lack of rain and dry summers suck all the moisture from the tall brush and by late fall, the vegetation is tinder dry with single digit humidity levels. Like clockwork, the second or third week of October each year in Southern California produces a unique weather phenomenon called the "Santa Ana". This is when the normal "onshore flow" of moist air reverses, and instead, due to a massive pressure build up in the Great Basin, an "offshore flow" occurs, making blast-furnace-hot winds off the California deserts blow out down through the narrow mountain passes and over the foothills toward the Pacific Ocean. These wind speeds increase dramatically to over forty miles per hour, with gusts in the narrow canyons and passes at almost twice those speeds. The ambient temperature reaches up to 110 degrees Fahrenheit in the foothill areas. This further rips the remaining moisture from the foothill brush and causes any fire, whether accidental or incendiary, to be a potential catastrophe. The Santa Ana winds occur three to four times each year, but seem to be most common and severe in October.

The same thing happens in Central and Northern California to a slightly lesser extent. Again, due to the vagaries of nature and atmospheric conditions, which more often occur in late summer and fall, the winds reverse their normal trends and blow stronger, toward the west. In the central and northern foothills, these winds have long been called "el Diablo" or the "Devil Winds." They are unpredictable, violent, swirling, and almost always a causal factor in fires or the spread of fires.

The Santa Barbara area, a wealthy coastal city surrounded by low mountains and endless miles of brush land, has its own odd wind patterns. The winds in this area during the spring and summer months are called the "Sundowners." This name is derived from the winds that occur in the evening hours, pushing hot air out of the hills down to the cooler coastal area. Sundowners are often harbingers of the more famous Santa Ana winds as they seem to occur a day or two preceding a Santa Ana event.

Another close cousin to the Santa Ana winds or the Devil Winds can be found on the east slope of the Sierra's. These winds are called the "Zephyr Winds." The Zephyr effect is found most often in the late summer and fall and causes strong winds to blow from the west (down slope) on most hot afternoons. Known locally as the "Washoe Zephyr," these winds gained national fame during the Nevada Comstock Lode gold and silver rush era and were immortalized in the written works of Mark Twain (who himself in *Roughing It* claims to have accidentally ignited a large wildfire during a Washoe Zephyr).

No matter what part of the state the conditions arise in, these winds almost immediately draw the attention of fire bosses, rural residents, and the media. As soon as the winds are noticed or predicted, a certain hubbub of activity begins to build. Firefighters in California call it a "Red Flag Condition."

Peculiar things occur during this condition. First, as always the local media babes get into their "brush turnout fire coats," stand at the side of a windswept canyon road, and give breathless live reports of "Firewatch 2013" (or whatever year it happens to be). Downed power lines and overturned semi-trucks are featured, and a worried looking fire chief is filmed giving a dire warning to "be on the lookout for wildfires." That report is followed up with a too-late warning to rural homeowners about brush clearance around their properties, and the need to have a disaster or evacuation plan in effect. Within hours the first fire occurs, and the swarm of fire suppression agencies responding to it is only rivaled by the swarm of media helicopters and trucks trying to report on it.

Often, the first reported fires occur because of violent winds toppling power lines in a rural canyon, or more embarrassingly, a rural rancher trying too late to mow the brush around his buildings. Either way, the majority of the fires are accidents of some sort. However, the media jumps on these events, and even veteran fire officials who have seen it all a hundred times start to lose their focus. They begin "seeing ghosts" and start to classify accidental fires as "suspicious" or "incendiary." Some even embarrass themselves to no end by telling a television crew that "only an arsonist would set a fire in a red flag condition." The reality is that the fires are most often some form of accident. The rabid news anchors now have a new banner—"Firestorm 2013."

By the second or third day of the Santa Ana event, the public has been bombarded by twenty-four-hour news footage of airborne firefighting activities, neighborhood evacuations, and walls of fire assaulting rural enclaves. Handsome fire department PIO's (public information officers) give sober accounts to the cameras of the ongoing battle with the flames. Hours of television footage depict dramatic animal rescues, helicopter insertions, air tanker Phos-chek (fire retardant chemical) attacks, chainsaw and dozer operations, and endless lines of weary wildland firefighters trudging up steep hills in high heat and swirling winds.

It is quite often during the second or third day of these major events that the weirdos emerge from their fetid holes and come out to torment us. Wannabe firefighters get into their purchased or stolen fake firefighter uniforms and start showing up at massive command posts to get in on the excitement. The "stringers" show up and get in everyone's way. Stringers are independent film crews who monitor scanners and then race to get involved in any police or fire activity. They often beat the regular media to the scene and frequently get some fairly dramatic video, which they later sell to the main television stations. A few of these stringers have some very shady pasts and quite often deliberately placed themselves in harm's way to get the most dramatic footage. Some of these nuts get themselves injured through their recklessness, while a few get themselves arrested for interfering with emergency officials. Still, a few actually are arrested as suspects in arson cases.

Hidden amongst all this mayhem and chaos are the "copycat" arsonists. These rare folks are the sick individuals who see all the excitement and want to have an intimate connection to

Prologue

it. They slink off into a quiet area of the foothills and start their own fire in the tinder brush. Quite often they park nearby and monitor the massive response to their fire. Some of these people are former firefighters, some are fire buffs looking to see the men at work, and some are just pissed off jerks wanting to settle a grudge. A few of the stories in this book will describe some of the oddest, craziest, cruelest, and most evil persons we have ever come across in the arson investigation field.

When I originally got into this field of expertise, I heard numerous accounts and laments from veteran arson investigators that the Santa Ana winds bring out all the arsonists and weirdos. I originally scoffed at the notion, chalking it up to yet another unproven and exaggerated bit of firefighter lore of the kind that seems to permeate this profession. To me, a veteran detective of over five thousand criminal investigations, a crook is a crook, and they commit their crimes for their own selfish little reasons. I did not believe at all that they were drawn to or enticed into committing their crimes by something as innocuous as the wind, the fog, the moon, the tides, or the dark of night.

But then, at that stage of my career, I had not yet met an excitement-based arsonist such as Rickey Jimenez, Jim Hough, Norman Henderson, or Doc Hallman. I hadn't yet crossed paths with wannabes and weirdos like "Alien Head Guy," Mike McNeil, or John Piller. I wasn't aware that paranoid schizophrenics like Chuck Galante, Tyrone Wilkerson, Qi Jun Li, and Steve Agredano actually followed orders from the voices in their heads. I hadn't looked into the eyes of the evil and obsessive maniacs like Gary Glazier or Tim Komonyi. I didn't understand that the dark hidden recesses of the foothills appealed to these guys and maybe even called to them. They could take refuge in the deep forbidding shadows of a narrow oak-choked canyon and emerge to create havoc when the conditions were just right. I couldn't comprehend that the start of a Santa Anas wind condition energized them and swept them along in their despicable acts.

Fireraisers, Freaks, And Fiends

Writers going back to the time of Mark Twain have commented about the allure of the western winds and the solitary areas. Some writers have romanticized it, while others have hinted at its more sinister characteristics. Many have talked about the electricity or energy created by the hot winds rushing down canyons toward the sea. Writers have long said that this energy lowers the last inhibitions of many shadowy characters and for some reason compels them into acting out their sick fantasies.

Literary giants from western writer Louis L'Amour to modern police master storyteller Michael Connelly repeatedly mention the desert winds in their tales. The winds have been mentioned in several songs and have been the backdrop of numerous stories and movies. Crime noir legend Raymond Chandler described the Devil Winds and their aftermath on Los Angeles better than anyone in his 1938 short story "Red Wind":

There was a desert wind blowing that night. It was one of those hot dry Santa Anas that come down through the mountain passes and curl your hair and make your nerves jump and your skin itch. On nights like that every booze party ends in a fight. Meek little wives feel the edge of the carving knife and study their husband's necks. Anything can happen.

Sixteen years ago, as I entered the arson investigation world, I didn't believe any of this nonsense. Today, after talking to over three hundred arsonists I personally arrested, and discussing hundreds of other cases with my peers in the field, I'm keeping a much more open mind. I know that some of these guys are driven by the oddest of impulses and that just about anything is possible. Now when the Santa Ana winds start to howl, I gas up my truck, repack my equipment and double check all my gear in preparation for a "call out" to a major fire scene. When the call comes, as it always does, I just know that by the time the winds die down there is a decent chance that I will be sitting in a small room, having an intimate conversation with a fireraiser, a freak, or even a fiend.

Prologue

Detectives and Investigators

As I write this, I've been a detective in a major department in the sprawling Los Angeles area for over twenty-one years. There have been thousands of movies, books, and television shows about detectives and investigators over the years. If the truth be told, my own path to becoming a cop and a detective began in my early teen years after I read my first Joseph Wambaugh novel, *The New Centurions*. From that point on, I endlessly watched crime dramas and read every book I could on the matter. Of course, other than Wambaugh's works, the vast majority of these depictions was and continues to be pure Hollywood fiction with very little connection to the real duties of detectives and investigators. Like everyone else, I believed that detectives were very much like the rock-star characters depicted in "Starsky and Hutch," and that a typical day was one spent driving in high-speed chases, shooting guns, and fist fighting with bad guys. Like so many other naïve men in the field, the thirst for action is what drew me to the profession.

The reality of the situation is that detective work is mostly mundane, cerebral, and unglamorous. The average detective I know is more a puzzle master than a rock star. His mindset is that of a marathoner and not a sprinter. Most don't have the best physiques because they miss their workouts opting instead to stay at work late, chasing leads. They don't get enough sleep, eat endless amounts of crappy junk food off taco trucks and crummy restaurants open at two in the morning in seedy areas, drink way too much coffee, and ruin their eyes by reading through an endless supply of documents off computer screens.

Great detectives are extraordinarily analytical people. The more common traits of successful detectives are the ability to not just look but to actually see things other people miss; to pick up subtle nuances and hear things in conversation that most people wouldn't notice; to show compassion and understanding to even the most heinous criminals in the world in order to forge a connection; and to always remember that the reason they are there is the victims. Other common traits are endurance, tenacity, patience, and the ability to talk and listen to people. The final trait is intelligence. The best detectives I know are also some of the most intelligent people I have ever met. They can sit in a stuffy, smelly, claustrophobic interview room and be fully focused on every word of a deranged maniac serial killer/arsonist/rapist etc.; yet simultaneously, another part of their mind will be thinking about three years down the road and wondering how an appellate court is going to view a particular statement or piece of evidence. They are already pondering and eliminating the potential defenses future sleazy defense attorneys have not yet even dreamed up.

In 1991 I was attending a two-week-long homicide investigation course in San Jose. One of the instructors for this course was a true legend in the homicide business, retired Los Angeles Sheriff's Homicide Detective Frank Salerno. Salerno had the distinction of being the lead homicide investigator on two of the most notorious murder series in American history. He successfully tracked down and convicted the two men responsible for the "Hillside Strangler" slayings in Los Angeles. A few years later he was handpicked to lead the even more notorious "Night Stalker" murder investigation. This most violent serial murderer of them all, Richard Ramirez, was also tracked down and convicted by Salerno and his partner. All three of these fiends ended up on death row as a result of Salerno and his various partners' thoroughness and tenacity.

When Salerno addressed our class of forty detectives, I realized that I was most likely the youngest and least experienced of the lot. He started out with a question: "Who in here thinks that if given enough resources and time, they can solve any crime?" Like an idiot, I raised my hand. I was the only one in the room to do so. I heard snickers and looked around to see thirty-nine more experienced detectives smiling at me like the punk kid I was. Salerno, who is a somewhat intimidating guy, walked up to me and stared. "Do you really believe that, kid?" When I sheepishly nodded, he said, "Good, I'll take you on my team anytime." Salerno then started out his lecture with some prophetic words for us: "You can't be a good detective without a big ego. If you don't think you can solve the case, then it won't get solved."

The Chase

Most really successful detectives I know are completely addicted to the chase. No matter what is going on in your home life, no matter how much you hate your boss, no matter how discouraged you get after failing to solve a case—or worse, losing in court—and no matter how exhausted, tired, and burned-out you feel, you always get a new burst of energy and adrenaline when you visit a particularly interesting, unique, or horrifying crime scene.

Sometimes you marvel in a perverse sort of admiration at the skill level or sophistication of a criminal. Other times you are quietly enraged at the hideous destruction the criminal wrought on the lives of his victims. You make a silent pact with yourself then and there to track him down and see him suffer in the tedious, dreary, and uncaring criminal justice system. Lastly, you look into the shocked and catatonic faces of the victims or survivors and a slow rage builds up, allowing you the strength of will to dedicate the next few months of your life making the criminal pay for all that he has done. You know the victims will never heal from what has been done to them, and you know that no amount of anguish and suffering felt by the criminal will make up for what he did, but you still vow to do everything you can to hold him accountable. That's what keeps detectives motivated and "chasing the case."

FIRERAISERS, FREAKS, AND FIENDS

One such chase in particular comes to mind. In 2000, Senior Special Agent Ron Michel of the National Insurance Crime Bureau (NICB) and I began investigating an organized group of construction contractors who torched about eighty homes and vehicles in the Los Angeles basin for the sole purpose of committing insurance fraud. It was an intricate scheme that spanned over four years and involved members of the "ring" posing as contractors and insurance adjusters to solicit homeowners. They would promise the homeowners free kitchens, bedrooms, garages, or a remodel, plus usually a five-thousand-dollar cash kickback, if the homeowners agreed to be out of town one night. During that night, a staged "accidental" fire would occur, usually causing about $175,000 in damages. The insurance companies would perform a token investigation, usually noting suspicious activity, but in the end, under the threat of law suits and intimidation by the contractors, they almost always paid. This crew of about a half-dozen associated criminals was so successful and brazen, that they openly bragged about their deeds to others on the street.

Early on, when SSA Michel and I began looking into the ring, we started contacting the homeowners, who were coconspirators in this massive conspiracy. Eventually, we began building a huge case as home owner after home owner began admitting their involvement. Soon, we began prosecuting the homeowners in an attempt to build a case against the contractors. As the case built, the contractors became aware that we were chasing them. They kept waiting for us to kick in their doors and arrest them. They even tried making overtures to us in an attempt to head off their own arrests. We ignored them and continued to doggedly build a circumstantial case against them. Eventually they learned that we had gotten into their bank records. Soon after they learned that we were interviewing various members of their own families and building cases against their elderly parents for money laundering. We even elicited the cooperation of members of their own families and organization. We learned later that our slow assault was driving the criminal leaders crazy.

Two years into the investigation, we dropped the hammer on them and arrested about thirty people in one large dramatic sweep. SSA Michel and I interviewed all of the suspects in a twenty-hour marathon. By the end, we were exhausted and nearly delirious. We approached several of the suspects with offers to cooperate in exchange for some sort of limited immunity. One guy, named Pete, abruptly turned us down. He then went back to his cell and thought about it for a couple more hours. He then asked for us again. Pete had a dramatic change of heart and became the first person in this organization to "turn rat" and cooperate. Others would soon follow.

About a year later, while still in the court process of this case, a district attorney asked Pete what his motivation was for cooperating. Pete told him that he and his buddies were aware that we had been chasing them for over two years and all had lost sleep and developed health problems because of the stress of being chased. He said that they had all contemplated turning themselves in *en masse,* just so they could get it over with and put an end to the pressure and stress of being hunted. They said they had seen us on the streets several times, and it was driving them crazy not knowing why we hadn't arrested them yet. It was only as they were all approaching mental exhaustion that we arrested them. Pete said most of them sat in the holding cells and announced that they were relieved the hunt was over. However, most of his partners also vowed to vigorously fight the case in court with very expensive attorneys.

Pete said he originally planned to fight the case as well, hoping to wear us down with some expensive litigation. When he first looked at us in the interview room, he saw that we appeared even more exhausted than he and his crew. In truth, I was sick and neither of us had slept much in the weeks prior to the massive raids. After Pete left us the first time, he finally realized that no matter how tired and exhausted we (the detectives) looked, we were never going to give up, and would push this case hard through the court system for the maximum time allowed. He said that we were just more determined to catch them than they were to avoid being caught, so he decided to join us in hopes of evoking some mercy.

Ron and I took this as a huge compliment. The case would go on for a couple more years and would result in the conviction of every member of the arson ring. It would be regarded as the most significant arson case in the United States for a couple of years, and we received several prestigious awards and honors because of it. Pete and his fellow rats, er, um, I mean cooperating witnesses provided valuable information against the ring leaders and earned the mercy of the court.

CHAPTER ONE:

Mission Men

The majority of criminals, particularly those who commit arson, put very little planning or forethought into their activities. They often commit their crimes in the heat of passion, using whatever materials they have on hand to accomplish their deed. That's why the bulk of arson attacks are labeled as "spite/revenge" attacks. These arsons are usually in response to a perceived wrong or a personal dispute. They are very similar to domestic disturbances in which the suspect is easily identified, commits his crime in the heat of passion, and leaves a large amount of evidence or witnesses to the event. A notable exception to this in the arson world is of course the arson-for-profit scheme, which often entails a large amount of pre-event planning, the establishment of an alibi for the property owner, the use of second parties or "arsonists for hire," exotic staging of the scene, and possibly the use of a device of sorts to delay the ignition of the fire.

Every so often in the world of arson we come upon a real gem. Men, who for whatever demented reason lurking in their minds, go on a mission. Not unlike a military or police raid, these "true believers" plan, scheme, prepare themselves, rehearse, and carry out intricate tactical operations against their targets.

These attacks are usually brought on by some form of psychosis, schizophrenia, paranoia, or other mental illness that compels the individual to conduct these raids. Sometimes the raids or actions are more than arsons, and involve the death or planned death of the victim. Sometimes, like a mass or spree murderer, the arsonist embarks on a one-way trip, where he has little expectation of surviving the event himself. Quite often, the same mental illness issues that compel these men to go on these missions in the first place work in our favor, causing them to "botch" the job, and thereby leaving us very little damage, a ton of evidence, and a great story to tell. These people are incredibly dedicated to what they believe and are extraordinarily dangerous. We classify these driven characters as "men on a mission," or more succinctly, "mission men."

Tyrone Wilkerson
"JPL Attacks"—Pasadena, 2006

Author's Note: This story is taken from author's own case files. JPL is an acronym for the Jet Propulsion Lab, a world famous Pasadena-based research and development center co-owned and operated by CalTech and NASA. Its main mission is to develop propulsion and robotic systems for space travel. It sits on the side of a mountain overlooking Pasadena and employs over five thousand people.

Tyrone Wilkerson was on yet another raid. This was his fourth such foray into the government stronghold. Each preceding venture had met with little opposition and without him being spotted by security forces. This time Tyrone was equipped with some additional equipment. He was dressed all in black, wearing his tactical kneepads, gloves, fence-cutting equipment, and this mission's "breaching tools." Tyrone was a soldier. He had planned and plotted these missions, and had added equipment where necessary.

Past missions at this installation had met with mixed results. Tyrone had successfully breached the several layers of security and had eluded the ground and vehicle patrols. He had been able to freely explore the defenses and access the "black ops dish" on two previous nights. However, both previous attempts to disable the dish had failed. The first attempt, on March 8, was admittedly crude. Tyrone had carried a hammer with him to assist him in breaching fences and to possibly damage the controls of the dish. When he got to the dish site, he saw that the controls were locked in the steel base of the stem of the dish. With no other tools available, he tossed the green framing hammer into the nearly forty-foot-diameter satellite dish, believing it would break a critical part, disrupt the radar waves, or jam the dish as it rotated. He then made good his escape.

The second attack, which took place on March 11, was much more professional. Tyrone had carried a large plastic pail containing eight glass mason jars. Each jar had been filled with a "napalm-like"* mixture of gasoline and diesel fuel. Tyrone had lugged this heavy pail over a half mile uphill and through the multiple layers of security forces to the dish site. He then threw the bottles up into the opening at the top of the stem of the satellite dish, a distance of over twenty feet. Two of the bottles failed to reach their mark and crashed down to the pavement below, splashing Tyrone with broken glass and the napalm mixture. Tyrone then opened his box of highway flares and threw a lit one into the opening of the stem. As Tyrone fled down his prearranged escape trail, he saw dark orange flames and black smoke extending out of the bottom of the multi-million-dollar dish assembly. His mission had been successful. Now if he could only escape without being caught. Tyrone safely made it back to his ex-filtration vehicle and was at his regular job site before anyone noticed he was missing. The next morning, Tyrone was extremely surprised and irritated. He climbed to a vantage point and viewed the target area to see how much destruction he had wrought. From this distance he could still clearly see the dish and could see that there was virtually no noticeable damage. He knew he had seen the large flames last night, and he had fully expected to see a smoking pile of twisted metal. Instead he could

Fireraisers, Freaks, And Fiends

only see the clean white dish, glistening in the morning sun as if nothing had happened. Surely someone had reported the large blaze to the fire department or media? He waited for two days for news of the event to be broadcast by the media. He hoped the press coverage would expose the dark secrets of this rogue government installation.

By early evening March 12, 2006, Tyrone had become extremely frustrated. He was now very sure that this cover-up conspiracy had permeated the Los Angeles Sheriff's Department, the Pasadena Police Department, the fire department, and even the press. He was extremely upset that no one had reported the major damage he was sure had been done to the dish. He had scoured the newspapers and listened to the local radio all day while working and had not heard a single word about his attack on the satellite dish. Somehow the government was even controlling the media. Tyrone had to make people notice! That's why the next event was going to be impossible to miss. Tyrone had a new plan. That night's attack would be so spectacular that thousands of people in the surrounding towns of Altadena and Pasadena would see the flames, making it impossible for the press to cover it up.

Tyrone prepared carefully. He had selected that night's target on the earlier recon missions. There was a large flammable liquid storage facility within a hundred yards of the "black ops" dish. Within that facility was a liquid nitrogen tank that held several thousand gallons of material. Tyrone knew that if he could breach the tank and ignite the liquid nitrogen, he would create a cataclysmic event that would burn half of the mountain down, thereby bringing international attention to the illegal actions perpetrated by the government at the site.

Tyrone labored as he lugged the tan duffel up the wooded slopes and through the darkened parking lots. The sharp hatchet, five gallons of gasoline, and sledgehammer were starting to get very heavy. However, Tyrone was a true professional soldier who knew his role. He had to press on through the pain in his lungs and legs and complete his mission—and quickly. He was a little late that night, and would have to rush to get the job done before the workers arrived. Additionally, Tyrone had another "hit" to make. He had to kill the man he knew was responsible for all this misery.

Tyrone had been forced into this drastic plan. He had tried to tell everybody about the dark secrets of the new dish. Months before, when he had first noticed the construction of the satellite dish from his Pasadena apartment, he knew there was something wrong. The ominous dish seemed to point directly at him and seemed to observe and record his every movement. Worried, he first contacted the FBI and then later the Secret Service. He explained that the dish was not on any government website and must be some sort of "black ops" or other rogue government project. While they were polite and took all of his information, he was certain that the agents did not take him seriously. They seemed more concerned about his mental health and criminal history than about the obvious threat imposed by the satellite dish. They assured him that they would "look into it."

Soon after his visits to the federal agencies, Tyrone began to realize he had made a mistake. He started to suffer severe and near-paralyzing headaches. Each time he got a headache; he would look up and see the dish pointed directly toward him. Eventually, he began to suffer severe pain in his genitals. He was unable to focus and could not have sex without a severe burning pain in his penis and testicles. Tyrone, desperate by now, went to the Pasadena Police Anti-terrorism Squad on several occasions. They too seemed sympathetic toward his plight, but again seemed overly concerned about his mental health and criminal record. By February of 2006, Tyrone Wilkerson decided to take matters into his own hands.

FIRERAISERS, FREAKS, AND FIENDS

JPL security knew they had a problem. Starting on March 8, 2006, security cameras had picked up fleeting glimpses of a dark figure wearing knee pads and running through parking lots in the early morning hours on at least three occasions. A check of the expansive site showed no obvious signs of theft or break-in. Security officials issued memos to JPL personnel, asking them to be extra vigilant and report any suspicious persons immediately to security and the local sheriff's station. The problem with security at this facility was that the site operations involved dozens of subcontractors, college groups, and scientists. Because of frequent turnover and changes in personnel, it was often difficult to tell who belonged or who did not belong if their security badges were not visible. Security supervisors frequently lamented that the academic types were so caught up in their work that they were somewhat lax on security functions, despite often being involved in "Top Secret" level work for the government.

Following several fleeting sightings of the ominous nocturnal invader, JPL security issued new memos regarding security and informed their local NASA investigator that there may be a security breach at the site.

In the early dawn hours of March 13, two technicians arrived at their work area early to get a large project ready. Both soon saw an adult black male walking toward them. They did not recognize him, and the scientists noted that he was not displaying a proper JPL security badge. They also noted that he was wearing some sort of knee pads and was carrying a large gasoline container and brown duffel. They immediately notified JPL security.

JPL security arrived and sized up the suspect. He was a male, black, about forty years old, and looked to be in excellent shape. He had muscles bulging from his medium frame. When they confronted him, he appeared to look right through them in a focused stare. They followed his gaze to a thirty-foot-high liquid nitrogen tank. When they asked him what he was doing, he replied, "I'm on a mission. I have to get to that tank." Security surrounded the man as he started to rant and seemed to get excited. They immediately requested help from the local Los Angeles Sheriff's substation. As deputies arrived, they contacted and patted down the male. They were surprised to find a package of highway flares tucked into his waistband.

When the male calmed down a bit, he finally told them that he planned to burn down the facility. The male, later identified as Tyrone Wilkerson, was arrested for trespassing and attempted arson and brought to the Crescenta Valley Sheriff's Station. Deputies requested an arson investigator to the scene. I got the call.

By the time I arrived, Wilkerson had been processed through the booking system. The patrol deputies said that Wilkerson was polite and cooperative, but rambled on incessantly about a "black ops satellite dish" and his need to complete his mission to destroy it. Prior to talking to him, I consulted his RAPS sheet and found him to have a lengthy history of narcotics arrests and assaults. I placed him in the video room and entered to begin our conversation.

After I introduced myself, Wilkerson just stared at me for several minutes, apparently sizing me up. Finally, he asked who I worked for and what level my security clearance was. "Top Secret, of course," I replied, playing along with him. Seemingly satisfied, Wilkerson went into a nonstop description of his raids on the JPL site. He told me that he knew the site had a secret satellite dish and that it was sending pain and fire into his head and genitals. He described how first his wife, then the FBI, Secret Service, and Pasadena Police had ignored his demands to do something about this rogue operation. He then said that he was a "warrior who had been given the mission to destroy the dish." He cited his leaders as Secretary of State Condoleezza Rice, General Colin Powell, and President George Bush.

Wilkerson eventually got around to describing his "raids." He said he had studied the JPL site and its security systems for months, and had "probed their defenses" on numerous occasions. Finally, he began a series of "recons and raids" the previous week. He said he always wore black clothing and kneepads. He usually entered the site after 0330 hours and "breached" the chain-link fences. On the first raid, he reached the dish site and threw a green hammer up into the dish to disable it. The next day he scanned the newspapers but found no mention of the event. On a subsequent raid, he brought his own "napalm" mixture to the site and started a fire in the base of the dish. He said he used a mixture of gasoline and diesel which was a "standard sabotage mixture." After that fire, he was sure he severely damaged the dish. He became convinced that the sheriff's and fire department were now involved in the cover-up as there was again no mention of the incident in the local media.

Wilkerson said that the final raid was going to be spectacular. He was going to attack the volatile fuel storage area just a hundred yards below the satellite dish. He planned to use the sledgehammer and axe to break the valves off the gasoline and diesel storage tanks at the site, and then ignite them with the highway flares. Once the fire was started, he would then break the valves off the liquid nitrogen tank, which would then cause a "nuclear detonation on the mountain that no one could ignore" (I didn't have the heart to tell the guy that liquid nitrogen doesn't burn).

Wilkerson then said that prior to leaving the site; he had one more special mission to accomplish. He needed to find a man and kill him. He wrote the man's name down on paper for me, David Washington. He said the man, an older black man who was a secret government agent posing as an electrician at the site, was the creator of the "black ops" program at JPL. Wilkerson said he was trying to find the man to kill him with the axe. Up to this point, Wilkerson was an amusing break from the usual thugs and criminals I deal with every day; however, when he described his intent to kill a man with an axe, he got my attention. He seemed completely serious.

While listening to him, I realized that Tyrone Wilkerson actually believed everything he had told me. I felt a little sorry for him, wondering at what point in his life his mind had begun to fail him. Speaking to him I had learned (and later confirmed) that he ran his own painting business, was a good and reliable worker, had a loyal church-going wife, and led an otherwise normal life. He obviously had a dark demon in him that fueled this paranoid fantasy world. I also couldn't help but be amused at the prospect of him breaking open the valve of a liquid nitrogen tank. The image of him ending up frozen like the liquid Terminator in *Terminator 2: Judgment Day* popped into my head as I studied him.

Additionally, I realized that Wilkerson fully intended to follow through on his plan, which was to start a cataclysmic fire at the Jet Propulsion Lab. He had admitted this and had also admitted to one previous act of arson and a separate previous act of serious vandalism. I also believed he fully intended to kill David Washington (if he existed) at the site with his axe.

Based on his admissions, I called JPL security and asked them to check the sprawling facility for any fire or vandalism damage. I further advised them that I believed the suspect had a vehicle parked nearby. Within an hour, they confirmed all my suspicions. They asked me to respond to the new satellite dish project site.

I arrived at the twelve-meter-dish site. The dish was at least a half mile uphill from the main JPL gate, and about a mile from any civilian property. The location was a secured concrete pad on which had been erected a massive satellite dish measuring forty feet across. This dish was mounted on a twenty-five-foot-high steel pedestal which contained the electronic "brains" of the dish. The dish was just going through its final testing as it had just been constructed over the past twelve months. The dish was worth in excess of $12 million. At the scene I was met by a special agent from NASA (I hadn't realized they had their own agents).

Fireraisers, Freaks, and Fiends

Project manager Neil Bucknam was also waiting for me. He had been advised to check his site by NASA security. When he arrived, he saw that the chain-link fence surrounding the pad had been cut, and found several items of interest on the concrete pad. He found an unburned highway flare, an empty box that had held two flares, a white five-gallon paint bucket filled with multicolored towels, and broken glass littering the base of the dish pedestal. The entire site smelled of gasoline and diesel fuel. He also noticed that there was fire damage at the top of the pedestal, which was over twenty-five feet above the ground.

I began my crime scene investigation. I found the broken remnants of three clear mason jars, their lids on the ground at the base of the steel mount. The area around each pile of broken glass was wet and smelled strongly of diesel and gas. The large paint bucket contained only torn towels, but they too were wet and smelled of diesel and gas. We called for a nearby "cherry picker" machine to access the dish. When I was lifted to the base of the dish, I found two more broken mason jars and about an inch-deep pool of gasoline/diesel on the steel floor of the base. In the middle of this pool was a partially burned highway flare. From this flare, a fire had burned upward into the electronic "brains" and control system of the dish. The fire had apparently self-extinguished at some point because of a lack of combustible material. I brought up the project manager, and he estimated the damage at well over $200,000. He attempted to operate the dish, but heard a loud "clunking" noise when he attempted to turn the dish. I told him about the suspect's claim of having thrown a hammer into the dish. He said that it was entirely possible.

My crime scene investigation consisted of taking numerous photographs of the evidence, collecting liquid samples from the wet substance on the ground and the liquid found in the metal pedestal, collecting the remnants of the burned flare for lab analysis, tracking footprints and tool marks at the cut fence, and collecting the evidence left behind by the suspect.

My analysis or profile of the incident was that it was committed by an extremely physically fit but disorganized offender, who had attacked a metal structure with the wrong type of weapon—in this case, fire. The scene profile was consistent with the suspect, Tyrone Wilkerson, and coincided with his admissions.

Based on the scene, I asked security guards and sheriff's deputies to scour the surrounding streets and parking lots for a Ford Explorer belonging to the suspect. The bucket containing the five jars and towels would have been fairly heavy, and he wouldn't have been able to carry it from very far away. Within minutes, deputies had located the Explorer in the closest civilian parking lot at a nearby high school. The suspect's wife was just attempting to move it when they arrived.

I drove the mile to that parking lot and spoke to the suspect's wife. She said that he'd called her from jail and told her to get the truck before we found it. She stated that her husband was a good man but had some legal and narcotics problems from the distant past. However, for the past few years he had maintained a straight life and ran his own paint contracting business. Within the past year, he had begun voicing his concern to her about the new large satellite dish being constructed at the nearby JPL site. He told her that it was making his head and genitals hurt. She also noted that he began to partake of marijuana over this same time period. Mrs. Wilkerson was concerned about her husband's continuing obsession over the dish, but did not think he would ever get involved in any sort of terrorist raids. She said he was a reliable worker and never missed a job. She gave me permission to search the vehicle.

I entered the Explorer and found several large paint buckets that were identical to the one found at the dish site. I further found torn towels that were an exact match to those found at the dish site. I found an empty plastic bag with a receipt for a new hammer, dated two days ago, and the empty hammer package. This seemed to support the suspect's claim that he threw his old hammer into the dish about four nights before. Lastly, I found a "Smart and Final" receipt for a case of glass mason jars, dated two days ago. The evidence in the vehicle was a direct link to the evidence found at the burned dish site.

I eventually filed arson, burglary, felony vandalism, and trespassing charges against Tyrone Wilkerson. He was held in custody with a $250,000 bail. At his arraignment, the judge sent him out to Dept. 95** for a psychiatric evaluation to see if he was fit for trial.

Two days later, with the help of special agents from NASA and the ATF, I located and interviewed Mr. David Washington in his south central Los Angeles apartment. The sixty-five-year-old man said he had been an electrician employed for several years at the JPL site, but had retired at least seven years prior to this event. He was shown photos of Tyrone Wilkerson, but claimed to never have met him. Mr. Washington had no idea who Wilkerson was or why Wilkerson wanted to kill him.

Three months later, Wilkerson was found fit for trial (sane) and was "held to answer" for his crimes at a preliminary hearing in Pasadena Superior Court. Following that hearing, Wilkerson's attorney convinced him to plead guilty to receive a four-year sentence along with much needed mental-health treatment. He agreed.

In a footnote to the case, at his sentencing, I made the mistake of wearing my black uniform (Wilkerson had previously seen me in a green sheriff's raid jacket). The docile Wilkerson, upon seeing the black uniform, became highly agitated and began yelling at his attorney about "men in black" and a "black ops" government conspiracy.

Tyrone Wilkerson sat in a prison psychiatric ward for years, biding his time and carefully planning his next raid. He was paroled in 2009. So far no sightings...so far.

MISSION MEN

***Historical note**: Napalm is a military slang term originating in the Pacific theater of WWII. Early in the war, Marine and Navy close-air support pilots were experimenting with the use of aerial dropped drums of gasoline as a means of dislodging stubborn, dug-in Japanese troops. A problem with this is that aviation gasoline is such a volatile substance that it flashed and burned away too quickly to really affect the deeply entrenched enemy. At some point someone got the novel idea to mix a thick cooking fuel used by local Pacific Islanders, palm oil, with the naptha (hence: napalm) and aviation gas from the Navy, causing the mixture to become much thicker and thereby more persistent. This crude mixture worked much better, and the Navy began asking American chemical companies, to include a group working out of Harvard University, to develop a better commercially-manufactured substance with similar properties. Many variations of the substance were developed and used during the latter stages of the war in both the Pacific and European theaters, and soon Napalm became the semi-official name for any ordnance that was basically a thickened or jellied gasoline. These munitions were a staple in the US military through the Korean War and into Vietnam. The horrific effects of this ordnance were brought to the public's eye with vivid television footage in the latter stages of Vietnam, and since then the use of air-dropped napalm in civilian areas has been discontinued.

On the streets, however, the word Napalm is still in use and is a generic catch-all term used by any number of bad guys and "closet commandos" to describe an improvised thickened fuel mixture. There is no singular recipe for napalm on the street, and I have seen improvised mixtures of gasoline with other fuels (diesel, motor oil, lamp oil) and thickeners, including shaved soap, rubber bands, Styrofoam, detergent, and just about anything else an idiot could dissolve into gasoline. The use of these mixtures seldom has the effect that the suspect intends and usually leaves a stinky, smoldering substance at the crime scene. Napalm mixtures are still found in any number of underground manuals to include *Poor Man's James Bond* and the like. As I said above, "closet commandos!" More about them in the "Whackjobs and Wannabe's" section of this book.

** **Slang note**: Department 95 in the Los Angeles County Superior Court system is the courtroom where all defendants suspected of having sanity issues are sent for a mental health evaluation hearing. Since many of the principal subjects in this book have severe mental health issues, and their actions are bizarre to say the least, several of these stories make reference to the defendant being "sent out to Dept. 95". It's a bit more politically correct than those antiquated descriptions such as Looney Bin, Nut House or Ding Ward.

Investigator's Analysis:

Solving the Wilkerson case took about five minutes. It wasn't exactly strenuous detective work. It was an extremely unsophisticated event, and he left tons of physical evidence at the scene and in his getaway vehicle. Besides that, he gave a nearly complete confession of his crimes and his intent to commit future crimes. There was very little expectation that he would get away with this crime. To the lay person and casual courtroom observer, this case is almost laughable. Therein lays the danger with this type of suspect. What they do is so bizarre and ludicrous that they are not considered to be serious threats by the court system or the media. Most people would consider Wilkerson to be an oddball who just needs a little help. On the contrary, an experienced investigator would find this type of person to be off-the-charts dangerous. He is on a mission, and in this case it is so dangerous that he has little expectation of surviving the event, one way or the other. This is the same sort of person who commits a dramatic murder-suicide or even a suicide-by-cop. These types of criminals are so committed and so dangerous that they need incarceration, extensive psychiatric treatment, and years of close monitoring.

MIGUEL ANGEL RODRIGUEZ-CINTRON
WARNER BROTHER'S STUDIOS, BURBANK, 2010

Author's Note: This case comes from the Burbank Police Department and my own courtroom experience as an expert for the prosecution in this matter.

A little after three in the afternoon on September 17, 2010, a blue Chevy Camaro approached the north gate of Warner Brother's studio in Burbank. The gate arm was down, and as the guard stepped out to contact the Hispanic driver, the car sped up and crashed through the gate arm at nearly forty miles per hour. The gate arm was shattered, and its debris spread several feet onto the property; the Chevrolet emblem for the Camaro was left lying amongst the wreckage. The Camaro disappeared into the massive, crowded studio lot as studio security scrambled to locate the car. Simultaneously, a phone call was placed by studio security to the Burbank Police Department.

One of Warner's security guards found the Camaro within about eight to ten minutes and followed it to an exit. The driver got out of the car, appearing confused and highly agitated. The guard confronted him and told he him he needed to go back to the north gate. The driver reentered the Camaro and drove in a very erratic manner toward the north gate, where he was stopped and detained by a phalanx of security guards that hemmed in his vehicle with their cars. The driver jumped out of the Camaro, removed a duffel bag from the interior of the car, and placed it into the trunk. He was then approached by studio security guards. The driver produced a New York driver's license that identified him as forty-three-year-old Miguel Rodriguez-Cintron.

When the Burbank cops arrived, they approached Rodriguez-Cintron and performed a cursory search of his person and vehicle. Among the items in his car was the dark duffel in the trunk area. It contained two new butcher knives, still in their packaging; a claw hammer; a black, semiautomatic "air soft" pistol that had its safety markings obliterated and appeared to be a real handgun; a red, plastic gas can that was wrapped in a plastic sheet and contained two gallons of gasoline; and four plastic, one-quart containers of charcoal starter fluid. In the same bag there were a blue butane lighter and a bag containing several boxes of wooden kitchen matches. In the console of the car was a bag with eight, separately-taped bundles of kitchen matches. Each bundle contained between seven and thirteen matches, and all were taped in a way so that the match heads faced in the

Fireraisers, Freaks, and Fiends

same direction and were free to strike on a surface. The matches were held together with brown plastic shipping tape and each bundle formed a unique "torch."

Slightly alarmed at what the cops had found, studio security summoned a K-9 handler contracted by the studios along with his bomb-sniffing dog. The dog was run past the Camaro and gave a positive alert for explosives. An evacuation was established, and the Los Angeles Sheriff's Arson/Bomb Squad was summoned. Due to the studios being a high-priority target, a full response from Burbank Fire also ensued, complete with a fire battalion, rescue ambulances, and a hazmat team.

Sheriff bomb squad investigators Sgt. Don Shively and Det. Marcus Friedemann arrived and cleared the Camaro of explosive devices. However, they pointed out to the Burbank cops several incendiary devices and other very suspicious items. They told the Burbank cops that these incendiary and flammable materials constituted prearranged incendiary devices designed to cause multiple fires. Rodriguez-Cintron was arrested for trespassing and possession of incendiary devices. During a search of his pockets after his arrest, officers found a computer "USB" drive and another bundle of taped matches.

The detailed search of Rodriguez-Cintron's car revealed more disturbing items. In the center console, where Burbank officers had located the seven separate bundles of wooden matches, detectives also found three torn strips of cloth similar to the "wicks" used in incendiary devices. Next to them in the center console was a small, handheld tape recorder.

Shortly after his arrest, Rodriguez-Cintron was questioned by sheriff's and Burbank police detectives. He was cooperative and told investigators that the items in his car were merely "camping gear." He could not explain why he had no clothing, food, tent, or sleeping bag. He then told a story about why he was at the studios. He said that he was a longtime Warner's employee and was there to have a meeting with Joel Silver. Joel Silver is a famous Hollywood producer who has made numerous blockbuster films, including Arnold Schwarzenegger's *Commando* and *Predator*, Bruce Willis' *Die Hard* series, Mel Gibson's *Lethal Weapon*, and Keanu Reeves' *Matrix* series among many others. Rodriguez-Cintron also claimed to be a longtime associate of director Martin Scorsese and to have contributed to about twenty-five recent films on the Warner Bros. lot. He said he was specifically there that day for an appointment he had to present two new scripts to Joel Silver. He said that when he had first arrived, he was confused and thought the security guard had waved him through and the gate arm was raised. He claimed not to realize that he had run through the gate arm.

Rodriguez-Cintron explained his actions after he was detained by security. He realized that the police might be upset at the contents of his duffel, which was on the front seat, so he decided to place the bag in the rear of the car. He admitted that this "camping gear" included a fake handgun, a set of knives, gasoline, and charcoal starter fluid.

During this brief interview, the veteran detectives observed that Rodriguez-Cintron seemed completely disassociated with the event, and appeared a bit odd. In the middle of a serious conversation, Rodriguez-Cintron looked at one of the Burbank dicks and told him that he recognized him as a stunt double for the film *The Matrix*. The detective jokingly agreed that he had been. Rodriguez-Cintron then claimed to have played the character of Neo in that movie, which everyone knew was a role played by Keanu Reeves. He was adamant that the studios had used computers to install Reeves' face over his in the film. It was soon clear to detectives that Rodriguez-Cintron was somewhat delusional. He appeared calm, businesslike, and well-dressed, but something was wrong. Rodriguez-Cintron asserted that the studios owed him over $300 million for past projects. He continued to ramble about the studios, Joel Silver, and the *Matrix* movies. All of this was a bit amusing to the detectives until Rodriguez-Cintron uttered, "I knew this would happen...now my story will get out. This will be in the news soon, and everyone will know that a person with a bomb smashed through a gate at Warner Brothers." He then claimed that he would only get "three to six months for this," and uttered, "So what? I will eventually get out, and it will be worth it."

Detectives were extremely wary of the claims being made by Rodriguez-Cintron. They dispatched studio investigators to Joel Silver's office to attempt to confirm any of the claims. Silver's staff reported the following. They said that Rodriguez-Cintron had come to the Warner Studios on September 2, 2010, and had purchased a ticket for the group tour. Sometime during the tour, he had walked away from the guided group and eventually showed up near Silver's car in the parking lot. He spoke to Joel Silver and pitched a *Matrix* idea to him. Silver, in an effort to get rid of him, told him to call his office about the idea. Rodriguez-Cintron left without incident. Four days later he called Silver's office and told a secretary that Silver wanted to meet with him. He left his cell-phone number for Silver to call back. When given this information at a later time, Joel Silver told his staff that the guy was crazy, and he did not want to meet him. The following day a male called Silver's office pretending to be Rodriguez-Cintron's manager, asking for a meeting. The day after that, Rodriguez-Cintron called again and was told that Joel Silver did not want to meet him

Burbank police detectives and studio security experts realized that Rodriguez-Cintron actually believed his own delusional claims that he was a writer and contributor to many major films. They determined that he had been rebuffed several times in the past two weeks by Joel Silver's office, and he had been unable to get Silver to listen to his ideas for a new movie. It appeared to them that it was possible Rodriguez-Cintron was coming to the studios with a fake gun, menacing knives, and incendiary devices in some sort of scheme to force Joel Silver to listen to his ideas.

They also reviewed several surveillance tapes and found that Rodriguez-Cintron's activities were unaccounted for during a six-minute time frame after he had crashed through the gate. They began to question people on the massive lot to see if anything else had occurred. Later that night, Warner security was contacted by another producer on the lot. That man stated that at about four-thirty that day, he came out to his car in the parking lot and found an empty plastic bottle of charcoal lighter fluid with some tissues next to it. He placed the items in the nearby bushes and went home. While watching the news, he heard about the incident at the studios and now believed the item may have been related. Security retrieved this item and gave it to Burbank detectives.

Burbank detectives later found the item to be an exact match to the charcoal lighter fluid found within Rodriguez-Cintron's car. It was also interesting to note that the lot it had been found in was clearly marked with a sign indicating "Producer Lot." The bottle was empty with the cap missing, and there was a small amount of fluid at the bottom.

At some point, Burbank Police Detective Ken Schiffner took over as the lead investigator on this ever-expanding case. He led a team that continued to question people at the studios. Two days later they found a studio employee who had witnessed a Hispanic male pouring a liquid from a plastic bottle onto a black Lexus car in the Producer Lot. As the witness approached him, the male tossed the container onto the windshield of the Lexus and entered a blue Camaro that was parked nearby. The car then sped out of sight. Not knowing of the incident at the north gate, the witness assumed the man was a car detailer applying some sort of cleaner to the car. He did not think anything was wrong until he heard about the arrest a couple days later.

Other facts began to emerge. Neighboring Paramount Studios' security reported that Rodriguez-Cintron had contacted them on September 12, asking for rental space to begin working on his new *Matrix* sequel. He called two of their assistants and told them he was making a hundred-million-dollar sequel to *The Matrix* and needed to rent some space. He also asked them if they could recommend an agent for him. They considered his request bizarre, as they were well aware that *The Matrix* was a Warner Bros. property, and anybody who was a producer in Hollywood already had an agent. He told them he was angry with Warner Bros. for not compensating him for his earlier work. They began to doubt his credibility and had security present when he showed up later that day. He was respectful and calm, but they soon realized he knew nothing about the movie business. They determined he was a fake and terminated their dealings with him.

A Warner Bros. tour guide was interviewed and she recalled that on the day Rodriguez-Cintron took his studios tour, he had told the group that he was a screenplay writer who was currently writing a book on the "dirty business that happens in Hollywood." He then got visibly upset during the tour and later told the guide that his book was about Joel Silver. He pointed at Silver (who was standing in a nearby parking lot) and told the guide that he had just spoken to Silver, saying that Silver had "tried to blow me off." He then asserted that he had written two- to three-hundred scripts that he had given to Silver and Martin Scorsese, and that the two would take his ideas and put their names on them. He was upset that he never got credit for any of his films made by these two men. Lastly, he told the guide that the two men would put him in "a hypnotic state" that caused him to continue providing scripts and material to them without credit or compensation.

The guide would identify Rodriguez-Cintron through police photo lineups. Producer Joel Silver was also interviewed by Det. Schiffner and his team. Silver easily picked out Rodriguez-Cintron's photo from the lineup and identified him as the man who had accosted him in a parking lot near the studio's tour group. He reiterated that he had never met the man before and knew him to have no connection whatsoever to any Warner Bros. productions.

Burbank detectives later searched Rodriguez-Cintron's small apartment and found that he had applied for food stamps and other welfare assistance. He had business cards with his name "Michael Cintron" and documents from a college. They also found that he had lived most of his life in New York City. A check with NYPD showed that they had a history with the suspect as well. Rodriguez-Cintron had a mental-health history in New York and had been admitted to psychiatric care facilities on multiple occasions. He had a past arrest for assaulting his girlfriend. His last known address in New York was at a homeless shelter just three months prior to his arrest in Burbank.

A review was conducted of the material on the USB drive found in Rodriguez-Cintron's pocket during his arrest. On it were letters to various studios claiming that he was a writer/producer and was making a *Matrix* sequel. In a rambling letter to CNN host Anderson Cooper, Rodriguez-Cintron wrote that he helped create over $153 billion in revenue with his film projects for which he was not compensated. He pitched a new book project to Cooper called "Hollywood Demons" that he promised would "blow his mind." Other items of note on the disk included his resume, where he lists an association with every major production company in Hollywood, and a long list of his film credits. Under his list for education, he names the "School of Life" and "Living within Social Societies." Lastly, he lists his title as "Ghost Consultant" and describes it as working behind the scenes on top projects all over the world.

Rodriguez-Cintron's writings claim that he had died seven times, fathered numerous Hollywood celebrity children, conducted time travel, and become both Tom Cruise and Colin Farrell in the past. In a scarier vein, he had at least two long lists on his thumb drive detailing celebrity names along with their associated office and home addresses.

The real clue to Rodriguez-Cintron's mental instability came from a series of rants he wrote about a clinical hypnotherapist who he had obviously been seeing. He claimed that this man was one of the demons pursuing him. I was later allowed to review all of the materials on the thumb drive and found that they were the usual ranting and delusional thoughts of many of the people I have dealt with in the past and describe in this book. He espoused the normal conspiracy theories, and described being pursued by demons and victimized by various institutions along with society in general. They were horribly misspelled, containing hundreds of grammatical and spelling errors in every document. Truly, they were your average hysterical writings of a mad man.

Detective Schiffner, the lead investigator, eventually took the case in total to the district attorney who filed several serious charges against Miguel Rodriguez-Cintron. Among them were charges of stalking, possession and the use of incendiary devices and materials, felony vandalism, and trespassing. At one of his hearings, an arson expert was not called into court, and the judge dismissed the bulk of the serious charges.

After the hearing, a disillusioned Det. Schiffner ended up attending a "Major Arson Investigation" course I was presenting in Los Angeles. In the course I profiled Tyrone Wilkerson's case, detailing his several arson-related attacks on the Jet Propulsion Lab in Pasadena. Det. Schiffner found close parallels between the two cases. He consulted with me after my class, and I agreed to help him get his case reassigned to a special district attorney who handled mostly arson-related cases. The case went to Special Arson Prosecutor Sean Carney from the Los Angeles District Attorney's Office. He re-filed the case with several arson-related counts and pushed it through several hearings, all the way to a jury trial. The trial was closely watched and monitored by several civil attorneys and the heads of security from more than one studio.

On May 2, 2011, DDA Carney called me into Pasadena Superior Court as the final prosecution witness. I was to testify as an expert arson witness regarding the materials found within the suspect's vehicle. My testimony lasted about an hour and a half. I opined that, given the materials that were in the possession of the suspect, along with his implied threats, erratic behavior, and other factors, I believed he was at the Warner Bros. studios that day to initiate a major traumatic event. The materials he had on hand were sufficient to construct at least six different incendiary devices made out of the cloth wicks and the various containers of charcoal starter fluid and gasoline. The eight special bundles of matches were designed to give him a large flame when struck, so as to facilitate the rapid ignition of the incendiary devices. Other strips of cloth were possibly brought to bind someone, and the fake gun (which was altered to appear very real) was likely to be used to control or kidnap someone. Finally, the knives and claw hammer were most likely there to torture or kill someone.

My belief was that the most likely scenario would be that Rodriguez-Cintron, irate and embarrassed after being rebuffed by Joel Silver, would forcibly enter the property with his car (which he did), find the office of Joel Silver or Martin Scorsese, use the realistic-looking pistol to force his way into the office, kidnap and bind either or both men, and then force them to hear his ideas or possibly sign documents. I believed that the knives and hammer were needed to force, torture, or kill the victims as the gun was a fake. I further believed that the incendiary materials were brought with him as a backup plan if all else failed. He would possibly attempt to burn the office, building, or anything else on the lot in order to gain the media attention he craved.

My final opinion that day was that this was possibly an end-of-life event in which the suspect had very little expectation

Fireraisers, Freaks, And Fiends

of surviving the incident, and that he likely would have ended the day in some fashion, either by suicide or taking a victim with him in a murder-suicide, and most likely through fire or by cop.

I expressed to the jury that it appeared that the defendant did not find the target he was looking for (Silver or Scorsese), so he did the next best thing and attacked a vehicle within the Producer Lot. It was also my belief that he had tried to actually ignite the black Lexus on fire, but was unable to do so. It was my past experience that charcoal lighter fluid was a very poor substance to use when attempting to burn a metal vehicle. This particular substance is manufactured in a way that requires a porous wicking material (like charcoal or a rag) in order to sustain a flame. It just doesn't work on the smooth metal of an automobile. I have known several would-be car arsonists who have failed in their attempt because they used charcoal starter fluid.

DDA Carney would later state that my testimony was "clear, concise, convincing, and the knockout punch" for the prosecution's case. The jury later gave similar reviews.

On May 3, 2011, Rodriguez-Cintron took the stand in his own defense in Department C of Pasadena Superior Court in front of the jury. He was well-dressed, clean-cut, and youthful in appearance. He told the jury the story that he truly believed. He told them he was a big-shot Hollywood producer and writer, and that Martin Scorsese and Joel Silver had in fact screwed him out of millions. The defense would later inform the courtroom that Joel Silver did have a rather poor reputation, even by Hollywood's low standards, as other parties have also claimed he stole their ideas in the past.

Despite the contentions of Rodriguez-Cintron and his attorney, the jury was not fooled. They recognized him as being out of his mind and extremely dangerous, and they quickly found him guilty on all presented counts. He was immediately remanded to custody. Shortly afterward there were some legal maneuverings that attempted to get him into a psychiatric prison. One way or another, Miguel Rodriguez-Cintron was led away to a secure room for a few years, where he is no doubt writing a few more screenplays.

Investigator's Analysis:
This event, like the preceding Tyrone Wilkerson case, ended up being a very dramatic incident that at the time garnered only a brief mention on the evening news casts. However, since the planned attacks failed, neither of them was remembered by the public forty-eight hours later. Nonetheless, the investigators from two agencies, and more importantly the highly paid studio security specialists, were extremely impressed by this attack. Had this attack been successful, it is quite likely it would have been a news event worthy of international press, and all the Monday morning quarterbacks wondering how the authorities could have not prevented the murder of a famous Hollywood producer or the torching of a major studio. The scariest part is that when he is eventually released from custody, there is little doubt that Miguel Rodriguez-Cintron will be as real a threat as the day he was arrested.

SECRET AGENT MAN: TIM KOMONYI
SAN FERNANDO VALLEY, 2005

Tim Komonyi was coming mentally unglued, slowly but surely. Anyone who knew him, lived near him, or worked with him was aware that Tim was cracking up. It was blatantly obvious to even the most casual of observers. It was obvious to everyone, that is, but Tim.

On January 27, 2006, my partner Mike Cofield and I met Tim Komonyi in a cramped break room in the smelliest, dirtiest section of the old Central Jail in downtown Los Angeles. We had just finished searching his mom's house in Sylmar and had found all the evidence we needed to prove that Tim was one of the more dangerous persons we had met in quite a while. But as we were sitting across from him at the broken conference table, sizing him up before starting the interview, we couldn't help but think how pathetic and ridiculous he looked, peering and blinking at us through old horn-rimmed glasses. He looked nearly identical to the Michael Douglas character in the movie *Falling Down*—, a real nerdy, "techy" type of geek. He didn't look at all like the out-of-control maniac we had been hunting for months. As it turns out, Tim's life wasn't that far removed from the pathetic but dark character in the movie.

Tim had grown up in the San Fernando Valley. He didn't talk about his childhood much, but, suffice to say, he seemed to have the broken-home childhood that seems prevalent in this day and age. What is known about Tim is that he was extremely bright, yet socially inept. He had behavior and emotional problems all of his life. He was not athletic, tall, and very white-boy geeky. He looked exactly like what he was—a nerdy engineering type who looked more at home behind a keyboard than in any sort of physical job.

Despite his straight-laced life, Tim somehow got into a lot of trouble. He started using methamphetamines and cocaine. In his twenties, he was arrested numerous times for car theft, burglary, and receiving stolen property. He was not involved in gangs or anything like that, but it seemed like he was going to grow up to be the tweeker/burglar* type. Eventually, based on the accumulation of his crimes, he was sent to state prison for a few years.

Tim never talked about his experiences in the "joint," but prison could not have gone very well for him. He was a very soft-looking white boy who was no doubt a daily victim in the predator-filled prison yards. We harbored few illusions about what his role was in the prison population. After Tim got out of prison, his life seemed to change for the better. At some point he started going back to school, and his keen mind really started to show. He enrolled in a local technical institute in the San Fernando Valley, and began taking advanced mathematics and technology classes. A later review of his grades showed that Tim excelled at microelectronics, circuitry, mathematics, and electricity. Tim's grades were close to straight A's throughout his three years at the school.

During this time, he met his future wife, Veronica Lopez. She was a goofy and not-so-smart Mexican girl from a very tough Pacoima neighborhood. Although she lived in a Hispanic gang-controlled area, she was a clean-living girl whose sole aspiration in life was to start a family and be a mother. She met Tim at her work, where he frequently flirted with her. From the outset, she liked Tim for his brains, and for his boyish and sometimes childlike behavior. Like many characters you will meet in this book, Tim led a secret and dangerous double life, at least in his fantasies. He told Veronica many stories about his "dangerous and crazy" past life, and she reveled in the idea that he was a bad boy who she had somehow tamed. The two eventually married and purchased a townhome in a nice complex, in a clean neighborhood, in the foothill suburb of Canyon Country. Tim was extremely handy and immediately set out to customize the townhome for the couple. They both wanted a child badly, and shortly after Veronica gave birth to a baby girl. The couple had few friends as Tim was your typical loner, and Veronica, who was never an outgoing or adventuresome girl, seldom hung out with anyone other than her sister and mother.

At some point during this time, Tim began to lose his mind. He was always pretty weird and quirky, but now he was starting to do some really bizarre things. True to his engineering roots, he was forever tinkering and making things in his garage. Soon, he started acting a bit like his old tweeker self and began collecting junk and odds and ends for no apparent reason. He spent long hours in the garage by himself, making bizarre things out of junk. He also started to go out at night and during his free time, and collected cans and other recyclables. He even started to rummage through dumpsters and trash bins.

Tim was having work problems too. He worked as a technician at a large medical center in San Fernando. Numerous times, female employees had reported that Tim would act overly flirty toward them. His own boss recognized that he often drifted from his area of work and was found sitting near women in other parts of the massive building. Some of the women thought he was just a harmless flirter, but others reported that they were very uncomfortable around him. Eventually, the human services director of the hospital became notified of his behavior and called Tim in for a talk. Tim arrived at the meeting and was very belligerent and hostile. He was extremely upset that he was being talked to and appeared highly agitated and paranoid. Tim also had put in for several different types of worker's compensation claims for odd injuries. Some of these were turned down as ridiculous, and again Tim was called in for counseling and a warning about his behavior.

After this latest warning, the security department at the medical center began to keep loose tabs on Tim. This did not go unnoticed by Tim and only served to fuel his paranoia. Tim began to act even more bizarrely than ever and started to walk around his work as if he were some sort of spy or secret agent. This all culminated with the hospital HR department head ordering Tim to a clinic for a mental health evaluation. Tim arrived wearing a long bulky trench coat of all things and began acting weirdly. A female acquaintance approached and asked Tim if he was okay. Tim winked and told her just to stand back and watch. Soon, because he was standing in a somewhat intimidating manner, security arrived. As soon as they did, Tim announced, "Stand back, I'm wired and rigged to blow." He indicated toward his bulky clothing, hinting that he had a bomb strapped to him. The Los Angeles Police Department (LAPD) was summoned, and as soon as they arrived, Tim threw himself on the floor and announced that he was just kidding. Tim was suspended by the hospital at that point, and a restraining order was obtained to keep him off the site. He eventually settled a hefty worker's comp claim with the hospital.

For the several months of 2004 and 2005 that Tim was off work, his behavior really started to deteriorate. He stopped bathing and was up all hours of the night tinkering in his garage. His paranoia increased to the point that he began calling the local sheriff's station to report suspicious persons and vehicles. The local deputies had over two dozen calls from Tim, reporting on virtually all of his neighbors. A local sheriff's detective sergeant knew Tim well and had several notes from him in which Tim volunteered to go "deep undercover" to root out drugs and car thieves in his neighborhood. Tim seemed obsessed with crime in his neighborhood despite the fact that the neighbors were mainly senior citizens, and the area was relatively crime free.

His wife Veronica later reported that Tim was using several types of prescription drugs during this period. The drugs were mainly for stress, anxiety, and depression. She believed that Tim was possibly supplementing his prescriptions with meth or some other narcotic. Veronica noticed that Tim had become increasingly paranoid, and he began to regularly accuse her of having affairs. Tim stopped working completely, and the couple began to fall behind on their mortgage. For several months they remained late on numerous bills, and Tim's behavior eroded even further. Finally, by early 2005, Veronica had had enough and took their daughter to go live with her mother in Pacoima. Within a month she had obtained the services of a divorce attorney and had decided to sell the townhome.

After Veronica left, Tim began to have conflicts with everyone around him. He immediately started an ongoing battle with the head of the complex' Homeowner's Association (HOA), a woman in her sixties. Tim began aggressively confronting her in public about all the problems in the area. He removed all his own sprinkler heads and let his sprinklers flood the common areas. He began pounding and sawing late into the night in his home and garage, generating numerous complaints from the neighbors. He began to act and talk in a very suspicious manner, intimating to neighbors that he was doing undercover work and that he was skilled in the use of guns and explosives. He told several yard workers that he possessed military explosives and numerous firearms. He finally told a male neighbor that his wife left him for a cop and that he was going to have to kill the cop to get his wife back. (In fact, his wife had no boyfriends at all, but her better-looking sister was dating a San Fernando police officer).

Despite Tim's menacing behavior, he garnished little attention from the local sheriff's. Most of his neighbors just thought he was a weirdo and did not take his behavior very seriously. Maybe it was his milquetoast appearance or his nerdy manner, but folks just did not perceive him as a viable threat. He was more of an annoyance. His middle-aged HOA president considered him one large pain in the ass. She was not afraid of him and confronted him on many occasions. He made several veiled threats to her, but she took none of them seriously. It would take her several months to change her mind about Tim.

In the meantime, Tim was losing battles on every front. His wife's attorney filed for divorce and custody of their only child. At the same time, his wife began negotiations with a real estate agent to sell the townhome. The first time that the female agent showed up at the townhome with Veronica, Tim was present and got into both of their faces in a very threatening manner. The real estate lady fled the scene, despite Veronica's pleas to her that Tim was not a serious threat. The next day, the real estate lady found her office vandalized and torn flyers for the townhome scattered in her doorway. She refused to represent Veronica after this.

Within a month or two, the townhome began going into foreclosure, because Tim had not paid the mortgage despite having received a recent large settlement from the hospital. Veronica and her attorney pleaded with Tim to sell the townhome and split the proceeds. The townhome had tripled in value since they purchased it, and both thought this was a fair deal. Tim refused all offers and said he would never let anyone else live in his home. Veronica then began negotiations with a property investor group named "Andrade Financial," which routinely purchased properties that were foreclosed or close to foreclosure. They waited until they heard that Tim was in a court hearing for unpaid tickets. He was sentenced to a few days in jail for the tickets, and Veronica and the Andrade rep went to the townhome to inspect it. They saw that Tim had nailed the front door shut and had covered all the windows with paint. They were able to access the townhome by prying the garage open. Inside they found that Tim had begun removing all the fixtures from the home and had torn all the interior furnishings out down to the faucets, electrical outlets, and carpet. They saw that he barricaded the interior front door by driving large bolts into the concrete floor, bracing the door closed. Tim had painted on the walls in red paint the words "Die in hell bitch!" They also noticed there were dozens of pellets from a pellet gun lying all over the garage.

After this inspection, the Andrade rep saw that there was thousands of dollars' worth of damage and lowered their bid on the townhome. Three weeks after this, a civil judge ruled in San Fernando Court that the divorce was final and that Veronica would have custody of the child. The judge further ordered Tim to sign the sales receipt for the townhome over to Andrade's lawyer. Tim refused, and the judge ordered the court clerk to sign for Tim. At that point, Tim collapsed in court and began crying, yelling, and screaming. He turned to Veronica's attorney; a middle-aged Chinese woman named Mak, and yelled, "Watch your back, Mak." Tim was held in contempt and escorted out of the court by bailiffs. Several days later he was released from jail and ordered to appear in another courtroom for outstanding traffic tickets. Irritated by this, Tim threw another hissy fit in front of the judge and was held in contempt again for several days.

When he got out of jail in early June, he went back to the townhome to find that Andrade's (the new owner) had changed the locks. Tim changed them back and reoccupied the townhome. Over the next few weeks, he could be heard using power tools, drills, and saws until five in the morning. One day, the HOA president, Veronica, and a female rep from Andrade's, arrived together to order him out of the townhome as it no longer belonged to him. At that time Tim told the three that he would "blow this place to Hell" before he would let anyone else live there. He began yelling and screaming at all three as they fled the scene and called the sheriff's. As they left, Tim yelled at the Andrade's rep, "I've got your (vehicle license) plate now." They saw him furiously writing something down on a notepad. Later that same day, Tim went to his upstairs window, opened it, and hung a realistic dummy from a noose out the window. All the neighbors panicked and assumed that Tim had hung himself. Several calls were made to the local sheriff's station. When deputies arrived with Veronica in tow, Tim calmly walked out and told them that he was preparing a Halloween prank and that his wife was mad at him because of it. Somehow, he managed to fool the cops, and they left without evicting Tim. A later chat with the deputies revealed that they just thought Tim was a harmless goofball and his wife a hysterical oddball.

Over the next few weeks, Tim alarmed some of the groundskeepers and residents by stating that, if he was evicted, he would "burn the place down, and they'll never figure out how I did it." He again claimed to people that he had been conducting secret surveillances for the sheriff's and had guns and explosives in his possession. Most of the male neighbors laughed him off as a very soft looking kook.

Sometime in late June, Tim was in court again and was incarcerated for refusing to pay all of his traffic tickets. This time he stayed in jail for about three weeks, which was just long enough for Andrade's to get in and start repairing the damage to the townhome. When the Andrade crew arrived in early July, they were stunned at the magnitude of the damage to the modern townhome. All interior furnishings, appliances, carpeting, and paint had been stripped away. All plumbing had been removed, and a synthetic concrete called "Quick Crete" had been poured into the empty pipes where the sinks and toilets had been, thereby destroying the home's plumbing. All of the electrical outlets had been ripped from the walls, and hardened plastic cement had been squirted into any openings. Additionally, Komonyi had cut all of the main power lines in the home just outside of the main power panel. Andrade owners would later call this their worst business loss as the townhome had now decreased in value by about $75,000 despite the strong real estate market.

Andrade sent teams of contractors to the townhome over the next month to rehab it for future occupancy. Due to the significant damage, contractors specializing in plumbing, electricity, and heating/air-conditioning were needed to complete the work. By late July, many of the repairs were finished with the exception of connecting the main power and furnace.

No one had heard from or seen Tim in several weeks, and all were hoping that this episode was winding down to a quiet finish. This was wishful thinking. In early August, he showed up uninvited to the West Hills Law Offices of Attorney Mak, who had represented Veronica Komonyi in the divorce. Mak was out of town, but Tim demanded from her secretary to know where Mak lived, what kind of car she drove, and what her schedule was. Tim only left after the secretary threatened to call the police. Late at night on August 10, attorney Mak had her fourth-floor office windows shot out with several marbles, apparently via a slingshot, causing nearly $5,000 in damage. At the same time, an unknown suspect had written on her sign the words "Die Bitch" and "Watch your back" after her name. On a different sign, over her name appeared the words "Mak, watch your back," scrawled in red marker. Attorney Irene Mak immediately recalled the words Komonyi had said to her in court a few weeks prior: *Watch your back, Mak.* She also recalled that Tim had written "Die bitch" in red on the walls of his home. Attorney Mak reported her suspicions to the LAPD, but they said there was not much they could do.

By August 30, things were really beginning to pick up. Attorney Mak's offices were again attacked late at night by marbles, causing over $4,000 in damages. The next week, she had a phone conversation with the eviction attorney used by Andrade Financial, Mr. O'Brien. That attorney mentioned in passing that his windows were being repaired in his law offices because "some nut blew them out with a slingshot and marbles." Mak and O'Brien talked further and found out that this incident occurred on the same night as Mak's, but forty miles away in the foothill city of Monrovia. The Andrade attorney said he believed that it had to be Tim Komonyi, since he had to force him out of his office the prior week. Tim had arrived at the office uninvited and sat in the lobby telling other visitors that he had been screwed by O'Brien. He left only after being told that police were responding. Upon leaving, he told O'Brien's secretary, "Watch your back." On the night after the vandalisms, O'Brien had received a telephone message from a male he believed to be Komonyi; the caller stated, "Watch your back...this was just a warning. Next time it will be real."

That same night as the marble attacks, another event occurred at the Andrade Financial business offices in nearby Glendora. This was the company that had purchased Komonyi's townhome after the eviction and had retained Attorney O'Brien to facilitate the deal. Their burglary alarm had sounded, and Glendora PD officers found that a window had been shattered by several marbles. They collected these items and left the scene. Several hours later, a fire occurred within the same office. The local fire department, unaware of the earlier vandalism, had classified the fire as an "accidental electrical malfunction."

These three similar attacks all occurred the same night, but were spread over a fifty-mile distance and in three different cities. The only connection these people had with each other was that they had all dealt recently in court with Tim Komonyi. Attorneys Mak and O'Brien attempted to bring these three events together. But, since they were all classified as misdemeanor vandalisms, and all occurred in three different police jurisdictions, they got very little interest from their local police.

Other things were also happening. The female Andrade rep that had gone along to help Veronica evict Tim back in June had her home and car vandalized in the city of Pasadena. The home had a window broken, and the car had windows smashed and tires punctured. Tim's ex-boss at the hospital in Mission Hills along with the human resource manager and the security manager (all women) each had their personal cars vandalized, with smashed windows and flattened tires, in the month of August. All of these incidents occurred at night and at their homes. It was later found that none of them had ever told Tim Komonyi where they lived.

At the time of all of these seemingly random attacks, Tim Komonyi was not being actively investigated by anyone. His crimes fit into that weird niche in law enforcement that, taken as an isolated incident, seemed too petty to put much time or effort into. Additionally, it would be several months before anyone put all of these events together. Tim was flying very low under the radar up to this point. That was about to change. Tim was about to be elevated to "master criminal" status—well, at least by the guys really starting to look at him. To everyone else, he was just an oddball and nerd.

On August 13 of 2005, my coworker Mike Cofield was the on-call arson/bomb detective. He is probably the smartest, most technically-skilled guy in our office. He got a call to respond to a townhome in Canyon Country where contractors had found a funny item within the floor of a townhome they were renovating. Not knowing what to do, they called the fire department, who in turn believed that this was possibly the site of a meth lab. They in turn called the bomb squad, which coincidentally is what firemen do every time they can't figure out what something is.

Mike and his partners arrived and found a vacant townhome that was under construction. Workers pointed out some mysterious wiring in the floor of the upstairs bedroom and some plastic bottles that were set in the floor. The bottles were mainly empty sports drinks. The wiring had been attached to the main power line to the home, which was under the floor in that area. The wiring led from the main power to a small metal horseshoe-shaped item. This horseshoe-shaped piece of metal was taped to the bottom of one of the bottles. The area around this item had been packed with cardboard and shredded sections of insulating foam. This stretched from one wall to another. All of this odd stuff was packed under the floor, and the opening had been sealed shut with a bonding material. The carpet had been replaced over this, completely hiding the hole in the floor.

Detective Cofield had no idea what this configuration was but realized that it didn't belong in the home. At the time, there was no one around to tell him the history of the home, so he chalked it up to a suspicious but unknown item in the floor. Luckily, he took pictures of the set up, and kept the horseshoe-shaped item. He left the scene, telling the firefighters that he didn't know exactly what he had, but couldn't see a bomb or any other hazardous device.

The contractors resumed their work for the next two days, continually pulling new odd items out of the floor and ducting within the floor. Two days later, an air-conditioning repairman was on site, fixing the vandalized furnace. When he removed the furnace cover, he found a sports-drink bottle full of gasoline inside the furnace. He removed it and continued his repairs. Several minutes later, he found a larger plastic bottle full of gasoline placed on top of the burners for the furnace. He then inspected the ducting that came out of the furnace. Inside that he found several more small plastic bottles full of liquids. Some were later discovered to be full of gasoline, some full of flammable brake fluid, and some were filled with rubbing alcohol. All of these items had been secreted within the furnace and ducting. The last item the contractor found was a small plastic bottle of gasoline with a strange metal horseshoe item taped to it. This item had wires leading from it to the main power of the home, just like the similar item found in the flooring. Again the fire department was called, and again the bomb squad was called. This time I was on duty.

When I arrived, the HOA president was milling around the scene, and she filled me in on the background of Tim Komonyi, including his threatening behavior and threats to burn the house down. I cleared the "device" and examined it for a long period of time. While doing this, the HAZMAT detail gave me the lab report on all of the flammable liquids. When I looked at the metal horseshoe-shaped item, I was stumped as to what it could be, but it looked vaguely familiar to me. I photographed the bizarre components in the floor and took the metal piece to my office. When I got back, I began to go through my old materials from classes and finally found what I thought this item might be. Coincidentally, I had just returned from an advanced arson class on the east coast. Part of it had to do with investigating appliance fires. I eventually recognized that the metal horseshoe-shaped item was in fact the heating element from an electric coffee maker.

The next day I called Det. Mike Cofield and told him about my discovery. He was amazed, because his item ended up being the same thing. I told him about my interviews with the contractors and the background on the home and the previous owner,

Fireraisers, Freaks, And Fiends

Tim Komonyi. A few days later, Mike and I sat down for several hours and diagrammed out what we had seen and how it was configured. It took a lot of thought, be we eventually came to the conclusion that someone, most likely Tim Komonyi, had constructed a long-term, incendiary delay device into the floor, ducting, and furnace of his home. We found this item to be so sophisticated and exotic that we really doubted that a civilian could have pulled it off. At that time, we had no idea about Tim's mindset and his heavy interest and knowledge of electrical circuits and engineering. For several weeks we doubted our own findings and consulted with several other experienced arson investigators. Few believed that someone could actually construct something like this into the floors and walls of a home and expect it to work at some later date. However, we all agreed that it was possible. The theory we settled on was that Tim built this as a hidden booby trap. He then disabled the electricity of the home in a very visible way, which would force the new owners to make dozens of repairs to the power panel and other visible wires. Eventually, when all circuits were reconnected and the panel was recharged, a current would be sent under the floors to the hidden heating elements, which in turn would ignite the plastic bottles they were taped to and would spill the gasoline and other flammable liquids throughout the ducting. The added Styrofoam and paper products found in the floor would extend and accelerate the fire from one exterior wall to the other, thereby causing catastrophic damage to the home.

We believed the similar bottles of gas found within the furnace were some sort of secondary or backup booby trap incendiary. This was designed to function when the furnace was powered up at a later date, causing a large fire in the furnace area. We believe that Tim's plan was for these items to function several weeks after he was evicted, and in a manner that may appear as the accidental failures of appliances. All in all, this scheme was far-fetched, crazy, but pretty damn ingenious.

Our problem was that we knew very little about Tim at this point. We also knew he hadn't been in the home in weeks, and from a legal standpoint, we knew it would be difficult to link him to this device in a court of law. Nonetheless, we set about attempting to prove our theory.

For the next four months, we interviewed all of Tim's neighbors, in-laws, and coworkers. From these interviews we pieced together a portrait of a very disturbed guy. Our first source of information was his ex-wife Veronica. Unfortunately, she was not the brightest bulb in town and was actually not very helpful. While she gave us a great description of his deteriorating life and all of his bizarre activities, she downplayed everything as just Tim's boyish behavior. She considered him more of a "naughty boy" than a real potential threat. She appeared to actually enjoy his many desperate attempts to get her back. She also seemed to revel in the fact that Tim believed she had many boyfriends, even though she wasn't that type of person nor did she have the looks to facilitate that life.

Veronica's sister and mother were much better sources of information. They passed on many tidbits that really alarmed us. These were things that Veronica did not deem important enough to mention. They said that Tim routinely followed the three of them on a near daily basis, and would often switch between as many as four or five different cars during the day. They saw him wearing many different disguises, including dressing up as a homeless man and a woman. They pointed out graffiti on their trash cans and on several light poles in their neighborhood that all formed the letters "VBSL." This appeared to us originally as regular tagger graffiti, but they explained that it meant "Veronica Bitch Slut Liar." They knew him to steal their mail and vandalize their vehicles. They described several high-speed chases where they had tried to elude Tim and he had tried to run them off the road. Each time that they reported him to their local police, Tim would talk his way out of it and describe them as crazy women.

Tim also took to wearing trench coats and walking around as some sort of spy or secret agent. They knew him to be in stores where they shopped and at places they frequented.

We saw Tim's actions as part of an overall pattern of paranoia, stalking, and obsession. We recognized this as consistent with many other cases of this nature that we had investigated. However, we still had nothing to link him to his old home and no real good reason to get a search or arrest warrant. Eventually, by Christmas of 2005, Tim's case began to fade, and there were no recent leads to go on. His bizarre antics were replaced in our office by more serious cases we were working.

However, Tim would not go away quietly. Just as we were starting to forget him, he reminded us again of what a jerk he was. On New Year's Day, 2006, he went on a bit of a spree. Three homes in his old townhome complex were vandalized with marbles obviously propelled by a slingshot. On the same night, two other neighbors had their car tires slashed. The victims of the marbles were the HOA president, her daughter who lived a few doors down, and her daughter-in-law who also lived in the complex. The car tires that were slashed belonged to two elderly neighbors who had lived on either side of Tim Komonyi's townhome. True to his cowardly form, Tim was only attacking women and the elderly.

Seven days later, a near identical second round of attacks occurred to the same victims. More marbles had shattered windows and the same vehicles had their tires slashed. By mid-January, Veronica called me, and for the first time was alarmed that Tim was starting to become dangerous. She said that the courts had restricted his visits again in late December, and since then he has told her that if he couldn't "see his daughter and wife (he still did not recognize the divorce), then no one would." He had been seen lurking around their home and climbing their back wall several times late at night. Veronica had hired a private detective who had started surveillance on Tim. On the second week of the surveillance, Tim had apparently caught the PI and pointed a gun at him, chasing him away. The next night Tim had been seen in the vicinity of Veronica's sister's home, and her car had been broken into. Many items were stolen, but some mail that had been stolen from Veronica's home the prior week had been left in the burglarized car.

Veronica was pleading with us to do something. Because she had called her local police so many times on Tim and had then refused to prosecute, they began to strongly doubt her credibility. I really didn't blame them, because she had been similarly flaky with our investigation.

My partner Mike and I got together and decided to write a warrant for Tim's home, seeking, of all things, the marbles that Tim had used to vandalize the twelve different victims in this case. We received a great deal of skepticism and heckling from within our own unit as we were major case arson/bomb investigators looking for marbles! We also included knives, costumes, disguises, and evidence of incendiary items on our list, along with surveillance items. As we watched his mom's home in Sylmar for confirmation that he lived there prior to the warrant service, we noted that there were other detectives watching the same home. We would later find out that the San Fernando Police Department was also planning a search warrant against Tim for a couple burglaries he committed, and a private investigator was still observing him. Apparently he was becoming a one-man crime wave.

On January 27, we planned to serve the warrant. As a normal course of business, the night before the warrant service, I ran Tim through a computer and found out that he had been arrested for auto burglary on January 25. He was currently in our own jail. That made the service of our search warrant a much lower-risk operation. We went ahead and served the warrant on the 27 and were happily stunned to find pretty much everything we had hoped to find...and more! In descending order of importance, we found the following items in Tim's personal property: a photo of the incendiary device in place in the floor, including *Tim's feet in the photo*!!!!!!; a hand-drawn schematic of the incendiary device and where Tim was to install it in the floor; a wrist rocket slingshot with three green marbles, identical to all of the marbles located during the fourteen different marble attacks; an "arson kit" which consisted of a small bag containing a mask, highway flares, and surgical gloves; a bag containing various wigs, masks, and disguises, a dagger-type knife consistent with the marks left on the many slashed tires; "Thomas Guide" maps with the pages to the various victims' addresses highlighted; both daytime and nighttime surveillance photos of Andrade Financial's offices and the vehicle driven by the "Andrade" rep; night vision gear, surveillance cameras, audio taping devices, and a complete notebook filled with Tim's frenetic notes and writings, most of which were detailed surveillance notes of times he had followed Veronica, her sister, and her suspected boyfriends. These surveillance notes contained references to his various disguises, references to vehicle chases and avoiding police, and dozens of license plate numbers. A last item of interest was a complete computer printout and file on the private investigator that had been following Tim. Tim had apparently done counter surveillance and had begun gathering information on the investigator, including work and home addresses, vehicle models and license plate numbers, and photos. When I later showed these items to the moronic boob masquerading as a PI, he almost had a heart attack and demanded immediate police protection.

 Additionally, Tim had within his possession numerous items linking him to more than one burglary. The last unique item in Tim's possession, which pretty much summed up his crazy life, was a self-help book entitled, *How to Win Your Wife Back*. Well, Tim was not going to win Veronica back. On the contrary, she was going to help see that he spent many years in prison.

So, now back to where we started this story—the interview room in Men's Central Jail. We were two of the most experienced arson investigators in all of California, and we sat face-to-face looking at one of the most pathetic suspects we had ever chased. It was hard for us to believe that this goofy-looking guy was the brazen and clever crook who had terrorized two dozen people for the past ten months. Even to us he didn't look like he was capable of scaring anyone. However, we attempted to interview him for about three hours. We came away with a series of almost juvenile denials from him in the face of reams of good evidence. We realized that he really was living in some weird fantasy world where he believed he was the good guy and was conducting secret agent operations to get his family back from all the bad guys.

Tim was of the mindset that if he just got his wife back, everything would be okay. He believed that there were forces out there trying to intercede and destroy his plans to get back with Veronica. Never mind that she didn't like him anymore and that their divorce had been final for several months now. Tim was the epitome of denial! However, we also learned that, despite his obviously warped sense of reality, he was extremely clever and cagey when being interviewed. He was very careful not to admit to anything more than what we already knew. He was very intelligent and very difficult to catch in conflicting statements, despite the fact that he spent three hours denying everything he had ever done in life. One of the only things he was proud of was the fact that he had turned the surveillance tables on the bumbling "private eye" who had been hired to watch him. Tim was obviously more skilled than the wannabe private dick.

We came away from our interview with the realization that Tim was intelligent, clever, bright, but undeniably crazy. He would take his denial of obvious facts to the jury box and would never admit to anything. This idiot was not going to take a plea bargain that would have probably saved him about eight years of time in prison.

FIRERAISERS, FREAKS, AND FIENDS

The district attorney's office, after reviewing the case, charged Tim Komonyi with over twenty-five felony counts, the most serious being attempted murder by arson, attempted arson of an occupied structure, use of an incendiary delay device, and several felony stalking counts. He was facing about nineteen years in state prison.

We went through a lengthy preliminary hearing in which a judge bound him over for trial and held him to answer on twenty-four felony charges. Over the following year, two different lawyers spent hours of their time explaining to Tim in legal terms that he would be royally screwed if he went to a jury trial and that they could get him as little as eight years in prison if he pled guilty. Nope, Tim remained true to his mania and refused all reasonable offers. In 2008 he was convicted by a jury after three weeks of trial. He was convicted of twenty-one felony counts which led to a sentence of eighteen years in prison. His own defense expert came to court and admitted that Tim appeared to have constructed a unique and diabolical incendiary delay device. The defense expert's only value to the defense was that he stated that he didn't think the device would have functioned as designed.

Tim Komonyi had several highlights to his trial. The first came on the opening day of the trial when an unknown female called the courthouse to report a bomb being delivered that day. This caused a four hour delay in the start of the case when the security officers at the entrance found an abandoned bag left at the metal detectors. It later proved to be someone's lunch. Although it was never proven, we found indications that Tim had a friend on the streets make the call in a crazy attempt to stop his trial. Another high point of the case was when Tim revealed to the judge that my partner Mike had attempted to seduce him during the interview. Tim was not aware that the entire interview was on tape and that the judge had listened to it. The visibly angry judge told Tim that he was the most unbelievable person she had ever met. Every time the judge called a recess in the trial, Tim would pull out photos of his daughter and point them toward the jury. When he did this, he feigned crying over her photo. This had the opposite effect than intended as the antics began to irritate the jurors. A last and more serious problem developed during the trial when we learned that a jail deputy had given Tim a lighter and some combustible materials so that he could "do experiments" for his defense. My partner Mike and I absolutely exploded when we discovered this. We contacted the jail commander and pointed out the idiocy of giving an incarcerated inmate who was suspected of attempted murder by arson, the means with which to start a fire. The young jail deputy was counseled over this lapse in judgment.

During the trial, Tim's beleaguered lawyer was left with little to work with as he admitted in open court that Tim was probably guilty of everything except the attempted murder charges. However, he tried to tell the jury that Tim was operating in a make-believe world, impressing on them the fact that nobody had really gotten hurt. He reasoned that because no one was harmed, the jury should give Tim a break. The jury found Tim to be a little different than we did. While we saw him as a somewhat dangerous and nutty nerd, the jurors later told us that, to a person, they found him to be creepy, evil, and dangerous as Hell. The judge apparently agreed and sentenced him to only one year below the maximum.

There is another James Bond footnote to Tim's case. While awaiting his trial, he remained in the county jail for nearly two years. He relished his role as a "trusty" (inmate that has been entrusted with minor duties) as it gave him free run of the massive jail and unlimited contact with thousands of vicious gang members, killers, and thugs. This wormy-looking nerd somehow ingratiated himself with one of the most dangerous prison gangs in the world, and was seen several times associating with hard-core, vicious murderers. At his sentencing, his worried attorney admonished Tim to stay clear of trouble in jail and keep to himself. We don't have much faith that Tim will heed that sage advice, as there have already been indications that Tim continues to want to play "secret agent" within the jail system. If he persists in this behavior in state prison, we believe that Tim will have effectively signed his own death warrant, or at least mortgaged off his meager manhood, as the gangsters are sure to find out about any treasonous acts and shank him to death or sell him as a prostitute in prison.

All in all, Tim's future doesn't look so bright.

> ***Tweeker:** The term "tweeker" is street slang for a methamphetamines addict; it is a sort of new version of the '70s era term "speed freak." This term is used frequently throughout this book. Sometime over the last fifteen years, methamphetamines eclipsed cocaine as the most dangerous drug in America. Whole swaths of the American heartland have been destroyed by this drug, and an entire generation has been enslaved by it. Tweeker behavior is described as obsessive activities, rampant theft and burglary, erratic violence, inability to sleep or relax, extreme paranoia, and very bizarre and confrontational attitude swings. Extended use leads to serious physical problems and major mental health issues, including paranoid schizophrenia.

Investigator's Analysis:

Tim Komonyi is one of the most bizarre and weird dudes we have ever met. Detective Cofield and I had a hard time wrapping our minds around his petty crimes at first. Later we had an even more difficult time convincing the district attorney's office that this guy was a real danger. At first we looked at him as an overgrown prankster who spent his time settling petty debts and picking on helpless women and the elderly. As we began to discover and track his escalating exploits, we honestly believed he was just weeks away from killing someone. His activities grew so bold, desperate, and overt that we were sure he was working his way up to a spectacular end-game event, that would surely make the news. We believed it highly likely that he was in fear of losing his daughter and would choose to murder her or himself rather than let someone else raise her. Eventually, the prosecutors also began to believe this same thing.

Qi Jun Li
Rosemead High School, Rosemead 2000

The San Gabriel Valley is a long corridor of suburbia that stretches about twenty-five miles from the eastern edge of Los Angeles to the San Bernardino county line. This valley is comprised of thirty-one cities and several large tracts of unincorporated county land. Over a million-and-a-half people live in this valley, and there is a huge population of Chinese Americans. The city of Rosemead sits in the middle of this valley, a couple miles south of the foothills of the San Gabriel Mountains. Rosemead High School is situated at the major intersection of Mission Boulevard and Rosemead Avenue. In April of 2000, the high school had just under two-thousand students in grades nine through twelve, and over a third of them were Asian.

The third week in April is always a sensitive time for law enforcement. There are many notorious anniversary dates during that week, which can often lead to high emotions and unpredictable incidents. Of note, April 19 is the anniversary date of several dramatic federal law enforcement incidents. In 1985, the FBI and ATF raided a massive, heavily-armed compound in Arkansas run by an anti-government religious group known as the Cross, Sword, and Arm of the Lord (CSA). Eight years to the day later, the Branch Davidian cult, another anti-government group, had a similar, heavily-armed compound raided by the ATF and FBI in Waco, Texas. This botched raid led to the deaths of seventy-six men, women, and children. In retaliation for the Waco debacle, Tim McVeigh chose that same date two years later to target the ATF. He initiated the massive truck bomb at the Murrah Federal

FIRERAISERS, FREAKS, AND FIENDS

Building in Oklahoma City, Oklahoma, killing 168 people and injuring nearly seven hundred others.

In the final week that this book was sent to the publisher, yet another horrendous event took place during this fateful time. On Monday, April 15, 2013, two bombs were detonated at the finish line of the Boston Marathon. The heavily televised event was depicted nationwide for the ensuing week. The bombs, which were packed with fragmentation and shrapnel in the form of nails and ball bearings killed three people and wounded 180 others, with a dozen sustaining life threatening trauma. Multiple amputations occurred as a result of these coordinated blasts. On April 18, federal investigators identified two brothers from Chechnya as the suspects. On that date one of the bombers blew himself up in the midst of a gun battle with police while his brother escaped on foot. During the shootout, one police officer was murdered by the brothers and another was seriously wounded. The second bomber was arrested after another gunfight with police a couple days later.

On April 16, 2007 a lone gunman shot and killed thirty-two students and faculty and wounded several others during a rampage on the Virginia Tech campus in Blacksburg, Virginia. The shooter committed suicide immediately following the shootings.

April 20 is not a whole lot different. It has the ignoble distinction of being Adolf Hitler's birthday, which still causes incidents sixty-plus years after his death. It also was the date two disenfranchised students in Columbine, Colorado, chose to attack their school mates with assault weapons, fire, and homemade bombs in 1999. This horrendous assault, known now as the Columbine Massacre, killed thirteen and injured a couple dozen more. In less sinister news, this day also has been adopted by potheads everywhere as the international holiday to celebrate marijuana.

One little known side note about the Columbine incident is that my agency, the Los Angeles Sheriff's Department, was invited by Colorado authorities to assist in the crime scene after the shooting. Experts from the LASD Arson and Explosives Detail (my unit) and the Special Enforcement Bureau (SWAT) flew to Columbine to assist in making the scene safe and to begin a "lessons learned" analysis of the event. As such, LASD became a national leader in developing the "active shooter" training now being taught to every school officer and most police officers in the United States. This training is designed to teach regular patrol officers how to immediately deal with an armed attack of any sort on a school campus, hospital, or major venue, as opposed to waiting for a SWAT unit. This training was in effect a year later in Rosemead.

Because Columbine was still very fresh in everyone's mind in 2000, school officials nation-wide were happy to see April 20 slide by with little fanfare and not much drama. This was true at Rosemead High School that day. That is, until the noon recess occurred.

Around a quarter to one in the afternoon on Friday, April 21, security guards at the Rosemead High School were lounging near the barrier fence along busy Rosemead Boulevard. The guards heard a loud screeching of tires and winced, as they expected to hear the impact of a car crash. Instead they heard a car engine revving. They soon saw a dark-blue, two-door Ford Escort enter the north parking lot at an excessive speed. The guards walked over to stop the car, but the driver stared past them toward a student lunch area. They assumed that the driver was lost or had taken a wrong turn. They were surprised when the car sped up, and they could see it spinning its tires. The car was now speeding up and racing directly toward the lunch quad! Other guards leaped out of the way just in time as the car burst through the fifteen-foot-high chain-link gate and fence that surrounded the common area of the school.

In bullfighter fashion, the stunned security guards avoided the car as it sped past them, leaving only inches to spare. The car was accelerating toward the nearby student lunch area, which was an open, outdoor courtyard. Even more stunning, the guards had an up-close view of an Asian adult male sitting in the driver's seat. The male appeared to be laughing and smiling and was repeatedly pounding two metal things together, making massive sparks. Within seconds, and before the car made it to the lunch area, the interior burst into flame, and the car quickly careened to the right, out of control. It slammed its right front fender into a low metal pipe and concrete barrier and came to a violent halt. The male driver leapt out of the vehicle on fire. Despite their shock, the guards reacted quickly and ran to the man, swarming him and helping to put out the minor flames on his body. They then called fire paramedics and the nearby Temple City Sheriff's substation.

Needless to say, this shocking scene was met with stunned silence by the over one hundred or so high school kids who remained at the lunch tables. Several hundred other students that had been sitting there just five minutes before had already started returning to their classrooms and had missed the calamity.

A school nurse was first on the scene and began to treat the burned and dazed driver. Los Angeles Sheriff's Deputy David Brakebush arrived next, and aided by a staff Mandarin translator (the school had many recent Chinese immigrants as students so it maintained translators on its staff), began to question the burned driver. The male identified himself as Qi Jun Li, and immediately said he was despondent over not being able to find his father. He told the deputy that he had lit a gasoline container in his car on fire, and wanted to drive the burning car into the student area, killing himself and all the male students. A student who also spoke Mandarin asked him why he had done this, and Li replied "I did it. I hate the students at the school."

Los Angeles County fire department personnel arrived and put out the car that was still burning fiercely while their paramedics began to treat the burned driver. After his men slammed down the car fire with firefighting foam, the captain looked in and saw three large plastic gas cans on the seats, along with some five-gallon metal propane cylinders. Thinking that there was a bomb of some type in the car, the fire captain asked the responding sheriff's deputies to call the arson and bomb squad. He also took steps to evacuate a large area and to call his own department's hazardous materials squad.

Sgt. Gene Leslie and Det. Mike Cofield arrived at Rosemead High around one-thirty in the afternoon. The odd event had caused a mob of media to begin descending upon the scene, and the arrival of a large truck with "Bomb Squad" imprinted on the side only caused the furor to increase. The only saving grace for the two detectives at this time was that nobody, including the firefighters, really knew what had happened and what exactly this stuff in the car was.

Cofield and Leslie examined the car and were a bit shocked at what they eventually pulled out of the burned hulk. They first noted that the car was a brand new Ford Escort with Illinois license plates. Sitting next to the driver on the floorboard was a single six-gallon plastic can full of gasoline. It had severe fire damage, but still held a few gallons of gas. There was another similar gasoline can on the rear seat that was heavily damaged by fire. Also on the front seat was a quart container of lighter fluid. Directly next to the gas can on the front passenger floorboard was a twelve-volt car battery with jumper cables attached to it. The jumper cables showed signs of heavy electrical arcing on the teeth portions of the clamps. The entire passenger compartment was soaked with about ten to twenty gallons of gasoline and smelled strongly of propane. The back seat had been pulled down by the driver and exposed the trunk to the passenger area. The arson/bomb experts soon noted some significant items hidden in that area.

The trunk of the car revealed more items. Four five-gallon propane cylinders with their valves spun to the "open" position were packed into the small trunk. A third six-gallon gas can was also in this area. For good measure, a gallon can of flammable paint stripper was open and sitting in the trunk along with a case of twenty large spray cans of Aquanet hair spray. It took Sgt. Leslie and Det. Cofield over an hour to "render the vehicle safe" and turn over the cleanup process to the hazmat team.

After interviewing about thirty students, faculty, and security guards, the two investigators came to the startling conclusion that the subject appeared to have arranged his vehicle into a "fuel/air bomb," or in other words, a weapon of mass destruction. The gasoline had been poured over the interior of the car, and the driver had been soaked in gasoline. The propane cylinders had been opened all the way and had purged their gasses throughout the vehicle. The suspect banging together two open ends of the jumper cables caused massive sparking and ignited the flammable vapors that filled the car. This was clearly a serious attempt at a suicide/homicide car bombing. The investigators speculated that the improvised device was in fact a viable fuel/air bomb, but that the conditions within were too rich of a fuel mixture to produce the desired effect of a massive flaming explosion.

The detectives continued with interviews and a crime scene investigation. They noted that the vehicle had traveled over two-hundred feet from the street and had finally crashed into the steel pole and concrete wall just fifty-one feet short of the nearest table of students.

The detectives drove to the nearby hospital to interview Qi Jun Li. Li was fairly mum but did tell the investigators (through an interpreter) that he had been driving past the school when he noticed that the students were looking at him in a derogatory manner, as if he were less than them. He told the detectives that he thought that he should do something about this perceived slight. He explained this as the reason he did what he did. The detectives obtained the permission of the subject to search his room at a nearby motel. The subject signed a consent-to-search form for room #28 at the Sunny Cal Motel in nearby San Gabriel.

Immediately following the interview, the two detectives booked Li for attempted murder and using a destructive device or bomb. He was held without bail in a jail hospital.

Following his arrest, the detectives continued their investigation. They wrote search warrants for Li's credit cards and bank records, trying to link him to the items in his car. Their work paid off as they found that Li had purchased the bulk of the components on the morning of the event. He paid over $200 for the propane cylinders from a K-mart. A nearby Auto Zone sold him the gasoline cans. Following that purchase, his Mobil card showed a purchase of over twenty gallons of gasoline. The remaining items were purchased at a nearby drug store and at a second Auto Zone store. In all, Li had spent in excess of $500 in the four hours prior to this attack in order to assemble the components of his incendiary bomb.

The diligent detectives continued to back track Li and his activities. They were able to do this by researching his vehicle and his other credit-card records. They tracked Li back to ten days before the event, when he rented the Ford in Marion, Illinois. His credit card then showed a trail of travel and motel stays from Illinois, south into Alabama, and then west to California. The car rental company remembered Li as he had requested a special rental so that he could drive the car to California. When they refused to give him free or unlimited miles, he became very upset and highly agitated. He left in anger but returned a little later in a good mood.

Further checking in the Midwest revealed that Li had recent recorded incidences of erratic behavior. The police in Herrin, Illinois, had been called to the Kew Gardens Chinese restaurant on March 24, 2000, because of a disturbance. The owner had fired Qi Jun Li, who was a food server at the business, and Li had attacked the owner in retaliation. When the police arrived to mediate the dispute, Li attacked the two responding officers with his fists and feet. He was arrested for the assault on the officers and on the owner of the restaurant. Employment records also showed that he had been employed in other Chinese restaurants in Illinois and in California.

On April 25, 2000, Det. Mike Cofield filed ten counts of attempted murder, a single count of explosion with intent to murder, and a final count of arson against subject Qi Jun Li. This was after a detailed evaluation of the incident and the numerous steps the suspect took to accomplish his act. The investigators were convinced that it was the suspect's premeditated intent to commit suicide in a spectacular fashion, and to kill as many innocent children as possible during the event. The charging counts were purposely stopped at the arbitrary number of ten students so as to cut down on the number of people testifying in court. The case was specially assigned to veteran Deputy District Attorney Marion Thompson, who has a well-deserved reputation as a dogged and tenacious prosecutor.

Facing life in prison without the possibility of parole, Qi Jun Li later pled guilty in a deal that would land him in state prison for life with the possibility for parole after twenty years served. He has never confided in anyone, that we are aware of, as to what his true intentions and motivations were on that day. He has obvious psychological issues.

Investigator's Analysis:

The investigators and firefighters that day knew that the kids at that school dodged a huge bullet, and it was likely just a few liters of oxygen, more or less, from becoming a major catastrophic event, with dozens of injuries or deaths. Had the fuel-to-air mixture been a little leaner, or had the firefighters not extinguished the blaze before the propane cylinders could "bleve"*, it is strongly believed that a vapor explosion would have occurred, ripping the car apart and sending a shock wave and fragmented metal from the car through the hundred or so innocent students who were sitting nearby.

This event could have been on a par with the Columbine massacre, and we could have had one more reason to dread the third week of April. As it is, because the bomb did not function as designed, it has become yet another "ho-hum, non-event" for the voracious Los Angeles media. Twelve years later it is difficult to find the single, short press referral to this attack in the news archives of the region.

>***BLEVE:** Boiling Liquid Expanding Vapor Explosion; an explosion caused by the external heating of a container filled with a volatile liquid or gas.

CHAPTER TWO:

Serial Psychos

Nothing interests an arson investigator more than a serial arsonist. The motive behind arson-for-profit is understandable and quite mundane—it makes good business sense in most cases to sell your property back to the insurance company. Juvenile fire-setting is also easily explainable as the vast majority of people on earth have some fascination with fire, and juveniles have the lowest abilities to repress their impulsive actions. Likewise, most cops easily understand why people set things on fire for spite or revenge. When you are really, really mad at someone, it is one of the easiest things you can do to strike back at them, even if they are twice your size.

Unlike all of the other motives for arson, serial fire-setting is the least understood and the most fascinating. In my first book, *"Torchered" Minds: Case Histories of Notorious Serial Arsonists,* I gave brief case histories of over sixty-five serial arsonists of every type. Since the release of that book, I have received a large amount of positive feedback from my peers in the arson investigation world. We agree as a group that the serial arsonist is the most enigmatic and misunderstood of all criminals. We'd love to have an honest conversation with each one to figure out the "why" of it all. Of course, when you do catch one and have a face-to-face conversation, the suspect is usually giving face-saving explanations for his actions, as he is often unwilling to discuss his most intimate secrets.

The serial arsonists in this chapter will cover the entire spectrum of social and economic classes in the United States. Their actions are a mixture of impulsive and compulsive forces. Their acts of arson range from unbelievably minor events to spectacular conflagrations. No two are alike in the world of serial arsonists, and only they know why they do the things they do.

Doc Hallman: aka "The Lunatic on Lavender Lane" La Canada, 2009

Author's Note: This case comes from the author's case files and those of his partners, Sgt. Mike Costleigh, Sgt. Joe Acevedo, and Det. Mike Cofield, along with Homicide Detectives Mike Valento and Todd Anderson.

Lavender Lane:
Early in the latter chapter of this book concerning Mad Men, I mention a major wildland fire in 1959 called the Woodwardia Fire. Exactly fifty years after the Woodwardia Fire, the massive Station Fire erupted in the same region and burned over the exact same areas in the Angeles National Forest, plus an additional eighty-thousand acres of forest over the next two weeks. Like its predecessor, the Station Fire was an arson event and claimed the lives of two firefighters, Los Angeles County Fire Capt. Ted Hall and Firefighter Arnie Quinones. This fire grew to be the largest wildfire in the histories of both Los Angeles County and the Angeles National Forest. As such, it drew massive media attention and caused a great deal of pressure to be put on the investigation team assigned to solve this event.

Like the earlier fire, a joint investigation between the Los Angeles Sheriff's Department and the United States Forest Service was undertaken. Because of the loss of nearly two-hundred homes, over one-hundred vehicles, and the deaths of two firefighters, a large task force of investigators was assembled. The forest service was tasked with conducting the fire scene investigation, which they quickly ruled as arson. The sheriffs, with Detective Mike Cofield and Sgt. Joe Acevedo from their arson/bomb squad and their homicide detail duo of Detectives Mike Valento and Todd Anderson, handled the large follow-up investigation, which included chasing dozens of clues and dozens more phone tips. I was assigned the supporting role of cataloging all known arsonists in the region and providing lists of potential suspects to a force of detectives who were physically chasing down each lead and eliminating each person as a suspect in this event. On the list of people and things to be checked out were the details from dozens of phone tips; the whereabouts of all registered arsonists in the area; the wannabes, groupies, and the other weirdos who hung around firefighters; and a few firefighters who had recently acted strangely. Additionally, we were using this pool of investigators to closely examine every arson event which had occurred anywhere near the area of origin.

In October of that year, just six weeks after the start of the Station Fire, an odd series of events was noted in the northern-most portion of the very affluent foothill community of La Canada. A series of bizarre events was unfolding on and around a small street called Lavender Lane. Of importance to the taskforce investigators was that this was the closest neighborhood to the origin of the Station Fire. The fire had been started just six miles up Highway 2 (Angeles Crest Highway) from Lavender Lane, with no other homes in between.

Lavender Lane and the surrounding neighborhoods are home to a mostly white and Korean population of wealthy people, including many doctors, lawyers, and other professionals. This area also sits in the foothills about a quarter mile from the start of the Angeles Crest Highway. By October, residents of the virtually crime-free neighborhood had begun to report to the local sheriff's that bizarre vandalisms were occurring to their cars, homes, and

FIRERAISERS, FREAKS, AND FIENDS

yards. The calling card of the vandal was not gang graffiti or "tagger" drawings, but in most events the initials "USC" were scrawled or scratched onto people's property. It should be noted here that in the greater Los Angeles area, the two main schools that are associated with the affluent and powerful are the University of Southern California (USC), and the University of California, Los Angeles (UCLA). This upscale neighborhood boasted numerous license plate frames and stickers associated with both prestigious schools.

As the case would unfold during the holiday season of 2009, I did a more detailed check of similar events and found no less than thirty similar attacks of minor arson or vandalism, many of the events involving the letters "USC." No suspects were ever identified in these seemingly random attacks. Additionally, neighbors were reporting that small items in their yards had been burned in minor arson attacks.

In the early evening hours of October 21, a witness was driving to his home near Lavender Lane. As he entered his street in the growing darkness he immediately saw a plastic political campaign sign in a front yard on fire. About twenty feet from the sign and walking away, was a white male who was walking a golden Labrador retriever. The man with the dog was wearing a blue Dodgers Manny Ramirez jersey and a blue Dodgers ball cap on his head. The man was calmly walking his dog away from the fire. The witness stopped and contacted the homeowner, informing her about her election sign being on fire. She told the witness that there had been several other fires on the street in recent weeks. The witness got back into his car and drove around looking for the guy with the dog. He found him on a street two blocks away from Lavender Lane. He drove up to the man and asked him about the fire. The man with the dog told him he didn't know anything about the fire and was heading to his house on the corner. The witness in disbelief confronted him and said that he saw him standing right next to it. At that time, the man with the dog said, "Leave me alone," and sprinted away with his dog, disappearing down Lavender Lane. The witness later called the arson squad with this information. At that time the witness described the suspect as a white male, about six-feet tall, thin, and maybe in his early twenties.

Task force detectives jumped on this info given that it was about the closest neighborhood to the start of the Station Fire. Arsonists are a rare breed and to have one this close to the start of the large fire is indeed peculiar.

A quick check with the victim and the local sheriff's station showed that over the past few weeks this had been the eleventh such "nuisance fire" in a four-block area surrounding Lavender Lane. All of the fires had occurred at night, and the items burned included fencing, campaign signs, mailboxes, and mail. My partners and I studied these events, and we agreed that this was the mark of a serial offender— burning items of little value in close proximity to his home. We concluded that the offender was probably capering on foot and taking his flame source (most likely a lighter) with him. We believed that the offender was someone living within this wealthy neighborhood.

Immediately we received a new clue. The witness who had originally spotted the man with the dog had been doing his own amateur detecting. He had been going out looking for the suspected arsonist and had identified a house on Lavender Lane with a golden Lab. We quickly did a background on the home and found that it belonged to a very high-powered attorney. According to neighbors, the attorney had a teenaged son who sometimes stayed at the home and was a bit odd. Arson Detective Mike Cofield and Homicide Detective Mike Valento got busy with this investigation. They put together a "six pack" photo run with the attorney's son included and showed it to the witness. The witness indicated the attorney's son and said that he looked pretty close to the guy. More importantly, the witness said he was positive that it was the same dog. The two detectives executed a search warrant at the attorney's home and later brought in the son for questioning. No significant evidence was located, and the attorney's son adamantly denied setting these fires. Oddly, the attorney himself was fairly cooperative and said that his son was having some behavior problems; he stated that it was quite possible his son had committed these crimes as he was upset over a family situation. Without any tangible evidence, the detectives decided to hold off on filing any charges against the boy. He still remained high on our interest list. About a mile from Lavender Lane is a Starbucks situated in a theater complex directly under the junction of the 210 and 2 freeways. Again, due to the affluence in the area, the Starbucks is frequented by a large number of wealthy doctors, lawyers, and the like. The baristas are the usual assortment of shiny-faced kids, young girls, and metrosexual males. The place was always busy, and there were plenty of regular customers. One customer stood out to many of the employees. He was a male known only as "Chris." By everyone's account, Chris had been a regular customer for about a year. He was a creature of habit and showed up about two to three times per week, always around seven in the evening. He ordered the same odd non-coffee beverage each time. Another unique thing about Chris was that he almost always wore a piece of clothing that said "USC" on it. Someone in the shop found out that he was a doctor of sorts as well as a rabid USC fan.

For the first half of the year, Chris was fairly innocuous. By midsummer the Starbucks employees had noticed that his behavior had begun to dramatically change. Chris began to come in and be nearly incoherent in his speech. Workers could not smell alcohol on him, but he had the mannerisms and speech of someone who was drunk or on drugs. His beverage order was unintelligible, so the workers just kept giving him the same drink he had always asked for. He always paid for the drink, but then would take a newspaper off their rack and leave without paying for it. This behavior continued for the entire second half of 2009. At some point the young workers asked their boss if they should confront Chris about the stolen newspapers and the management said to just let him be. The employees said that Chris seemed totally out of it at times and could not speak coherently.

One day in November, the Starbucks workers noticed a small fire burning in the trash can in the bathroom. It was extinguished with a cup of water and they figured a customer had tossed a lit cigarette into the can. A few days later a similar incident occurred. This time, the employees knew that Chris was the only customer in the store. When they compared notes with the other employees, the managers realized that Chris had been present at both of these fires. Because so many cops from the LAPD, the sheriff's, and Glendale Police Department frequented the business, the manager asked them for advice. Because the business was just within the sheriff's borders, the local deputies advised the manager to call them when Chris arrived again, and they would respond to, identify, and talk to him.

On December 11, Chris arrived again and appeared incoherent. While the workers slowly worked on his order, the manager called the local deputies who sped to the scene. When they arrived, they identified Chris as Dr. Christiaan Hallman, a Pasadena-based dermatologist. He was also wearing his usual USC garb. The deputies realized that he appeared stoned but not drunk. He told them that he had been taking some sort of psychiatric drugs on the advice of a psychiatrist. The deputies released him to his wife who was also a medical doctor. The deputies also learned that the Hallman's lived in the corner house on Lavender Lane.

On December 12, the Starbucks received several phone calls asking for the manager. The employees recognized Chris' voice, and he was extremely belligerent. Later, when the manager arrived, Chris called again and told him that he was very mad at him for calling the cops the previous night. Chris made vague threats and then called the manager a "nigger." Later that same night, three employees watched as Chris drove up in his car, walked directly into the bathroom of the Starbucks, and emerged after about twenty seconds. Immediately, the employees saw smoke and fire coming from the trash can. They watched Chris as he walked into the parking lot, scratched another customer's car with his keys, and then left the scene.

Christiaan Hallman:

On December 14, I got assigned the Starbucks arsons. After I interviewed the employees, I learned that there had been at least three identical fires in the bathroom and that Chris Hallman was present during each event. I also learned of a fourth trash-can fire in their outdoor courtyard about a month prior to these recent fires. I drove to the local sheriff's station to check for similar incidents. I soon realized that Hallman lived directly in the middle of all of the eleven other arson events that were occurring on Lavender Lane. A review of the reports showed an extremely interesting fact. In most of these small arson events on Lavender Lane, the victim's property had been vandalized with the letters "USC" scratched into car hoods, fenders, and nearby fences. This immediately grabbed my attention as every witness so far had mentioned that Hallman always wore USC garb.

One fire/vandalism stood out from all the rest. There was an incident at a home much further away from Lavender Lane. In that case someone had lit two small fires, one to the mail and one to some vegetation, and had then ripped a USC license plate frame from the victim's car and had used it to scratch "USC" into the car. The MO was the same as the other events, but the distance was at least a mile from the Lavender Lane events. I spoke to detectives Cofield and Acevedo and told them about Hallman. They agreed that he seemed a likely candidate for their eleven arson events and numerous other vandalisms in the neighborhood involving the letters "USC." The two detectives drove to the arson scene that was a mile away from Lavender Lane, since it didn't fit the same geographic profile.

At that location the detectives interviewed the upscale homeowners who of course had no idea why anyone would do this to them. The wife said she was a USC graduate, as was her brother. Somewhere in the conversation, she mentioned that her brother was a doctor. At this point the stunned investigators asked her brother's name. She said he was Christiaan Hallman. She also said that Hallman was very upset with her for a family incident which had occurred a few years prior. She has had no contact with him in the past few years.

The Arrest of Christiaan Hallman:

On December 14, Homicide Detective Valento, Arson Sergeant Mike Costleigh, and I drove to Christiaan Hallman's Lavender Lane home and arrested him for the Starbuck's arsons. As we were booking him in at the station, we noted that he possessed a USC logo watch, tie, credit cards, and other items. He said he was a huge fan. The interview was nothing short of fascinating. We were sure he would immediately ask for an attorney, but instead he agreed to talk to us without an attorney. After we told him what we wanted to discuss with him, he admitted to starting a fire at Starbucks which we had no record of. He said he "accidentally" started the fire in an outdoor trash can about three months prior. After further prodding, he eventually admitted to intentionally starting the fires in the bathroom as well. In all, he was connected to five minor arson fires at the Starbucks.

We were struck by the dispassionate, aloof manner in which he discussed these crimes. Hallman acted like a detached doctor giving an analysis of his own behavior. In the end, he said he had no idea why he was doing these things, and he asked us for our opinions as to why he was so compelled. When we told him that we had done several cases like his in the past, he was shocked and stated, "You mean there are other people like me?" He indicated that he knew what he was doing, but didn't know why, and was surprised that other people had done similar things. He appeared more fascinated with his own behavior than upset or despondent over it. It was the most non confrontational interview we had ever had. We were like doctors sitting around discussing an interesting case!

Hallman made the quarter-million-dollar bail the next day and was free. We took his photo to the original witness who had earlier identified the lawyer's son, and showed him a new "6 pack." This witness then identified Hallman as the person he had seen light the sign on fire a month prior. Even though Hallman was almost twenty years older than the lawyer's son, we realized that he (Hallman) still looked very young and bore a resemblance to the other male. We also learned that Hallman owned a blue Dodgers jersey and hat, and also had a golden Lab that was almost a clone of the dog owned by the lawyer. The two families lived just a few houses away from each other on Lavender Lane.

Two weeks after I arrested him, Hallman, while out on bail, was involved in a hit-and-run accident with his car. He was again arrested for this incident and for being under the influence of alcohol and prescription drugs while driving. I learned that that same week, the Starbucks suffered another fire in one of their outdoor trash cans. Alas, there was no witness to the event, but for me there was little doubt that Hallman was melting down fast.

In early January, 2010, we rearrested Hallman on new arson charges. By that time, we had re-interviewed some family members, and they gave us a better picture of his life. Always a high achiever in school, Hallman had obtained academic scholarships to prestigious USC and its medical school. He eventually graduated second overall in his class. However, around 2006 his family noticed that he appeared to be abusing prescription drugs. He was confronted during an intervention and went off the deep end. He banished his sister and her husband from his life, and eventually his wife (also a doctor) forced him into drug rehab. She had a lot to lose if anyone found out about his problems as they co-owned a large medical practice. Hallman had been using psychiatric drugs for a few years and had occasionally mixed them with other meds he was self-prescribing. When he took these drugs, he became unable to speak coherently and conducted himself in a bizarre manner. This was consistent with his actions in front of the Starbucks employees.

When we rearrested Dr. Hallman, he was not nearly as cooperative as he had been the first time. He denied remembering any of the other incidents and even began telling us that he sometimes "blacks out" and is not responsible for his actions. He had clearly been advised by an attorney. We did notice that he had traded in a damaged car on the day after New Year's. Oddly, within blocks of his home, a male pedestrian had been killed by a driver in a hit-and-run involving a car similar to Hallman's old one. The traffic investigators as yet have been unable to link Hallman to this incident.

Following this last arrest, we served a search warrant at his home. Since this case originally was an off shoot of the Station Fire arson/murder investigation, the warrant service was led by homicide detectives Mike Valento and Todd Anderson. Three arson investigators, including me, went along to assist. The Hallman's were a family of two doctors with three children. Their home was a very old home that had been extensively remodeled over the years. It was not an overly large or ostentatious home, but it was worth nearly a million dollars. The most significant evidence found in Hallman's home was in fact what was missing. Specifically, we were looking for an LA Dodgers Manny Ramirez jersey that the witness had seen on the arson suspect at the campaign sign burning. We were unable to find this item. However, all other members of the family possessed similar Dodger's jerseys, with the notable exception of Chris. We inquired about this with a housekeeper, and she confirmed that he did own a jersey of that exact style, but she had not seen it in weeks.

It was easy for the housekeeper to know it was missing since the Hallman's closet was nothing short of bizarre. The large walk-in closet had the wife's clothes on one side and his on the other. All were meticulously folded or perfectly pressed and hanging in dry-cleaning bags. The weird part was that of the hundreds of items of clothing that were his, almost 99 percent were jerseys, tee shirts, sweaters, jackets, shorts, slippers, ties, and socks, all sporting the USC logo. He appeared to have no other clothing whatsoever except for one sport coat and a lab coat for work. Everything else was USC garb. He even had USC bedding, rugs, pennants, watches, and every other item available for purchase at the university's bookstore or sports store. It appeared that Chris Hallman had a less-than-healthy obsession with USC. There were also some bottles of prescription medications and a diary of sorts that gave us intimate details of problems involving Chris, his wife, and his problems. It was clear that he had been away from his family for an extended period in the past, probably at some sort of treatment center. Other than the odd clothing, their home was extremely barren of warmth and personality. There were very few pictures on display, and the home was very uninviting.

By March of 2010, a total of fifteen arson and a dozen felony vandalism charges were filed against Dr. Christiaan Hallman, hereafter known to us as the Lunatic on Lavender Lane. The case went to Deputy District Attorney Sean Carney, a specialist in arson cases. As in any case involving wealthy clients and their high-priced attorneys, the legal maneuvering commenced. Hallman's attorneys went proactive by delaying his court proceedings and having him voluntarily enter another substance abuse program.

We later learned that his attorneys were fighting wars on two fronts. As soon as Hallman was arrested, an automatic notice was sent to the California State Medical Board, who immediately launched their own investigation. I was contacted by their agents who requested copies of our investigation. They later conducted their own undercover investigation and suspended Hallman's medical license, pending a formal hearing. Hallman's attorneys, fearing his livelihood would be cut off, immediately began preparing to defend him in both criminal court and at the state's medical hearing.

In a legal gambit, Doc Hallman pled "no contest" on December 22, 2010, to one felony count of arson to property and one felony count of vandalism. As part of this negotiated plea deal, Hallman would receive four years of formal probation, two-hundred-and-fifty hours of community service, and was ordered to pay court costs. Deputy District Attorney Carney also got the defense to agree to pay restitution to the victims in all of the alleged counts, even if the charges were later dismissed. Many of the victims had their cars "keyed" and windows smashed. These acts of vandalism amounted to tens of thousands of dollars in damage. Oh yeah, Hallman also got one day in jail! In the deal he was also ordered to undergo substance abuse and psychiatric counseling. All of this was in exchange for dropping all of the remaining arson and vandalism counts. It pays to be rich and have good attorneys*.

Doc Hallman faced one more serious hurdle. In the second week of February, 2012, the Hallman case was set to be brought before a panel of the California State Medical Board. I was subpoenaed to testify as an expert witness in the case. Again, Hallman's well-paid attorneys did their job. Prior to the hearing, Doc Hallman reached a settlement with the State Medical Board, and agreed to have his suspended medical license put on probation for a term of between five and seven years. He also agreed to complete a medical testing course which would cost him about $20,000 out of his own pocket. He further agreed to adhere to drug, alcohol, and psychiatric standards and evaluations. The board did not expect to reinstate his probationary license until at least late 2012. By the time this book is published, Hallman will be back practicing medicine.

Investigator's Analysis:

Doctor Christiaan Hallman's story proves that serial arson cases span all racial, ethnic, and class lines. He was a wealthy, white, forty-two-year-old, highly educated professional who up until 2009 was never suspected of criminal activity. It is my opinion and that of my colleagues that Hallman had been committing minor crimes on and off all of his adult life. We believe he will likely resume his erratic activity if he fails to stay on his medications or fails to manage the stress in his life. Some months after his arrest, I was contacted by a distant member of Hallman's family. This person was not at all surprised that Christiaan had significant issues as an adult, as this person knew Hallman's father quite well. This person reported that Hallman's father led a completely out-of-control life that included criminal activity including shootings, theft of dynamite, stalking, and other serious crimes. It was reported that, just prior to this latest binge of attacks by Hallman, his father, a homeless transient, had been found dead on a park bench in Santa Barbara. Like all serial arsonists, Christiaan Hallman's life was no doubt influenced and shaped by this dysfunctional childhood family situation.

>*Author's Note: During the same time frame as the Hallman case, a homeless black woman named Rosemary Longstreet faced justice in Los Angeles for setting four trash cans on fire. Considered a serial arsonist by the prosecution and me, Rosemary accepted a plea bargain for her string of fires. Since she was indigent, she had only the public defender's office to represent her. In stark contrast to Doc Hallman's plea deal, Rosemary Longstreet got three years in prison for setting far fewer fires than the good doctor. Likewise, in 2012, I was involved in a serial arson case in Lancaster in which a poor white man named Jesse James Ellison, with considerable mental health issues, had been linked to about fifteen small grass and trash fires. His guilty plea got him four years in prison. Doc Hallman's well-paid attorneys brokered his expensive deal for just a single day in jail. Sigh…

Norman Ralph Henderson
Lake County Serial Arsonist, 2007

Author's Note: The information presented in this case comes from the files of CALFIRE Investigator Chris Vallerga, interviews with him and one of his former partners, Investigator Brice Trask, and news accounts of the events.

About a half-hour north of the sprawl of Sacramento on Interstate 5, a northbound traveler will come to State Highway 20. By turning left (west) on SH20, the traveler will soon leave the flat Central Valley and cross into the foothills. Several miles west is a large body of water known as Clear Lake. This volcanically-formed body of water has long been known as a mineral spring area, and the lake is surrounded by small towns, resorts, and vacation properties. The entire lake region is at the edge of the heavily-wooded Mendocino National Forest. Because of this dominating geographic feature, the entire county is known as Lake County. At the lower, east end of Clear Lake is the small town of Clearlake. The town of Clearlake has about fifteen thousand residents. In 2007 authorities knew that at least one of them was a serial arsonist.

The story of the final spree of the Lake County Arsonist began in 2007, on the eastern edge of Clear Lake. Winding Road Motors is a used car dealership in Clearlake. A part-time employee named Norman Henderson worked odd jobs at the car dealership. One day, Henderson got into a bitter argument with his boss and left the dealership. Some days later, two motor home units on the lot caught fire and were destroyed. Those two fires were investigated by Captain/Investigator Brice Trask from the Lake County Fire Protection District. Investigator Trask ruled both fires to be arson events and started an investigation. At the time of this fire, there were no good suspects in the case.

Besides being the local arson investigator, Trask was also part of a loosely-linked group of area detectives known as the Lake

County Arson Task Force. Included in the group was a representative from the state agency CalFire, Investigator Chris Vallerga, Lake County Sheriff's Investigator Corey Paulich, and Chief Deputy District Attorney Richard Hinchcliff, the local arson prosecutor.

All of the little communities surrounding Clear Lake are semi-rural with one edge of each town abutting the lake and the other edges usually terminating at the base of the slopes leading to the wooded foothills of the Mendocino National Forest. One such town, just a few miles from the town of Clearlake, is the small community of Lucerne.

Leading north out of Lucerne is a scenic back way known as Bartlett Springs Road. This rough road undulates over hills and valleys for about twenty-five miles, connecting Lucerne to the high country reservoir known as Indian Valley Reservoir. The road passes through the forests and rises in altitude from about 1,500 feet to nearly 5,000 feet. On the way visitors can view the bedraggled remnants of the old Victorian-era spas and resorts that proliferated in the rugged backcountry over a hundred years ago.

On July 28, 2007, a fire broke out at the old Bartlett Springs Resort Lodge along Bartlett Springs Road. This historic landmark was founded in the late 1800's after its namesake had discovered what he believed were healing mineral waters on the property. According to newspaper articles following the fires, the resort was restored by the current owner in about 1985. The owner, Mr. Zane Gray (not the author), was coincidentally a volunteer firefighter in the area and helped protect his restoration project from a major fire in 1996. After the 2007 fire, no ignition source or device was found during the investigation, but the fire was ruled an arson attack by a local investigator. Because of its remote location, there were no witnesses to the event and no workable suspect information.

Shortly following this fire, on the same property a second arson attack occurred. This time the building that housed part of the old Vittel water bottling company was burned to the ground. The circumstances of this fire were nearly identical to the first fire on the resort.

Finally, on September 11, 2007, a third fire in as many months took place at the remote resort. This time the carefully restored historic gazebo was destroyed by flames. Again the circumstances of the arson attack mirrored the previous two events. Northshore Fire Chief Jim Robbins was particularly incensed by these fires, as his firefighters had fought valiantly in 1996 to save these very same structures from the massive "Fork" wildfire in the area that destroyed over 80,000 acres of the forest.

After the gazebo fire, authorities suddenly became fully aware that they had a serial arsonist at large. This caused tremendous concern as the fall of 2007 was one of the worst years for wildland fires in recent memory. The small arson task force met secretly, compared rare leads, and combed the area. They began a series of surveillance operations in the area and were funneled some tips and clues by citizens. Most of these were somewhat vague and didn't pan out. The team did learn of a suspicious Toyota pickup seen in the area of the fires, but never could locate it or find out its license plate. Several vehicle stops were made throughout the fall, but all of the drivers checked out okay. One day, two Cal Fire investigators were speeding to an unrelated incident in the area when they passed a Toyota truck that looked somewhat suspicious. The truck was on Walker Ridge Road, a feeder road that eventually leads into the Bartlett Springs area. This remote road had been the site of a couple of suspicious brushfires in the recent past. The truck had a camper shell that did not fit it correctly and had been jerry-rigged into place. The investigators were only able to get a partial license plate, and were unable to determine who was in the vehicle. They stuck that partial tag number into their burgeoning case file along with the other fragmented tips and leads.

The investigators were stymied by the remoteness of the area and the usual lack of personnel and resources to cover such a vast wilderness. By the time a fire was noticed up on Bartlett Springs, the suspect would have at least a seventeen-mile lead with which to make his getaway.

Another problem that afflicted the task force was that some of the fire scenes had not been properly investigated and documented by the original agencies that responded to the fires. Additionally, a local fire official had also leaked to the media that the task force was in the area conducting surveillance operations. This is a very common mistake that continues to occur with fire administrators who are not aware of how to properly conduct an investigation.

For some reason, the arsonist didn't strike again. The area survived the dry fall season and made it safely into the wet and cold winter season without a trace of the arsonist.

By April 10, 2008, their reprieve was over and the arsonist struck again, this time torching a remote vacation cabin in the Bartlett Springs area. A second identical attack to another vacation cabin soon followed, and the case was back in full gear. Again the arsonist left no evidence behind for investigators to exploit.

On April 23, 2008, a semi-truck driver traveling along rural Highway 20, just west of the town of Williams in Colusa County, spotted a man in a pick-up truck leaving a burning roadside fruit and vegetable stand. The suspicious man had stopped to pick up an aluminum can, but for which he wouldn't have been seen at this event. His vehicle's information was called in to the California Highway Patrol (CHP), and CHP officers soon stopped the vehicle as it was headed toward Clearlake, detaining the only occupant—sixty-one-year-old Norman Henderson. Henderson was carrying wooden matches, a lighter, and some cigarettes. He was arrested for the arson of the fruit stand, which happened to have been closed for the season. The fire had caused minor to moderate damage. Henderson was booked into the Colusa County jail, and prosecutors subsequently filed two counts of arson against him. It was soon learned that Henderson had past arson convictions. He was released from jail a few days later, pending his next court date on the case.

Because the officials in this region were highly sensitive to arson cases in the wild land areas, most firefighters were well aware of the previous year's arson activity in neighboring Lake County. Even more suspicious was the fact that Henderson lived in Clearlake and was a convicted arsonist. Based on this, Fire Chief Jeff Gilbert of the town of Williams astutely notified members of the Lake County Arson Task Force of the arrest, saying, "We may have your guy." Task-force officers jumped at this news. Task-force Investigator Brice Trask ran the name and found an immediate link to fires in his area from the previous year. Norman Henderson was listed on records as an employee of Winding Road Motors, where there were still a couple of unsolved arsons. Inv. Trask contacted the owner of the car lot who confirmed that Norman Henderson had worked for him in the past as a laborer, stating that he had fired him for poor performance. The owner said that Henderson had been a bit upset at the time. He also confirmed that the firing of Henderson had occurred before the arson attacks at the car lot. Trask was ecstatic with this information. The investigators also looked at Henderson's truck. It was in fact the same suspicious vehicle they had seen on an earlier surveillance mission in the Walker Ridge area. The partial license plate in their files from that surveillance matched Henderson's truck.

Immediately upon his release from jail in Colusa, Henderson was contacted by members of the arson task force. He agreed to an interview with task-force members. Investigators Chris Vallerga, Brice Trask, and Corey Paulich conducted a team interview of Henderson regarding several fires in the Lake County area. After obliging Henderson's request for a pinch of Copenhagen tobacco and a six pack of Coca Cola, the investigators sat back and let the suspect begin pouring out a lifetime of arson events. Sheriff's Sgt. Paulich started the interview, and shortly after Henderson admitted to starting the two arson fires at the car lot the year before. He also admitted to starting the fires up at Bartlett Springs the previous summer. The other two investigators then entered the interview room, and soon Henderson was speaking freely about his wild land fire-setting behavior.

Investigator Vallerga, a seasoned veteran of other wildland serial arson cases, was interested in the "why" of the arson acts and also the exact details of each event. Henderson was mostly accommodating in his replies. He described himself as a true pyromaniac who often heard voices that instructed him to light fires. His arson episodes were impulsive, and he admitted that he had been fighting the urge to light fires for many years. He described how he picked targets so that he would not get caught. He further was very worried about his own safety, and described bypassing some targets that would endanger him. He was also careful not to enter some of the dilapidated cabins, because he feared they would collapse on him. This was important to the investigators, as they believed that Henderson had some mental health and social issues, but he was clear-headed enough to take steps to ensure his own safety during his attacks.

Henderson admitted that he had lit one of his first fires back in 1965. He was arrested and convicted for torching a rural barn in the Butte County town of Gridley. Gridley, which is about sixty miles east of Clearlake, is a typical Central Valley agricultural town of 6,500 people which sits astride California Highway 99, at the base of the foothills to the Sierra's. This conviction would be his first in a lifetime of arson activity.

At some point Henderson left the foothills of California and ended up three hours east, in the desert wastes of Fallon, Nevada. The records get fuzzy around that time, but what is known is that, between 1991 and 1994, Henderson was arrested and convicted for threatening a seventy-three-year-old female. He was also convicted for at least two different arson attacks resulting in some more prison time. The first was an attack on a vacant building. His next assault was of a much more sinister nature, as he was arrested and convicted for setting fire to a casino in Fallon.

Henderson would then spend several years in the Midwest, but during the interview he was not very forthcoming about his activities around this time. Somehow, he fell off the radar until 2006, when he showed up in Lake County, California. Investigators would later describe Norman Henderson as a very simple man of fairly low intelligence. He maintained a living through the odd menial job, including washing cars at the car lot and yard work. His main occupation seemed to be his daily ritual of driving around and collecting aluminum cans for recycling, a hobby he called "canning." It was this ritual that got him caught. His last fire was the vacant fruit stand. He lit the structure on fire and started to drive away. On his way out, he spotted a couple of aluminum cans in the area and stopped his vehicle to retrieve them, despite the burning building nearby. This obsessive compulsion, to pick up about ten-cents' worth of aluminum, cost him his freedom for the next two decades of his life.

After admitting that he was a pyromaniac, Henderson cleared up the remaining unsolved arson fires in the Lake County area that had taken place over the previous year. He said he was upset from an argument with his boss at the car dealership, and one night lit two motor homes on fire with a match. Later, while out "canning" on the rural mountain roads and he could no longer deny the urge, he would start fires, always with a match. He eventually admitted to two small brushfires, all of the fires at the Bartlett Resort, and a few fires started at some small outbuildings. He admitted to a total of ten fires in Lake County.

Based on this admission, along with his connection to several of the arson scenes, and taking into account his past documented history of arson activity, the task force investigators were well aware that they had a life-long serial arsonist on their hands. He was a lower performer in work and in life, and his method of ignition was extremely simple—just a simple match put to any available combustible materials. Investigators speculated that, over the past four decades, Henderson was likely involved in dozens of other fires for which he was not confessing. Still, his statements solved the fires in their area.

The task force didn't stop at the confessions. As true professionals, they were aware that there was very little crime-scene evidence to link Henderson to these scenes. They needed to confirm the information he had given them. Shortly after his confessions, Henderson agreed to accompany the investigators to the scenes of his fires. A lengthy day with him at the fire scenes satisfied the investigators that he was in fact the person who ignited the various blazes. At each site he explained where he had lit the fire, how he had gathered and arranged fuels to allow the fire to build, and what his method of ignition was. The team was surprised to learn that Henderson's urges lay only with setting the fire, not in the results that followed. He seemed unconcerned if the fire was big or if it destroyed anything. He was only interested in the act of fire-setting itself.

After his startling confession, Henderson was booked into the Lake County jail and held on $100,000 bond. After sitting in jail for several months while his defense attorney reviewed the prosecution's case, Henderson opted to plead guilty to most of the fires in a plea bargain. He entered his guilty plea on October 3, 2008.

On Friday, January 9, 2009, Norman Ralph Henderson was sentenced to twenty-four years in state prison for the ten arson fires he had set in Lake County. He won't be eligible for parole until he has served twenty years, or when he is over eighty years old. As a parting gift, the sentencing judge also ordered him to pay restitution to the victims in excess of $540,000.

Investigator's Analysis:
Norman Henderson is a typical example of what most arson investigators believe is the most common subtype of serial arsonist. It is a group of lower-intelligence, lower-performing people who have obvious mental health issues. His crimes lacked planning and sophistication, and his fires tended to be fairly small in scope. This type of offender will light dozens if not hundreds of fires throughout their lives, with lengthy gaps between fire-setting activities. Their fires usually occur when there is a stressor in their lives such as the loss of a job, relationship issues, or the abuse of alcohol, prescription drugs, or narcotics. Norman is slightly different than most in that he used a vehicle. Most of his peers conduct their arson attacks on foot or use a bicycle or public transportation.

The task-force officers caught him the old-fashioned way. They worked their scenes, amassed tips and leads, and finally got a lucky break. However, it was their work in the interview room which was the real key to this case. Any investigator can prosecute a case when the suspect is observed setting a fire. A truly gifted investigator can take that event and solve all the cases in the series through a proper interview and follow-up investigation that positively links the suspect to all of his fires. Investigators Trask, Vallerga and Sgt. Paulich did an excellent job in all aspects of this case.

A SECRET LIFE
JAMES KENNETH HOUGH, BUTTE COUNTY, 2005-2007

Author's Note: This story comes from the case files of Deputy Chief Alan Carlson, Cal Fire (retired). Additional details were gleaned from an online story by writer Gordon Gregory, published on November 1, 2007, on newsreview.com.

The foothill region surrounding Sacramento was a veritable hot bed of arson activity in the 2000's. As was covered in my first book *"Torchered" Minds*, firefighter serial arsonist Robert Eason set over 140 brushfires in the foothills about twenty-five miles west of

Sacramento in the two decades prior to his arrest in 2006. Near the end of Eason's string of capers, starting in 2005 and lasting until his arrest in 2007, another firefighter arsonist, Ben Cunha, was setting at least fifteen wildland fires in the foothill region about forty miles east of Sacramento. Both of these guys were typical firefighter arsonists who used automobiles to set fires in large clusters during the daytime on rural roads in the secluded foothill areas. Both also used a delay incendiary device they designed to give themselves enough time to get out of the area of the fire before it started. The serial arsonist Norman Henderson, as discussed in the previous chapter, was involved in a smaller arson spree just fifty miles northwest of Sacramento in Lake County. He, like most serial offenders, did not use a delay device, and instead relied on a "hot set," using wooden matches to light materials he gathered at the scenes.

At the same time that young Ben Cunha was starting his final spree in 2005, another series of suspicious wildland fires started in the foothill region about forty miles north of Sacramento, in the Yuba City/Marysville area. Again, Cal Fire investigators were called in to investigate this arson series. Before it ended, the series would stretch over four counties and encompass sixty wildland fires. The arson spree in that area would last until August 10, 2007. It would conclude with the unexpected death of a man later that year.

Jim Hough was just an average guy. In his mid fifties, he lived a very stable life—at least it appeared that way. He had been married to the same woman for twenty-nine years, and had worked at the same soda-bottling plant for close to forty years. He was reliable and trustworthy, and he had been eventually promoted to the position of plant manager. He had successfully raised two sons, one of which was a senior in high school and the other a corrections officer for the Yuba County jail. He enjoyed family events, the outdoors, camping, and his dogs. He was mostly a model citizen, with nothing more than a minor blemish on his record. But he also had a secret life.

On the Fourth of July in 2005, a pair of wildland fires erupted in the Sutter Buttes area of Sutter County. Sutter Buttes is volcanic parkland just west of Yuba City. Normally, with the area's heavy use of fireworks, firefighters and investigators dread the midsummer holiday. Literally hundreds of extra fires spring up on and around the Fourth of July every year. Because of this, two fires on the Fourth didn't mean a whole lot to anyone, especially for a recreation spot like the Buttes. But two days later, a third fire on the sixth of July and a fourth fire on the seventh finally gained some fire investigators' attention. All of these fires were within the same camping area of the Buttes. The investigators actually found the ignition source of the third and fourth fires (no easy task in a wildland fire), and were a little surprised to see that both were set off by an identical item. The ignition source for both these fires was a small firework known as a "ground bloom flower." These small cylinders are lit by a fuse, and when thrown on the ground, they begin spinning violently for about ten seconds, spewing flame an inch or two in all directions. They sound like an enraged swarm of bees buzzing all at once. Thrown on concrete or dirt, they are just a fun item that amuses kids. However, when these items land anywhere near dry brush and grass, they more often than not ignite the vegetation. Based on the similarities between the four fires, their close proximity to each other, and the discovery of the same type of ground bloom firework at two of the scenes, the local fire department became concerned.

Sutter County fire investigators contacted arson experts from Cal Fire to assist them. Cal Fire, the state fire agency in rural California, focuses mainly on wildland fire investigations. They are the chief experts in wildland fires, and their investigators examine hundreds of fire scenes each year. They also assist small fire departments whose investigators are overburdened or simply don't have the resources or experience to conduct these difficult investigations. Cal Fire eventually assigned Captain Shannon Garrett as the case officer for this investigation.

Fireraisers, Freaks, and Fiends

Shortly, Cal Fire administrators became very concerned about these seemingly small events. Because their jurisdiction crossed many county lines, they were aware of a spate of similar fires in nearby Yuba and Butte counties. Cal Fire had already targeted a potential arson series in those counties and had deployed surveillance assets into those rural areas.

The term "surveillance assets" needs some explaining. If this were a city environment with a large police force, a "surveillance asset" would normally mean an undercover officer of some sort, on foot or in an undercover vehicle, staking out an area. On a more serious case, it might mean several officers and possibly some aircraft conducting mobile surveillance of a subject. However, in the rural counties, where skilled manpower is at a premium and following someone on a lonely forest road is way too conspicuous, the investigative agencies often employ fixed cameras at road junctions and at the mouths of canyons. These items are rarely used to catch someone in "real time," but are designed to gather information (specifically license plates) in a discreet manner, so that after an event investigators can review the data and find out who was in the area prior to the arson attack. These devices have been employed many, many times and can produce excellent results if used properly. They can at least give the investigators a starting place in an investigation.

The trick to using a static camera in an investigation is to keep the item secret. People in rural areas are keenly aware of the hazards posed by arsonists, armed marijuana growers, thieves, and poachers, and they are often quick to spot any unusual activity—including undercover cops installing items along the road. Placing these cameras and recovering the data without being noticed is a skill that takes some learning. There is nothing worse than having spent hours or even days setting up a covert law enforcement operation, only to find that all of the locals in the rural area have guessed what you are up to. Some citizens are not keen at all on any government entity "spying" on people and will warn others in the area. Some may even try to destroy or steal the surveillance equipment for their own use. Local officers or firefighters who become aware of a surveillance operation also pose a risk, as they may accidentally "spill the beans" when bragging to someone in the area.

More seriously, Cal Fire has arrested several firefighters over the years who were engaged in arson activity in these rural areas. In these cases, like any other, investigators were well aware that their subject may in fact be a local firefighter. Because of these obstacles, the Cal Fire surveillance experts seldom tell anyone, except for their immediate bosses, where they are working and what they are doing. Sometimes they have to quietly slip in and out of small towns without notifying the local authorities.

Making the decision of how to handle a case like this often depends on the size and scope of the case. The bigger the case, the higher up the chain the decisions are made to employ resources, budget overtime, and bring in additional personnel. In this case, Cal Fire had Battalion Chief James Engel working as the incident commander and Battalion Chief Joshua White as the operations chief. Their job was to facilitate the needs of the lead investigator, Captain Garrett. Soon, these two men realized that a potential serial offender was operating in a three-county area surrounding Yuba City. Eventually the case would expand and come to the attention of Alan Carlson, the Cal Fire deputy chief for the northern region's law enforcement program.

Based on their case analysis, the investigators expanded the surveillance assets into Sutter County. They installed their remote cameras surreptitiously and were able to keep the rumors and information under control. Cal Fire also brought additional cause-and-origin investigators in to assist Sutter County officials with the processing of the fire scenes. Following standard investigative steps, the investigators began seeking witnesses who may have seen something suspicious around the Buttes. While no great leads developed that year, one partial tip came in. A witness had a vague memory of a dark Toyota 4Runner being driven by an older white male, and carrying a younger white male passenger. This vehicle was seen in the area around the time of the fires. This vague tip was stuck in the case file with all the others.

This case was not going to be easy, and it was not going to be quick. The fires continued for a few weeks, and soon the Cal Fire guys discovered there were similar fires across adjoining Tehama and Colusa counties, expanding the arson area to five counties. The fires were identified as part of the series because of the similarities in time of day, method of ignition, and seclusion of the sites. Ground bloom flowers had also been found at many of the fires sites.

As quickly as they started, however, the fires soon stopped, and the arsonist went dormant for the fall and winter months. Chief Carlson and his people had planned for this. The chief was a twenty-five-year veteran and had participated in several wildland serial arson cases, some of them spanning over a decade. He and the lead investigator knew well that wildland serial arsonists are a very odd group, and sometimes go months between arson sprees. Often after the arrest, confession, and analysis of the offender, investigators discover very good reasons for why the arsonist ceased his activity for a time. Sometimes he was a seasonal worker who left the area for a while. Sometimes he only lit the fires when he was having family or work problems and would stop when things got better, only to start again when invariably things went bad again. Sometimes the arsonist was a true excitement junky and only wanted to start fires on the hottest, most dangerous days of summer. Really, each arsonist is unique and each has their own reasons for beginning and stopping their activities. The arson investigators in this case hunkered down with their files of leads and tips and waited for the next fire or break in the case.

By mid-July of the following year, they knew he was back. Fires were springing up in some of the same areas as before. Ground bloom flowers were found again and again at fire scenes. The series was exactly like the year before. Again, just like the previous year, the fires continued for several weeks and then just stopped. Again, the Cal Fire investigators amassed their information and reviewed and reread reports, only to find that, once again, there were simply no solid leads in this perplexing case.

Chief Carlson had another technique that he had found useful in the past. Like many seasoned arson investigators, he had gone through training in the analysis of crime patterns. There had been a large amount of research on serial offenders in the past three decades, and the behavior analysts believed that many serial arsonists tended to operate in specific geographic areas and during specific time periods. All good arson investigators, when they detect a pattern, begin to amass information as to the location and time of day of the fires. They also sometimes take into account the actual day of the week that the attacks take place on. All of this information is analyzed in an attempt to see a pattern of behavior. That pattern of behavior is used to aid the investigation and eliminate potential suspects in the case. For instance, because of the vast distances between fires, it was clear that the arsonist was an adult with access to a vehicle. This would easily eliminate most juvenile offenders, thereby cutting the suspect list in half. It is a well-accepted fact in the arson world that half of all offenders are juveniles. Additionally, it is widely accepted that most arson series occur near the offender's home, school, or place of work. Carlson conducted a "geo-spatial" analysis and found that there were two distinct clusters or "anchor points" where many of the fires were occurring. One was near the small community of Live Oak, and the second was near the northwest edge of the town of Marysville. The chief also found that almost all the fires occurred during daylight hours, which is consistent with most wildland serial offenders.

After two seasons, an armchair analysis of the case concluded that the arsonist drove a vehicle, had connections to Live Oak and Marysville, had freedom during the day to commit his crimes, and had access to ground bloom flower fireworks. His activities spiked around the month of July and faded later in the summer and fall. While this information was hardly earth-shattering, and only narrowed the suspect field down to about fifty-thousand people, it did give investigators a place to start. They refocused their surveillance assets into the hidden roadways near the anchor points of activity.

The fall of 2006 passed, and the spring of 2007 emerged with the investigators knowing fully well that the arsonist would be at it again in the warmest months of the summer. They were not disappointed.

The summer of 2007 would send the "ground-bloom-flower arsonist" into his final frenzy of incendiary attacks. He started a bit early that year, and the first two fires were noticed in the Sutter County, Sutter Buttes area—the site of his first attacks. Ground blooms were found after two fires begun on June 28. The only deviation from the past fires was that these two both occurred in the late evening.

The holiday that summer started a busy week for the arsonist. On July 4, he hit again in the afternoon just two miles east of the Buttes in Live Oak. Another ground bloom was recovered at this scene. On July 5, he went a couple miles further east into Butte County and set an afternoon fire with a ground bloom lit in a grassy area. On July 6 there was another deviation, as a ground bloom flower was found after an afternoon brushfire in Yuba County, about ten miles south of the Buttes. On July 7, he was back in the Sutter Buttes area and lit three different grass fires within a half hour, all before nine o'clock in the evening. Only one ground bloom was found at these three scenes. Before noon on the 8, the arsonist struck again with a ground bloom in the Sutter Buttes area. This was followed by an identical event and ground bloom two hours later in the same area. A total of eight fires in four days were attributed to this arsonist.

There was a short respite as the task force struggled to keep up with their documentation and the complaints of the suppression chiefs who wanted somebody caught. But the arsonist, having gathered his energy, started again on the eleventh of July. He lit two fires just two-hundred yards apart from each other in the mid afternoon, about five miles east of Yuba City, in the forested foothills. Twenty minutes later, another blaze was spotted about fifteen miles away, further east into the forest and at a higher elevation. Ground blooms were found at both of these sites. The arsonist was clearly mobile and was now beginning to explore some more heavily-forested areas, where the fires had the potential to become really massive. A half hour after that, the fourth fire of the day set with a ground bloom was found back in Butte County. The investigators were now sure that the arsonist was driving out as far as twenty or thirty miles into the mountains, and then returning to the Yuba City area. They could infer that he had some sort of base or deep connection to that area.

Another break ensued, and there were no more incidents until July 27. On that day, two more fires broke out just after noon a couple miles east of the Buttes. Later in the day, a third fire was spotted yet another couple miles east, and a fourth fire broke out late in the afternoon back in the Buttes. Ground blooms were found at all of these fires.

The trend continued in the Yuba City/Sutter Buttes area with four fires erupting on July 31, two on August 3, two on August 4, and then five on August 5. August 7 was another bad day, as five fires were found burning in the heavy brush and trees about twelve miles northeast of the Buttes and Yuba City. All of these events were linked by the ground bloom flowers that the investigators kept finding at the fire scenes. By the first week of August, suppression teams in the area were practically reeling. Investigators were also besieged and had documented at least thirty-six fires in five adjacent counties, all linked to the same unknown arsonist. There were no great leads and no workable evidence.

Then finally, the break came. Because they continued to believe that the suspect had links to certain specific areas, the investigators monitored surveillance cameras in those areas. They finally got time to review the footage from the hardest hit areas. After the August 3 fires, investigators realized that they had caught on hidden cameras a similar vehicle in the area of two of the arson attacks. The vehicle was a black Toyota 4Runner. The vehicle was registered to a man named James Hough who lived in the nearby town of Live Oak, one of the two anchor points in Alan Carlson's pattern analysis. Surprisingly, investigators learned that Hough worked at a soda-bottling plant in the town of Marysville, which was the location of the second of Chief Carlson's anchor points. The vehicle was also similar to the suspicious vehicle seen in the Sutter Buttes area in 2005 during the first fires in this series.

A background check revealed nothing dramatic. In fact, Hough didn't seem to match any of the accepted traits of a serial arsonist. He was a long-time family man, had a son who was in law enforcement, and had been married to the same woman for almost thirty years. He was gainfully employed and was in fact the plant manager at the bottling plant where he had worked for thirty-three years. There was no indication that he was a wannabe firefighter or had ever applied to be in the fire service. He did not appear to have any major grudges against the government or anyone else. Investigators would later learn that Hough was an accomplished competitive archer, loved his dogs, and loved to hunt, fish, and camp. He seemed to be a man with an established family, positive hobbies, and a stable life. Basically, Hough just didn't fit the profile.

However, because they were desperate, and Hough was the only workable lead they had, investigators jumped on it with all of their available resources. They brought in some help and began a vehicle surveillance or "loose tail" on Hough during the daylight hours. They were soon rewarded for their efforts, as they followed Hough into the Buttes area where he seemed to just drive aimlessly around.

Meanwhile, other investigators were working up a court order to place a monitoring device on Hough's vehicle. Once that was accomplished, Cal Fire specialists conducted an operation called a "black bag job." This operation is a high-risk ploy in which investigators and technicians actually approach a suspect's vehicle surreptitiously and attach a monitoring device to it. In this case, a GPS tracker was attached to Hough's 4Runner so that he could be monitored from a remote distance. This worked well in the wild land, as it allowed investigators to follow him at a further distance (loose tail) so as not to spook him.

The investigators stayed with Hough until the morning of Friday, August 10, 2007. Hough got into his 4Runner as usual and drove to work in Marysville. At ten in the morning, he left work early to drive to a recreational area near the town of Chester where he would meet his family for a weekend of camping. Hough first stopped at home, changed, and loaded two of his dogs into his SUV. Hough then began driving north to the city of Chico. After a couple hours of driving, he made it to Chico and then turned northeast on Highway 32 into the Sierra foothills, toward the small town of Chester. This winding highway drove through heavy forests in the rugged low mountains just south of Lassen Volcanic National Park.

This surveillance operation continued until about three in the afternoon, when the investigators saw Hough pull to the side of the road in a remote area. The investigators passed Hough and parked, waiting to see what he would do. They weren't prepared for what happened, as within a few minutes he came driving up the road toward an investigator and performed an abrupt U-turn, nearly striking the undercover vehicle. (This, oddly, was an exact copy of a similar near-crash into an undercover vehicle initiated by serial arson suspect Ben Cunha just one month later in nearby El Dorado County.) The team tried to follow Hough as he engaged a series of erratic U-turns in the roadway, driving back and forth in the same area. They soon figured out why. After his third U-turn, investigators found a small brushfire racing up a steep slope along the edge of the roadway Hough had just passed. This fire burst into the mature forest and began to spread rapidly. It would eventually consume nearly a thousand acres of woodland and become known as the Colby Fire. The fire closed the highway for three days and eventually cost the United States Forest Service $1.3 million in suppression costs.

On scene, Investigator Josh White, who was running the surveillance, notified Chief Carlson about the latest fire. They decided then and there to arrest Hough, as his actions were clearly a danger to all of those around him. He was stopped without incident at around six in the evening, as he approached the town of Chester. The team was very surprised to see a loaded semi automatic pistol on the seat next to Hough. Hough agreed to return to Butte County following his arrest. A search of his vehicle was very rewarding for the team. Investigators found ground bloom flower fireworks hidden in both an overhead compartment and a wheel well.

Hough drove back to Butte County with Chief Carlson and Investigator White that night. He was in a district attorney interview room by ten. The interview was recorded on video. After initial denials, Jim Hough began talking about his fire-setting habits with Carlson and White. Noting that the man was older and had probably had an old-style upbringing, the investigators decided to try a tact that had been successful with other older offenders. They appealed to his traditional childhood upbringing by asking him to take responsibility for his actions. Using this method, the investigators were able to get Hough to admit to and describe his fires. At one point, he calmly allowed, "Well, I guess I'm guilty."

Hough told them that on the Fourth of July in 2005, he purchased his first bag of ground bloom flower fireworks from a roadside stand. He lit them, usually with a cigarette lighter, and tossed them into the dry grasses along the roads around the areas where he was camping. He did this over and over again for a few weeks until his bag of fireworks ran out. He claimed to have not lit any more fires until the same time the following year, when he purchased another bag of ground bloom flowers. Again he deployed them until his bag ran out a few weeks later. He mimicked this activity again in 2007 with another bag of ground blooms until he was finally caught. This admission answered the nagging question of why the arsonist had gone dormant for so many months each year.

Like many serial arsonists, Hough had no explanation for his activity. He said he could think of no reason why he would do this—he just did. He said that he would feel a little adrenalin rush immediately after starting a fire, but it faded soon and he was left with only the thought, "What the fuck did I do that for?" Over the course of the detailed interview, Hough admitted to lighting at least thirty-six fires since July of 2005. He said he exclusively used ground blooms, and lit all of his fires in dry grass along roads, during daylight hours, while in his vehicle. He learned through his activity that the fires grew larger in a shorter period of time if they were ignited at the base of hillsides.

During part of the interview, while the investigators were addressing the most recent blaze, the Colby Fire, Hough gave this surprising explanation: "I hated that mountain." That was the only real reason that Hough ever gave for any of his fires. At the end of the interview, Hough agreed to take investigators on a tour of his fire scenes and to describe each one in detail.

After his admissions, Hough felt that he ought to be released home. He was stunned when he discovered that his crimes were felonies, and he was facing the possibility of several years in jail. He mumbled at one point, "I'd just as soon shoot myself."

He was booked into jail and investigators soon filed nine counts of arson of a forest against him with Butte County District Attorney Mike Ramsey. Bail was set at $675,000. The DA promised to file additional counts in the future as they were assembled. Chiefs Carlson and Engel as well as Investigator White believed that Hough could be positively linked to about forty-six arson scenes. Hough, who was irritated that the bail was so high, withdrew his offer to take the investigators to his fire scenes. Eventually, thirty-three felony counts of arson were filed against Jim Hough.

In the early morning hours of Friday, August 24, 2007, just two weeks after his arrest, Jim Hough reached a climactic decision. He knew he was caught and knew he likely couldn't escape the fate that awaited him, many years in a prison. This was an unendurable sentence for a man who had spent much of his life in the outdoors among the hills, trees, and mountains of north central California. He was also aware that any court battle would be embarrassing and a financial hardship on his wife and sons. Hough made a noose out of some jail sheets and tied one end to his cell bars. He then deliberately strangled himself by forcing his own body weight against the noose around his neck. Found unconscious by jailers during a routine check, he was rushed to a nearby hospital. Unresponsive, he was placed on life support machinery at the hospital long enough for his wife to arrive and give the final consent for the machines to be turned off. Jim Hough died shortly thereafter, taking the details of his secret life of serial fire-setting to the grave with him. In the short note he left his family, he gave no reasons or details about the arsons, only saying good-bye and apologizing for having let them down.

To this date, Hough's family cannot fathom his arrest. They are convinced that nothing in his history foretold of this type of behavior. They have long maintained that he was an excellent employee, good husband, and dedicated father.

However, a deeper look at Hough provides some telltale warning signs. He did have an old brush with the law when he and one of his sons were arrested for poaching, which is hardly an accidental act. He also kept a loaded gun on the seat of his truck with him while he was committing his arson attacks. This may have been some sort of defense system if he was stopped immediately after starting a fire. Hough's family history is also indicative of some issues. Jim Hough's father was a heavy drinker all his life and was in bad health at the time of Jim's arrest. Jim had a younger brother who committed suicide five years before the fires started. Jim himself was known to be a bit of a heavy drinker at times, and he had confided that he was not happy with the recent changes made by management at his bottling plant.

All we have at this point are the speculations of those who knew and chased Jim Hough. The real secret to Jim Hough's behavior remains just that, a secret.

Investigator's Analysis:

Every experienced detective and investigator I know is well aware that a large number of people have three facets to their persona. They have their public persona, which is comprised of how they act and are perceived at work, school, with their friends, or casual acquaintances. They also have their private persona, which is a more intimate look at how they act behind closed doors, usually with their family, lover, or very close friends. Quite often a person's public persona is markedly different from his private persona. Finally, many people have a rarely acknowledged or discussed secret persona. This is where they get really interesting. Most people attempt to hide or at least downplay their secret life. Investigators, when searching a crime scene or digging deeply into a suspect's past, often stumble upon this secret side that is incredibly different from everything else in the suspect's life. Quite often this secret life involves out-of-character sexual desires, fetishes, or deviant tastes that the person may want to hide. Other times it involves illicit affairs or underhanded business deals, or even the use and abuse of illicit drugs or alcohol. Every once in a while, it involves serial criminal activity of the "thrill nature," including shoplifting, serial theft, prowling, peeping, burglary, stalking, vandalism, or even rape, arson, and murder. How many times has the media covered a story in which a child molester, serial rapist, or serial murderer is identified and his clergyman, wife, children, parents, or coworkers express complete amazement and denial that the person they have known closely for all these years is a serial offender? Jim Hough's case is a classic example of a "secret life."

The Sunset Strip Arsons
West Hollywood, 1980's-2012

A small slice of land existing within the city of Los Angeles at the base of the Hollywood Hills was inexplicably left unincorporated when the city was formed in 1850. Bordered on its east side by glamorous Hollywood and on its west side by posh Beverly Hills, the area which is just under two miles wide and about a half mile top to bottom, came under the jurisdiction of the Los Angeles Sheriff's Department by default back in the 1800s. It remains so today.

The sheriffs in the early 1900s patrolled a vast county of mountains, beaches, deserts, and about fifty small towns. The department, which would grow to nearly 9,000 deputy sheriffs, had only a handful of patrolmen in those days, and as a result it paid little attention to this unincorporated area completely surrounded by the city. The city of Los Angeles developed a large police department which aggressively enforced the various laws of the city. Likewise did the neighboring city of Beverly Hills. For instance, gaming and gambling were illegal in the city of Los Angeles, while during the 1920s these activities were not banned in the unincorporated areas patrolled by the sheriff.

As could be expected, in the years following Prohibition and into the Great Depression, the few citizens of Los Angeles who did have money wanted to spend it. They took great pains to attend casinos and gambling boats off the California coast and at Catalina Island. This became overly burdensome for gamblers, and a gaming spot was needed closer to home. Entrepreneurs began building bars, card rooms, and nightclubs in the live-and-let-live unincorporated "west Hollywood" area. As most of these businesses began to flourish along the main east-to-west artery in the area known as Sunset Boulevard, the natural name for this zone became the "Sunset Strip."

Like any successful venture, the opportunists and criminals began to notice all the money being spent in this area. Soon, east coast gangsters followed by organized crime syndicates began hooking their claws into the Strip. This brought with it the arrival of every kind of vice for every taste. By the 1930s and decades before the existence of Las Vegas, the area became notorious as a bawdy sin city.

The history of that notorious and colorful era is filled with rampant rumors, speculation, and outright criminal cases involving organized crime, murder, bombings, arsons, and the alleged illegal activities of the vice squads of the three major entities in the area—the LAPD, the LASD, and even the LA District Attorney's office. They were all trying to get a piece of the lucrative action at the gaming establishments. The modernization and reform measures of police departments, as well as a ban on gambling, put an end to much of this mayhem, but the wild nightlife of the Strip would survive.

By the 1960s most of the serious vice ventures had departed. However, the area soon became a haven for music clubs and bars that featured up-and-coming bands, singers, and music acts. These clubs flourished through the '60s, into the sleazy 1970s, and the metal boom of the 1980s. Many famous rock-and-roll acts got their first gigs in the pay-to-play clubs on the Strip such as the Rainbow Bar and Grill, the Whiskey a Go Go, the Key Club, the Viper Room, the House of Blues, the Troubadour and the Roxy. These clubs continue to serve as stepping stones for famous rock acts, even today. They were joined by a number of comedy clubs in the 1980s.

In 1984, the Strip finally got an official name as it was incorporated into the city of West Hollywood. The council elected to keep the Los Angeles Sheriff's Department as their policing agency. A unique, tolerant, and open city, it is one of the few mostly gay communities in the world. Modern West Hollywood still embraces its raucous past, and the area continues to flourish with nightclubs and restaurants. The area is like much of the rest of Hollywood in that there is also a huge population of Eastern Europeans, specifically Russians and Armenians.

West Hollywood also has another interesting feature. It has a higher than normal number of serial arson cases in its history. Between 2008 and 2010, it was difficult to figure out if a fire along the Strip was related to a marijuana shop dispute, a Gypsy feud turned violent, or just another of the many street denizens torching trash cans and dumpsters.

On December 30, 2011, five arson fires broke out within an hour in a small three-block area near the Sunset Strip. The first three fires were set in a carport, in trash cans, and on a cleaning truck. The suspect, a drunk college-aged kid, was apprehended rather quickly as he was attempting to light his final fire. This drunken spree was as a result of the young man being tossed out of a nearby party. He was in the custody of LAPD by about three in the morning. Within minutes of his arrest, two additional fires were spotted burning on Hollywood Boulevard in trash dumpsters. Both of these fires were witnessed, and the suspect, a deranged homeless man, was also quickly nabbed. Both of these men were in jail on arson charges for the next several days awaiting their trials. This became very important to them, as within about twenty hours of their arrest, a single person went on one of the most impressive arson rampages in American history. The previous night's arsonists would have the airtight alibis of being in jail to spare them the suspicion that arose when, over the next seventy-five hours, a total of fifty-two arson fires were set in the West Hollywood/Hollywood area. This orgy of arson stopped four days after it began with the arrest of a German citizen named Harry Burkhart. I was the lead investigator for the Los Angeles Sheriff's Department on the case which has come to be known as the "Hollywood Fire Devil" event. Along with my partners, Detective Dana Duncan and Detective Cindy Valencia, I processed several arson scenes within just a few hours. We also literally stayed awake for the next eighty hours as we combined with the LA City FD, ATF, and the LAPD to lead a task force of nearly four-hundred investigators over the next few days. I later interviewed Harry Burkhart along with the other lead investigator from the LAFD, Investigator Dan Gaytan. A day after his arrest, I filed the first thirty-six felony charges against Harry Burkhart for this series of fires. More charges would follow.

As of January of 2013, Burkhart has been charged with exactly one-hundred felony counts relating to these arson attacks. He sits in jail awaiting his hearings and trial. If he is convicted, he will be known as the most intense and energetic arsonist in the history of the United States—it appears that no one has ever before lit more significant fires in such a short period of time. All of the charged fires were ignited under cars with the use of a unique incendiary device. In each of the charged cases, most of the cars were parked within or under occupied commercial or residential structures. Many of these fires did tremendous damage to the buildings they were set within.

Sadly, because the case has not run its proper course in criminal court, I cannot give the specific and highly interesting details of this incredible event. Suffice to say that it will be known as one of the most significant arson cases in history when it is over.

The link between the Burkhart case and this chapter is that the Hollywood Fire Devil's first several fires occurred in West Hollywood in the blocks surrounding the Sunset Strip. Like I said, this area has a long history of serial arson behavior.

In the 1980s, an unknown serial arsonist lit over thirty fires in just thirteen nights on the streets of West Hollywood. LA sheriff's arson investigators, Bobby Taranto and Ron Ablott, later developed leads and information that led them to a male named Dave Schwartz. There was an odd twist to this set of fires. Ablott said that the arsonist was targeting a specific type of vehicle for his fires. In this case it was Jeeps. All thirty of these fires were set in Jeep vehicles. Schwartz was detained by the sheriff's investigators and questioned regarding the fires. He was eventually let go due to a lack of evidence. No charges were ever filed in this case, but suffice to say that once he was let go, Schwartz fled the area, never to be seen locally again and, amazingly, the arson fires stopped. Investigators would never learn if he truly was the arsonist or why he targeted Jeeps. This mystery is typical of the area with its ever-transient and fluid population.

Charles Galante, The Lion that Roared West Hollywood, 2010

Author's Note: This case comes from author's case files.

On a hot July evening in 2010, sheriff's deputies at the Los Angeles Sheriff's West Hollywood Station were sitting in their air-conditioned front desk area, monitoring phone calls and the radio. The modern operations center was filled with the latest equipment, including a high-resolution video monitor that viewed images from the eight security cameras surrounding the station. For the previous two hours, the desk deputies had been irritated by a recurring sight. One of their security cameras was focused on the courtyard just in front of their front doors. This was the main access point for the public. Sitting on a bench in that courtyard for the past two hours was a local transient they all knew as "Chuck." He was a miserable, crabby, stooped-over old man who was frequently urine-soaked and belligerent. He was short in stature, but appeared even shorter as he walked, as he was completely hunched over as if his back were injured.

Chuck was one of those colorful local characters well-known to all the young deputies at the station. He was fond of standing on the street and shouting obscenities at anyone who dared to look at him. The young, muscular deputies usually just laughed him off when they drove by and he challenged them to a fight or screamed loudly at them.

This night Chuck was starting to get a little too obnoxious. He sat or paced in front of the station and yelled at all who walked past him. Finally, the desk deputies had had enough of him and sent one of their newest trainees outside to chase him off. They watched the cameras with amusement as the bulky deputy attempted to cajole Chuck out of the courtyard area. Chuck could be seen yelling and gesturing wildly, getting in the deputy's face. Despite his antics, Chuck eventually shuffled off camera toward his usual hangout a block away behind, Koontz Hardware. The deputies went back to their normal duties.

About a half hour later, the deputies looked up and saw Chuck again in front of their station. This time he had a wad of newspapers that he was stuffing into one of the trashcans in the station courtyard. As the deputies watched, they saw smoke and flames starting to billow out of the trash can. This time they sprinted outside, just in time to see Chuck scampering off the property. The pissed-off deputies yelled at Chuck to stay away or he'd be arrested. Chuck stood on the sidewalk and began yelling curses at them, giving them the finger.

In truth, none of the deputies wanted to actually arrest this disgusting guy, as he frequently spit at them, screamed incessantly, and was often reeking of urine and feces that were also occasionally visible on his clothes. When they feigned as if they were going to chase him down, he finally took off. The deputies put out the trash-can fire with an extinguisher and promptly forgot about the incident. After all, it was only trash that was burned. They saw that the can had been stuffed with the "underground" newspapers that were common throughout the area. These types of newspapers are provided free on nearly every other corner in urban areas and cater to a sort of counterculture. In Hollywood, there are several of these publications, and they each have several pages devoted to local music clubs, bands, sex shops, marijuana dispensaries, and several pages of ads for defense attorney. A particularly colorful section of the newspaper is the section often referred to as the "back page." This section is the "personals" section that advertises erotic services including strippers, massage parlors, and escorts. Hollywood and West Hollywood, being very liberal locales, give equal amount of advertising to both male and female escorts (prostitutes), and include transgender and transsexual "providers." While of course prostitution is illegal in California, the papers skirt the issue by referring only to "erotic encounters," "mutual massages," "friends with benefits," and the like. In this case, just like the small, nuisance fire, the underground newspapers were soon forgotten.

Two weeks later, on August 10, 2010, I caught a case in West Hollywood. It was a fire in a large vacant building on Sunset Boulevard, about six blocks from the sheriff's station. Fires in vacant buildings were not uncommon, as they often become home to gangsters, prostitutes, and transients. The fires are normally associated with someone cooking or heating in the winter months, or occasionally someone using an open flame to cook their methamphetamines or cocaine. These fires tend to stay fairly small in size and are not that difficult to investigate. Since West Hollywood is an extremely liberal city, it has become a destination for all sorts of freaks and fiends who enjoy the live-and-let-live policy that defines the city. Among this group is a large population of homeless persons or transients. Because of this large number of transients, fires in vacant buildings are more common than in many other cities.

The building in this case was a real eyesore. It was a long-vacant, three-story, split-level structure that was part office building, part residential motel, and part apartment complex. It was extremely difficult to navigate through and appeared to be one of those structures that had been added onto over and over throughout the past fifty years. Despite its age and condition, it was still a very pricey piece of property as it fronted the famous Sunset Strip. This building was worth an easy $5 million, even in its dilapidated condition.

The fire in this structure was relegated to the first floor, just inside the main doorway. It was begun in a hallway among a large pile of papers and debris. The fire had spread from this origin into a half dozen other rooms. I sifted the origin looking for cooking items or a small stove. There were none. In fact, the only items in this fire scene were dozens and dozens of the "underground" newspapers from the racks outside. Most were opened to the escort ads section, showing half-dressed young males. My conclusion was that someone had purposefully set fire to these newspapers. I also believed that this person had a bit of a fixation with the ads for male prostitute. This was a whole lot more serious than a transient accidentally starting a fire smoking crank (methamphetamines).

As I was in this seemingly vacant building performing my investigation, my curiosity got the better of me, and I began to walk through, checking out the dozens of vacant rooms. Knowing that a lot of illegal activity, including narcotics sales and prostitution, took place in the building, I brought along my flashlight and carried my gun in my hand. Sure enough, when I got to the second level of this gloomy structure, I heard the sounds of a struggle of sorts. I silently approached, thinking there might be a rape in progress or some other nefarious act. I soon entered a dark room with a stinking mattress on the floor and two small candles casting big shadows. I was treated to the mind-altering sight of a male prostitute and his "date" (a sixty-year-old business man) engaged in mutual oral sex. Of course I scared the hell out of them when I shined my light on them and announced, "Police!" A few awkward moments later, I confirmed that there was not an assault or rape in progress and left the two men to their pleasures. They claimed to be long-time lovers and that, of course, no money was exchanged. Not surprisingly, neither one of them knew the other's name. But then again, it is Hollywood....

A month after this fire, I saw a call come in for a fire at Koontz Hardware, just a stone's throw away from West Hollywood Sheriff's Station. A trash dumpster behind the building had been set afire. This was not normally a big deal, but in this case the burning dumpster caught the eaves on fire, and the flames quickly spread into the building, causing quite a bit more damage. Store security cameras did not show the fire starting, but it did show that the large dumpster was just off camera. A review of the security footage showed several transients in the area before the fire. One of these transients, a very small, elderly male with extremely hunched posture, was seen shuffling off camera toward the dumpster. A minute or two later, he was seen walking away from the dumpster and out of view. Within a minute or two of him disappearing, the glow of a large fire was seen emanating from just off camera. Although we had not actually seen him light the fire, we knew we had to find and interview this particular male. Even in a city with a large transient population, we figured that this guy should stand out quite a bit given his age and posture.

Arson Detective Gary Spencer drove to West Hollywood and immediately started questioning people in the area of Koontz Hardware. Nobody had actually seen the fire ignited, but they all knew the guy in the picture. They identified him as "Chuck," and he was a notoriously aggressive and loud transient who had been around for over twenty years. Spencer learned that Chuck's real name was Charles Galante. Galante had been involved in a public masturbation incident and theft at a nearby store. Spencer went there and confirmed with store security that Galante had entered a dressing room in the store where he was observed fondling himself. Store security also stated that there may have been a small fire in the store as well. They had intercepted and questioned Galante as he had tried to steal some clothing from the store. Detective Spencer began an intensive search for Galante. He didn't have to look far, because within four days of the Koontz fire, Galante was in the sheriff's station.

On September 14, 2010, Charles Galante was observed while in the West Hollywood Sheriff's Station committing a lewd act. In the late evening of that day, two citizens were in the lobby when the bathroom door opened. Charles Galante stood in the bathroom doorway with no pants on, rubbing his limp penis vigorously, while staring at the pair. The outraged citizens informed the deputies at the counter, and they leapt out and grabbed a yelling and screaming Galante. Galante began screaming anti gay slurs at the deputies. The deputies were shocked to see that Galante had smeared fresh feces all over the walls of the restroom and on himself. He again was combative and challenged the much larger deputies to fight him. They arrested him for the lewd conduct and being drunk in public. Later, while being fingerprinted by a young female jail officer, Galante pulled out his penis again and began to masturbate, much to the shock of the young lady.

By early the next morning, I was called to the West Hollywood station to interview Galante. Galante was indeed a disgusting little man. Having been in hundreds of interviews with dirty, filthy criminals, it takes a lot to sicken me. Galante did it within just a few minutes, as he sat down in the interview room and promptly pissed his pants. He announced this fact loudly, as if to challenge me, and he sat and wriggled around while urine overflowed from his plastic chair. He just stared at me and grinned. When he saw that I wasn't going to react, he seemed a bit disappointed. We then sat and talked for over two hours, while he soaked in his own urine with feces visible on his pants. He had earlier refused to change his soiled clothes into a jail uniform, as he did not believe he was a prisoner.

While ignoring the odors and his frequent yelling, I soon became fascinated with Charles Galante. Eventually he gave me his life story. Galante was born in Michigan but moved out to California when he was very young. He grew up in the Burbank area and attended college briefly. He said he did poorly in college, because he was bored as he was so much smarter than his instructors. There may be some credence to this claim, as Galante then told me that he joined the army in the 1960s and, because of high aptitude scores, was soon selected to be a cryptographer or code breaker. He graduated from the very difficult and technical cryptography school in the army and soon received a Top Secret clearance. He was then deployed overseas where he completed a college degree. As soon as his tour of duty was up, he left the army and decided to take his skills to a local machine repair business. Galante said he did well with the machines but hated working with people and having supervisors. He admitted that he frequently got into screaming matches with his bosses and was unable to remain employed due to his behavior. Charles Galante said that by the 1970s, he had made the conscious decision to leave employment and live on the streets of Hollywood. He said he did this because he hates stress and supervision, and as a homeless person could freely roam about and do as he pleased. By his own statements, he has been on the streets for over thirty-five years.

Throughout this long interview, Galante would launch into explosive tirades and screaming fits. He cursed me and threatened me despite my having about eighty pounds on him. Finally, I just asked him bluntly why he thought he could intimidate me or the other cops. He just said, "It's worked for me for almost forty years." Galante then explained that he was a small and weak person on the streets, and had learned long ago that if he acted crazy, most people would leave him alone. He said he had developed a "lion complex" years ago and figured if he roared load enough, he could scare people away from him. Galante said the stunt had been working well for so long that it had become part of his persona. He then showed me several tattoos on his body. He actually had a lion tattooed on his left arm.

I then began asking him about his fire-setting behavior. He freely admitted that he had lit hundreds of fires. He showed me another tattoo of a Greek figure he called "Helena, the God of Retributive Justice." He said that he was a direct descendant of that god and that it was his mission to mete out revenge and retribution where necessary. He said that one of the ways he doled out his justice was through fire. He also said he was born under the zodiac fire sign, in a unique alignment of the stars, and that he was predisposed to be associated with fire.

I got Galante a meal, and as he ate he began talking about his fire-setting. He told me that he had never burned a building (all serial arsonists say this) and that he had only burned trash, filth, and pornography. He denied setting the Koontz Hardware fire, but admitted that he may have accidentally tossed a lit cigarette into the dumpster. At that juncture, I pulled out one of the underground newspapers from the area. Galante said that those items were pure pornography and that he was ridding the world of them. He then told me about a half dozen small fires he had lit in the previous few days, all using the underground newspapers as kindling. He described the fire in front of the sheriff's station and several other trash-can fires around the area. He gave me exact dates and locations for these events. I then showed him a picture of the vacant building fire from two months prior, in which underground newspapers had been used. He immediately became enraged and said of the building, "That's where faggots go. I don't go there." Oddly, upon further questioning, Galante revealed that he was gay, or at least bisexual. He also admitted to using male prostitutes on occasion.

Galante impressed me with his obvious intelligence and his near-photographic memory. He spoke to me somewhat fluently in French, Japanese, and English and could recite a large amount of historical trivia. He was obviously well-read and educated. He was also completely out of his mind. He admitted that he had severe mental health issues, had attempted suicide on several occasions, took several psychiatric drugs, and had been under the care of a psychiatrist for over twenty years.

When I left Galante that day, I contacted investigators Dave Liske and Tim Crass from LAFD's arson unit. Their area bordered on West Hollywood, and some of the events Galante admitted to had taken place in their area. Within hours, they located and confirmed several events. On July 21, a trash dumpster was found burning on a commercial property. On August 8, a male transient was observed setting fire to a trash can at the same location, a realty complex. A security guard took a cell-phone photo of the suspect. I looked at the photo, and it was clearly Galante. On August 20, the same guard saw Galante light another trash can on fire in the area. There was a fourth fire at the same complex a week later on August 27.

That same afternoon, after leaving Galante in the West Hollywood jail, I learned that he had tried and failed to start some mattresses on fire. He had apparently smuggled a lighter into the jail in his rectum. He was clearly out of control. After this event, several sheriffs' deputies approached me and told me they were aware of some other fires lit by Galante that they hadn't thought were important enough to report to the arson unit. They then related the story of the trash-can fire at the sheriff's station. Another deputy told us that he had witnessed Galante start a fire in a trash can about a month before, but had only arrested him on narcotics charges.

Within just a couple days, we realized that Charles Galante had set at least a dozen fires in the Hollywood area in the last two months alone. He was truly a serial arsonist.

Investigator Crass, Detective Spencer, and I all filed our cases with a special arson district attorney, Sean Carney. Although we linked him to twelve fires, we only filed the five best cases against him, as after that many, it becomes a moot point. The case got a little weirder, as at first the courts sent Galante to a mental health facility for diagnosis. Somehow the shrinks sent him back as mentally stable, and the judge, impressed by Galante's brains, allowed him to act as his own attorney or *pro per*. The preliminary hearing was nothing short of surreal, as a ranting and raving Charles Galante, who frequently soiled himself at defense counsel table, gave me and the other investigators a thorough cross examination. He actually did a fairly credible job. Despite himself, however, while attempting to ask us questions, he frequently admitted to his own acts of arson. Somehow we all made it through the preliminary hearing with our dignity intact. A few months later, Galante took a plea deal and admitted to the arson counts in exchange for a two-year prison sentence. Because of all the time in the psych ward and in jail awaiting trial, Charles Galante will be released before this book is even published. There is little doubt that the "God of Retributive Justice" will be angrily shaking his fist on some street corner, and seeking atonement soon after, somewhere in the Hollywood Hills.

Investigator's Analysis:

Galante's case points out some traits usually associated with serial arson activity. He is a very small, weak, and somewhat disabled man, which are all very common traits among serial arsonists. He suffers from several psychiatric issues and is gay or at least bisexual, again somewhat common traits among serial arsonists. Lastly, he is extremely intelligent and well-read, which coincides with the theory that many serial arsonists are actually more intelligent than the average criminal. He has also rationalized his fire-setting activity by claiming that he is cleaning up pornography and only burns garbage. Charles Galante is a representative of the most common subtype of serial arsonist; the "firebug."

Scott Andrew Arnold, Serial Arsonist
West Hollywood, 2008

One of the more famous clubs on the Sunset Strip is the Viper Room. The club was opened under this name in 1993 by an ownership group which included actor Johnny Depp. Since its opening, this club has been a hangout for the young Hollywood crowd of up-and-coming stars and celebrities. It will also be forever known as the club where young actor River Phoenix died on Halloween in 1993. Like all clubs in Hollywood, the Viper Room has heavy security at the front door. Like all the clubs most often frequented by very well-to-do clientele, the security at the Viper Room is instructed to dissuade the riff-raff and other undesirables from entering and mingling with the "pretty people."

A little after midnight on the morning on March 11, 2008, big Joe Mezzakappa was working the front door of the Viper Room. His job was to keep the peace, protect the high-end clientele, and ensure that any shady characters were kept out. About this time, he was approached by a fairly clean-cut, husky, white male who was dragging a large duffel bag behind him. The man wanted to enter the club. Noting that the somewhat bedraggled male looked like he might have been sleeping on the street for the past few nights, big Joe told him that it cost ten bucks to get in. The male looked irritated, started to walk away, then turned back to the burly security supervisor and said, "If you hear fire trucks coming, it wasn't me." He then walked into the alley at the rear of the club. Big Joe was immediately alarmed by this statement as he was well aware that there had been several fires in the alleys along the Strip during the past month. There had been at least three or four this week alone in the dumpsters behind the famous clubs.

A minute or two later, at the rear of the club, a floor manager was walking a female cashier to her car. They encountered a husky white male carrying a large duffel bag in the rear parking area. The male seemed agitated and had been hiding behind a metal dumpster when they approached. As they got close to him, he leaped out from behind the dumpster and began shouting and cursing at them. The floor manager saw the male disappear down the alley and a few minutes later, he heard fire engines and police cars approaching. They were responding to two trash dumpsters on fire at a nearby business. The floor manager went into his office to check his security cameras for the Viper Room and found the same white male now back in his parking lot near the dumpster. He went outside with security to confront him and saw that he had again disappeared from the lot, but now their dumpster was on fire. About a half-hour later, a fourth trash dumpster was found burning in the alley behind porn king Larry Flynt's Hustler store. This fourth fire actually caused some significant damage, as the dumpster was up against a carport that eventually caught fire. This was less than a block away from the Viper Room. All four of these fires had occurred within about forty-five minutes.

Soon a group of patrol deputies from the nearby West Hollywood Sheriff's Station began to deploy to the alleys of the area. They too were aware that there had been a string of recent fires in the alleys along the Sunset Strip. At least a half-dozen fires had occurred in the area over the previous month or so. The first one or two did not arouse suspicion, as the local cops and firemen just assumed that someone had carelessly discarded a cigarette into a dumpster full of combustibles. But after the third or fourth fires, the county firefighters started to get downright irritable at having to get up at two in the morning to put out these nuisance fires. As is often the case in these minor fire events, neither the deputies nor the firefighters had deemed these incidents serious enough to notify their respective arson investigation units.

Deputy Pete Briones saw that the fires were heading in an easterly direction. He sped a few blocks ahead of the last reported fire and entered the alley with his lights out. Almost immediately he spotted a male standing next to a trash dumpster with a piece of burning cardboard in his hand. The male dropped the burning cardboard into the dumpster and the contents started burning. Briones leaped out of his car and grabbed the suspect, who he now saw was lugging a large duffel bag. The suspect was identified as twenty-six-year-old Scott Arnold. Almost immediately Arnold told the deputy, "I'm not an arsonist; I just like watching the fires." Deputy Briones noted that Arnold was obviously drunk and had a plastic butane lighter in his hand. Arnold was belligerent and verbally abusive, and he soon began to curse and spit at Deputy Briones. Briones booked Arnold at the West Hollywood Sheriff's Station and notified the Los Angeles Sheriff's Arson and Explosives Detail. My partner at the time, Sgt. Craig Anderson, took over as the lead investigator on this small serial arson case.

Between the patrol deputies and Sgt. Anderson, they linked the suspect to the other fires by showing six-pack photo lineups to all the witnesses. This was the same guy who had approached the front door of the Viper Room and made the odd comment about fire engines. This was also the same guy who was seen on video footage near the dumpsters of the Viper Room and the Hustler store. It seemed like a fairly clear-cut case.

Sergeant Anderson also began to collect information on the previous fires in the area, since they appeared to fit this suspect as well. Because no one had reported these fires to an arson investigator, there were no reports to study. Additionally, because so much time had passed, there was no usable video remaining. Sgt. Anderson drove to the only fire station in the area, Los Angeles County Fire Station #7, and spoke to the various shift captains.

They assured him that there had been at least six, and maybe up to a dozen, dumpster fires in alleys along a six-block stretch of the Strip over the past two months. All occurred late at night, and all were set with an open flame applied to the paper and cardboard within the dumpsters. Sadly, no one had maintained records of these events, and there was just no way to recall the exact names of witnesses and victims.

Anderson then studied the background of suspect Scott Arnold. Like most of the people wandering the streets of Hollywood, Arnold was a transplant from somewhere else. He had been born in New York and at some point a few years ago had made his way to Southern California. He had arrest records dating back five years in the Los Angeles basin. Arnold had obvious issues with alcohol. He was convicted of drunk driving in 2003. This was followed by no less than five arrests for public intoxication, all in various beach cities near Los Angeles. Sprinkled among these were at least three arrests for disturbing the peace or public fighting. Not surprisingly, there were no arrests for fire-setting. This is very normal for serial arsonists. Very few serial arson offenders have past arrests for fire-setting activity.

Anderson was not going to get any insight on this guy from the suspect himself. As soon as he started to advise Arnold of his rights in preparation for an interview, Arnold invoked and declined to talk. With little more to link him to the other fires in the series, Sgt. Anderson took the case to the district attorney at Beverly Hills court. Like most prosecutors, the filing DA was wholly unimpressed with the size of Arnold's fires. Sgt. Anderson spent some time trying to educate the DA on his assessment of Arnold's fire-setting behavior and the fact that he was and would continue to be a problem fire setter who would likely graduate to more serious targets and larger fires. Sgt. Anderson wanted to file all five of these fires as separate arson attacks, so as to maximize Arnold's jail time. Despite this argument, the prosecutor dismissed the advice of the expert fire investigator and decided to count all five fires set in one night as a single event. This is common in a spree arson case. The DA filed only a single count of arson in this case. Seizing upon the fact that his client was given a huge gift, the public defender quickly pled out Arnold to a very minimal jail sentence.

Scott Arnold was quickly back out on the streets of Southern California, where he was soon arrested on multiple occasions for more public disturbances.

The Gypsy Arsons

Few American law enforcement groups have penetrated the shadowy world of the *Roma*, or Gypsies. The term "Gypsy" has historically referred to roaming bands of extended families that have long traveled the world and been involved in such lucrative pursuits as fortune-telling and palm-reading. Traditionally Gypsy families were associated with Eastern Europe, and the areas known as Romania and Transylvania. Throughout the ages, these families have migrated across the globe and modern Gypsy clans can be of Italian, Russian, French, German, Spanish, or other roots. Modern Gypsy families have moved on to many other fields of employment and have somewhat assimilated into modern society throughout this country; however, some still cling to the traditions of the old world. The overriding factor in the life of a modern Gypsy is the family or clan. Family traditions and bonds are extremely important, and any deviation from the established norms of the clan tends to cause a lot of crises within the Gypsy community. Many Gypsy feuds are fought as the result of an insult, perceived slight, or one party failing to abide with the wishes of his family, one clan in a dispute with another, or someone not obeying the wishes of the leader of the local Gypsy community.

Gypsy feuds have come and gone throughout the history of the people. In more recent times, the use of arson as a tactic has emerged during some very contentious Gypsy feuds. In 1993, in southern Florida, a war between Gypsy fortune-tellers broke out in Broward and Palm Beach counties. The cause of the small war was attributed to a Gypsy family opening a fortune-teller shop in too close a proximity to another family's shop, and all without the permission of the local Gypsy leader. In a forty-eight-hour period, three fortune-teller shops were attacked the same way, with a brick or rock thrown through a front window, followed by the application of a flammable liquid in through the broken portal. Around eight o'clock in the evening on Friday, December 10, an unknown arsonist attacked the Psychic Readings shop in Lantana, Florida, causing $50,000 in damages. This was followed an hour later by a second identical attack at Nora's Astrology in Boca Raton, causing over $150,000 in damages. By early Sunday morning, a third arson attack had struck the Psychic Shop in Fort Lauderdale, causing a very small amount of damage.

Florida detectives who specialized in Gypsy investigations told the media that they had learned that the head of a local Gypsy clan had not received his proper "tribute" when another clan set up the shops in his area. This affront appeared to be the cause of the multiple arson attacks. At some point the affront must have been corrected, because the fires stopped as quickly as they started (with no one arrested or charged), and the Gypsy families in the area went back to business as usual.

In more recent years and in southern California, a similar Gypsy feud appeared to be the main causal factor in a series of arson attacks.

In 2005 a car was torched in the Hollywood area just off the Strip, and behind a fortune-telling business run by a Gypsy named Debbie Riste. Riste has a long and colorful history with the police as both victim and offender. She appeared to a have had several disputes with other Gypsy family members over the years. It was her car that was torched that night, and she soon told the LAFD and LAPD about a potential suspect, another Gypsy.

Several months later at the same shop, a Gypsy man named Buddy Mitchell was arrested for an arson fire, again attacking Debbie Riste, who was apparently his sister-in-law.

At 8913 Sunset Boulevard, West Hollywood, sits the Russian Tea Room Psychic Reader. It is owned by a local Gypsy clan leader named Tony. This small shop sits just three doors down on one side from the famous Whiskey a Go Go, and three doors down on the other side from the Sunset Super Shop, a medical marijuana dispensary. The Whiskey is of course world famous for its contributions to the history of rock music, and the Sunset Super Shop is famous only for being the target of about a dozen arson attacks during its short tenure. The story of that shop will follow this one.

LASD arson Det. Mike Digby was trying to get a handle on a rash of arson attacks in the Hollywood area. Specifically, he was trying to get information on fires that were occurring at fortune-telling businesses in the area. In 2007 he began investigating a fire at the Psychic Reader on Sunset after it had its front windows smashed by a brick, and gasoline was poured into the shop, and set afire. This fire amounted to very little damage, and Det. Digby found the shop owners not very forthcoming. Eventually Digby would learn that this attack was related to a feud in the local Gypsy community. It seems that a young Gypsy couple had married without the permission of an elder in the clan. This ignited a simmering feud between two longtime rival families. This attack seemed like a fairly minor event until a few weeks later when just down the street on the LAPD side of Hollywood, a near identical arson attack occurred at another palm-reader's shop. This time the results were more dramatic, as a woman who was sleeping in the back of the shop died during the fire. This arson/murder case was investigated by the LAFD and LAPD. They too learned that this attack may have been related to a feud between two clans.

A detailed investigation could not penetrate the clans, but detectives would find a series of vandalisms, burglaries, and an ongoing list of threats in local police records. All of these instances were related to a shadowy feud between a few of the Gypsy clans in the area. Around the same time, rumors of vandalisms and fire bombings at other Gypsy-related shops extended from Hollywood, West Hollywood, Beverly Hills, West Los Angeles, the Marina, and areas to the north and south.

On November 30, 2009, at eleven thirty in the evening, an unknown arsonist attacked the Main Street Psychic business in Ventura, California, a coastal town of a hundred-thousand people just forty miles north of Los Angeles. The owner of that business was a Gypsy, and she also owned an additional psychic shop in the mountain community of Ojai. The Ventura City Fire Department conducted an initial investigation and determined that the arsonist had thrown a brick through the front window of the shop and sprayed a quart bottle of charcoal starter fluid onto the floor of the business. The fire caused about $10,000 in damages. True to character, the shop owner was less than cooperative with investigators, and no leads were developed. This case quickly and quietly closed due to a lack of cooperation by the victims.

Within about a year, the fires and attacks on the various fortune-telling businesses in the Hollywood area stopped as abruptly as they started. Whatever feud or perceived slight had generated this recent spate of attacks must have been settled or atoned for. Still, a bit of confusion reigned as will be shown in the following story that starts immediately next to one of the Gypsy shops targeted in the earlier attacks. To complicate things, the local Gypsy leader "Tony" actually reported the first arson attack in the following story of marijuana-shop fires. Like I mentioned, it does get a bit confusing along the Sunset Strip.

Fireraisers, Freaks, and Fiends

The Marijuana-Shop Arsons
Hollywood, 2007-2012

The 8900 block of Sunset Boulevard is one of the busiest sections of the Strip. On its eastern corner at 8901 Sunset is the world famous Whiskey a Go Go rock and roll club. On the west edge of this block sits three other famous rock clubs—the Roxy, the Key Club, and the Rainbow Bar and Grill. Across the street is the Viper Room and another landmark, porn king Larry Flynt's world-famous Hustler store. Most of these venues are open late, into the wee hours of the morning. There are always people in the area, including dozens of security guards, and the area also has a liberal number of security cameras. With all these eyes watching this block, one would think it might be difficult to pull off an arson attack. Actually, it was quite easy to pull off—several times.

Smack dab in the middle of this famous block, and directly next to the previously-burned Russian Tea Room Psychic Reader, sat a blue building which housed three different addresses. One address is for a Vietnamese nail salon called "Melody Nails." Five feet away, the other two addresses were jointly owned by a business called the "Sunset Super Shop." By late fall of 2012, both of these businesses had been torched in firebombing attacks no fewer than seven times. The owner of the blue building also had his personal homes firebombed on another five occasions.

The Sunset Super Shop, like so many others in the greater Los Angeles area, is euphemistically called a "non-profit medical-marijuana collective." In the late 1990s, the voters of California passed Proposition 215, also known as the Compassionate Care Act. This act opened the door for the semilegalization of marijuana for medicinal purposes. While the merits of marijuana as a legitimate medical treatment will not be debated here, calling these shops "not-for profit ventures" is the most ludicrous statement in history. These shops are absolute goldmines for the owners and investors, cagily known as the "collective." There is no debate that these shops barely break even selling medicinal marijuana out the front door to patients with valid prescriptions. However, there is also no debate that these shops rake in tens of thousands of dollars a week buying and selling large bundles of weed out the backdoors. Such seemed to be the case with the Sunset Super Shop.

In 2006, the Sunset Super Shop was operating under a different name. It was called the West Hollywood Center of Compassionate Healing, and the license for the shop was held by a man named Andrew Kramer. Kramer was a young up-and-comer in the medical marijuana industry and had previously been involved in shops in the San Fernando Valley. He had a bit of expertise in dealing with cities and obtaining the proper licensing for the marijuana businesses; he even testified a few times as an expert and consultant in the field of running a dispensary. In late 2006, the DEA determined that Kramer was operating his several shops as drug-trafficking businesses rather than as medical dispensaries, and they began a series of raids on his shops. In January of 2007, the DEA raided Kramer's Sunset Strip shop, along with a couple others he owned or controlled. The feds seized over 830 pounds of high-potency weed worth something over a million dollars during the raid. They began building a criminal case against Andrew Kramer and would eventually raid his homes and other shops several more times over the next five years. After this 2007 raid, Kramer cut a deal with the owner of the building on Sunset, a man named George Lanning, and eventually turned over control of the shop to Lanning and his family. Kramer was to stay on as an "adviser and consultant" to the Lannings and would receive almost $40,000 per month for his expertise. This deal eventually soured, and the two (Lanning and Kramer) began a vicious, four-year, civil court battle over control of the lucrative Sunset Super Shop. In the midst of this civil dispute, the Lannings began having serious issues with all of their properties. From 2008 until 2012, the Sunset Super Shop was attacked by fire on seven different occasions. On several other occasions, thugs were seen throwing bricks through the windows, throwing paint on the signs, and then smashing the windows with various items. The Lannings' nearby home was firebombed on four other occasions, and a vacant home they owned was torched to the ground. In total there were twelve major arson events associated with the Sunset Super Shop. This ongoing series escalated into a major home-invasion attack on the Lannings and three different instances in which thugs drove stolen cars into the front of the Sunset Super Shop.

Beverly Hills Detective George Elwell and I have been involved in this case since 2010, and we have prosecuted at least seven persons for these attacks and interviewed several other suspects on the streets and in prison. Additionally, other investigators on this case have identified several other marijuana shop fires in the Hollywood area linked to this same organized scheme. As of writing of this book, this case has not been presented in court in its entirety. As of January of 2013, up to twenty serious attacks have been linked to the dispute between the Lanning family and Andrew Kramer. In the early spring of 2013 Andrew Kramer and four other of his alleged hired thugs were arrested in a sweeping raid by the Beverly Hills PD, LASD arson unit and the DEA. Kramer is being held on a seven million dollar bond for his role in masterminding and financing the three year assault by fire of the Lanning family. A lengthy criminal court battle is expected.

Investigator's Analysis:

While they have no connection to each other, the six different arson series described above all took place along the fabled Sunset Strip and straddle a time period of just twenty years. All of these arson attacks occurred within about a mile and a half of each other and all involved angry, upset, or deranged men. There's just something about this area.

BEN CUNHA, FIRE FIGHTER ARSONIST
EL DORADO COUNTY, 2005-2007

Author's Note: The following case was taken from Superior Court case files, press releases, newspaper stories, and the official case files of Cal Fire, the State of California's Fire Agency, formerly known as the "California State Fire Marshal." This agency is a statewide agency primarily responsible for fire suppression and investigation in the rural state lands. Cal Fire investigators also gave personal interviews to this author regarding this and other cases presented in this book.

The mid 2000's were a tough time for Cal Fire investigators in the Sacramento region. From 2005 until 2009, there were no fewer than four major wildland serial arson investigations going on within about forty miles of Sacramento. It was sometimes difficult to tell which series belonged to which arsonist, and which fire belonged to which series. Cal Fire investigators had been chasing a serial arsonist on State Highway 16 for over a decade. This area was about between twenty-five and fifty miles north and west of Sacramento. In the fall of 2006, they would arrest and later convict a local volunteer fire captain named Robert Eason for several of those brushfires. He was accused of setting over 143 wildland fires over an eighteen-year period with the use of various incendiary delay devices. Unique among Eason's incendiary devices were several mosquito coil/match devices found at fire scenes and during a search of Eason's home. Eason would be sentenced to forty years in prison for his fires. Eason's case is covered at length in my previous book, *"Torchered" Minds: Case Histories of Notorious Serial Arsonists.*

Like many brushfire arsonists, Eason was a serial fire setter who lit his fires using a delay incendiary device during daylight hours and by use of a vehicle. Additionally, like other firefighter arsonists, he set fires in his own district and then responded to and fought his own fires. Foolishly, he was also the first person to report the fire in several cases, bringing attention to himself.

FIRERAISERS, FREAKS, AND FIENDS

The arrest of Robert Eason in 2006 did not end Cal Fire's serial arson problem. Nor did it end the embarrassing saga of a serial arsonist/firefighter in the area around Sacramento.

As the Eason case was coming to a head in the fall of 2006, Cal Fire investigators realized that they had another series of wildland fires occurring in an area about fifty miles north and east of Sacramento in El Dorado County. El Dorado County is truly in the foothills of the Sierra Madre and in the midst of historic gold country. These foothills consist of grasses, brush, mature oak trees, and the beginnings of heavy pine timber. Like all the foothill regions in California, this area is ripe for wildfires during the dry, hot summer or fall months, and these wildfires often explode into catastrophic firestorms.

Just before two o'clock on a hot Saturday afternoon in August of 2005, a brushfire broke out at a road junction on Sand Ridge Road in El Dorado County. The temperature at the time of this fire was over 104 degrees with 14 percent relative humidity. Thankfully, the winds were negligible. No ignition device would be found in this small, one-acre fire, but it would later be linked to the series by its close proximity to two other fires that occurred the following year.

Eleven months later in July of 2006, at one-thirty on another hot afternoon, a brushfire was spotted along another rural road in El Dorado. This fire was found burning in a stand of oak trees and burned five acres before it was stopped. No ignition device was found here either, but this location would burn again in a later fire and a device would be found. Two days later, with the temperature near one-hundred degrees, another fire was spotted burning near Sand Ridge Road at just before three in the afternoon. This twenty-four-acre fire was located very near the first fire site in this series, and it burned into a stand of oak trees on a slope just below a residential structure. Cal Fire Captain and Investigator Tom Oldag found a time-delay incendiary device at this scene. This device consisted of a single cigarette without a filter surrounded by four paper matches affixed to the cigarette with black tape. Oldag, who was aware of the Eason fires that took place about eighty-miles away, was sure that this was not Eason's type of device. He now became concerned about a copy-cat arsonist in the area.

A month later, on August 9, just before one in the afternoon on a blazingly hot day, a vegetation fire was spotted in a stand of oak trees on Martinez Creek Road. It was the same location as a fire in 2006. This small fire burned less than one acre, and Investigator Oldag found a time-delay device which was a clone of the device found a month earlier. As crews were arriving to the scene, they learned of a second nearby fire.. The second fire that day, which was burning in oak just a mile away, was investigated by Cal Fire Investigator Gianni Muschetto. He found an identical time-delay device at this scene as well.

Just two weeks later, another brushfire was spotted on another hot day at just before three in the afternoon. It was also in the same area as a brushfire that burned the previous year. This time investigators from the US Forest Service were on the scene. They located an identical time-delay incendiary device as found in the other fires. Like some previous fires, this device was placed in oak trees at the base of a slope. Above the fire were residential structures. This fire was stopped at about six acres and did not damage the homes.

Cal Fire and USFS investigators were extremely worried. They realized that they had an emerging series on their hands and the suspect was getting extremely dangerous. The fires were all linked by location, time of day, ignition fuels, similar device, and ambient temperature. The only factor that was good news for the investigators was that the fires were all set on days with very little wind, which every firefighter knows is the main critical factor in the spread of wild land fires. These investigators shuddered, as they knew that the Santa Ana wind season, which normally occurs in September and October, was fast approaching. They expected the worst. The arsonist apparently had other things to do, as they did not hear from him again for nearly nine months.

The fall, winter, and spring passed without a hint of the arsonist. However, as soon as the first signs of summer arrived, he came back. On May 21, 2007, a brushfire was reported just east of Highway 49 in El Dorado County. This fire started at just before three in the afternoon on an eighty-degree day. No incendiary device was found in this six-acre fire, but it burned near the same locations as three other fires in this series; devices were found at two of the other scenes.

Exactly two weeks later, at the same time of day, a small fire was found burning in a field of mowed grass in El Dorado County. Investigator Tom Oldag, who would eventually become the lead investigator on all these fires, processed this very small scene and found a delay incendiary device identical to the previous ones. They knew for sure their arsonist was back in action.

A month later, just prior to the Fourth of July holiday, again at four in the afternoon on a ninety-degree day, a fire erupted in another stand of oak in El Dorado County. This time, the arsonist set his time-delay incendiary device in a very dangerous area, at the base of a very steep slope. This fire destroyed over 125 acres of woodland on this relatively calm day.

Five days later, the danger continued as another large fire broke out at two in the afternoon as the thermometer topped 102 degrees. This occurred in the exact same area as an arson fire the previous summer, and investigators noted that the terrain was again steep and filled with oak. Again, an identical time-delay incendiary device was found at the base of the fire pattern in this eighty-acre blaze.

The pace of the arsonist was quickening, and his fires were getting bigger and more dangerous. It was clear to Investigator Oldag and his peers that this fire setter was growing more experienced with his crimes and was picking terrain and fuels that caused larger and more dramatic fires. Ten days after the July

6 fire, another blaze erupted near Highway 49. This time the arsonist torched twenty acres of oak woodland. Again the fire occurred at two in the afternoon on a hot day. Again, an identical time-delay device was found in the area of origin. This target area also matched two other arson scenes in the series.

Two weeks later the investigators got their first real break in the case, after yet another fire. On Tuesday, July 30, at around three-thirty in the afternoon on a ninety-eight-degree day, a fire was spotted burning in an area of oak and brush. This twenty-acre fire was stopped just short of several homes in the area of Cameron Park. No ignition device was found, but investigators matched this fire to their series through all of the other factors. This fire also produced their first real lead. A witness reported seeing a yellow-and-black motorcycle in the area just before the fire broke out. The motorcyclist was seen driving in and out of the area twice, with the fire being observed after his second visit. The investigators had found motorcycle tracks near the area of origin. They collected this forensic evidence.

Three weeks after that fire, another fire was spotted on Sand Ridge Road, near the site of three previous arson fires. This twenty-acre fire started at just before three o'clock in the afternoon on a ninety-seven-degree day, and a delay incendiary device was found at the area of origin.

Because Sand Ridge Road was an area obviously favored by this arsonist, Cal Fire investigators decided it would be the optimal location to place one of their high-quality static cameras. They had this camouflaged item in place weeks prior to the latest fire. They recovered the camera and reviewed the film. The film showed a small Toyota pickup being driven by a young white male passing through the area four times just prior to the fire being reported. This truck had two notable distinctions. The first was a large, diamond-plated chrome toolbox in the bed area. The second was something the investigators suspected they'd find, but were hoping they wouldn't. The camera clearly showed that this suspicious vehicle was sporting a small fire-helmet decal on its rear window. They recognized this as one of the union decals frequently displayed by firefighters in California. They would later recall that they were saddened by this revelation, but not really all that surprised.

The plate of the truck was run through a computer, and the vehicle was found to be registered to a man named Frank Cunha. The investigators knew it wasn't Frank Cunha driving, because the male in the truck appeared too young to be the Frank Cunha some of the investigators knew—Frank Cunha was a retired fire chief from a nearby department. The investigators, using a professional surveillance team, tracked the truck to a location where they also spotted a yellow-and-black Kawasaki motorcycle. The motorcycle was owned by a young man named Benjamin Cunha, who they knew to be the grandson of Frank Cunha. They also knew that young Ben had been a seasonal firefighter. Surveillance team members soon spotted Ben driving both the Toyota truck and the motorcycle on various occasions. They now had a possible suspect, who drove vehicles linked to at least two of the fires in their series. This was not definitive proof of anything, but it meant that they now had a workable lead in the case.

The fires continued. On August 29, just a week after the latest fire, a brushfire erupted on another rural road in El Dorado County. This small fire, set at two in the afternoon on a scorching 102-degree day, burned just an acre of oak and brush. It was stopped in the nick of time as the arsonist had set his device at the base of a steep slope, just below some homes in the area. Captain Oldag found another incendiary delay device in the area of origin. This was also the same area as an arson fire set in 2006. Prior to this fire being observed, the Cal Fire surveillance team had been following Ben Cunha as he drove his motorcycle into the area. They watched him fuel up at a rural convenience mart/gas station and were astute enough to collect his credit card receipt from his purchase.

The team attempted to follow Cunha as he left the gas station and drove down a secluded rural road. They lost sight of him, but within minutes found a very small fire burning in the area he had just passed through. Although they had not witnessed the actual ignition, they knew that their suspect had passed right by the area of origin.

By this time, the investigative team realized that Cunha was their most likely suspect. The surveillance of Cunha continued for several more days as Lead Investigator Oldag began assembling his case and preparing a search and arrest warrant. They had early on recognized the possibility of a firefighter arsonist. They knew that firefighter arsonists would have more knowledge of fire behavior and incendiary devices than the average person. It was clear early on that the arsonist had developed his skill and was using a fairly reliable device. This device was consistent with devices often shown to firefighters during their arson training. Also, the target selection and choice of ignition areas showed that the arsonist was someone who knew which fuels would burn the best, how slope and heat affect the growth of fire, and why setting fires below residences was so devastating. They also recognized that their arsonist was setting more and more dangerous fires, and his pace of fire-setting was speeding up. The investigators were terrified that the arsonist would choose a day when the winds were howling, leading to a cataclysmic event.

Investigator Oldag also began an in-depth study of his one potential suspect, Benjamin Cunha. Ben Cunha was a twenty-five-year-old man who had grown up in a family of firefighters. His father, Ed Cunha, was a retired fire captain with twenty-three years of service in the Diamond Springs Fire District. He currently sat on the fire district's executive board. Ben's grandfather, Frank, had retired in the same district after twenty years as a local firefighter. Currently, Ben Cunha was a volunteer in the same Diamond Springs Fire Protection District where his father and grandfather had served. Prior to 2007, Ben also had part-time employment in the area with Cal Fire as a seasonal firefighter. He had also worked a brief stint at the local El Dorado Fire Department as an apprentice. Oldag secretly consulted local fire officials and learned an extremely interesting fact. Ben Cunha had grown up and currently lived at a home on Wedge Hill Drive in Placerville. One local fire chief recalled that over a decade ago, when Cunha was around ten or eleven years old, he and another Cal Fire chief in the area had recognized Ben Cunha as a "problem-child fire setter." They suspected him of setting several fires in and around his family's home and had even watched the young boy to see if they could catch him in the act. The chief said that Ben Cunha had been such a problem a decade before that they actually had to enroll him in a juvenile fire setter counseling program.

Investigators also learned that Cunha maintained a MySpace page. He listed himself as a firefighter at Station 74, and also claimed to work as a stunt driver.

The "red flags" in this case were mounting quickly for Captain Oldag. Placerville, which was where Cunha lived, was dead center in the middle of this cluster of arson fires. At least fifteen fires were identified as being the work of one arsonist, and all had occurred within just a few minutes of driving from Cunha's home. Cunha's past history of suspected fire setting was a huge red flag, as the investigators were aware that most serial arsonists begin their careers at a very young age, continuing sporadically all throughout their lives. The time-delay incendiary device investigators kept finding was the most common type associated with firefighter arsonists. Another interesting note was Cunha's driving habits. For some unknown reason, serial arsonists who drive are almost always reckless drivers and notorious speeders. Cunha bragged about being a stunt driver and was seen speeding on numerous occasions. The surveillance team actually observed Cunha getting a speeding ticket from a local officer.

The surveillance of Cunha continued as Oldag continued to build his case. Of note, investigators logged notes indicating that Cunha frequently wore firefighter tee shirts, boots, and other accessories, even when not working. He routinely drove off by himself at a high speeds on either his motorcycle or in a truck. The vehicles were spotted parked along remote and deserted roads.

More uncomfortably for the surveillance crew was the fact that Cunha seemed to only hang out with firefighters and at fire stations. The team followed him to other firefighters' homes, fire stations, fund-raisers, and other such events.

By September 2, Oldag had his search and arrest warrants prepared and signed. Now, he waited for the right opportunity to execute them. The investigative team did not have to wait long. On Sunday, September 9, 2007, the surveillance team was again in position to follow Ben Cunha. As the temperature climbed toward ninety degrees, an area command for firefighters ordered a five-engine strike team to leave the El Dorado County area. This "draw down" of resources was normal to cover an emergency in another jurisdiction. On days like this, the authorities in the area that is drawn down gamble that there won't be any fires in their area. As is normal in the foothill regions on hot days, every firefighter from every conceivable agency was aware of the local draw down. It was presumed that Ben Cunha was quite aware of the lack of fire resources in his area.

The time line for that day is quite telling. At ten minutes to three in the afternoon, the draw down was announced. At three o'clock exactly, the local fire command asked the nearby Diamond Springs Fire Department to staff an additional engine in order to cover the loss of resources. Ben Cunha was closely associated with this department. Thirteen minutes later, the surveillance team saw Cunha leave his home for the first time that day. He rode his motorcycle to a nearby gas station and filled up. He left the station and began driving at a high rate of speed, and within twenty minutes he crossed a small bridge into a remote area. By this time, Oldag and his partners had utilized a fixed-wing aircraft to help them monitor Cunha. Cunha parked his bike in a turn-out and disappeared into the woods. He emerged several minutes later and left the area on his bike. Seventeen minutes after Cunha's bike was first seen parked in the remote area, the aerial surveillance craft spotted smoke coming from that exact spot. No other persons had been witnessed in the area before the smoke was seen.

Oldag and his crew knew that this was the most compelling evidence they would get. They were aware that the type of devices used by Cunha would give him from six to twenty minutes of a delay before igniting. This time delay, along with the speed of his motorcycle, would let him get up to twenty-five miles away by the time the fire started. Oldag decided to execute his warrants, and he ordered the surveillance teams to close in on the speeding biker. He also joined two investigators at the fire to begin suppression and attempt to locate an ignition device.

The surveillance team was surprised to see Cunha stop just a few miles away on a turn-out that had a view of the area of the fire. Cunha appeared to be watching the area of the fire. Cunha left the turn-out and was seen driving erratically, nearly colliding with one of the surveillance vehicles. After Cunha drove back into town, investigators were finally able to catch up and stop him. He was immediately taken into custody, exactly one hour after he left his home following the announcement of the draw down.

Because air tankers had made heavy drops of water and retardant directly on the area of origin, the investigators were unable to locate a source of ignition for this final fire. However, investigators did find Cunha's motorcycle tracks at the turn-out near the fire. They again collected this forensic evidence and were later able to positively match Cunha's motorcycle tire treads to tracks found at two other arson scenes in the series. Within the next two hours, the investigative team served a search warrant on the home of Benjamin Cunha.

A later analysis of Cunha's time records showed that he was not assigned to a fire station when most of the fires were reported. However, in his role as a "call" firefighter, he responded to and was paid on many of these arson events. He usually was a driver for firefighting equipment.

In March of 2008, Ben Cunha pled guilty to just two counts of arson and was sentenced to a relatively light sentence of six years in prison for his fire setting. In a galling move by the court, the bulk of his sentence was suspended under several conditions. Cunha was to be an arson registrant for life and had to wear a tracking device during fire season. The investigators who worked so hard on this case remain bitter to this day about Cunha's very lenient sentencing. Rumors were rampant that some retired fire chief had gotten into the judge's ear and possibly influenced the sentencing of young Ben Cunha.

Cunha did not seem to understand the extraordinary break he had received. Within just a few months, he was rearrested by the local cops for violating his probation, being a felon in possession of firearms, and facilitating the sale of stolen property. This time the court was not nearly as lenient. His bail was set at a staggering $10 million. At the time this book was written, Ben Cunha was in custody fighting additional charges and facing a very lengthy prison sentence.

Investigator's Analysis:

The Cunha case is an excellent example of a typical wildland serial arson investigation. These cases can last several seasons and cover wide areas. Investigators and their bosses must prepare to maintain the investigation of a case over several years. Cal Fire has had several similar cases to this over the past decade, and it is fairly adept at dealing with such events.

FIRERAISERS, FREAKS, AND FIENDS

This case also highlights your typical wildland serial arsonist. The most common offender for this type of arson is a white or Hispanic male operating during the afternoon hours, usually arriving at the scene in a vehicle, and often using a delay ignition device. The wildland serial offender is often employed in or near the wild land—often associated in some manner with the fire service, forestry service, or a law enforcement entity, and has some past training in the construction or use of ignition devices. This person is usually the polar opposite of the urban serial arsonist, who operates at night, on foot, and almost never uses any form of a device.

Lastly this case highlights some continuing problems in the fire service and arson investigation fields. One is the hiring of at-risk individuals for fire-related jobs. Cunha's juvenile history of repeated fire events was a major red flag that something was seriously wrong with him. His driving habits alone suggested that he had maturity issues. Despite this, he was repeatedly associated with various fire agencies and was obviously trying to become a full-time firefighter. I recently received correspondence from a fire chief who had worked in the same region of the state as the Cunha case. He lamented openly that he was aware of several cases where young, reckless firefighters, were ushered into the job by their father (a firefighter or chief) despite having many serious issues in their backgrounds. This retired chief called this practice of "legacy hiring" a serious issue within small fire departments. Another issue brought up by the Cunha case is the training he received with ignition delay devices. I will reiterate here, as I have done in several places in the past, that we (arson investigators) should never be involved in teaching anyone, particularly firefighters, cadets, college students etc. how to use, design, or construct delay incendiary devices. There is no legitimate reason for the continuation of this practice. A final note is that firefighters caught lighting fires have historically gotten very light sentences from judges. Their cases are usually depicted by defense attorneys as "a good man who cracked under the pressure of the job," or someone who "was only involved in training to fight the boredom." I recommend that these people get exactly the same punishment as any other offender in similar circumstances.

Aljuboori
San Gabriel Valley, 2001

Author's Note: This case comes from a joint investigation conducted by LASD Arson Det. Mike Cofield and Alhambra FD Chief John Kabala.

A serial arsonist is one of the rarest criminals you will ever come across. Despite many Hollywood fantasies to the contrary, the serial arsonist is rarely an out-of-control maniac intent on burning a city to the ground. In fact, in most cases, serial offenders rarely burn structures at all, but instead vent their malevolence on items of little value, including brush, trash, abandoned cars, trees, discarded mattresses and sofas, shrubs, and the most popular target of all...the ubiquitous trash dumpster.

By everyone's account, Aljuboori was a creepy little bastard. That is the most common and apt description of this oddball. His full name is Kareem Abdul Aljuboori, a native son of Baghdad, Iraq, who somehow ended up living in the San Gabriel Valley at the base of the foothills. The SGV is a sprawling collection of little cities starting about five miles east of downtown Los Angeles. Historically, the area had been mostly used for agriculture, and it was home to a mixture of white and Hispanic people of both the blue-collar and upper-middle social classes. After WWII, the agricultural orchards were plowed under to make way for the expansive housing tracts that were built over the next thirty years. The area became a mixture of residential neighborhoods and manufacturing facilities. In the mid-1980s, many of the cities had begun rapid transitions to heavy Vietnamese and Chinese populations. Now, the area is about 75 percent Asian. In the middle of all that, someone dumped a crazy Iraqi.

Aljuboori had a knack for irritating everyone he came into contact with. He was a little bitty guy, standing about five-foot-two and weighing about 130 pounds. He liked to drink, ride around on his bicycle, and generally piss everyone off, because he is what we refer to as a "lightweight 5150."* That is, he is a functioning nut case. He has obvious mental health issues, but they are not severe enough to stop him from functioning on the streets and staying out of psych wards. He's also a sexual deviant and serial arsonist!

We came across Aljuboori when he pissed off a bartender at a small watering hole in the Temple City area. He had been tossed out of the place and was last seen leaving on his bike. About five minutes later, a large dumpster in the alley behind the bar was on fire. As the firemen put this out several minutes later, they could see another dumpster burning in the same alley a block away. When they got to that scene, they saw the guy they later described as Aljuboori sitting on his bike, watching the fire with a cell phone in his hand. When the fire captain went to talk to him, he pedaled away.

He would have gotten away with that fire had he not showed up at the same bar two weeks later and done the exact same thing. This time the barkeep called the local sheriff's and gave him a description and the name "Abdul." Arson Detective Mike Cofield picked up the case the next day and went over to look at the scenes. Dumpsters aren't much fun to investigate, as they smell and usually burn up pretty well. Mike talked to the bartender and realized that the suspect may have lit three additional fires. He saw another bar about six blocks away and found out that "Abdul" was a customer there too and that he had been "eighty-sixed" out of there on several occasions. Now that they thought about it, the bar had had fires set to their stacked pallets and dumpsters shortly after tossing him out. Det. Cofield photographed old fire damage at those scenes and then drove to the nearest fire station. He looked at their records and found a total of six similar dumpster fires in alleys all along Las Tunas Drive within the past month, all after midnight. The bartenders and the firemen believed that there were more fires, but this was all that could be confirmed.

Impressed, Cofield realized that we had a serial offender on our hands.

A records check and a brief chat with detectives at the nearby sheriff's station uncovered that "Abdul" was in fact "Aljuboori," a person who lived on Las Tunas Drive and was well-known to the patrol deputies in the area. He was a frequent pest to the sheriff's station, as he routinely called 911 to report all sorts of emergencies, including fires. He had one past arrest for the forcible rape and sodomy of a mentally disabled girl several years before, but the case was eventually dismissed. Cofield quickly recognized both of these traits (sex offenses and fake 911 calls) as being consistent with serial arsonists. He also learned that Aljuboori was a "ding" (nut case) and frequented the area on a green Huffy bicycle.

The area where Aljuboori was operating was on the edge of another city called Alhambra. The chief arson investigator in that town, John Kabala, was very proactive and ran a small task force. We visited him one day and asked about fires in his area. He laughed loudly and turned over a photo of Aljuboori that was sitting on his desk. The chief said, "We're up on this guy right now. We think he is good for eleven dumpster fires set in alleys within the past two months in our town."

He explained that Aljuboori had reported several of the dumpster fires to the local police. At some point, when apparently the Alhambra cops didn't come to one of his fires, he walked into the police station to talk to whoever was in charge. Aljuboori then came into contact with the watch commander for that night, who happened to be an attractive female sergeant. Aljuboori took an immediate shine to the sergeant and told her that someone was starting fires in the area. He told the sergeant that he often drove around on his bike, and he offered to help her by reporting any suspicious activity. The attractive sergeant, with enough years under her belt to recognize a "ding," gave him the usual lip service and said that any help he could offer would be wonderful.

The very next night, the closest dumpster to the police department went up in flames at around two in the morning. Aljuboori dutifully pedaled into the police station shortly after the fire began in order to report it, and he seemed dismayed that the pretty sergeant wasn't on duty. He asked when her next shift was, and promised to be back. Sure enough, the next time the pretty sergeant was on duty, another fire started in the same dumpster close to the police station. Over the next two weeks, two more dumpster fires would occur in the exact same dumpster, with Aljuboori either calling in or coming in to report the incident.

No fool, the female sergeant soon realized that Aljuboori was more than just a creepy little annoyance and was probably setting the fires. She reported her suspicions to the Alhambra arson investigator. Coincidentally, another investigator on the chief's small task force worked in the neighboring city of San Gabriel. This investigator too had pegged Aljuboori as a person of interest in at least five dumpster fires in his city. Aljuboori had been seen by patrol officers in the areas of two fires, and he had reported three others. All were set in alleys, and two occurred behind bars that had tossed Aljuboori out for being a creep.

All told we had about twenty-two arsons linked to Aljuboori. He also had residences in the dead center of two of the arson clusters. Detective Cofield and Alhambra Chief John Kabala sat around and came up with a game plan. Since Aljuboori moved mainly at night on a bike, he was going to be very difficult to watch. The chief solved the dilemma by telling us that he had access to a pole camera that he was currently looking for a place to install. Since by now we had decided that Aljuboori was fond of the female police sergeant, we decided to enlist her help in catching this guy. Kabala set up the pole camera on the same dumpster near the police station that had been burned four times in the past three weeks. Next, he contacted the police sergeant and asked her to place a follow-up call to Aljuboori, asking him to "keep an eye out for suspicious activity" as she was on duty that week.

The call completed, the task force sat back to wait. They did not have to wait for very long. Two nights later, the same trash dumpster near the police station was found burning at about three in the morning. After Kabala was notified, he pulled the tape off the camera and spotted our man Aljuboori. He had ditched his bike a block or two away and approached the spot on foot, passing by the camera several times while carrying a white bag. Eventually, he entered the little fenced-in area where the dumpster sat, and he stayed out of view for a minute. When he reemerged, he was walking away very quickly. Nothing happened, as apparently his fire had burned out. About seven minutes later, he returned to the scene and entered the fenced-in area again. This time he emerged and stood staring back at the dumpster for about thirty seconds. Soon a glow was seen coming from the dumpster, and Aljuboori left the scene quickly. The fire grew and eventually consumed the contents of the dumpster. We had him!

For some reason it took us several hours to find Aljuboori that day, but it only gave investigators time to write a warrant for his place. We didn't expect to find much, as it appeared to us that Aljuboori was using a "hot set" method, which is to say that he was using an open flame like a lighter or match instead of a delay device. This is pretty typical for this type of arsonist.

We eventually caught him, and he was a belligerent little prick. He refused to admit to anything, even after he was shown the video. Mike Cofield is one of the most patient and low-key interviewers in this business. Even he became exasperated by Aljuboori's antics. When Cofield really pressed him, Aljuboori dropped to his knees and begged us to shoot him in the back of his head "like they do in Iraq." He blamed Mexicans for making things messy and getting him in trouble. All in all, he was displaying all the symptoms of a raving maniac.

The two agencies charged him with eleven counts of arson, and he eventually pled to two of them and received a four-year sentence, which was pretty stiff for burning garbage. We told the prosecutors that he was going to continue this activity, eventually burning more serious things, and that he would be a growing problem for years.

After about two-and-a-half years of prison in the psychiatric ward, Aljuboori was released back to the Los Angeles area. Within just a few months, he was arrested in several jurisdictions for street crimes such as urinating in public, being drunk in public, and placing phony 911 calls. There is no doubt that those areas experienced dumpster fires, but nobody can remember them. Alas, we have not seen the last of Aljuboori.

***Note:** 5150 is the California Welfare and Institutions Code for someone who is forcibly hospitalized for a seventy-two-hour period of evaluation for suspected severe mental health issues. It has become another slang term, comparable to nut, ding, whackjob or psycho.

CHAPTER THREE:
Whackjobs and Wildmen

Investigators are required to work around every possible type of person in the world. These people are from differing cultures, religions, social statuses, and any number of groups of people with a "protected status." We tread lightly when dealing with these differences and are often encumbered in our work by using extraordinarily politically-correct terminology that no one in the general public uses. Generally, people who have developed significant mental health conditions are officially referred to as "patients," "wards," or "individuals under mental health evaluation." However, we occasionally run into criminals whose behavior is so outlandish and shocking, even in the world of crooks, that we feel justified in branding them with the old colloquialism "whack job." Not exactly political correct, but sometimes it's simply the most apt description.

Pro Me Thius, aka Greek God of Fire
Laurel Canyon, Hollywood, 2009

Author's Note: This case comes from the files of Investigator Tim Crass of the Los Angeles (City) Fire Department's Arson Squad.

Some guys just beg to be arrested. At about seven in the evening on May 24, 2009, a small brushfire broke out on a steep hillside in the Laurel Canyon area of Los Angeles. Ever since the

1960s, fire officials in Los Angeles had dreaded the call of any sort of brushfire in the Hollywood Hills. A major fire in these foothills is the worst case scenario of all fire emergency planners in Los Angeles. The steep terrain, coupled with the dozens of winding narrow roads that crisscross the area, are a fire chief's nightmare. Sprinkled along every foot of these roads are thousands of homes, ranging from small studio apartments to the mega-mansions of the rich and famous.

Los Angeles is the only major city in the nation with a mountain range in the middle of it. The use of the word "mountains" may be a bit of an exaggeration, but the very rugged hills are completely covered with ten to fifteen-foot-high brush, dry grasses, and chaparral. Any fire started on the lower part of these mountains will immediately race uphill, potentially trapping the tens of thousands of homeowners up above. The fleeing citizens also block the responding emergency vehicles, as the roads in this area are barely a lane-and-a-half wide. Truly, a fire anywhere in the low range of mountains stretching from West Los Angeles to the Hollywood Hills would have the potential to cause hundreds of fatalities.

As it was that spring day, it wasn't quite fire season, and the brush burned fairly slow. It burned slow enough that, by the time the Los Angeles Fire Department arrived on scene, it had only spread to about half an acre. As they arrived, firefighters were approached by a disheveled character, who confronted them in a vaguely threatening manner. A citizen had seen the lone male standing next to the fire while it was in its incipient or beginning phase. The citizen would later describe to investigators that the male appeared to be simply staring into the small fire. The citizen also identified the male as a denizen of a small homeless encampment situated next to the brush fire. Firefighters, concerned by this threatening male, and believing that he appeared to be the person who started the fire, called the arson investigators from LAFD to the scene. By the time they arrived, it had grown dark and the threatening male had faded away into the shadows. The arson investigators were unable to find the man in the dark and decided to return in the daylight. Prior to leaving they briefed the local LAPD commanders to have their patrol units keep an eye out for this person.

They couldn't locate the suspect that night, but LAFD arson investigators and some LAPD units continued the search the next morning. This was no small task, as the area of the fire, which was at Mount Olympus Drive and Laurel Canyon Blvd, was at the very base of the hills that overlooked Hollywood. This was no more than a quarter mile from the famous Hollywood Boulevard, an area rife with many people who fit the description of the suspect. As such, there were literally hundreds of homeless and transient persons wandering about within just a few short blocks of the fire scene.

Shortly after ten thirty in the morning, the original citizen who called in the fire called the LAPD and told them the strange male had returned to the scene of the fire. Patrolmen responded, detained the suspect, and called the arson investigators back to the scene. The cops sized him up as the standard transient haunting every quiet corner of Los Angeles. The tall thin man had the usual sun-burned complexion of a person who slept outdoors. He was dressed in the typical rough and layered clothing of a transient and had the usual wild-eyed look of many of the homeless people in the area. His hair stood out a bit, as it was wild and unkempt, but appeared to have been freshly dyed, as its odd dark color was in stark contrast to his graying beard and mustache.

It was when they asked his name that the cops became aware that the man was in need of mental health treatment. Like many homeless people, the man spoke in a loud and agitated manner. He proclaimed loudly that his name was "Prometheus," which didn't seem to impress the patrol officers much. When they asked him to spell it, he obliged, but somehow the name was misspelled on the booking sheet. True to police procedures, a suspect has to have a first, middle, and last name, so one of the officers wrote his name out in three sections, the last name being "Thius," the first "Pro," and the middle "Me." Being as they worked in Hollywood—the world's capital of weirdos, oddballs, and freaks—the officers didn't bat an eye at the bizarre name. They were obviously not students of ancient Greek mythology. They transported and booked Mr. Thius at the Hollywood Station along with all the other colorful characters from the area.

LAFD Arson Investigator Tim Crass was the on-duty investigator that day. He met Thius at the Hollywood Station and conducted one of the more bizarre interviews of his career. He was a bit more impressed, if not amused, by this man. Investigator Crass was aware that Prometheus was a figure from Greek mythology, known for, among other things, stealing fire from the gods. In popular culture, Prometheus is the Greek God of Fire.* Over the years, as researchers in the fields of psychology and fire investigation have sought to put a reason or rationale behind fire-setting behavior, the subject of Prometheus and other gods associated with fire come up quite often. The "father of psychoanalysis," Sigmund Freud, and his famous peer, Carl Jung, attempted to tackle the relationship between fire-setting and sexuality. In a 1992 thesis entitled "Arson and the Arsonist," British researcher and senior fire investigator Mick Gardiner writes, "Freud and Jung focused upon the legend of Prometheus, the Greek Titan (credited as the founder of civilization in that he stole fire from the Gods), to explain certain traits of those who misuse fire. This explanation which draws attention to such traits as confused sexuality and insecurity has become labeled the 'Prometheus Complex'."

I personally have no knowledge about this particular Pro Me Thius and his sexual inclinations, but suffice to say that many of the persons in this book have obvious sexual-identity issues. It is one of the true puzzles in the arson investigation world that has not been satisfactorily explained by anyone.

When Investigator Crass interviewed his subject, the man reiterated with some vigor that his name was in fact Prometheus and that he was the Greek God of Fire. Crass would later be surprised to learn that the man's California driver's license did in fact list his name as Pro Me Thius, listing his former name as Darby Ralph Tennal. At some point this man had formally changed his named with the DMV. A check of the man's wallet showed a credit card also in the name of Pro Me Thius.

A computer check of Thius showed that he had been a transient in the Los Angeles area for several years and had a few past arrests for obstructing police officers, using fake bus passes, and some violations of panhandling ordinances—all typical transient offenses. In 2008 he was charged with assaulting someone.

Investigator Crass attempted to get at the "why" of the fire set by Pro Me Thius. He began the interview by advising Thius of his Miranda Rights, which the subject soon waived, stating that he had no objections to speaking with the investigator. Thius told Investigator Crass that he lit the fire and that it was his intent to "blacken" the hillside as part of an "art project." He showed some clarity when he told the investigator that he was well aware that it was safe to light the fire that day as the wind had not been blowing. It was his intent to let the fire burn to the top of the hill and then call 911 after about a minute, whereby the responding firemen would extinguish the blaze, thus completing the "art project." Thius also gave a reason for his name change. He said that he had taken the name not because he loved fire, but because Prometheus was known as a "benefactor of humanity."

He was subsequently charged with arson to forest or land. Later that summer Thius was sent to Department 95 (the psychiatric court), where he was referred to a state prison hospital for psychiatric evaluation. He spent about one year in the psych ward and was eventually brought back for trial. He was released to the streets pending his trial. He failed to show up at his next court date and was rearrested while wandering the streets. On

May 24, 2011, Pro Me Thius was convicted of the felony count of arson to forest or land and placed on thirty-six months of probation. He wandered out of the courthouse and hasn't been seen in Los Angeles since. Within weeks he failed to show at his probation appointment, and they posted a warrant for his arrest. A couple of months later, he was picked up in Maine for his probation violation, but Los Angeles authorities refused to extradite him back to California. It is clear that the officials didn't want the fire god back in the tinder dry California foothills. Today, somewhere lurks the modern day Greek God of Fire, Pro Me Thius, with a price on his head. He has two "no bail" warrants for his arrest and another $40,000 warrant for trespassing. Let's hope he doesn't unleash his legendary and frightful power over fire during the next red-flag condition.

> ***Note from the literature professor**- Prometheus is not actually an Olympian god. He is a titan. He symbolizes human progress. Hephaestus is the Greek God of Fire. That fact being clarified, popular belief and the freaks of Hollywood still like the Prometheus "fire god" angle.

Tevin the Demon
Santa Clarita, 2009

The most intriguing person in the field of arson is the serial offender. Normally viewed by the public as a sinister, dark person who burns homes in the dead of night for glee or out of some maniacal desire to see things burn, the true serial offender is most often someone much less imposing.

In January of 2009, my partner Sgt. Derek Yoshino and I had identified a fire setter in the upscale Northbridge neighborhood of Santa Clarita. This city is known for its sprawling, master-planned housing tracts, and the Northbridge section is one of its showcase neighborhoods. The entire neighborhood is made of newer large homes built completely around a large greenbelt called the paseo system. The paseos were built to connect hundreds of homes in the area by a rural walking path and greenbelt. They are ideal for biking, walking, and dog walking. The paseos were designed to be accessed by dozens of well-maintained sidewalks from any number of streets that gird the area. The paseos pass through parks and school yards, and abut dozens of backyards. The paseos are heavily wooded and very well maintained by the city of Santa Clarita.

As I stated earlier, we had found an arsonist in this area who lived about four blocks from the nearest Paseo entrance. He was a real gem! This forty-five-year-old male was a former probation officer from Massachusetts who was married and had two beautiful ten-year-old kids. I mention this fact because this guy and his wife were hideously ugly and both suffered from some real mental instability. It amazed us that these two toads could produce such beautiful kids. Anyway, this guy's neighbor had a beef with him for a dozen bizarre little things such as stealing sprinkler heads, turning them the wrong way, and stealing mail—basically all sorts of nuisance-type crimes. I said he was a *former* probation officer because he had been on "stress leave" from that job for the a couple years.

One night in late December of 2008, this probation officer had a dispute with a couple of neighbors. The neighbors, some tough-looking martial arts guys, decided to confront our freak about stealing their mail and sprinklers. Like the oddball he was, he refused to answer the door and sent his hefty wife out instead. Not wanting to get into it with a woman, the martial arts guys let the occurrence slide for a few more days. Later that night, after the wife went to work, the neighbors' car alarm started sounding. They looked out to see a small fire burning under their "brodozer" (a large, raised-up Ford F-250 truck). My partner, Derek Yoshino, was called, and he later found a burned wooden jewelry box under the truck containing mail and other papers from the probation officer.

In early January, we interviewed the probation officer at his home. This guy was a mess. The moment you saw him, you immediately thought "child molester." He was a fat, dirty, disheveled, middle-aged guy who refused to look you in the eye. He started whining and denying things before we even began asking questions. His wife soon interceded, and it was clear that she ran the household. She was pushing a solid 250 pounds on her five-foot-two frame, and acted more like his mother than his wife. Their house was a pigsty, and they both admitted to having problems with their past rental homes.

We soon got a clear picture of this guy. He sat at home watching TV all day and only went out at night to walk his dog in the paseos. His wife slept all day and worked as a nurse all night. Their house smelled like cat piss, stale cigarettes and spilled soda. There were cigarette burns on the carpets and in the furniture. Amazingly, their two kids walked down to meet us looking like two little models. They were twins, a boy and girl, but both looked like they were child actors. We immediately felt bad for the kids, as we could see that their parents were a real pathetic pair.

We didn't arrest the guy, instead deciding to investigate further before dragging him in. We felt very strongly that this guy was an arsonist. He was a true coward who acted out his sneaky dirty deeds under the cover of darkness when his wife was at work. We felt sure we would see him again.

Within three weeks, we felt justified in our assessment. Reports started to come in from the patrol officers that someone was burning items within the paseo system in Northbridge. By early February, there were seven cases of burned plastic dispensers on the paseos. The dispensers were blue plastic and held blue plastic dog-poop bags. These were placed for convenience about every two-hundred yards along the paseos. Most were in locations hidden from the roads by the heavy trees and brush on the paseos. Since he lived within a block of the paseos, we immediately thought of the probation officer.

I started going back to the scenes in daylight to seek clues and evidence. The paseos were extremely neat and were maintained on a daily basis. This enabled us to pinpoint the time of the fires and notice any potential evidence. Each scene was nearly identical. Each scene had a plastic dog bag dispenser mounted on a pole situated next to a metal trash can. After examining the scenes, we began to identify some trends. Each scene had several cigarettes strewn nearby. In nearly every case, the cigarettes were either Newports or Camels. We also found brown paper grocery bags from Ralph's grocery either in the trash can or strewn nearby. Additionally, at every scene we found a few twenty-two-ounce malt liquor cans of an odd brand. Lastly, at one of the scenes we found a white cloth work glove, and at another we found the cut off finger of a white cloth work glove. There were no matches found at any scene, so we assumed the suspect was using a lighter to set the fires.

Over the next few weeks, we tried to find a pattern. Every morning I would have the city workers walk the paseos and inspect for new damage. We soon had seventeen fire incidents on about a one-mile path. We narrowed the activity to a single pathway and to the nighttime hours. We were now pretty confident that our probation officer's hours were consistent with these fire incidents.

By March we were able to get enough bodies together to conduct surveillance of the area. Normally arson is considered a serious crime, so getting surveillance detectives isn't that hard. However, in this case the dollar value of the property burned was fairly insignificant, and my boss wasn't going to waste money on hiring a professional surveillance crew. I was able to train a crew of deputies from the local station to assist me. As we were gearing up to stake out the probation officer's home, a patrol officer hit me up at the local station. The word was out that we were looking at someone, and he wanted to know if it was "that kid" he and his female partner had identified. Since the probation officer was hardly a kid, I asked the patrolman who he was talking about. He then gave me a copy of a report he had made about a suspicious kid in the area. He said he had busted the kid the previous month for carrying a fake gun in his waistband and for being drunk in public. Later the patrolman had responded to one of the first fires, and it had turned out that it was the kid who had reported it. He had taken a picture of melted blue plastic on the kid's shoes. The patrolman and his partner felt strongly that this kid was the arsonist.

Stunned, I reviewed the original patrol reports in depth and realized that this kid was the same person who reported at least two of the fires. It has been common in the past for serial arson offenders to insert themselves into the criminal investigation by reporting the events. I could have kicked myself for missing this glaring clue! An even more startling revelation by the patrolman was that he had followed up on this himself and found out that the kid worked at a nearby Ralph's grocery store. (Remember the Ralph's bags at several of the fire scenes?) On a weird note, at the time of his arrest, the kid had been carrying a masturbation device known as a "pocket pussy," and it was heavily lubed and ready to go.

Taken aback at having been probably looking at the wrong suspect, I called off the surveillance operation on the probation officer and decided to look into this kid a bit further. As luck would have it, the wife of a detective I knew worked at the same Ralph's and was able to give me some insight into this kid. He had worked every night we had a fire and usually left the store by eleven at night. He was a Mormon kid from a good family but had been having problems recently. He lived nearby and always walked home after work. He was also a heavy smoker.

That night, four of us set up a short surveillance of the kid. He got off work at the Ralph's at eleven. He then sat outside and chain smoked Newport cigarettes for over an hour. Finally, he went back inside and reemerged carrying a brown paper Ralph's bag. As he walked away, we saw that he had at least two pairs of white cloth work gloves extending from his pockets. We followed him for six blocks until he entered the paseo system at the very first entrance he came to. After a period of time, undercover officers rode bikes into the paseos behind him and found him drinking from a malt liquor can and talking on a cell phone. He stayed in the paseos until about three in the morning. We knew then that he had to be our guy. We still could not get over how bizarre it was to have two arsonists in such close proximity to each other.

A few nights later, we set up another surveillance operation on this kid whose name was Tevin. Tevin followed a nearly identical routine—he got off work, smoked about a pack of cigs just outside the grocery store, and then left the store carrying a brown Ralph's bag. This time we had pre-staged detectives in the thick woods and brush of the paseos. As soon as the kid entered the paseos, he sat down and opened his first beer. Our guys watched as Tevin sat and drank and smoked in the same spot for the next two hours. Most of the time, he was talking on a cell phone. At some point he started crying as he was talking. It was clear to us that this kid was arguing with a girlfriend. Soon, after he had drunk at least four cans of malt liquor, Tevin surprised us all by pulling down his pants and beginning to masturbate. After finishing, he zipped up, drank another beer, and wandered off down the paseos. By about three in the morning, he emerged again and walked home. There were no fires on either of those first two nights of the surveillance operation.

We watched Tevin for another three nights. A strict pattern developed, and we soon were able to predict where he would sit and talk and drink. At no time did he ever meet with anyone nor did anyone else enter the paseos after eleven. Because it was too costly to follow him every night, we were able to only follow him about once every three or four nights. The fires continued on some of the nights we were unable to follow him.

Within a couple of weeks, we were 100 percent convinced this kid was our serial arsonist. He was an absolute loner. He drank massive amounts of alcohol. We were stunned that a 140-pound kid could drink between four and six twenty-two-ounce cans of malt liquor each night, as each can was equivalent to around four regular beers. He also smoked one or two packs of cigarettes each night. Lastly, he seemed to have an obsession with masturbation. All of this behavior was contradictory to his Mormon upbringing.

On the fifth night we followed him, he followed his ritual exactly. By two in the morning, we were soaking wet from lying in the sprinklers watching this guy. Then, his mood changed. He was on his phone with a girl when he began crying and yelling. After he hung up, he grabbed the Ralph's bag and jammed it into a trash can. He pulled out his butane lighter and lit the bag and trash can on fire. Finally! We followed him away to see if he would do it again and then arrested him on a street a few blocks away. It is a rare thing to actually catch a serial arsonist in the act of lighting a fire.

We felt that it would be a difficult interview, as we had all watched him drink four large cans of malt liquor. We were wondering if he would be at all coherent. To our amazement, when we met him in the interview room, he appeared completely sober, with only a vague odor of alcohol on him. We later learned that he had been drinking for some time and had an extremely high tolerance for alcohol. He hid his symptoms so well that his tee totaling parents had no idea he even drank.

The interview was a truly pathetic affair. In about thirty seconds he had confessed to upward of twenty arson fires. He said he was unsure of exactly how many or even why he was starting them. He said it was "better than what I used to do." He wouldn't elaborate, but we knew that he had been detained as a fourteen-year-old for molesting a younger family member. His church had intervened and attempted to counsel him, but we knew that this kid was having some severe problems. We video recorded this interview and gave a copy to his attorney.

During our interview, Tevin made a unique statement to us. He said that he had been a real disappointment to his family and church and that he knew he had a real demon inside of him. Later that same day, we searched his room at his house. In an otherwise clean, orderly, and distinctly Mormon home, his room was a real hell hole. It was strewn with piles of trash, fast food wrappers, pornography, knives, and sexual paraphernalia. He was obsessed with masturbation, and we found several videos to that extent. Oddest of all, and perhaps most telling of his true persona, Tevin had a very large, garishly-bright, red statue of a demon sitting on his dresser. This item sat about four-feet high and had to have cost over two-hundred dollars. It dominated the room with its sinister features and was no doubt the true inner personality of this very young, very soft-looking kid. Maybe this was the demon he had referred to in his interviews.

Needless to say, Tevin pled guilty to arson at his first court appearance. In a deal with the special arson district attorney assigned to the case, we forced Tevin into mental health treatment as a condition of his probation. Since he could have been sentenced on every arson count, we had a heavy hammer over his head. In the end, he did about eighty days in jail and was released back to his parents and the probation department in the late summer of 2009. He was such a soft character that we knew prison would not go very well for him. However, we were also about 100-percent sure that he would re-offend if not treated.

As we predicted, Tevin's problems would continue. As soon as he was released, he tried to register as an arsonist as prescribed by state law. Due to a court glitch, the judge forgot to mention that requirement to Tevin during his sentencing, and the State would not accept his later attempt to register as an arsonist. Tevin started to attend court-ordered counseling but was unable to make the payments. Because of this, the counseling program dropped him from their classes. Of course the probation department did little or nothing to monitor him, and within just a couple of weeks from his release, we had dog-crap bags burning in the paseos again. It took a month or more for anyone to notify the arson squad. When they did, we immediately began to track down Tevin.

It wasn't hard to find him as he was rearrested in December of 2009 for commercial burglary. He had walked into a Wal-Mart and stolen clothes, shoes, and a realistic-looking pellet gun. All of this was captured on store security cameras. I interviewed him again, and again he fully admitted to his crime, although he was adamant that he had not lit anymore fires. We knew he was lighting the fires but had no witnesses to them.

This time though, the court result was different. We went back to the same arson district attorney, Sean Carney, and told him about Tevin's latest arrest and our suspicions about the new fires. They dropped the heavy hammer on his head and offered him a thirty-two-month sentence in prison as a result of the violation of his probation on the original arson case. Because he was facing over ten years in the new case, he wisely took the deal and was sentenced to state prison. It will likely not go well for him there. He will finally have to deal with real, tangible demons other than the one inside himself.

James Edward Patti
Valencia, 1999

In the foothills thirty miles north of downtown Los Angeles, lies the town of Valencia. A master-planned community developed in the 1970s, Valencia became the destination of tens of thousands of upper-middle-class people fleeing the festering cesspool of the San Fernando Valley. Although the Valencia area has grown exponentially since then, it still remains a relatively crime-free area where families can play in parks and walk on the paseos unmolested. In later years, Valencia would proclaim itself "Awesome Town" in a well-scorned and obnoxious advertising campaign designed to lure shoppers and homeowners to the area.

Although the area was fairly crime-free, I can attest that drugs, legal or illegal, abounded in this area during the 1990s. Prior to becoming an arson investigator in 1997, I spent two years as an undercover narcotics detective in the Valencia area. I noted that, while street drugs were difficult to find, the area was awash in prescription drugs. The Valencia area was filled with troubled teens and housewives who spent their days partially anesthetized on any number of drugs for anti-anxiety, stress, ADHD, ADD, migraines, insomnia, and depression. Many kids in high schools were taking and selling these prescription drugs without any medical need for them. I performed dozens of undercover stings targeting pharmacists, doctors, and nurses who were illegally writing "scrip" for thousands of pills. Among its less awesome features, Valencia was well-known as an active member of "medication nation." By many law enforcement officials who still work there, Valencia and the entire Santa Clarita Valley are believed to have an extraordinarily high rate of teen suicide, with the rampant misuse of medications being a major factor in these tragic deaths.

On February 27, 1999, just after midnight, someone set fire to the exterior of a large three-story building on Lyons Avenue, in the Valencia area. This area has almost no such incidents, and it was a truly unique event for that city. The fire was not that dramatic in size or scope, and the county firefighters easily extinguished it within minutes, leaving very little damage to the structure.

Luckily for us, there was an eyewitness to the event. The witness was passing by and saw a lone male pouring liquid from a square container onto the entrance of the building. The witness parked his own car and watched the male light a match. This then ignited the vapors of the liquid. The witness heard a "whoosh" and saw a large fireball burst upward onto the doors of the building. The witness then saw the male enter an older Chrysler and drive away. He reported his observations to the responding fire personnel and sheriff's deputies.

I was the on-duty arson investigator assigned to this case, but the patrol deputy neglected to call me until morning. The next morning I was taking my two young sons to day care when we passed the building (at the time it was near my home). I stopped by and saw that there was fairly little fire damage, and because it was a small scene, I deputized my two sons on the spot and decided to use them to help me photograph and sketch the scene. Pretty fun stuff for a four- and a six-year-old! My sons were both surprised to recognize the building as the one that housed their pediatrician. I would return later after dropping the boys off to finish a more detailed origin-and-cause investigation.

The fire was confined to an area surrounding the glass front doors of the modern building. I could smell the strong odor of gasoline coming from the front door. This odor was tracked to a wet stain that started at the base of the glass doors and then angled with the pavement down toward the parking area. I could see that a large quantity of gas had been used, and I estimated it to be between two and five gallons. It was clear that someone had poured gasoline on the doors, and most of the gas had run into the street prior to the ignition. My youngest son, only four years old at the time, walked over and pointed to a single paper match at the edge of the pour pattern. He had found the source of ignition, and he knew enough to tell me to put my gloves on before picking it up. I photographed and collected this rare find.

I was well aware that most arsonists who use a flammable liquid routinely leave the container at or near the fire scene. I had found dozens of gas cans and other containers at, in, or near arson scenes. Because of this, my sons and I walked around the parking lot, hoping to find the vessel the gasoline came in. At the rear of the building, my six-year-old pointed out three odd items lying in some shrubs. They were in fact the plastic pieces from the spout of a gasoline can. We never did find the can, but we knew that someone had brought it to the scene and then taken it away. These pieces were held as evidence and processed for fingerprints.

I finally delivered my sons to their day care and returned to do a more complete investigation of the area. I noted immediately that the facility was a medical office building that held at least thirty suites. Like I do at every arson scene, I tried to profile the scene and the victim. In most cases, arson is a very personal crime, and the target of the arson attack will usually be the key to finding a motive. Of course the motive is the key pointing toward potential suspects.

Part of my process is determining the level of sophistication of the arson attack. In this case, the sophistication level was not very high. The attack was made with gasoline poured on a surface that had little chance of spreading the fire. The entire building was fairly new and made of stucco and brick. These surfaces do not burn well at all. The use of a flammable liquid on the exterior of any structure is a poor way to start a fire. Most of the gasoline flashes off or burns away too quickly, so that sustained burning does not take place. The best way to burn a building down is from within. This suspect did not enter the building. I soon came to believe that it was not a typical "insurance job." I also did not believe that this was a prank or juvenile-related fire, due to the extreme use of gasoline. My working theory was that this was likely a personal attack on someone who lived or worked within the building. The attack was one of rage and was not well thought out or planned.

Besides the fact that the fire had little chance of succeeding, the manner in which it was ignited was extremely dangerous to the arsonist. He had to pour a large quantity of gasoline on a non-absorbent surface, then put the can down or away and strike a match. The vapors created by the pouring would be extensive, and the chances of a flash fire or mild explosion were very high. I deemed it quite possible in this case that the arsonist may have burned himself while setting this fire. Again, this fire scene pointed toward an inexperienced fire setter and a person of rash or impulsive behavior. This was not a sophisticated event at all.

Now that I had my ignition scenario figured out, I had to figure out who or what the exact target may have been. With thirty or more medical suites, each with several employees, my task may have appeared quite difficult. However, I knew that this was a rare event and was therefore probably preceded by some sort of confrontation or disturbance. I knew that it probably would not take long at all to discover who the intended victim was.

In this case, it took almost no time at all. I scanned the glass sign outside of the building to look at all of the offices and noticed quickly that one suite held an agency entitled, "Los Angeles County Mental Health Services." Since there were no other psychiatrists or psychologists listed on the sign, I felt that this was a likely place to start. The mental health office was in the center of the building and away from the point of attack. I contacted the office manager and asked her if she had had any recent problems with patients. Like all medical and mental health facilities, this agency was very reluctant to give me information. The office manager surprised me by saying, "Give me your number. I will make some calls and get you some information by tomorrow." True to her word, she called me the next morning and explained that the office was very suspicious of a patient, but she had had to get clearance from her supervisors to speak to me.

The manager then told me about a patient named James Patti. She said that Patti was a long time patient who lived in the area. She said he had just had a violent episode in their office over a change in his medication. He had begun throwing items and threatening the staff. The head doctor had then called the local sheriff's to report Patti's dangerous behavior and asked to have him forcibly placed into a seventy-two-hour mental health evaluation center. When the deputies went to his nearby home in Valencia to arrest Patti, his parents said he had left the area for San Diego. This, by the way, was the same evening on which the fire had taken place.

 I then contacted the witness in this case and interviewed him. He said he was not exactly sure of the make and model of the car, but thought it might be a Chrysler product from the mid- to late-1980s. However, he was very clear that the car was dark maroon in color, had a slanted front end, and had tilt-up headlights. The witness further said that the car drove away with its lights off, and he had been unable to get a license plate number. He said the driver was a white male in his thirties with a muscular build and very dark hair cut into a high flat-top. Lastly, the witness said the suspect yelled something at him as he drove away.

 I got to a computer and found the DMV photo for James Patti. James Patti was a white male, thirty-two years old, and wore his dark black hair in a high flat-top. Furthermore, I checked cars registered to Patti and found that he owned a 1988 Dodge Daytona. This car model does indeed have a slanted front end and tilt-up headlights. James Patti became my prime suspect.

 I drove to Patti's local address and spoke to his parents. They admitted that James had long suffered from several mental illnesses and had been diagnosed as "psychotic" in the past. They said that he did fairly well when he took his medications, but they were also aware that he had recently been off his medications and had a few violent episodes as a result. They told me that, at the time of the fire, they believed that James was in San Diego with some relatives. They also confirmed that he drove a battered, maroon Dodge Daytona with tilt-up headlights.

 I recognized that Patti's parents had been long-suffering as a result of his mental health issues and behavior. They truly believed (or hoped at least) that he had been one-hundred miles away in San Diego at the time of the fire. They didn't think he was capable of this kind of rash and violent act. I had other thoughts. Several days later, I got a surprising phone call from James Patti's father. He had called relatives in San Diego, and they confirmed that James had been down there in the days before and following the fire, but that he and his car had been missing for about sixteen hours the night of the fire. This painful admission from his father confirmed that James had plenty of time to get to Valencia, light the fire, and get back to San Diego. Even Patti's parents now believed that he had lit the fire.

Because the eye witness had identified Patti as the arson suspect from a "six-pack" photo lineup, I set out to obtain an arrest warrant for James Patti. On March 16, I was still waiting for a judge to sign my arrest warrant. Late that night I received a call from Patti's family informing me that James had been arrested in San Diego. He would be easy to find in their jail. I felt at this time that it would be an easy arrest. I would just drive down to San Diego, interview Patti in custody, and then file my case before he was released. It certainly seemed simple at the time.

At three in the morning on March 17, I awoke and called the jail in San Diego. They told me that Patti was at a small branch jail. I called them, explained my case, and told them I was on my way down. They told me that he was being held for assaulting a police officer and would be in custody for a few days at least. With that information, I sped down Interstate 5 for what would be a quick interview.

I drove the one-hundred miles in about ninety minutes and got to the substation just before five in the morning. As I entered, I asked for the jailer. The jailer was a nice guy, but he sheepishly told me that he was sorry, but that I couldn't come into the jail area. He seemed embarrassed about having to tell me this, and he then told me that the watch commander wanted to see me. I entered the office of the lieutenant from the Chula Vista Police and realized immediately that I was in for a tough day. He was your typical prissy administrative asshole, who purposely made me stand there for about five minutes before even looking up to acknowledge me. I belong to the largest sheriff's department on earth, and my unit, the arson/bomb squad is one of the two premier investigative units in the department, the other being the homicide detail. We are generally well-respected and well-treated by almost every agency we come in contact with. Apparently this lieutenant was not impressed in the least.

Without looking up, he began to lecture me that it was not his job to detain suspects for other agencies to come and interview at their whim. He asked if I had an arrest warrant, which I did not because the judge had not yet signed one. He then told me that he had no intention of allowing me to interview James Patti in his jail. This admin geek then spent about ten minutes explaining to me how to run a proper investigation and how to properly follow policies and procedures. Realizing that my blood was starting to boil and that I was a guest in his station, I calmed myself and explained the case and danger level of this arson suspect. The lieutenant was wholly unimpressed. He let me plead with him for about another twenty minutes before he dropped the bombshell. He said with satisfaction that, just minutes prior to my arrival, he had ordered the release of the suspect, so it was a moot point. The suspect had left the building.

I walked out before I punched the guy's smug face in. On my way out, I was stopped in the parking lot by the jailer. He apologized, stating that he had reported to the lieutenant that I was driving down from Los Angeles. He said that the lieutenant had asked him if there was a warrant in the system for Patti. When the jailer said there wasn't, the lieutenant told him to release the prisoner on a citation, as the jail was overcrowded. The jailer tried to argue on my behalf, but the lieutenant just told him that he didn't work for the LA Sheriff's Department. I later learned that this particular lieutenant had a personal dislike for a couple of

Fireraisers, Freaks, And Fiends

LA sheriff's detectives from years ago and was going to take his revenge against the entire nine-thousand-man agency. What a world-class punk!

I did learn while in the police station that Patti had reported a local address about ten miles away from the station and just a couple miles from the Mexican border. I decided to go down to his address and pick him up myself. At that point, good fortune came my way. A couple of task force auto theft detectives were in the jail booking a prisoner when they heard of my plight from the jailer. The two approached me and offered to go along with me to find and interview Patti. I gratefully welcomed the help as I was three hours from home and my radios didn't match any of the San Diego frequencies. Since I knew that Patti was erratic, extremely muscular, had recently assaulted a cop, and was a psych patient, I definitely needed the help.

We drove to Patti's local address and contacted a cousin of his. That cousin brought James Patti out onto the porch for an interview with me. Patti confessed to the arson attack almost immediately and said he felt very badly about it. He said he was very upset with the doctors for changing his medication and just wanted to feel normal again. He seemed docile and contrite. We took him into custody and headed back to the local station to book him. My plan was to hold him in the local jail for a few hours until I could get a prisoner bus or a couple of uniformed deputies down to transport him back to Los Angeles. I was driving a van at the time and did not have the required safety features necessary to safely haul a prisoner.

It was just my luck that the same jerk of a watch commander was on duty when we returned. As I was walking my guy in to be held in their jail, he forcibly stopped me and said he was not going to allow me to book or even hold the inmate at his facility. I again explained my problem about awaiting a proper transport for the inmate, and his curt reply was, "That's your problem, not mine." Again, with my blood boiling, I turned around and left before I did something stupid.

I walked out and told my new partners my latest problem. They said, "Don't worry we'll book him under our names at the main county jail." As we turned to go to our cars, the watch commander gave his parting shot: "Don't bother. I'm sending out a teletype to all jails in our county to not accept your prisoner. Release him or take him back to LA." That was it. I lost it for a second and stormed over to the useless prick. When I saw him recoil as I approached, I said, "You don't really go home at night and tell your wife and kids that you are a cop, do you?" It was pretty juvenile of me, but it somehow made me feel better. He practically had a coronary and could only stutter, "There will be a complaint waiting for you when you get back to your office." I just laughed and drove off.

By my own department rules, it wasn't recommended that I transport a prisoner without a partner. This was especially true if I was out of county and didn't even have the proper equipment with which to secure him. Compounding this issue was the fact that Patti, while sitting docile and quiet the entire time, was a rippling mass of muscle. His arms were huge and shredded. Plus, let's not forget his unpredictable behavior.

However, this jerk cop from San Diego had created a problem for me, and I was stuck in a position with few options. Besides, if you ask any supervisor I have ever worked for, they'll tell you that I was never a big follower of administrative rules. So, following my personal axiom that "rules are for fools," and the time-tested motto that it is "better to ask for forgiveness than permission," I came up with a plan. I figured that if I drove really fast, I could get back to LA and book my prisoner before anyone knew what I was doing.

Despite my bravado, I was a little concerned about James Patti. I looked in the rear of my van for extra handcuffs or something to secure him. Since I also work on the bomb squad, I was issued a minivan of sorts to carry all the necessary equipment for doing arson and bomb investigations. Luckily I found a set of waist chains that our custody deputies use to transport prisoners. I cinched Patti up with them, effectively wrapping them around his waist and holding his hands apart at his sides. This gives a bit of comfort on a long ride. Then, fearing he may try to jump out of the car at some point, I wrapped about half a roll of duct tape around him, literally taping him to the seat. He looked like a mummy as we sped up the I-5 freeway a hundred miles to Los Angeles. I had overlooked one minor detail. I forgot that there was a US Border Patrol checkpoint on the freeway about fifty miles above San Diego. Since my van was unmarked, I fully expected to get jammed by the border cops as I drove through their checkpoint at about five miles per hour, with a guy duct-taped to the seat. He must have resembled a kidnapping victim, but the bored border guards only gave me a surprised glance and waved me through.

For his part, James Patti was an extremely chatty and calm prisoner. He started out a bit glum, but perked up when I bought him a Carl's Jr. burger, fries, and Coke in San Clemente. Since he couldn't use his hands, I duct-taped the Coke to his armrest where he could just reach the straw. Eating the fries and burger were a huge struggle for him, but I put them close enough so he could figure out a way to eat them. This task kept him busy for about a half hour. After that, he began to tell me about all the other crazy things he had done. The thing that really caught my attention was that he had recently walked into a gun store and asked to see a pistol. When the salesman handed it to him, Patti had sprinted out the door with it. He said that he had thought about shooting his doctor or someone with it, but then he had decided to just throw the gun in a dumpster after a few days. Patti couldn't remember where this had happened or where he threw the gun.

When I finally got Patti to an LA jail and booked, I sighed in relief. The only hard part was taking the duct tape off his hairy arms. Patti surprisingly didn't whimper at all and just shook my hand when it was all over. The next day, I filed my arson case against him and told the DA that he needed extensive mental health treatment during his incarceration. Patti and his attorney did not fight the charges. A few weeks after his arrest, he quietly pled guilty in a San Fernando court to a felony charge of arson to a structure. By September of 1999, he was given a ninety-day mental-health diagnostic commitment to the state prison at Chino. Following that, in early 2000, Patti was sentenced to sixteen months in state prison. True to the leniency typically extended to arson offenders nationwide, Patti was released from prison after having served about one-fourth of that term and placed on parole. However, like most offenders, he violated that parole almost immediately and was incarcerated in state prison within just a few weeks of getting out.

I never did get that complaint from the lieutenant near the Mexican border.

Investigator's Analysis:

James Patti is yet another guy walking the streets whose sanity and actions are balanced on a precarious mixture of medications and therapy. He can go months or years with no problems and then have a complete meltdown. When frustrated by the medical and mental health system, he lashed out in the only way he could display any real power—with fire. This is a very common outcome for people dealing with similar issues.

The small side story about the administrative and logistical issues I faced on this case was included as it represents something that happens every day to working investigators and detectives. People like that guy in Chula Vista haunt public service and are known as "can't do" people. They spend hours of their day telling you all the reasons why they can't help you or you can't do something, instead of thinking five minutes for a positive solution to a problem. Every case I've ever worked has similar issues and frustrations. A detective has to deal with legal constraints, internal department guidelines and rules, jail policies and rules, political roadblocks at the prosecutor's office, mental health rules and regulations, and finally a mired-in-the-mud court system. It's a wonder that anyone gets successfully prosecuted. I've spoken to a lot of retired detectives who all said that the cases and criminals didn't burn them out; it was the ancillary administrative issues that got worse each year that eventually exhausted them and caused their retirements. I couldn't agree more.

JUSTICE FOR A BUDDY
BUDDY THE BASSETT HOUND
VENTURA COUNTY, 2012

This story comes from the investigative files of the Ventura County Fire and Sheriff's Departments.
In its exhaustive studies of serial killers in the 1980s, the FBI's Behavioral Analysis Unit (Profilers) learned a lot about the roots, development, and causal factors that created hundreds of serial killers. One disturbing thing they found was that most serial killers had a significant amount of serial fire-setting activity in their very early years of life. This activity was but one leg of the homicidal triad that the BAU identified during its revolutionary studies. The other two legs of the triad were frequent and late-stage bed-wetting issues, and the very disturbing behavior of torturing, poisoning, and murdering animals.

The most prolific serial arsonist ever documented, David Berkowitz, aka the "Son of Sam," was not only a serial killer of people; he readily admitted to a lifetime of torturing and poisoning all of his mother's pets, without her ever suspecting the truth. His history is heavily documented in a number of books including my own, *"Torchered" Minds: Case Histories of Notorious Serial Arsonists*. Indeed, more than a few of the serial arsonists described in both of my books engaged in animal poisonings, tortures, and worse. The worst criminal I have ever met, Gary Glazier, is described in a chapter in this book. He had an alleged thirty-year history of luring, trapping, torturing, eviscerating, poisoning, and murdering an estimated one hundred pets in his neighborhood. He was also a serial arsonist and alleged serial child molester. Arson is truly the crime of the weak and cowardly, and any related assaults are usually targeted toward victims who are unable to defend themselves such as meek women, children, and helpless animals. Like all arson-related crimes, the following case is one of sneakiness, cowardice, and a person who needs some serious, long-term, mental health treatment.

Ventura County is a semi-rural, coastal county located about forty miles north of Los Angeles along the legendary Coast Highway 101. It is patrolled by the Ventura County Sheriff's Department and a few small police departments. The fire service is provided by the very modern Ventura County Fire Department. While there are several large, modern beach cities and towns, about half of the county still clings to its very rural roots. It is partly filled with the last remaining citrus groves, strawberry fields, and pumpkin patches that exist in Southern California. Due to its semi-rural nature, the sprawling residential neighborhoods come directly up against the agricultural land as well as the dark and gloomy canyons and foothills.

Like in many of the stories in this book, the Santa Ana winds were just starting up on October 27, 2012, at 3:30 a.m. A resident was awakened by a dog barking in a strange manner in the dark and secluded *barranca* (ravine) behind his Camarillo home. He looked out to see three small fires and the figure of someone running away to the west. The resident grabbed an extinguisher and went out to investigate. He put out the first two small fires and approached the third, which he believed was a burning piece of wood. He spent the last of his extinguisher on this and was alarmed to find that the wood was in fact a small whimpering dog. As the man tried to soothe and care for the hot and smoking animal, the dog ran away to the west. The resident called the Ventura County Fire Department and the Ventura Sheriff's. Firefighters would find three very tiny spot fires along the trail in the darkened *barranca*. They also found a bottle of lighter fluid.

Arriving sheriff's deputies from the Camarillo substation got a simultaneous call to the home directly across the *barranca* to the west and three houses south of the fire. This call was for a family disturbance, with a man reporting that his teenage son was out of control. When the deputies arrived at the home, a mother and father were confronting their adult son, and at the same time were trying to soothe an obviously burned Basset hound. The father, James Delgado, told the deputies that he and his family believed his eighteen-year-old son, Andrew Delgado, was responsible for the injuries to the family pet. They described Andrew as being a longtime drug addict and as having used drugs earlier that evening. They said that Andrew was on probation for several crimes, including theft and drug use, and earlier that night they suspected that he was high on at least marijuana. The long-suffering parents, tired of Andrew's antics, kicked him out of the home earlier in the evening. By a quarter past two in the morning, the family relented and allowed Andrew back in. They noticed that for some reason he went immediately to his room and changed his clothes. At a quarter past three, the father awoke to see Andrew holding the family's Basset hound, which look and smelled burned. Andrew told his father that a neighbor had found the dog outside and brought him home and that he was injured. The family reported that the Basset hound's name was Buddy, and that he was an adopted rescue animal that the family cherished.

Fire personnel and sheriff's deputies arrived and questioned Andrew. They immediately noted the vague chemical odor of solvents on the clothing that he had changed out of earlier. He gave them a rambling and unbelievable story of the night's events. Highly suspicious, the cops summoned arson investigators to the scene. In Ventura County, arsons are investigated by a joint team of a fire department investigator and a sheriff's arson/bomb detective. On duty and responding to the scene that night were Sheriff's Deputy Darrin Smith and Fire Investigator Christine Saqui. The two investigators immediately surveyed Buddy's injuries with alarm. The dog was suffering from severe burns and peeling flesh on his head, ears, and face area. Blood was seeping from his mouth and ears. Investigators saw that the burns extended down to the neck, legs, paws, and along the sides of the poor animal. Most shockingly, there were burns to the dog's eyes and under his ears, as if those sensitive and hidden areas had been particularly targeted for assault.

The animal was lethargic and unresponsive to his own name. He was suffering silently from his painful wounds, and the experienced investigators could see that he was slipping into shock and was likely dying. The investigators recommended that the family get Buddy to a veterinarian hospital immediately.

Based on the types and manner of the burns, the investigators immediately suspected that Buddy had been sprayed or doused with a flammable liquid of sorts, but they were unable to smell anything like gasoline or a similar fuel.

Another brother in the family later directed the arson investigators to a trail leading to the *barranca* behind the family home. Along that wooded trail, the investigators were unable to see the three small fires described by the witness, but they did find a burned dog leash. The brother identified the green leash as Buddy's. Along the route, the investigators recovered a two-quart plastic bottle of Kingsford Odorless Charcoal Starter. This item was clean and newer in appearance; it had not been on the trail for very long. It still contained an amount of liquid in it, which appeared to be as advertised. Both investigators were quick to note that this was an odorless product, which explained the lack of smell on Buddy. This was collected as evidence along with the burned dog leash. Next to the bottle of charcoal starter was a fresh paw print that was similar in size to the Bassett hound's. This was photographed as evidence as well. When the two investigators and the brother returned to the residence, the brother pointed out that their charcoal starter was missing from the family barbecue. The two investigators took note that there was an imprint in the dust at the barbecue exactly the size and shape of the bottom of the bottle they had found along the trail. It was clear to them that this was where the charcoal starter had come from. They photographed this evidence as well.

That night the two arson investigators sat down with Andrew Delgado. Prior to this they had interviewed his parents and brother, who told them a bit about Andrew's background. Andrew had been having mental health and behavioral issues on-and-off for a long time. These were exacerbated by his frequent use of illegal narcotics, including heroin, methamphetamines, and several prescription drugs for anxiety and other minor psychiatric issues. He was a bit of a loner and was heavily into "death metal" music and clothing. His family, and later his friends, reported that he had stolen from all of them. He was not trusted at all, even by his own family. The family also told them that Andrew was also in the habit of lighting small things on fire. They were aware that he had recently lit a frog on fire that he and some friends had found nearby. Earlier on this evening, his mother had found a burned dollar bill in his bedroom.

The initial interview with Andrew Delgado uncovered only an ever-changing and rambling story. He could not explain the fresh scratches and cuts on his hands and arms and had no credible explanation for why he had changed his clothes immediately after coming home. The clothes he had changed out of were found to be wet, and he said it must have happened when he was jogging in the dark. He maintained that he saw Buddy on fire at some point, but then said that he thought he saw suspects running from the scene, insinuating that they must have been the ones to ignite Buddy. This didn't hold up against his earlier story to his dad. Both investigators eventually confronted Delgado about his ever-evolving story, and at some point the interview terminated. The investigators left to begin putting a credible case together, believing they had the likely suspect already known to them.

The next day, Investigator Saqui was refueling her vehicle at a county gas pump when she learned from an animal shelter official that Buddy the Bassett hound had finally died, despite an intense day of medical treatment in a hyperbaric chamber. This expected but still very sad news impacted the arson investigator who, over the previous dozen years on the job, had gained a bit of a reputation in her department for saving and caring for small animals that had been rescued from fire-ravaged homes and farms. A notorious animal lover, Investigator Saqui made the local papers several years prior when she was photographed rescuing a bunny rabbit after a fire. This grim news about Buddy incensed her, and she immediately focused all her efforts toward building a strong case.

Over the next week, Investigator Saqui and her partner Investigator Alan Campbell worked with a succession of sheriff's detectives to canvass the area of the fire, map out the events, and conduct several interviews with witnesses and friends and acquaintances of Andrew Delgado. During this time they found additional physical evidence at the fire scene. They finally pieced together that only the dog had been set on fire, and that it was his travels through the wooded area and the falling pieces of burning hair and dog leash that likely ignited the smaller fires seen along the path. There was no source of ignition at any of the scenes, so they knew that the suspect had taken it with him. They suspected a match or lighter had been used.

At the same time, they began to amass a pretty detailed profile of Delgado. He had a long history of erratic, bizarre, and sometimes violent behavior, even with his own family. Sheriff's investigators learned that he had been adopted at an early age and that there was a strong likelihood his biological parents had a history of mental illness. They heard several anecdotal stories from friends that there had been a few instances recently in which Andrew Delgado had captured, tortured, beheaded, and then burned small frogs and lizards in the area. A check of his criminal history showed that he had been on a rapid downward spiral in his life over the past year. From June to July of 2012, Andrew Delgado had been arrested and booked for receiving stolen property, resisting arrest, twice for petty theft, vandalism, and at least twice for being under the influence of dangerous drugs. He admitted to being a heavy user of marijuana, and also to taking multiple prescription drugs for anxiety. Relatives and friends stated that he was also a user of methamphetamines and possibly heroin. All of the above described behaviors are heavily consistent with persons involved in arson and serial arson activity. He was shaping up to be a very strong suspect in this case.

VCFD arson investigators contacted Delgado again on October 31 and obtained a DNA sample from him to compare with the charcoal starter container and other evidence from the scene. As a precaution they also took a DNA sample from the witness in the case who had tried to help the dog, in order to exclude his DNA. The evidence was taken to the local crime lab, which would later confirm that Buddy had in fact been doused with charcoal starter liquid.

They had now proved that this event was an actual arson attack, and not an accident of any sort, and they had a viable suspect in the case. Their next step, which is almost always the most difficult, was to link the suspect to the crime scene. As the fire investigators worked, the case stayed under the local radar, and they struggled to get resources to assist them in some unique parts of the investigation. At some point, however, the story eventually leaked out to the media, and a firestorm erupted as the odd and cruel nature of the attack made state, national, and then international headlines. Local groups established rewards and posted flyers throughout the area. The group that had initially rescued Buddy, and then later transferred him to the Delgado family, was incensed by this barbaric attack. Bassett Hound Rescue of Southern California began its own independent investigation of the case. The lead spokeswoman for the organization began appearing everywhere in the media, drumming up a lot of attention for the case. They eventually posted a $10,000 reward for information about the case, and it eventually climbed to a $24,000 reward. This caught the attention of some important people, including Hollywood celebrities, and even the governor of California's office called the investigators to check on the status of the case.

While media hoopla is always distracting to working investigators, in this case there were some side benefits. The sheriff's brass gave the case a bit more priority and assigned a few more people to help the arson investigators, including a polygraph examiner. The DNA samples, which would normally take up to eight months to process, were put at the head of the line. The lab would quickly confirm that Delgado's DNA was on the dog's leash and charcoal starter bottle. A special detail of sheriff's detectives, along with probation officers, descended upon Delgado's home on November 8, 2012, to conduct a probation search, since he was on active probation at the time of this incident. Detectives recognized that he was under the influence of narcotics at the time and arrested him for being in violation of his probation.

When he was brought in to the local sheriff's station, veteran Detective Sergeant Pete O' Sullivan sat down and had a detailed interview with Delgado. O'Sullivan was completely armed with all the facts of the case, which now included the arson investigator's findings, lab results, and interviews from Delgado's friends. This time the rambling, ever-changing stories and half-truths from Delgado met up against fact and information. Each time

Delgado came up with a new story or theory about the incident, it was quickly shown to be untrue. At the end of the interview, Delgado finally conceded that he had in fact caused Buddy to be lit on fire. While his statement was a bit self-serving, he nonetheless confirmed the very facts of the case.

Part of his self-serving statement insinuated that Buddy may have accidentally knocked over a gas can in the yard and got some of the liquid on him. Delgado acknowledged that he had thrown a lit cigarette in the dog's direction, and stated that it was what must have started the fire. When further confronted, he admitted to the sergeant that he had wanted to see his dog burn. He said he had then made up the elaborate alibi to hide this fact. He also said that he was a bit out of his mind that night, as he had argued with a girlfriend, smoked some pot, and taken a handful of Xanax.

Sergeant O'Sullivan, not being an arson investigator, didn't quite know how to deal with this partial confession. He called in Investigator Saqui, who responded by immediately following up on the ignition scenario provided by Delgado. A veteran with over a dozen years as an arson investigator, Saqui knew well that a smoldering ignition source, such as a lit cigarette, would not ignite the vapors of a flammable liquid like gasoline or charcoal starter. Furthermore, there was no evidence that any gasoline was on the dog, only the charcoal starter, and this had to be physically squirted out of the plastic bottle, which the crime lab confirmed bore Delgado's DNA profile. Investigator Saqui confronted Delgado on these points, and he finally admitted that he "might have sprayed him" with charcoal starter and that he "lit him with a match." He ended his statement with a soft, "I did light Buddy on fire." All the while, he continued to blame his actions on his drug use that evening.

Finally, on that rainy November day, Buddy got some justice. Investigator Saqui left the interview and returned to the scene of the crime to check some information. On the street leading to the site, she found a sad memorial set up for Buddy along with a poster and a reward flyer. The memorial consisted of pictures of Buddy, a stuffed puppy, a dog bowl, some flowers, and a cross. It sat forlorn and drenched with rain on a street corner—a sad reminder of an incredible act of cruelty. Saqui knew that nobody would get the reward. The case had been solved with old-fashioned police work.

No competent investigator ever clears a case with just a confession. They will always try to corroborate any alibis or excuses given by the suspect. The investigation would drag on for a few more weeks. The VCFD arson investigators, Saqui and Campbell, began to test their case and to work through with any issues that might come up in trial. They wanted to be able to prove when faced by dubious prosecutors or defense attorneys that the original "accidental ignition scenario" described by Delgado was not valid. They set up a series of filmed tests at the arson unit. For this they gathered a variety of dog hair from a local shelter and began testing its ignition properties with charcoal starter, gasoline, and cigarettes. After many tests and becoming nauseated off of the cigarettes, they confirmed what they had always known. Cigarettes would not ignite dog hair, and they would not ignite either the charcoal starter or the gasoline, whether mixed with the hair or not. It would take an open flame via a match or lighter to have caused this fire. These filmed tests were given to the prosecution as proof that Delgado's original scenario was impossible.

Andrew Delgado was re-arrested on charges of arson and animal cruelty. He was charged shortly thereafter by the Ventura County district attorney. On January 4, 2013, Delgado had his lawyer tell the court that he was not going to contest the two charges. She entered a "no contest" plea on his behalf, and the case was set for sentencing on March 6, 2013, in which Delgado faced up to three years in state prison for his actions. On that date the Ventura DA gave a lengthy and passionate plea to the judge to sentence Delgado to the maximum sentence. Additionally, an online petition submitted to the judge had one hundred-six thousand signatures of dog lovers from all over the world imploring the court to impose the strictest sentence possible. Not surprisingly, the judge noted the plea of the people, but showed great leniency and gave dog-killer Andrew Delgado a very light sentence of about eighteen months in jail, with a few months already served. He will likely be out in less than a year.

Investigator's Analysis:
Arson investigations are a sometimes complex and awkward mix of fire and police duties. Some agencies conduct them using only cops, while others conduct them using firefighters turned investigators. Each has a lot to offer an investigation of this nature, but sometimes you need a mix of skills and experience. Large agencies have their detectives hold a dual role of cop and fire scene investigator. In Ventura County, I believe they conduct arson investigations in the most practical way, which is to team up an experienced fire scene investigator from a fire agency with an experienced detective from a police agency, thereby getting the best of both worlds. It worked out very well in this case history. They did an extraordinary investigation at the scene, and complemented it with thorough follow-up interviews and a complex testing of theories. This all culminated in an excellent interview that led to a legitimate confession. Textbook investigative work!

At Andrew Delgado's sentencing, there is little doubt his lawyer lamented mental health issues or the fact that this was an isolated, drug-induced act. A sober evaluation of the event and his actions in the months leading to the event tell a scarier story. I've known thousands of hard-core drug addicts, and most of them do not commit crimes of this heinous and cruel nature. While drug use is a huge factor in breaking past the last barrier of moral inhibitions, there is little doubt that this was not an isolated incident and that this young man has given us a dark warning of the evil thoughts in his head. No matter how much time he gets in prison, or hopefully a psychiatric prison, he will be someone with a very high risk of reoffending—most likely in an even more gruesome crime. He bears serious watching and will remain a threat for years to come.

NATE THE NUT AND THE CONSPIRACY
VALENCIA, 1998

Valencia is where all the chic people from Santa Clarita live. Santa Clarita is a master-planned modern community of about 170,000 people, tucked into cookie-cutter neighborhoods in the foothills about thirty miles north of downtown Los Angeles. It is known as one of "America's Safest Cities" and is billed as the best suburb in the LA area in which to raise a family. The nightlife is fairly bereft in this town, and the businesses usually close at sundown. By 1998, the population was about 80 percent Caucasian with a sprinkling of Hispanics and Asians. At that time there were very few black families in the Valencia area.

Valencia is not a town for single people, and virtually every part of the community is geared toward families with children. However, it was the fastest growing real estate market in the United States for a twenty-year period, and people were getting rich off their investments in just a few years. For these reasons, Robert Goldbaum—a tall, single, Jewish man—moved into a very high-end condo complex in the upscale Valencia Summit area. By November of 1998, he had made a lot of money on his place and enjoyed an expansive three-bedroom luxury condo. Another neat thing about the Valencia area was that about half the cops and firefighters from the LA basin called it home. At any given time, about 15,000 cops or firefighters lived in the area. As it happened, Goldbaum lived above the unit of a California highway patrol officer named Matt Hill.

Goldbaum is a tall, awkward, unassuming guy who comes off as very cerebral, but not exactly the most physical or masculine man in the world. When I met him, he was nervous, jittery, and fairly soft in his appearance and mannerisms. At the time of this case, he was involved in money management and real estate investment.

The Santa Clarita area is patrolled by deputies from the massive Los Angeles Sheriff's Department. While the sheriff's enjoy a strong reputation nationwide as one of the most aggressive and progressive law-enforcement agencies in the world, the Santa Clarita substation was known in those days within its own department (of 25 other substations, each with about 250 deputies) as a slow-paced duty post, where some of the lesser inspired deputies chose to work. I'm telling you all of these little details because, for some odd reason, they all factored into this bizarre case of a ludicrous criminal conspiracy.

In the fall of 1998, Goldbaum started to have problems. He was contacted by an old friend named Michelle, who confided to him that she was having marriage problems. She was married to a highly emotional Filipino guy named Jim Del Rosario. They lived nearby in Northridge, and Jim made an excellent living as the owner of a heating and air-conditioning contracting business. Michelle and Jim had known Goldbaum for years, and when she and Jim began having problems, she went to Goldbaum for moral support. Jim eventually found out and called Goldbaum, telling him that he would kill him if he kept interfering in his life. This was followed up by numerous threatening calls from other persons. On November 1, Goldbaum woke up to see the words "fucken fag" spray-painted in black on the stucco wall just outside his front door. On the door itself, someone had painted the words "child molester." Goldbaum went to his car in the garage and found all four tires slashed. He knew right away that someone working for Jim had done this to him. Goldbaum continued to speak to Del Rosario's wife on the phone, and soon he began receiving more threatening phone calls. Again, he knew it was Jim. A mutual friend called Goldbaum and told him that Jim Del Rosario had been bragging about the attacks, promising that there would be more to come. On November 2, Goldbaum's neighbors reported to him that a man matching Del Rosario's description and two Mexican gangsters had been knocking on Goldbaum's door. Goldbaum dutifully reported these incidents to the deputies in Santa Clarita. On their advice, Goldbaum petitioned the Newhall Court to issue a temporary restraining order against Jim Del Rosario on November 5, 1998. Del Rosario was served this order and reacted in a predictable manner.

At eight in the evening on November 8, 1998, Goldbaum heard a heavy pounding on the door of his condo. Not expecting visitors, he looked through the security peephole and was startled to see the unfamiliar face of a very large, very scary looking, black man. The man was thickly built with wild hair in a "jeri curl," a battered face, and missing his front teeth. Goldbaum told the man, "No thank you," through the door. The man again knocked loudly and said he was looking for a female, demanding that Goldbaum open the door. Goldbaum wisely refused and told the man to go away. Several minutes later, he heard yelling and screaming outside and heard a hissing sound coming from his front door.

Downstairs, off duty CHP Officer Matt Hill and his buddy, another off duty cop from the LAPD, were watching a football game on TV. They heard the loud pounding and didn't think much of it. About five minutes later, they heard a man yelling and screaming, and heard an odd crackling sound. They ran outside and saw a small line of fire leading from the base of their door upstairs to a larger fire burning on the landing above them. More to their amazement, about thirty feet away, they saw a black male yelling and pounding furiously at his pants, which were on fire. CHP Officer Hill was pretty sure that this guy did not live in the high-end condo complex, and both cops were seasoned enough to recognize the burning man for what he was, a street thug. They watched as the man put the fire out, and then they both yelled at him that they were cops and to freeze. The man's immediate reaction was predictable. The man started running out of the complex. Officer Hill and his buddy, while in shorts and sandals, took off in pursuit. Simultaneously, one of the two put in a 911 call to the sheriff's and described the suspect as a black male wearing gold pants and a colorful Rasta-type shirt running through the complex.

Meanwhile, upstairs Robert Goldbaum began investigating the disturbance near his door. As he moved toward it, he could see that the small windows in the top of the door were filled with fire, and the flames were extending into his apartment over the top of the door. The door was visibly flexing, and he could see dark smoke seeping into his home. Trapped, Goldbaum ran to the only other exit—a sliding door leading to his balcony. While his apartment was technically only on the second floor, it sat over thirty feet above the ground, as the complex sits atop its parking garage. Goldbaum began to weigh his options as his unit started to fill with smoke; he decided against the thirty-foot drop into the rock-and-cactus garden below him. He stayed on his balcony and prayed for the fire department to arrive.

Within a few minutes of the commotion, several neighbors with fire extinguishers descended upon the scene. They were able to successfully extinguish the blaze prior to it penetrating Goldbaum's metal door. They eventually knocked long enough to coax a visibly-shaken Robert Goldbaum into exiting his condominium.

Meanwhile, the pursuit was unfolding below with comical results. Officer Hill, who at some point realized he did not have a badge or gun with him, was following the running suspect. He watched at one point as the suspect tripped over a raised speed bump in the complex' driveway and fell flat on his face. The suspect managed to get up quickly and sprint off down the driveway toward the main road. Hill heard sirens and assumed that sheriff's deputies would soon arrive. He abandoned his pursuit after a few hundred yards.

On the main road below the complex, an eyewitness relayed the following odd encounter, which was later confirmed by the suspect himself. The witness saw a sheriff's car speeding his way with lights and siren on. The patrol car slid into a tight turn toward the sprawling complex and skidded to an emergency halt as a wild-looking black male wearing a colorful Rasta shirt and gold pants came running down the driveway. Both the male and the sheriff's car were traveling so fast that they crashed into each other. The witness saw the male get up after running into the side of the car and then place his hands on the front fender of the patrol car, as if waiting to be searched or frisked. The witness watched the patrol deputy exit his car (with the lights and siren still on) and furiously wave at the black man to "get out of the way." The black man took his hands off the car, watched it speed noisily into the complex, and then he jogged away down the street. The witness saw one more speeding patrol car pass the black man as he jogged into the darkness. Classic! Somehow the intrepid deputies of sleepy Santa Clarita seemed to miss the likely only black man in the Valencia neighborhood, while responding to an emergent call of a black male suspect dressed in gold pants and colorful shirt. Very solid police work indeed!

Back at the condo, some semblance of order returned and someone began to set up a containment of the area, not realizing of course that the sole suspect had jogged away minutes before. A total of about a half dozen of Santa Clarita's finest sat on a four square block perimeter for the next three hours while a helicopter searched overhead and K-9's scoured the surrounding neighborhood for the long-departed suspect.

Finally, someone realized that they needed to notify the arson squad, and I got the call. I made it to the scene in short order and conducted my investigation. By this time, Goldbaum had filled in the local deputies on the background of this event. He strongly believed that the black male was one of the many air-conditioning employees who worked for Jim Del Rosario. It seemed like a logical place to start the investigation. Arson is an extremely personal crime (like murder), and in most cases the victim knows exactly who lit the fire. It's either himself (for financial gain) or a very pissed-off acquaintance whom he just bilked on a business deal or whose wife he just had an affair with. People light fires when they are really pissed off at someone. This seemed to be the case here.

I noticed that the fire had started at the base of Goldbaum's door on his mat. The fire had done significant damage to the metal door and came just short of breaching it before it was extinguished. I couldn't help but notice the graffiti that was still painted next to the door: "fucken fag." (In my mind I was envisioning a possible boyfriend/boyfriend dispute.) While going through the debris, I could smell a strong odor of gasoline. I also found the heavily-burned remnants of a yellow plastic anti-freeze jug on the mat. This was obviously the vessel that had held the gasoline. When gasoline is not in a normal gas can, it has most likely been recently acquired, so it was likely that the gas in this case had been purchased from somewhere nearby. I was also able to find two burned paper matches on the stairs leading up to the doorway. These appeared to be the source of ignition for this fire.

The fire scenario was fairly simple in this case. A suspect had poured gasoline from the antifreeze jug onto Goldbaum's concrete porch. Some had been absorbed into his door mat, and the remainder had run down the concrete steps and pooled on the porch below Goldbaum's—the one belonging to CHP Officer Hill. The suspect, no doubt the "wild-looking black malein the gold pants and Rasta shirt," had poured the gas and then ignited it using the matches. The ignition not only ignited the gasoline vapors on the door mat, but also ignited the gasoline vapors that had pooled around the suspect and on his clothing, thereby causing him to do the "dance of the flaming asshole," as noted by Officer Hill and his friend. While you are unlikely to find that colorful phrase in the scientific books and manuals on fire scene investigation, this is not an uncommon phenomenon when arsonists pour too much gasoline during their nefarious deeds.

A search of the area for a possible suspect vehicle came up empty. This puzzled us since we were sure the suspect wasn't local and had to have driven to the complex. However, an odor of gas was found outside the parking garage near where the victim had parked his car. In this spot we found where the antifreeze container had been sitting on the ground prior to the fire being set. Near it, we found some Camel cigarette butts and a couple more paper matches. We started to think that this was where the suspect had waited or possibly parked his car.

My investigation and interviews lasted until about one in the morning. By this time the suspect had not been located, and the containment had been broken down, the evening-shift deputies having gone home. A few of them drove to a nearby Denny's on Lyon's Avenue and the 5 Freeway and to have an early breakfast.

The next day, I would learn that a "wild-looking" black male wearing gold pants and smelling of gasoline had walked into the Hilton Garden Inn, about a half-mile away from the arson attack. He loitered in the lobby and basically scared the two women working behind the desk. The night manager approached him and asked him if he needed assistance. The black man said he was looking for a ride to a Denny's, but was out of cash. The manager called a local taxi and paid the cabbie to give the man a ride to Denny's. He then pulled five dollars out of his pocket and gave it to the man. The man seemed pleased with the generosity of the manager. The manager was just happy to get the menacing-looking man out of his lobby.

The night manager of the Denny's was a recently-promoted white male named Darryl. Darryl saw the very tough-looking black man enter his restaurant at about eleven that night and watched as he sat at the far end of the counter. Darryl took the man's order himself, and the man asked for a Coke and some French fries. The bill came to a little over six bucks. The man gave Darryl a five-dollar bill without comment. Darryl took the money, added his own in to make up the difference, and settled the man's bill. He couldn't help but notice that the man had some blood on his gold pants and smelled of gasoline.

Darryl thought of calling the local sheriff's to report the suspicious man, but then recalled his very recent supervisor's training. Denny's had been the recent media target of a nationwide claim of racism. This highly publicized case was a result of the efforts of many black dignitaries, led by the vocal Reverend Jesse Jackson, in proclaiming that Denny's treated black customers very poorly and in some cases refused to serve them. The Denny's executives nearly broke their spines bending over backward to appease the black community and the agitators, who were basically holding them up for extortion. In the end, the Denny's management paid millions of dollars to settle claims, enrich the pockets of black "leaders," and start a positive campaign to show that they were not racist bastards. All this occurred in the few months leading up to this night. The night manager, Darryl, was keenly aware of the concern of his corporate bosses.

Darryl kept a close eye on the black customer. He saw the man devour his fries and use the pay phone on several occasions. He saw the man eyeing other customers, and he still appeared to be hungry. Out of a sense of appeasement, Darryl decided to spot the man a meal. He had the cook make up a large Grand Slam with extra everything and delivered it to the customer. The man told him he was out of money, but Darryl told him it wasn't a problem. He watched the man inhale the meal and down a couple more Cokes. Still, by one in the morning, the man had not left. Darryl was greatly relieved at about a quarter past one to see three sheriff's deputies enter the restaurant and approach the man. As they got to him, they turned and sat down in the booth next to him. They glanced at him and proceeded to order an early breakfast for themselves. (Inexplicably, all three deputies had come off a long shift, and all had spent the last three hours of it in a long, boring surveillance operation searching for a "wild-looking, black man with a colorful Rasta shirt and gold pants." It still boggles my mind how they could not equate the man in Denny's to the suspect from the containment...sigh.)

Feeling much more relieved, Darryl spent the next few hours bringing food to the sheriff's deputies and the black man seated ten feet from them. By five in the morning, Darryl was getting off shift, the sheriff's had long since departed, and the black man was now standing outside near the phone.

Around that time, the day shift manager, Bertha, had arrived. A tough, stout woman, she was the only Mexican on the Denny's management team, despite the fact that all the cooks and busboys were from Mexico. She was a dedicated long time employee of this Denny's and was proud to have been promoted to assistant manager. When she took over, Darryl told her the story of the black male. He then happily went home to bed. At about six that morning, the breakfast rush was in full swing, and Bertha was busy. She finally looked up to see a dirty-looking black male seated at the end of the counter. He asked her for some more free breakfast. Bertha, recognizing a thug when she saw one, asked him if he had money. He said he did not, and Bertha tossed him out. She then called the local sheriff's to report the vagrant. Fortuitously, the deputy taking the call from Bertha was working overtime and had been involved in the containment the night before. He immediately recognized the description of the male and sent a team to arrest him. A team of five sheriff's deputies descended upon the Lyon's Avenue Denny's and hauled a very compliant Nathaniel Garner to jail for arson and attempted murder. He was booked and immediately went to sleep for the first time in about five days.

About the same time, I was awakened from my sleep after working most of the night and informed that the arson suspect had been captured. I drove to the nearby sheriff's station and began my interview of Nate Garner. I had spent most of my first ten years in the department working the heavily gang-infested, cocaine-fueled streets of South Central Los Angeles, primarily in the areas surrounding Watts and Compton. Upon seeing Garner stumbling half-asleep into the interview room, I immediately recognized him as a denizen of those dangerous streets, and most likely not from the bucolic Santa Clarita area. Given his smell, appearance, and, most significantly, his glazed eyes, I concluded that he was most likely a crack-cocaine addict. I noted that, although he wasn't tall, he was thickly muscled and had the battered face of a guy who had seen, and probably engaged in, a lot of violence in his life.

We went through the Miranda ritual, and I asked him about the event. "What's to tell?" he said. "You got me, and I'm going back for life. There's really nothing to say." Indeed, Nate Garner had a pretty impressive criminal record. He was thirty-eight years old and had spent about eleven of the last fifteen years in state prison. He had just gotten out of Patton State Prison Hospital (for the criminally insane) on a seven-year hitch for manslaughter. He had apparently beaten someone to death in a fistfight. He had several felony convictions dating back twenty years. He was correct—he was probably going back to prison for life.

We bantered back and forth a bit, and Garner revealed that he had been a professional boxer in his late teens and had received a brain injury in the ring, for which he was on permanent state disability. He said that before he went to prison the last time, he had become addicted to crack cocaine and was doing "thug work" for local drug dealers to support his habit. He said that he had left Patton addicted to psych meds, and immediately began using crack the moment he hit the streets. He acknowledged that he had mental health issues and that he was being used by guys on the street to do dirty jobs. I wondered if there was anything scarier to a soft-looking white guy like Goldbaum than looking out his peephole to see a crack-addicted, former boxer, ex-con, psych-med taking, street thug like Nate Garner? Nope, that was probably as scary as it gets.

When I asked him about the fire at Goldbaum's, he freely admitted his actions. He refused, as per the code of the street, to discuss the names or actions of others. Soon Garner asked me for some food. Apparently he was an insatiable eating machine. I told him that I would get him some sandwiches, but that he would have to have something to trade. Garner smiled and said, "You get me some sandwiches, and I'll tell you what you want about the other guys…under one condition. I'm going away forever. I just want you to put me in the same cell as them for a few hours." I told him I'd start with the food and we could talk about the condition later. I left the interview room and had some inmate workers make up a plate of beef sandwiches and grape drink. I brought them back to Garner, and he began to talk.

Garner said that he was hired by a guy to go to Bakersfield to "beat up a fag." He said a guy named "Leroy" hired him off the street in the Watts area and drove him up to Bakersfield to do the job. He barely knew this "Leroy" but thought he knew where Leroy's mother lived. He said they had driven in Leroy's white van toward Bakersfield. They arrived at a Denny's and made a phone call. Two Mexican guys drove up in a van and gave them some money and written directions. Garner said the Mexicans looked like gangsters and that the one in charge told Garner to call him "Mr. X." The van they were driving had some writing on the side, like a business name. Garner and Leroy then followed the Mexicans to the condo complex. Mr. X pointed out the victim's car in the garage and told Garner they wanted it burned. They said that when the fire was burning, they wanted him to wait outside of an apartment and beat up the tall dude when he came out. They told Garner that the tall guy was a child molester and a fag and had messed with the wrong person. For all of that work and risk, Garner was given three rocks of crack cocaine and $75 in cash. They gave him the coke up front and promised the cash when the job was complete. Because nobody likes a child molester, and he was craving the crack real bad, Garner said he didn't hesitate to take the job.

What struck me about this story was that Garner had no idea what city he was even in. Santa Clarita is about eighty miles south of Bakersfield. The fact that he was being preyed on by these co-conspirators for a meager seventy-five dollars was deplorable, but not exactly unheard of in the world of crime and addiction.

Garner inhaled the crack cocaine. He said the plan went sideways almost immediately. The parking garage was locked, and he couldn't get to the victim's car to burn it. He went back to Leroy and the two Mexicans and told them the news. They discussed what to do next while Nate smoked some cigarettes. Finally, they told him to knock on the victim's door, pretending to look for someone, and then to beat up the guy when he opened the door. Nate agreed. He said he tried to get the victim to open the door, but the guy seemed too scared to. He went back downstairs and told the other guys that it wasn't going to work. They gave him the gas can and ordered him to go up and torch the home. Garner complied.

He said he poured the gas and dropped the yellow container on the porch. He walked down a few steps and lit some matches. He was immediately covered in flames and then saw that his pants were on fire. He ran downstairs, put himself out, and heard two white dudes yelling at him. One was holding a badge, so Garner started running. He said he ran down the steep driveway and found that both getaway vans were gone. He kept running and then tripped over a bump in the driveway, falling hard and injuring his legs. He showed me his scuffed shoes and torn and bloody knees. He said he ran out of the complex and immediately ran into the side of a police car that had just arrived. He knew he was caught, so he just put his hands on the hood like he had done so many times before in his life. He was shocked when the cop began yelling at him to get out of the way.

Nate said he ran to a nearby hotel, and the manager gave him some money and got him a taxi. He rode it to the Denny's and tried several times to call his mom to pick him up. He kept telling her that he was at a Denny's in Bakersfield but wasn't sure exactly where. He said that the Denny's manager was really a nice guy and kept giving him free food. Garner said he ate about three different free meals at Denny's until the Mexican lady kicked him out in the morning. He thought he was going to get arrested at one point when three cops came in and sat next to him, but they ignored him.

When all was said and done, Garner said that he could direct me to Leroy's mother's house in the ghetto. He said that he could help us make Leroy talk if we would just leave him in a cell alone with him for a while. The one thing Garner said he wouldn't do was testify. That went beyond his code of right and wrong. He said he was just happy to get back to prison so that he could get off crack again. Garner also commented that when he got out of prison (if ever), he was going to talk his mom into moving to Bakersfield, because everyone had been so nice to him, giving him money and food all night.

Two days later, following Garner's directions, I found Leroy's house and identified him as thirty-three-year-old Lee Hogan, a man with a very minimal criminal record. We simply knocked on the door, and one of the first things he said was, "I knew you guys would find me." Hogan was not at all a street thug and came off as a sort of two-bit hustler who liked to wear fancy clothes. After we explained to him that Garner was requesting him as a cellmate, Hogan, already compliant, quickly became a proactive member of the investigative team. He visibly shuddered at the prospect of seeing Garner again. Before we could even get him back to the interview room for a proper debrief, Hogan had laid out the entire conspiracy. Hogan told us that he worked for a man named Jim Del Rosario in the heating/air-conditioning business. The company was called Bernardinos Heating and Air Conditioning. He said that Del Rosario was a little punk of a boss who liked to yell and scream a lot. He had two foremen, who both looked like old-school Mexican gangsters. The main guy in charge under Jim was a former *vato* named Roger. Hogan said that Roger carried himself like a gangster, even though he was close to forty years old, and he often bragged about his family's connections to the street gangs in Sylmar.

Hogan, who was a recent part-time employee of the business and the only black guy on a dozen-man crew, heard rumors over the past month that his boss was having problems with some guy. Jim had mentioned that his wife was fucking around with a "fag" and that Jim wanted to kick the guy's ass but was afraid of getting sued. At some point, Hogan had heard Roger bragging that he had done "a little work" for Jim, which Hogan took to mean that they had kicked someone's ass. Roger said that Jim had paid them well for the work.

A week ago, Hogan was called to the Northridge home of Jim Del Rosario, where Del Rosario told that his wife was fucking a "pussy Jewish guy." He told Hogan to see Roger about a special project he had in mind. Jim then walked away and stood about thirty feet away while Roger pitched a plan to Hogan. Roger asked Hogan to hire another black guy to beat up the Jewish guy for three-hundred dollars. Roger also promised Hogan that if the job went well, he would be hired full time with the company. As soon as the plan was being discussed, Jim, who apparently couldn't contain himself, reentered the conversation and told Hogan that he could just punch the Jewish guy in the gut and face a few times. He specified that he didn't want the guy killed but did want some physical evidence of a beating, such as a broken nose or black eye.

Jim, then remembering that he didn't want to be involved, pointed out that Hogan was to do this for Roger and not him.

Jim then said, "I'm not involved," and again walked away while Roger finalized the plan. Roger specified how they would attack the victim or his car. He wanted it done the upcoming Saturday night, as Jim would have the rock-solid alibi of being in Las Vegas that night.

Hogan, who had no criminal activity of this sort in his past, was shocked. He believed that these guys had chosen him because he was black, and they just assumed that he knew a couple thugs. Still, Hogan needed a full-time job, and he did know this insane guy named "Nate the Nut" who would probably do anything for money. Hogan, despite the fact that his common sense was screaming at him not to, agreed to join the conspiracy. Roger gave him three-hundred dollars to hire the "hit man," Nate the Nut.

On Saturday night, he located Nate the Nut standing on a corner on 109th street in the Watts area. He pitched the idea, and Nate agreed almost immediately. Nate jumped in the car and immediately asked Hogan for the money or a rock of crack. Completely scared of Nate Garner, Hogan took him to a corner and gave him a hundred bucks so he could score some crack. Garner returned with a crazy look in his eyes and seemed extremely ready to go. On the drive up the freeway, Hogan became extremely frightened of the obviously out-of-his-mind Garner, who kept asking for more money so he could buy some more crack. He also wanted food very badly. Hogan finally pulled into a Denny's parking lot in Sylmar and got Garner some burgers from a McDonalds across the street. They were soon joined by Roger and some other scary-looking Mexican gangster who Hogan learned was Roger's cousin. The gangster cousin asked Hogan if he had a gas can. Hogan looked into his own van and only saw a yellow antifreeze jug. Roger told him to fill up his van at the Mobil station and put some gas in the antifreeze jug. Hogan became alarmed and asked what the gas was for. Roger said that since Jim was out of town, something needed to be done tonight for sure. He said that if the victim wasn't home, they would burn his car or something. By this time Hogan was completely freaking out, but then Roger promised him that Jim would pay him $5,000 if everything went well.

While driving the ten miles from Sylmar to Santa Clarita, Hogan became almost paralyzed with fear. He kept looking at Nate the Nut, who was flexing and breathing hard like he was getting ready for a boxing match. Somewhere in his mind, Hogan conjured up images of Nate crushing the poor guy's face and killing him. Still he kept driving, following Roger's van. He marveled at the fact that the idiot had brought his work van.

When they got to the apartment complex, Hogan got even more worried. This was a really nice area, and there were no black people (or even Mexicans) around at all. Roger pointed out the victim's BMW in a parking garage and told Nate to go vandalize it. Nate demanded some more crack, and Hogan gave him a couple rocks he had held back. They all watched in amazement as Nate sucked the potent drug down in about five seconds. He then happily trotted off to wreck the car. Soon, they saw totally out-of-place Nate the Nut trying to find a way into the locked garage. He returned and told them everything was locked. Now Roger and his cousin were worried. They needed the job done tonight. They finally told Nate to knock on the door and punch the guy in the face when he answered. After Nate trotted off to the designated door, they all expressed the hope that Nate wouldn't kill the guy, as he looked just a little too eager to beat somebody up. Minutes later, a wild-eyed Nate returned again, saying that the guy just wouldn't open the door. Silently, Hogan breathed a sigh of relief and hoped the night was over. Roger and his cousin consulted again and then told Nate to go torch the guy's doorway to get him to come out. Nate didn't hesitate a bit. Hogan said he almost had a heart attack at this point.

A minute after he had disappeared, they saw a flash of flame and heard yelling. They then saw Nate the Nut dancing around wildly on the sidewalk with his pants of fire. They heard then saw two white guys run out in shorts, yelling, "Police, freeze." This was all too overwhelming for both Hogan and Roger, and they both fired up their vans and sped out of the condo complex, leaving the flaming Nate the Nut to his fate.

By now Lee Hogan had realized what a huge mess he had gotten involved in. He said the case made the papers the next day, and Jim called him up screaming at him for hiring a maniac and trying to burn the guy to death. Jim wouldn't listen when he tried to explain. Hogan told Jim he was going to leave the area, as he was sure that either Nate would kill him for leaving him at the scene or the cops would find him. Jim told Hogan that was a good idea and told him he would give him $5,000 if he would leave for Reno. The day after the fire, a petrified Hogan met an even more petrified Jim Del Rosario at a Wells Fargo bank in the San Fernando Valley. Jim came out and handed him $5,000 in cash and told him to leave town immediately, mentioning that Roger and his cousin had done the same.

Hogan took the $5,000 and paid about $3,500 toward his mother's back rent. He then spent most of the rest on clothes and going out that night to party and clear his head. The next morning he was too broke to flee, and a few hours later, we showed up at his door.

Hogan told us that he could get Jim Del Rosario into a compromising phone conversation that we could record. I called my buddies in the major crimes unit, and we got a motel room in South Central and set up a monitored recording in it. That afternoon, we sat around for a couple hours while a very nervous Lee Hogan began calling Jim Del Rosario. He left several messages on Jim's message service and got no reply. He then told the service to tell Jim that he was going to the cops if Jim didn't call back. Jim called about ninety seconds after that warning.

Immediately Jim began to caution Hogan about being on a phone and to not discuss anything unless in code. When the two couldn't figure out a code, Jim became frustrated and just foolishly started blurting out things. Soon he was admitting to most of the conspiracy over the phone. It was clear that he had not ordered the arson, but he did admit to wanting Goldbaum beaten up badly. When Hogan told him that the cops were at his home, and he couldn't go back to get the money he stashed there, Jim freaked out. Hogan (at our direction) asked to meet Jim again to get an additional $3,000 and some clothing and luggage so he could return to his native Belize. Reluctantly, Jim agreed to meet him the next night at the Sylmar Denny's with the money and luggage.

After the conversation ended, we began tearing down the "wire." Before we could even start, however, the phone rang again. This time a male with a thick East Coast accent called. Over the course of several minutes, this male engaged Hogan in an almost ludicrous conversation where he didn't state, but clearly insinuated that he was some sort of "heavy" or "muscle" for Jim Del Rosario. He spoke in Italian Mafia lingo and told Hogan that he "fixes problems" for Jim and "sends people on long vacations." He warned Hogan about talking to the cops and about bothering Jim in the future. He confirmed that Hogan would get his money the next night, but wanted him out of the picture fast after that. Hogan was actually petrified by this hoodlum, but we three detectives almost couldn't contain our laughter. We hadn't heard of any "wise guys" or Italian Mafioso in Los Angeles in recent years, and it was clear to us that, whoever this guy was, he had clearly seen *Good Fellas* way too many times. This was getting better by the minute.

We agreed to keep Hogan out of jail with the promise that he would meet us the next night in Sylmar. I then began to set up the "sting" operation on Jim Del Rosario and Roger, who I identified as Rogelio Alvarez. I drove by Del Rosario's home and photographed his work vans. I took these photos and photos of Lee Hogan and Roger Alvarez back to the jail and showed them to Nate Garner. Nate the Nut smiled as he identified "Leroy" and "Mr. X." He relished the chance to see them again in order to pay them back for stranding him at the scene of the crime. I didn't have the heart to tell Nate that there was no way I was going to allow anyone in a cell with him—I didn't need a jailhouse murder and its subsequent civil lawsuit on my hands.

Oddly, the sting operation was set to take place in the most crime-ridden parking lot in all of Los Angeles. A little side note here: The Denny's in Sylmar sits alongside the northbound Interstate 5 Freeway, at the Roxford exit. It is not in the ghetto, and it is not an area known for crime or a hangout for thugs. However, for some reason every drug dealer and crook in the greater Los Angeles basin seems to know this place and picks it to conduct meetings and transactions. I had worked in an undercover role as a narcotics detective for almost five years before joining the arson squad and had conducted no fewer than thirty undercover or sting operations in the parking lot of this restaurant. Almost all were at the insistence of the drug dealer, burglar, prostitute, pimp, or weapons dealer we were setting up. We never knew why, but obviously the bad guys had a network, and they liked this location. Perhaps because it was a very visible, busy place and was easy to find. Even more amazing, I can count no fewer than three occasions in which I was there for one deal, sitting in a surveillance mode, when I observed a totally unrelated criminal transaction take place. One of these was an unrelated drug deal between white bikers and Mexican gangsters, and another was a transaction between a prostitute, her pimp, and a "john."

Another unique fact about this particular Denny's is that it is allegedly a place where some of Charlie Manson's people stopped after the Tate-LaBianca murders to dispose of some of the evidence in that famous case. A firearm used in one of those murders was disassembled by a Manson girl and left in the tank of a toilet for several weeks before it was found.

Apparently regular folks liked this place for a rendezvous as well. One day, while waiting for a meth dealer to show up, we saw what appeared to be a man and woman conducting a consensual sexual transaction. We saw two cars show up, park near each other at the Denny's (in broad daylight), and then watched as a very attractive young female exited her car and got into the other car with a much older, well-dressed male. She immediately reached down and grabbed his crotch while he sped out of the lot to a motel about a block away. Out of curiosity and a bit of boredom while awaiting perpetually tardy drug dealers, two of our surveillance experts followed the pair, and kept a blow by blow (pun intended) narrative of the action, assuming it was a high dollar call girl and her date.

The man and woman sped behind the motel, and she obviously couldn't wait to get into the room as she began to orally service him there in the parking lot. This was a little surprising since it was in the middle of the day and the woman did not look like a street hooker but more of a high-class escort. We fully expected the two to get a room. Eventually, after the two realized that some grungy-looking Mexicans were watching them, they started to get out of the car and enter a room. Our grungy Mexicans (actually highly skilled undercover detectives) identified themselves to the couple and inquired about their activities. Much to all of our surprise and amusement, the couple was in fact a local dentist and a medical sales lady from his office. Both were in fact married to other people, and our presence nearly gave them both heart attacks. None of us had the heart to do anything about it, and we let the relieved pair go. No doubt the mood was broken that day. But I digress.

As this arson case unfolded, the bad guys again selected this Denny's as a meeting place. We smiled at the irony, realizing that this case had been revolving around Denny's restaurants since it began. So on November 18, 1998, we surrounded the Denny's with a team of skilled undercover investigators, including four sprinkled within the building, and sent Lee Hogan in to meet with Jim Del Rosario. He was wired for sound with a high-tech recorder attached to his belt and disguised as a pager. A lone white male in a leather jacket was the sole patron at the counter, and he was reading a paper and eating his meal. Hogan sat a few stools away, ordered a meal, and walked outside to call Del Rosario. He got no response from Jim. This sequence would repeat itself several times over the next seventy-five minutes. Eventually, Hogan and the undercover officers inside could eat no more food and could not stick around without appearing really suspicious. Hogan came out and called me to ask for advice. We had a team at Del Rosario's home, and his car had never left the driveway. We realized that Jim wasn't going to show, so we shut the operation down and contemplated our next move.

However, as Lee Hogan was settling his bill at the counter, the lone white male walked up behind him to pay. He then whispered into Hogan's ear with a very thick East Coast accent that his name was "Guido" and that the cops were around. In his best "Godfather" voice, he advised Hogan to leave now and never come back to Los Angeles, or else! The tone was menacing to say the least. The man then calmly walked outside and entered a red Camaro convertible and drove away. Now, this little interaction went somehow unnoticed by the undercover detectives in the restaurant, and Lee Hogan had taken his "wire" off after he was instructed to leave the restaurant. He also took his sweet time walking to his car, leaving the lot and meeting me down the street. He then said, "Did you get that guy? It was the East Coast hit man." In reality, we didn't hear or see the guy do anything. Hogan then explained what had happened. It was apparent that "Guido" was sent there as Jim's agent to intimidate Hogan.

Luck was not totally against us, as I still had one undercover car watching Del Rosario's home. Within a minute of my conversation with Hogan, the man watching Jim's home reported a red

Camaro convertible entering the driveway and a man matching Guido's description get out and go into the home. We knew that this final connection between Guido at the Denny's and now at Del Rosario's home completed an overt act toward this conspiracy. We encircled Jim Del Rosario's home and called him and Guido to come out. They meekly appeared at the door and gave up with no resistance. Guido immediately began to shake and quiver. Del Rosario began blurting out very ill-advised statements about the conspiracy, including how he had "only wanted that fag beaten up" and the he "didn't pay them money... just loaned it to them." His lawyer would come to despise him for those and other blurted statements.

Guido turned out to be another Jewish boy named Robert Barry Syderman, formerly of New Jersey. In reality he stood about five-foot-eight and only weighed about 155 pounds. He talked a whole lot taller. His criminal record was quite interesting and consisted of numerous theft and fraud arrests, terrorist threats, and a few assaults. Not exactly mafia material, but no slouch either. At the time he was working as a used car salesman and had stolen or "unlawfully removed" the Camaro he was driving from his boss's lot.

Syderman was bold and bad in front of Del Rosario, acting like things such as this happened to him every day. He cockily swaggered out to our car in his East Coast leather jacket and wisecracked until the door was closed. His façade immediately changed when we told him he was being booked on attempted murder and arson charges along with criminal conspiracy. Almost immediately Syderman put forth his best used-car-salesman schmooze and began to tell us that this was all a misunderstanding and that a disgruntled employee named Lee Hogan had been trying to involve the boss in some crime. Syderman was quick to point out "how all them black dudes lie and steal." Syderman soon began to sweat when we told him that he was an active party to a conspiracy and that we considered him as an agent of the Italian Mafia; we told him we were going to book him in jail as a Mafioso. The ramifications of this would have been that he would be specially booked into a "high power" wing of the downtown jail with other organized crime figures, including the one or two Italian Mafia hit men who were actually currently in jail. Syderman soon became so nervous that he nearly puked in the back of our car. He stammered and stuttered through the car ride, providing a detailed interview stating adamantly that he was not mafia and was in fact just putting on a "Gumba" act to intimidate Hogan. He described himself as just a "Jew Hustler" trying to get a little money out of life.

Eventually, Syderman agreed to cooperate and laid out the details of the scheme to us. He admitted that Jim had sent some black guys to beat up Goldbaum after they had vandalized his car. Jim had paid for everything and then let his Mexican foreman handle all the details. He believed that that would keep suspicion off him. After the incident made the papers, Jim had panicked and asked Syderman for advice, as he too believed that Syderman was an experienced crook. Syderman advised him to pay off the idiots and have them leave the area. Syderman knew that Jim paid nearly $20,000 in total to finance the entire fiasco. He and Jim had also gone to a criminal defense attorney in the San Fernando Valley and had sought legal advice about this caper before their arrest. After Hogan had called Jim, Syderman agreed to "handle the Lee problem" for Jim. He said his goal was to case the Denny's looking for cops and then to scare Hogan away. He believed he had seen surveillance officers and identified three people (who were not cops) as cops inside the Denny's.

A similar interview with Jim Del Rosario yielded many self-serving statements. Jim admitted that he had wished openly among his employees that something bad would happen to Goldbaum, but he said that he never dreamed that anyone would act upon his wishes. He conceded that he had only loaned money to both Hogan and Alvarez, as he was a very generous boss and both men had family problems. Del Rosario eventually admitted that he only wanted Goldbaum beaten badly and had in no way endorsed the arson attack. Both men were booked into jail. They were bonded out within hours by their attorney.

Over the next few weeks, I spent time solidifying my case. I wrote a warrant for Del Rosario's account at the Wells Fargo bank branch. It confirmed that he had withdrawn $5,000 on the day Hogan said he was paid. It also showed several other large transactions that week, totaling over $20,000. I spent the next two weeks looking for Rogelio Alvarez with an arrest team. They didn't find him, but he soon found us. On November 27, I received a fax message from Alvarez. The message was a self-serving admission about the incident. He claimed to have been paid by Jim Del Rosario to only show Lee Hogan and another man the Goldbaum car and condo. He said he had no idea a beating or arson was to take place. Alvarez confirmed that after the event, he had been paid $5,000 by Del Rosario to stay in Mexico for a few months. His fax claimed that he was well on his way there. Indeed the fax was sent from a business just an hour north of the Mexican border. Roger Alvarez would not be found for almost eight years. By then all the witnesses would be gone and the evidence destroyed. The best we could do when he was found in 2006 was to have him deported back to Mexico.

The court proceedings dragged on for nearly a year. Del Rosario had hired a pair of typical, bad-suited, hair-piece-wearing attorneys whose main job seemed to be to drag out the case in order to siphon more and more money out of Del Rosario's bank accounts. Fine with me! Nate the Nut Garner pled guilty first and received a thirty-year sentence for arson. His ghastly criminal history predestined how long he would spend in jail. Surprisingly he seemed happy upon sentencing, and he smiled and waved at me several times. Lee Hogan was convicted of criminal conspiracy and given three years in prison. His sentence was suspended based on his slight criminal record and his level of cooperation. Little Robert "Guido" Syderman was thoroughly embarrassed in court when the judge read aloud about his "tough-guy act". This antic would land him a two-year sentence for conspiracy, with one year suspended.

Finally, after threatening to sue me and allegations by his attorneys and their "expert" that our wired conversations were faked, we finally brought the FBI in to validate the wired tapes as authentic and pristine. After this, and probably because he was running out of money, the sleazy attorneys for Del Rosario persuaded him to take a guilty plea for criminal conspiracy and a three-year sentence. The coward still had a trick up his sleeve, as his wife advised me that he was soliciting many business owners and local politicians to write letters to the judge asking for leniency on his part. This tactic can be very effective, so for the first time in my career, I felt compelled to address a letter to the court and spell out in detail every step Jim Del Rosario took to pay people to have them do his dirty work. The judge read my succinct letter in open court and noted that there were over seventy letters supporting Del Rosario. My tactic apparently worked, as Del Rosario fully expected to walk out of the courtroom with a suspended sentence. On August 6, 1999, he was enraged at both me and his attorneys when the court sentenced him to two years in state prison plus a year of probation.

My only regret was that he probably wasn't going to meet or be cellmates with Nate the Nut Garner in prison. Although the two never met and didn't know each other, the many long hours alone would surely have brought out the truth and would surely have allowed Nate to learn that he had received only $75 out of the more than $20,000 Jim Del Rosario paid out for the scheme. I'm sure Nate would have known how to get a little justice for himself.

Investigator's Analysis:
In Southern California we have the Hollywood influence. By that I mean that we have some very strange criminal cases that are not that common in other areas. Rich people—wanting to settle a grudge, destroy a business, or get even with an unwanted spouse—tend to do what they see on TV and in the movies, employing hit men, arsonists for hire, and other paid thugs. These sorts of stupid actions only add further opportunities for the cops to find and locate the suspect, who then in turn always "flips" on the guy who hired him in exchange for leniency. These days, with law enforcement's ability to track cell phones and the prevalence of video cameras, finding co-conspirators is easier than ever before. In the poorer areas and ghettos, the crooks usually commit the crimes themselves, and there is no one to tell on them or testify against them unless they unwisely run their mouths. This case is one of dozens of major crime cases that I have been involved in over the years in which the cowardly man behind the conspiracy doesn't have the guts to settle his own beefs and instead involves a phalanx of underlings and thugs-for-hire. Between paying his thugs, his greasy lawyers, and his loss of income while he spent his pithy few months in jail, Jim Del Rosario dumped a cool $50,000 into this caper, all because he was irritated with a family friend. The true pity is that he didn't get to spend a single hour in a dank cell with the animal he hired for $75, Nate the Nut.

THE DEVIL NEXT DOOR
STEVEN AGREDANO
SOUTH EL MONTE, 2012

The vast majority of people who commit arson are one-time offenders who do it for either financial gain (insurance fraud) or for revenge because of a personal grudge like the one in the previous case. In these cases, the choice of target, time of the attack, and level of sophistication of the event will most often point toward a likely suspect. The trick then for an investigator is to positively link that suspect to the crime.

However, there are a few kinds of cases out there that investigators truly hate. Those are the ones in which the fire is set for no apparent reason whatsoever. These types of arsons make no sense, and there are no logical leads to follow when trying to assess possible suspects. Such is the case with this story.

On March 8, 2012, my new partner Det. Dana Duncan and I were working the night duty. Just prior to coming on at three in the afternoon, we learned of a large residential fire which had occurred in the San Gabriel Valley area known as South El Monte. This unincorporated stretch of county land lies about fifteen miles east of downtown Los Angeles in the flat lands at the base of the looming San Gabriel Mountains. This area has long been a blue-collar, Hispanic area of residential neighborhoods filled with working folk. In the past twenty years, like the majority of the San Gabriel Valley, tens of thousands of Chinese, Vietnamese, and Korean immigrants have been slowing giving the area a much more Asian flair. Still, working-class Hispanics continue to dominate the neighborhoods.

The fire was reported as a typical event by our patrol deputies. The fire was noticed at about one thirty in the afternoon. The patrolmen reported that the home was vacant at the time of the fire, and the county fire captain was calling the event an arson attack, as he had found gasoline poured throughout the interior of the home. Immediately, two thoughts crossed our minds. The first was that the time of day was not consistent with an arson event, as the vast majority occurs during times of darkness. The second was that the home was reported vacant, which immediately caused us to consider an insurance-fraud scheme as a possibility. Even before we arrived, we had begun to mentally profile the event. Of course, only a complete and thorough "cause-and-origin" investigation would give us the truth.

As we were making our way toward the scene through the normally congested Los Angeles area traffic, we learned of an update to the fire. The patrol deputies had been contacted by a man at the fire scene named Gabriel. Gabriel lives about forty miles away. Gabriel said he had been called by his brother, Steven, who said to him, "I burned the neighbor's house. It's on fire." Gabriel, who was well aware of Steven's past erratic behavior, was worried about Steven hurting himself or others. He immediately drove to his mother's home (which is next to the burned property) to see if it was true. When he arrived, he saw the fire trucks and sheriff's cars. He approached one of the deputies with his information. Gabriel also gave the deputies Steven's address and "horsepower" (police slang for name, date of birth etc.). He mentioned that Steven had become increasingly paranoid and had begun reporting that he frequently heard voices that threatened him. Patrol deputies went next door and contacted Steven's mother, Helen, and found out that Steven lived in a small home at the back of her property. He had left the area in his truck around the time of the fire. Helen also informed the deputies to be careful with her son, as he was suffering from severe mental health problems and had reported to her that he was hearing voices. She also said he had been drinking that day and was on active parole. She said he had a past history of rampant drug abuse. She also mentioned that he had been upset about something that morning, and she had seen him break the windshield of his truck.

The deputies did some checking and learned that Steven was on parole for a well-publicized car chase a few years before in which he had evaded dozens of cop cars for about an hour on the Los Angeles freeway system. The chase terminated in front of his mother's home where he attempted to attack several armed officers from the West Covina Police Department. The entire incident ended dramatically when the police officers were able to subdue Steven with several shots from beanbag shotguns. He was sentenced to a few years in prison for this event but had been released on parole several months prior to this fire.

Upon hearing of this, we thought *Great, we have an active parolee, with a past assault on police officers, a history of alcohol and drug abuse, who is paranoid, drunk, and possibly "hearing voices."* We advised the patrol deputies to begin an active search for the man and to use extreme caution.

At about four in the afternoon, we arrived at 10328 Weaver Avenue, South El Monte. It was a large, slightly-overgrown property with a sixty-year-old home on it. The home and property appeared to have been vacant for about sixth months, but it seemed cared for. It was not abandoned and had none of the signs of burglary or vandalism normally associated with abandoned homes. We later learned that the elderly owner had died some months previous, and the home was in probate, pending the settlement of the estate. The heirs occasionally came over to mow the lawn and to insure the home was secure.

We saw immediately that a large portion of the home had sustained heavy fire damage. The damage was concentrated in a west bedroom. This bedroom was completely destroyed from top to bottom and had undergone a phenomenon called "flash over." This occurs when there is so much heat and air in a room or compartment that every single thing reaches its ignition temperature and bursts into flame. The temperatures in a room that reaches flash over hover around 1,200 degrees Fahrenheit. The fire spread from this room into a bedroom hallway and up into the attic via an open attic hatchway. Because of this, the entire attic and roof was destroyed, but the remainder of the home was intact. There was heat and smoke damage throughout. The damage estimate for this fire was over $200,000.

We smelled a strong odor of gasoline in this room and quickly tracked it to a five-gallon, red, metal "jerry can" propped up against the exterior of the windows to that bedroom. The gas can still had almost four gallons of gas in it, and it showed signs of having been on fire. The deputies told us that they had seen the can on fire when they arrived.

Dana and I began to process the scene. We took photos of the exterior of the home, the yard, the utilities, and finally the gas can. We then entered the home and systematically went through and examined every area of the home, starting with the areas that were the least damaged. All of this is standard fire investigation protocol. Among the things we were looking for was, of course, any damage caused by direct flame, heat, smoke, or fire suppression activity. Besides that, we were looking for red flags or indications that something else was amiss. For example, fires in vacant homes are somewhat common events for a variety of reasons. Often, juveniles will exploit a vacant home as their secret little playground and commit minor acts of vandalism in them, including small fires. Gang members, drug dealers, users, and prostitutes will also utilize vacant properties to conduct their own nefarious activities. Homeless transients often find a vacant home and "squat" in it for a means of shelter and comfort. Each of these types of people causes fires either on purpose or by accident during their illegal activities. Each leaves noticeable clues to their involvement. What we were really looking for were signs of a staged fire for the purpose of insurance fraud or some other financial gain. It is not unheard of for a property owner to stage gang or juvenile activity in a vacant property, with the later intent of burning down the home so that he can collect the insurance proceeds. All of these fire motives are in our mind every time we examine an abandoned property after a fire.

In this case, we found none of this type of activity. The majority of the home had no flame or heat damage at all. There was medium smoke damage throughout, with only direct fire damage to one bedroom, the hallway outside that room, and throughout the attic. We also found no signs that anyone had broken into the home, with the exception of the fire suppression crews.

We documented the home and then proceeded to the rear bedroom, which we determined was the room of origin. Like I stated earlier, this twelve-by-ten-foot bedroom had completely flashed over. Everything in the room was badly burned. As soon as we entered, we smelled the overpowering odor of gasoline. We reconstructed the room and found that the gasoline odor was prevalent on the carpeted floor at the base of the only window in the room. We went to that spot, cleaned the floor of debris, and took several samples of the debris. We captured these samples in clean metal cans, sealed them, and later transported them to the crime lab for chemical analysis. The floor area below the window also yielded some interesting evidence. We found a pattern of shattered window glass that did not have smoke damage on it embedded into the carpet. This told us that the window had shattered before the fire had ignited.

Directly outside of this window was the jerry can, still mostly full of gasoline. We went outside and processed the area. We took an ounce sample of the gas from the jerry can, and then poured the remaining four gallons into another gas can on the property. We only needed the small sample for testing. Even though it was obvious that the fluid in the can was gasoline based on its smell, color, and the container it was in, the proper rules of evidence dictate that we have an actual forensic chemist test the fluid in a crime lab. We also took the large, now-empty jerry can and held it for a fingerprint and DNA exam. The likelihood of finding this evidence on the can was somewhat remote, but it is a standard criminal investigation procedure. If we didn't do this, it would be the very first question any competent defense attorney would ask us at the preliminary hearing.

After we had removed the jerry can and its liquid sample, we examined the area outside of the window. The best evidence in any criminal case continues to be physical evidence. It doesn't lie. We were looking for anything a criminal may have left behind, from footprints, to gloves, to blood etc. We were rewarded for our efforts. We saw that next to the window was a large amount of broken window glass that did not have smoke stains on it. This positively proved to us that the window had been shattered prior to the fire.

At this point we had collected all the evidence at the scene that we could find. We began coming up with our "ignition scenario." We had a slight problem in that we were unable to find an ignition source. We knew that in order to ignite gasoline vapors, an open flame was needed. We were unable to find a match, candle, lighter, or any other flame source for this fire. We formed the opinion that the suspect likely took it with him, which would normally indicate the use of a butane lighter. So, based on what we could find, we determined that an unknown suspect carried a full, five-gallon gasoline container to the scene, broke the exterior bedroom window of the home, poured about a gallon of gasoline into the home via the broken window, set the can down outside the window, and then ignited the vapors of the gasoline with an open flame, most likely a cigarette lighter. The suspect then left the location carrying his lighter with him. This is a standard and very unsophisticated scenario. What made this case odd was the time of day. The overwhelming majority of arson attacks are committed in the dead of night, so as to avoid detection. This attack was done in broad daylight in a busy neighborhood.

I am a great believer in profiling crime scenes in order to classify the crime and thereby form a pool of potential suspects. There are a limited number of arson motives, and by closely studying the target of the attack, the sophistication of the ignition scenario, and carefully assessing the victim, an experienced detective can usually locate a suspect or identify a suspect pool.

In this case the attack was unsophisticated in that the suspect did not enter the home. The suspect used very obvious and crude ignition materials and left a large amount of visible evidence at the scene for investigators to exploit. The home had been unoccupied for months, and so the victim portion of this crime was very hazy. It was unlikely that this was a spite/revenge arson, as no persons lived at the home and the arson was not preceded by vandalism attacks. We saw none of the normal indications of fraud, so we quickly ruled out the heirs as potential suspects. The size of the gasoline can ruled out young kids as suspects. The time of day was the largest factor to consider. This was such an incredibly high-risk attack that we knew the suspect had to be either extraordinary angry, irrational, drunk, or mentally ill.

Sticking to basic investigative principles, we had the waiting patrol officers conduct a "canvass" of the neighborhood. This soon proved fruitful as they quickly found a gardener nearby who had witnessed the entire event. He told investigators that he had seen an adult Hispanic male break out the window of the home and tilt a large metal gas can into the window. The male then lit the fire and calmly walked away from the scene. The gardener, who did not come forward but was cooperative when approached, said that the suspect walked into the rear house of the property next to the burned home. This was the same location where we were told Steven lived.

We then focused on the gas can. The gas can was unique in that it was at least thirty years old and was made of metal. These used to be known as "Jeep cans," because they were found attached to old military jeeps. These cans are becoming very rare. We approached Steven's brother, Gabriel (the man who originally called the sheriff's about the fire), and asked him about the can. He said his brother had kept an old metal "Jeep can" in his garage. He said that the can was normally empty. Gabriel then went into Steven's garage and found the Jeep can to be missing. We showed him the metal can we had found at the fire scene, and he confirmed that it looked like Steven's. We then sent detectives out to the local gas stations, realizing that most arsonists get their gas from sources near the attack site. Again we were rewarded.

A station about a mile away reported that a heavily-tattooed Hispanic man had purchased five gallons of gas about forty minutes prior to the fire. We later drove to that station and interviewed the clerk. She later picked out a photo of Steven Agredano as the man who had purchased the gasoline. She said he was driving a white Toyota SUV and was using an old metal gas can. She described him as looking scary and disturbed.

Now we were beginning to get comfortable with this case, as the physical evidence was beginning to corroborate the original statements made by witnesses. We just had to locate the suspect in this case, Steve Agredano. As we were wrapping up our scene investigation at about sunset, the arrest gods smiled favorably upon us and delivered our man. Without any fanfare, Steven Agredano drove up to his house in his white Toyota SUV and got out, acting like nothing at all had happened. Two burly uniformed deputies grabbed him, hooked him up, and tossed him in the back of a patrol car. We walked over and got our first look at the man. He was a husky, clean-cut guy who had a significant number of tattoos. What caught our attention was that he had a wild smile and a crazy look in his eyes, as if he were thoroughly enjoying the moment. We asked his name, and he gave it to us, but then he began giggling like a crazy man. The patrol deputies transported him to the nearby Temple City Sheriff's Substation where we interviewed him.

Prior to following Agredano to the substation, we conducted interviews with both his mother and brother. Both were extremely cooperative and seemed relieved that he had been picked up without any drama. Both said that he had been arrested a couple years before after leading a local law enforcement agency on a lengthy, televised vehicle pursuit that terminated right in front of his home. Agredano, a heavy user of methamphetamines at the time, had jumped out of the car and begun attacking the dozen or so police officers who had been chasing him. They were able to subdue him only after shooting him several times with a beanbag shotgun and releasing a patrol dog to attack him.

His long-suffering family, who by all appearances seemed to be hard-working, law-abiding citizens, told of how Steven had been slipping deeper into paranoia and mental illness because of his long history of drug and alcohol abuse. They said he had talked of suicide several times and in the past had attempted to "blow the house up" by opening all the gas valves and trying to start a fire. Other times he had made mild attempts at slashing his own wrists. He had also mentioned that the cops were going to have to kill him someday. His mother was aware that he had been placed into a seventy-two-hour psychiatric hold on at least two prior occasions after similar destructive and self-destructive behavior.

Most alarmingly, his mother said that he had begun drinking heavily after complaining to her that he continued to "hear voices" from unseen people who appeared to be threatening him. She said that early that morning, she had heard noises and saw that he had smashed the window of his truck. He had also kicked dents into the side of the well-cared-for vehicle. She said it was then that he began drinking, and she knew something bad was going to happen.

The family was genuinely afraid of what Steven would do and believed that he would either kill himself or force the cops to kill him. He had called two different family members on the day of the fire and told them that he had burned a home and would not be coming back. He called his son and told him good-bye, that he would never see him again. He had also told a daughter that he wasn't going to make it through the day. We genuinely felt sorry for his family, and we were also relieved that Steven had decided to come in peacefully.

Later that afternoon, Detective Duncan and I interviewed Steven in the jail at Temple City. He was polite and controlled, but it was easy to see that he was at the edge of cracking up.

He had a demonic look about him and was proud to show us a satanic pentagram tattoo he had on his hand. He said that he was relieved to go back to prison, as he could now get Satan's horns tattooed on his forehead. One particularly unnerving characteristic about Steven was his otherworldly grin and low, giggling, maniacal laugh that seemed straight out of a Hollywood portrayal of a psycho. He laughed and giggled and grinned for no apparent reason, and he genuinely seemed to relish the crazy life he was living. He did give off the appearance of someone who was slightly possessed.

While never truly admitting to the arson, Steven gave us a rambling two-hour statement. He said he was surprised to have survived the day, as he'd felt that he was going to be attacked or killed by unknown evil forces. He said he had a gun stashed nearby and would use it rather than be arrested. He eventually told us a weird story of how this day came to be. He said that he had been hearing threatening voices beginning several weeks prior. The voices said they were going to harm him and his family. He heard them when he was driving around and heard them when he was asleep. The day before the event, a strange thing had happened to him. He said he heard an explosion and saw a blue bolt of lightning coming from behind a home across the street. Since then he said he had been energized and believed that he was about to be attacked by unknown forces. After this bolt of energy, he began hearing specific threats coming from the empty home next door.

The voices taunted and threatened him all night, and he attempted to drown them out by consuming alcohol. They wouldn't stop, and when he awoke in the morning, they were louder and more persistent. He became upset, went outside, began kicking his truck, and finally broke the window of the vehicle. The voices from the vacant house next door persisted. Steven told us that he had then wanted to go out and attack the people he felt were behind these voices. He got into his truck and drove off, planning to attack a woman from work. He said he was going out to slash the tires of her car and break the windows. He would not tell us who this woman was or where she lived.

Steven then told the more frightening story of how, after he couldn't find this unknown woman, he drove around to visit old friends in the area. When he got to their homes, he seemed to find that all were vacant and abandoned. He said this made him very mad, and he wanted to attack the homes. Eventually he came back to his own home and was arrested. We asked Steven if he had purchased gas the day of the fire. He admitted that he had and named the same gas station where he was observed filling the jerry can. Steven did confide that he was willing to be killed by police. At some point he stated that he had been carrying a gun. He said that if the cops came after him, he was going to take a couple of them with him. He proudly showed us old two-year-old scars from where the cops had had to shoot him several times with beanbag shotguns. He said he wasn't going to let the police do that to him again. He also admitted that he had called two of his children and told them he would never see them again.

Steven's matter-of-fact description of his chaotic last twenty-four hours was a bit unnerving. We also knew another fact that added to our unease. During the same hours Steven had been driving around, there had been no fewer than five other unexplained fires within five miles of where he lived. He would not admit to setting any of these, and as of the writing of this book, we have been unable to conclude if he was ever involved in those incidents.

We beseeched Steven to admit to his fires, and we would advise the district attorney to ask for psychiatric treatment as part of his incarceration. However, his past prison experiences worked against us. He said, "I like you guys and want to come clean, but that would make me a snitch, and snitches die in prison." Apparently he believed admitting to the crimes amounted to snitching on himself, and with this prison logic in mind, Steven never admitted to the primary act of arson. He did throw us a bone by saying that he was going to plead guilty at his first court appearance, his reasoning being that he was "a man, and that's what men do."

On April 12, 2012, in an El Monte court, prior to the start of his preliminary hearing on this case, Steven Agredano held true to his promise and did not contest the charges against him. His lawyer had him plead guilty to one count of arson to property, which in California is a serious and violent felony. Taking into consideration his prior state prison record, the DA demanded that Agredano take the midterm sentence of four years and eight months in state prison. Both Det. Dana Duncan and I strongly recommended that the man be incarcerated in a psychiatric prison facility, as it was clear he had violent mental health issues.

We imagine we will see or hear from him again in a few years, and we fully expect to see Satan's horns tattooed on his forehead.

The Weather Watchers
Dale Frey-Glendale, 1985 to present

In 2010, I was cleaning out some old files at the arson squad. Among the many odd things I found was a videotape with an intriguing, handwritten title. The tape was marked, "John Orr Interviews: a Serial Arsonist." Since John Orr is considered to be the most significant fire fiend to ever haunt the California foothill region, I could not wait to view this tape. The tape is a twenty-minute production made by John Orr and an unknown female investigator in an interview room at the Glendale Police department in 1985. Orr, as many readers will recall was a Glendale (California) Fire Department captain and arson investigator from about 1980 to 1991. During his time as an arson investigator, he was also secretly setting hundreds of arson fires. He was suspected of having lit over 2,500 fires during his lifetime and was convicted of four different arson series, and four counts of arson/murder. He is currently serving a life sentence in prison for his crimes. In the video, made several years before Investigator Orr was arrested for his fires, he was conducting an interview of an alleged serial arsonist. John Orr's face never appears, but he narrates part of the tape and asks questions of a young arson suspect for about half the tape. Investigator Orr shows the suspect a map of the Glendale City College and skillfully inquires about a small series of very minor arson fires on the campus in the summer of 1985.

During the initial questioning, conducted by the female detective, the young man, identified only as "Dale" and with his face hidden for most of the tape, admits to starting a fire in some juniper bushes on the campus with a cigarette/matchbook delay device. He states that he is sorry and adamantly denies lighting any of the other suspicious fires in the area. Despite this, the tape shows that there were at least three other identical cigarette/matchbook delay incendiary devices on the table. Dale denies knowing anything about these items.

After a brief cut in the tape, the female is gone, and John Orr resumes the interview alone. During this second round of questioning, Investigator Orr is able to get Dale to admit to at least four other arsons on the campus, all using the delay incendiary devices on the table. John Orr begins to pursue Dale about some other arson fires that had been set to brush, trash, and an abandoned property in the neighborhood surrounding Dale's home. Dale acknowledges that he is aware of several fires that occurred near his home, and he states that he and his brother had been questioned by police several times over these fires. He again adamantly denies any involvement in these fires.

After viewing this tape, I realized that it was an absolute gold mine of information for arson investigators. First, it captures the unique circumstance of a notorious serial arsonist conducting an interview of another serial arsonist—fascinating! Second, it gives some insight into the character of John Orr, arson investigator. The tape is of average quality for the 1980s, and somehow Orr had gotten his name and title lettered into the production. A second item to note is that—in addition to the other investigative props he used, such as the incendiary devices, a map, and some photos (Orr makes great use of all of these items)—John Orr had placed his bright-yellow, arson-investigator fire helmet in the center of the table throughout the interview. The camera pans down to it on more than one occasion. This event had to have been an incredible power trip for the egotistical Orr.

During this amateurish production, the camera moves quite a bit, and for about a minute, it reveals the cadaver-thin face of the young man known as Dale. As soon as I saw the face, I recognized the man as Dale Frey. Frey was a convicted arsonist from the Glendale area and an arson suspect in several other cases. Even more interesting, seventeen years after the taping of this original confession, Dale Frey made another similar confession. On this later tape, he confessed to a different brushfire in the Glendale area. I viewed both tapes and was stunned by the consistency of the so-called "Weather Watcher Arsonist."

Dale Frey lives with his brother in the Lake View Terrace foothills near Tujunga Canyon in the Los Angeles basin. Dale Frey and his brother are really weird men, and they have both have been on the police/fire radar for over thirty years. John Orr and other arson investigators first began running into the pair in the early '80s and found them to be two codependent men, both with the appearance and mannerisms of mentally-impaired, special-needs people. In all honesty they have the odd look of possible in-breeding and speak in a hesitant and stilted manner; they always have the look of a "deer in the headlights." Orr noticed then, and LAFD investigators later confirmed, that a large number of unexplained nuisance fires had occurred near the street the Frey brothers lived on. Dale was arrested on an arson count by Orr back in 1984. He subsequently pled to a very reduced charge of recklessly setting a fire. In 1997 LAFD investigators linked them to a fire started in a vacant structure across the street from their own home, but they were unable to prosecute them for that act. In 2002, a jailhouse informant approached a sheriff's detective and told him that the Frey brothers started fires along the 210 Freeway in 1999. Indeed, the LAFD had had several unsolved brushfires along that stretch of road that year. Dale Frey was later contacted by sheriffs and fire department investigators after the statute of limitations had expired and admitted on tape to one brushfire on the 210 Freeway. LASD and LAFD arson investigators developed information in 2002 linking one or both of the Frey brothers to several unsolved brushfires in the 210 Freeway corridor and served a search warrant on their home. No evidence was found linking the pair to the most recent series and both brothers denied involvement. The search of their home turned up some other oddities and uncovered that the pair were engaged in some very obsessive behavior. Among their belongings were numerous photos capturing fire scenes during their very beginning stages, including fires developing in vacant structures. This would tend to indicate that the pair was at the fire scene at the very beginning of the fire, also implying that they may have lit the fires. The pair was known to despise transients, and they both voiced their opposition to vacant structures in their area. Detectives also found compiled records of weather reports in the Los Angeles basin dating back several years. The Frey brothers were self-professed "weather watchers" and had dutifully recorded detailed weather information every day of each year over the past several years. This information included temperatures, humidity, wind conditions, barometric pressures, and more, and each measure was taken and recorded several times a day. The brothers explained that this was just a hobby—not at all related to anything sinister.

While this sort of hobby on its own is at worst odd and may in fact have nothing to do with setting fires, Los Angeles arson investigators have noted a whole subtype of person obsessed with weather patterns, particularly during the dangerous red flag conditions. Investigator Dave Liske from the arson unit of LAFD has been maintaining an unofficial watch on persons involved in rabid weather-watching since about 2009, when a weather-watcher in the areas east of Los Angeles was suspected of setting a wildland fire at the height of a red flag warning. This weather-watcher's online posts and webpage depict him as a part-time weather-watcher, part-time fire and disaster photographer, and part-time arson-watch volunteer. By keeping their eyes on this guy, local investigators discovered that he belonged to a small clique of men with similar interests. Each of these odd guys was looked at by investigators, and each was found to be obsessed with weather, fire scenes, and the excitement surrounding both of these things. To date only one or two of these colorful characters has been linked to arson activity.

To date Dale Frey is a convicted arsonist and has admitted on tape to two different arson fires set seventeen years apart. His brother (purposely not named) has never been convicted of a crime. Both are believed to be longtime arsonists who have probably set small fires on-and-off for most of their lives.

Author, graduating Bemidji State University as *"Outstanding Student in Criminal Justice-1982"*

1st Lieutenant United States Marine Corps - 1985

FIRERAISERS, FREAKS, AND FIENDS

"Honor Graduate" of Los Angeles Sheriff's Academy,
Class #230- April 1986
L-R **Los Angeles Sheriff Sherman Block**, **Author**,
1st Lt. (now Colonel) **Paul O'leary** USMC

Narcotics Bureau 1996.
Holding high grade weed and a Tec-9
seized from a marijuana grow house.

Narcotics Bureau 1997. Stalking armed pot growers in mountains above Los Angeles.

Arson Explosives Detail (Bomb Squad) circa 2006

L-R Det. Mike Digby with author 2011. Planning investigation of $10 million church arson.

L-R Author with Det. Rick Velazquez- 2011

L-R Sgt. Derek Yoshino and **author-2010**.
Burning phosphorous military shells washed up ashore.

L-R Sgt. Mike Costleigh and **author-2010**.
Training in Israel with National Police.

L-R Author and **Det. Rob Harris- 2008.**

L-R Det. Dana Duncan and author with LASD rescue helicopter-2012

Det. Mike Cofield and accelerant K-9 "Pax"-2012. Mike is probably the most gifted investigator I have ever met.
(photo courtesy Mike Cofield)

Det. Mike Digby-2013. This is one guy you don't want chasing you. He just won't quit.
(photo courtesy Mike Digby)

Gary Gene Glazier- 2005. The most evil man I've ever met.
(author's case file)

Gary Glazier's incendiary device in his truck.
(author's case file)

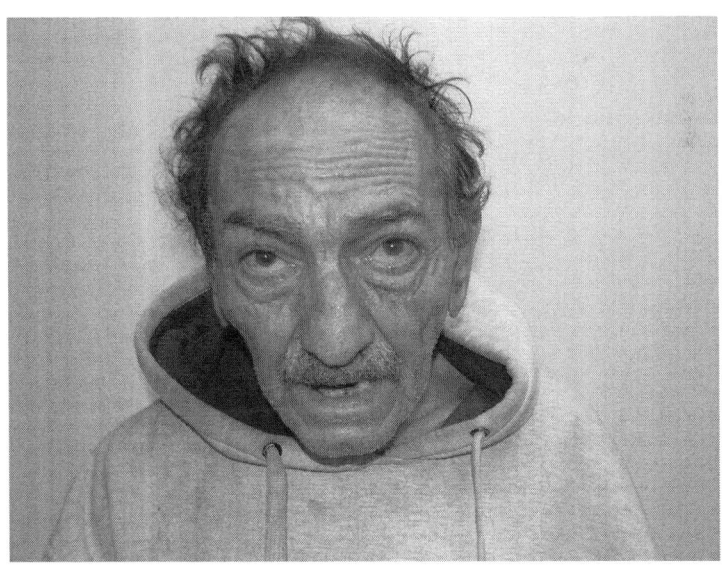

Charles Galante aka *"the God of Retributive Justice"*
Hollywood- 2009
(author's case file)

Doc Hallman aka "Lunatic on Lavender Lane"- 2009
(author's cae file)

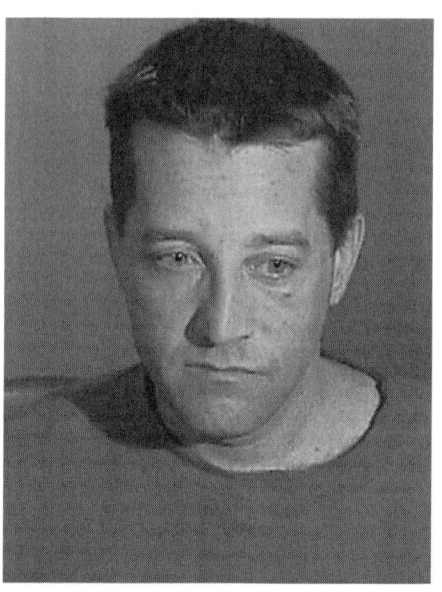

Tim Komonyi *"James Bond"* 2007
(author's case file)

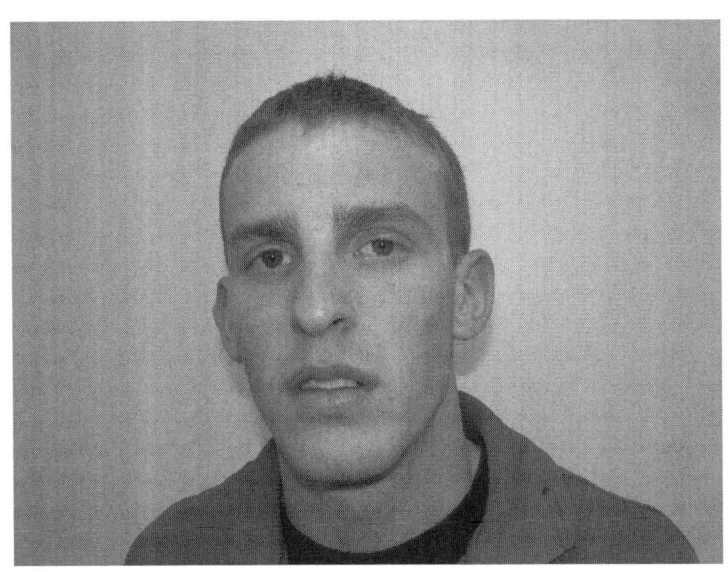

Tevin Gibson 2009
(author's case file)

Tevin's Demon-found in his bedroom *(author's case file)*

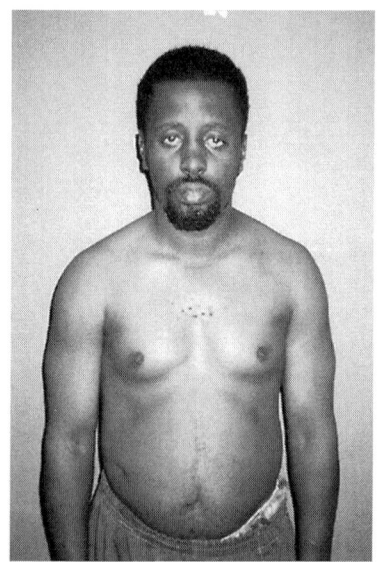

Nate the Nut Garner- 1998
(author's case file)

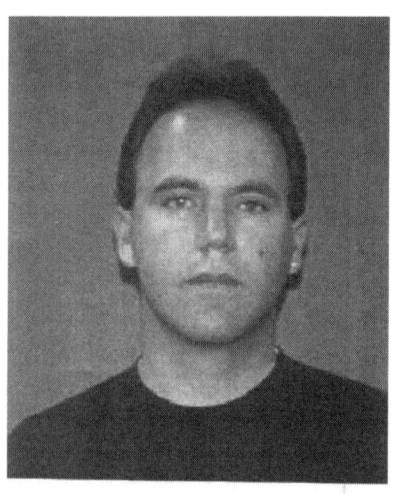

Johnny on the **Spot Piller-2001**
(author's case file)

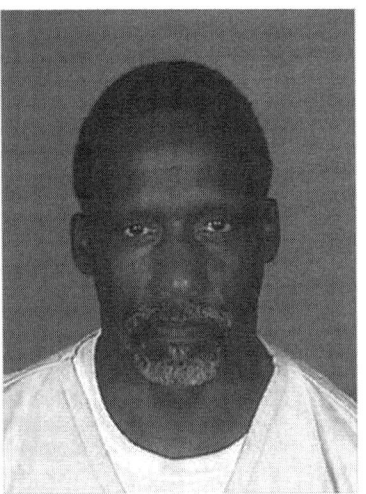

Tyrone Wilkerson *"Mission Man"*-2006
(author's case file)

Fake CalFire car owned by a *"Wannabe"* who posed as
Fire Captain for years

Suicide car bomb driven by Qi Jun Li- 2000
(courtesy Mike Cofield)

18 gallons gasoline, 20 lbs propane, 1 qt. charcoal starter,
1 gallon acetone and 12 cans "Aquanet" hair spray
(courtesy Mike Cofield)

Andrew Delgado – dog killer 2012 *(courtesy VCFD)*

Buddy the Bassett Hound *(courtesy VCFD)*

Buddy's streetside memorial *(courtesy VCFD)*

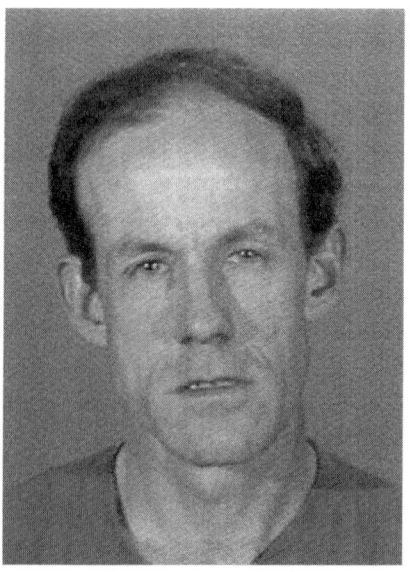

Dale Frey aka "Weather Watcher"- 2002
(author's case file)

Ben Cunha- firefighter serial arsonist- 2007
(courtesy of CalFire)

Det. Ed Nordskog 2012-instructing at an arson investigation school

L-R Los Angeles Sheriff Lee Baca and **Det. Ed Nordskog**
"International Arson Investigator of the Year"; "Law Enforcement Officer of the Year"-2004

Universal Studios Fire-2006
L-R Det. Jim Gonzales, Sgt. Craig Anderson, author as Lead Investigator, **Det. Rob Harris, Det. Irma Gonzales.** (Irma was injured and later retired due to a major explosion at this scene an hour after this photo was taken)

CHAPTER FOUR:
Wannabes and Weirdos

There is one phenomenon that is truly unique to the world of arson investigation and fire and police services as a whole. There are thousands of individuals who have dedicated their lives to being firefighters, police officers, investigators, and other public servants. They have uniforms, badges, paraphernalia, vehicles, union stickers, identification cards, and everything else needed to be professional firefighters or police officers. They spend hours a week in fire-service chat rooms and on fire-service websites, and they frequently monitor all calls for emergency services via scanners. Many have taken tens of thousands of firefighting action photos and miles of videotape capturing suppression activities. The only problem is that none of these men are actually firefighters or police officers. Many have made vague or half-hearted attempts to join agencies or at least become volunteers. Most have fared very poorly, and the agencies let them go for any number of reasons. Still, even after these rebukes and setbacks, most people functioning in this arson subtype continue to masquerade or pose as firefighters or cops.

Many notorious arsonists and other criminals have histories of obsession with the fire service, and many even attempt to become some sort of auxiliary firefighter. Serial arsonist Paul Keller had a lifelong fascination with the Seattle area fire departments, and he twice attempted to gain employment with them in the months prior to his final arson binge; he set seventy-six structure fires. The quality and quantity of his personal collection of firefighter gear and memorabilia reportedly eclipsed that of many large fire museums. Other notable serial arsonists, including Thomas Sweatt and David Berkowitz, also had long obsessions with firefighters and the fire service.

We in the business run into some variation of this type on a monthly basis, and this subtype shows at every single major fire event. Many are harmless aficionados who want to get a taste of the perceived excitement and danger that they believe occurs during every waking moment of an emergency responder's day. Some are very successful businessmen, doctors, or attorneys who always wanted to be first responders, but instead allowed their families to guide them toward more traditional (and lucrative) paths to success.

While most fire buffs and aficionados are somewhat embraced and accepted by the fire service as harmless, others have an obsessive, dark, and even illegal side to their activities. Some go so far as to actually start fires so that they can interject themselves into the scene in a heroic capacity. Others falsely assume heroic roles in major fire events, and give themselves fake titles and identities within a fire agency to try to impress their families or steal glory from the actual firefighters who are truly risking their lives.

You can find these guys associated with nearly every level of firefighting. They are usually quite well-known among firefighters and investigators in the area, and they are often tolerated with bemused acceptance. We in the business have many nicknames for these types of faux-heroes. They are known as "posers," "heroes," "closet commandos", "armchair warriors", "buffs," and our favorite, "wannabes."

During every major brushfire in the Southern California area, I will eventually get a phone call, tip, or message from a citizen, fire captain, or police officer who will spot or meet someone involved in bizarre activity around the fire. There are several documented cases of people actually owning their own fire engines and forming their own "department." Of course the subject always assigns himself as "Chief." They frequently post themselves in neighborhoods during large wildland fires and offer to protect people's homes. Other wannabe's drive around in retired paramedic trucks—or style their own vehicles to look very much like a fire department vehicle, complete with red paint and diamond plate trim—all the while wearing some form of firefighter uniform.

The Nordskog Syndrome

After several years of gathering tips about these oddball wannabes, I had accumulated a large folder full of them. In the folder I would place the original "tip," followed by a photo, a criminal history (if any) of the subject, a synopsis of the subject and his actions, and any tidbits that we had gleaned from interviews with him or an associate. This bulging folder evolved into a thick file and eventually a box full of these guys. We really could never come up with a name or title for this group and we just called them "wannabes and weirdos." My old partner Rob Harris became somewhat fascinated with these very colorful fellows and even investigated a few himself. One day, in a fit of mirth, Rob saw a reference to the malady known as Munchausen's Syndrome. Jumping on this phrase, he proclaimed our box full of wannabes and weirdos to have the recently-discovered condition known as "Nordskog Syndrome." As the keeper of the file, I claimed the honor of having this "syndrome" named after me. Rob wrote this title on the file and for a few days was contemplating getting an entry for it on Wikipedia. To this day, the guys in the office label all of these characters as having "Nordskog Syndrome."

On a recent large fire that burned for nearly six weeks in the mountains above Los Angeles, a narcotics sergeant called me to report a "person of interest." Due to the large number of illegal marijuana fields in the local mountains, the Los Angeles sheriff's has a dedicated narcotics team that literally looks and acts like a bunch of Navy Seals. The deputies wear camouflaged uniforms and carry semi-automatic rifles and packs full of water, food, radios, and supplies. They then set out into the rugged mountains to find and arrest the hundreds of marijuana growers that infest the remote corners of the Angeles National Forest. These are highly dangerous operations that on occasion break out into gunfights between the narcs and the heavily-armed pot growers. I had worked one of these units prior to joining the arson/bomb squad, and I still had several friends doing the same work. In 2007 there was a rash of arson fires in a particular canyon around the same time that a massive fire was burning several miles away. I had mentioned to the narcs operating in this area to keep a lookout for possible arson activity. The narcotics sergeant contacted me with the name and vehicle plate of a suspicious person they had come across. Just before sunset one evening, the narcs emerged from a darkened canyon onto a roadway, where they were waiting to be picked up by their ride home. They saw a car parked on the rural roadway and a lone male slunk low in the driver's seat. Still heavily camouflaged, they crept up on the car and got to the driver's window prior to being seen. They looked in and saw a forty-year-old white male masturbating as he stared off toward the west. The narcs shocked the hell out of the guy and pulled him from the car. There he sheepishly stood on the roadway, with his pants down and a half dozen completely camouflaged men staring at him while holding semi-automatic weapons. After identifying him as a local mechanic with just a minor criminal record, they began to question the man. He confessed that he just loved watching the distant brushfire. He said he had thought about it all day, and when he got off work, he drove up to the mountain road and just stared at the massive fire burning miles away. He said he wasn't bothering anyone and just need to release a little stress. The narcs uncomfortably noticed how excited the man got when he talked about the fire. You can bet that I have kept his information in my book of suspicious people ever since. The following stories are from some cases that are a tad more bizarre than the norm.

MICHAEL MCNEIL, UNITED STATES FOREST SERVICE, ET AL CALIFORNIA, 1996-2008

Author's Note: The following lengthy case history was compiled from the incident and police reports of the LASD, USFS, ATF, FBI, congressional investigators, civil attorneys, newspaper/Internet accounts, a book written about the Esperanza fire by author John N. Maclean, and from personal conversation with several federal agents, sheriff's detectives, jail investigators, fire chiefs, federal and state arson investigators, and Michael McNeil himself.

The arson investigation world was rocked to its core in 1991 with the arrest of highly regarded arson investigator and Glendale fire captain, John Orr. Seven years later, after many grueling court battles, Orr was convicted of four different arson series and the murders of four persons during the act of arson. Suspected of setting well over 2500 arson fires, John Orr was eventually sentenced to prison for life. He would become the most notorious serial arsonist of all time and forever represent a stain on the firefighting and arson-investigative community.

The Orr case finally brought to light the dark secret phenomenon known as the "firefighter arsonist." While this has been a known problem within the firefighting community for decades, its true scope has been minimized by fire officials for years.

Prior to his arrest, John Orr was a well-respected investigator and fire-investigation instructor. He routinely wrote and published papers in firefighting magazines and lectured often on the subject of serial arsonists and their delay devices. As a result of his work, it had become an accepted fact that serial arsonists usually employ some form of delay incendiary device that can often be found at the scene of their fires. In reality, and looking backward over the twenty years since Orr's arrest, very few serial arsonists actually use delay devices. In contrast to this, and probably as a result of John Orr's influence on the field, many serial arson offenders who have connections to firefighting do use delay incendiary devices. This may be a reflection on "learned behavior." Years later it seems that John Orr may have spawned a copycat or two.

In 1996, while John Orr was already convicted of four different arson series and sat in jail while he awaited trial on his murders, a strange character showed up at a rural fire department in Utah. Chief Louie Ford of the all-volunteer Smithsonian Fire Company of Apple Valley, Utah, was approached by a twenty-three-year-old man named Michael McNeil. McNeil, who lived with his young wife and grandfather in nearby Hurricane, was volunteering his services to the fire company. Chief Ford would later recall that his company was so rural and so small that they were desperate for any kind of help, so they immediately took on McNeil. The chief would admit that it was normal for agencies such as his to hire first and check backgrounds at a later date.

Chief Ford was immediately impressed; McNeil seemed highly intelligent, very gung ho, and even had a large amount of his own firefighting gear. He even had the look. McNeil wore his hair in a razor-sharp flattop, and even sported the standard firefighter short, brush mustache. McNeil told him that he had been trained in wildland firefighting at some agency in California. The chief would later recall that McNeil was always very vague about his past. McNeil also told the chief that it was his long-term goal to become a fire investigator. While the chief was impressed with McNeil's enthusiasm, he sensed that something was not exactly right with McNeil.

Even though McNeil only worked for Chief Ford for about three months, the chief easily recalled three odd incidents about McNeil when questioned over fifteen years later. Shortly after being hired, Ford recognized that McNeil possessed some degree of skill with electronics and computers. One day, they were asked to assist a local woman whose phone was malfunctioning and kept dialing 911. Ford asked McNeil to accompany him to the women's home. Soon, McNeil had the phone working properly, and Ford was impressed by McNeil's very inquisitive nature with the woman. He said it was obvious that McNeil would soon make a fine investigator, as he was able to converse easily with the woman and get a great deal of information from her. However, a few days after this incident, the chief was alarmed when McNeil approached him and showed him a large amount of the woman's personal information he had obtained through a computer search. He said McNeil was extremely gifted at pulling information off of computers. He warned McNeil to destroy the information, as it was none of their business.

A few weeks later, McNeil bragged that he had connections that would get the entire company some new fire boots at a greatly reduced price. The chief then gave McNeil a check from the company's fund, and McNeil promised to purchase the boots. Weeks later, when no boots had arrived, Chief Ford confronted McNeil, who said that he had given the check to his wife and she had spent it. When Ford threatened to report this to the police, the boots arrived within a few days. Later, the chief would realize that McNeil had attempted to steal from them.

The final suspicious event occurred about three months after McNeil joined them. One day, he rushed into the fire station and told everyone a brushfire was burning a mile or so away. They immediately thought this was odd, as they knew McNeil lived in the opposite direction and the terrain would not have allowed him to see the fire from the direction he drove in to the station from. When the company arrived at the several-acre brushfire, McNeil announced that he was going to the area of origin to look for an ignition device. The chief directed him to start fighting the blaze, as they were not even aware of the cause of the fire. McNeil ignored the chief and immediately marched to an area several yards into the burn pattern where he reached down and picked up a delay incendiary device. He proudly held it up and displayed it to the shocked chief and a fire investigator from a nearby jurisdiction. The device was a unique item made of a cigarette with matches affixed to it, all wrapped in a funnel of paper designed to catch the wind.

Almost immediately, the local investigator and Chief Ford realized that there was no way in the world that anyone could have found this thing so fast. Ford would admit that it was the only delay incendiary device anyone in his company would ever find in two decades. The other investigator told Chief Ford that it was obvious that McNeil had placed this device at the scene. After this fire, Chief Ford called McNeil into his office and asked him point-blank if he had lit the fire. McNeil never answered, but only hung his head as if guilty. Chief Ford immediately terminated him from the company, and McNeil left without denying his actions. That is the last time that Ford ever heard from McNeil.

Had Chief Ford had the luxury of conducting a background investigation into Michael McNeil, he would have discovered that McNeil had a significant criminal history at the time he volunteered. Records would show that a sixteen-year-old Mike McNeil had graduated from a law enforcement explorer course in the San Gabriel Valley of California in 1990. In January of 1993, at nineteen years of age, McNeil had been arrested in the San Gabriel Valley foothill town of Sierra Madre. The arresting charges were for receiving stolen property and burglary. Eight months later he was convicted of felony burglary and placed on three years of formal probation. Despite this, the United States Bureau of Land Management (BLM) gave him employment in the Barstow, California, area as a water tender operator for the fire service in May of 1995. He lasted just two months and was then hired by the

Apple Valley Fire Protection District to the position of reserve fire inspector. A month later, while he was still on felony probation for the 1993 burglary charge, McNeil was arrested by sheriff's deputies in the small desert town of Adelanto, California, for carrying a loaded firearm in a vehicle. Inexplicably, the convicted felon would never be charged for this offense, and the case was dropped by the local district attorney.

After leaving Utah, McNeil returned to Southern California to be near his parents in the San Gabriel Valley. By early 1997, he was a volunteer fire-prevention officer at the South Pasadena Fire Department. He brought with him his wife, Lori, and their two sons, Daniel and Paul. By any account, the marriage was not a good fit. In October of 1997, McNeil's wife, after one of their frequent arguments, threatened to leave him because he was unable to maintain employment. McNeil pulled out a 9mm pistol and threatened to kill her, their sons, and himself in a murder/suicide.

This threatening incident went unreported to police for a couple of months until Christmas Eve of 1997. That day Michael had been fired from his latest job, which he had held for exactly twenty-four hours. He showed up distraught at his wife's employer's Christmas party and they immediately got into a fight. When she refused to leave with him, he threatened to go home, get his gun, and kill her, the kids, her mother, and himself. This time Lori called the Arcadia Police Department. McNeil was arrested, and a loaded 9mm Ruger pistol was seized from him. He was charged with making terrorist threats and for being an ex-felon in possession of a firearm. At the time of his arrest, he identified himself as a reserve firefighter from the city of Alhambra. He even showed the officers an identification card proclaiming McNeil a reserve inspector from that agency. Seeing that the card looked homemade, the officers confirmed with Alhambra Fire Chief John Kabala that the card was phony and that McNeil had never been an employee with his agency. Arresting officers also noted that McNeil drove a bright red Jeep Cherokee with firefighting stickers affixed to it. Another interesting thing occurred during the booking process. While filling out a routine booking form that asked if the arrestee had ever been a police informant, McNeil claimed to be an active informant for the Federal Bureau of Investigation.

McNeil made bail from that event but did not stay quiet for very long. He and his wife continued their tumultuous relationship. Just two weeks later, on January 14, 1998, McNeil was again arrested by Arcadia Police. After an argument with his wife over the phone, McNeil had called 911 to report that she was attempting suicide at her work. When the cops responded to her work (a bowling alley), they found that all was normal and she was carrying out her duties. When later confronted by the officers, Michael McNeil admitted that he had made up the emergency because he was upset with her. He was arrested for falsely reporting an emergency. During that arrest and booking, he identified himself to officers as a US government firefighter.

Shortly after his release on bail for that latest offense, McNeil prudently admitted himself into the Las Encinas hospital for psychiatric evaluation and counseling.

In April of 1998, McNeil was convicted of the felony charge of terrorist threats. He was placed on formal probation for three years and given six months in jail. In August of 1998, the probation was revoked, and he was sentenced to state prison for two years. This was the second felony conviction for Michael McNeil. Based on a review of criminal justice records, it appears doubtful that McNeil ever served time in state prison as he should have. His records show that he was sentenced to state prison, but they do not reflect an official state prison number or a release or parole date. His first marriage to Lori collapsed at that time.

For the next decade, Michael McNeil continued on a similar path; he still had relationship problems, a suspicious work history, and the uncanny ability to avoid criminal prosecution. He applied with numerous fire agencies for work and later claimed affiliation with several, including the Riverside City FD, Utah Department of Natural Resources, Moreno Valley FD, and the Santa Monica Mountains Conservation Authority. All of these jobs were short-lived, and there were very few people who actually recalled knowing McNeil. His job title varied between fire prevention specialist, fire warden, fire specialist, and other equally vague titles.

McNeil was a convicted felon when he signed on with Utah's Rural Volunteer Fire Department in 1996. By 2001, he was a twice-convicted felon who also had documented domestic violence issues, multiple documented threats of murder and suicide, a shoddy work history, two alarming arrests involving firearms, and at least one admittance into a psychiatric hospital. Despite this dangerous history, which would have been obvious through even the barest of computer searches, McNeil was able to bypass a background investigation, and in 2001 he was hired as a firefighter for the United States Forest Service.

McNeil's first assignment with this federal agency was as a firefighter at a small station fifteen miles north of Castaic in the Angeles National Forest. He soon came to the attention of USFS Investigator Ron Huxman, the law enforcement specialist in the Angeles National Forest. Huxman later realized that the 2001 to 2002 fire seasons in the Angeles National Forest were the most active in terms of arson events in many decades. He said that soon after McNeil joined his team, he was notified by McNeil's peers at the station that they had serious concerns about this man. Huxman said that McNeil fancied himself a fire investigator and provided documentation professing his expertise in this field and several other fields of law enforcement. Somehow, McNeil had paperwork and certificates that showed he had attended several nationally known fire and investigation schools. During 2001 and 2002, Huxman was alarmed to note that McNeil had a suspicious knack for "discovering" arson fires and incendiary devices

Fireraisers, Freaks, And Fiends

in the forest. Investigator Huxman began an investigation into McNeil, but he could never legally link him to any of the arson fires in the area.

By 2003, under suspicion by Huxman and others, McNeil left the USFS and began working in the Palm Springs area as a fire patrol officer for the US Fish and Wildlife Service in the Cleveland National Forest. McNeil spent two years with this agency, and then left in 2005 under some sort of settlement. This agency has never revealed anything about McNeil's employment or mysterious dismissal.

In 2004, McNeil met a Russian* woman on the Internet, and they started a romance. He claimed to have arrived in her native Kazakhstan (former Soviet republic) in 2005 to pick her up and bring her to the States. Strangely, he allegedly called her from the airport in Kazakhstan to report that he got called back to the States because his mother was ill. The Russian woman, Yevgeniya, later came to believe that he had never made it to Kazakhstan at all and had fabricated the entire story. Yevgeniya eventually made it to the United States to meet McNeil in early 2006, and the pair married two months later. Yevgeniya had come to believe that McNeil was some sort of "agent" for the United States government.

Somehow government bureaucrats screwed up again and rehired McNeil into the forest service in late 2005. This time he was assigned to the San Bernardino forest as a fire prevention technician. Again, he was able to produce several official certificates and documents describing him as a graduate of several federal schools, including a school of fire investigation. McNeil was assigned to the Banning Pass fire station. Shortly, due to his insistence that he was an arson expert, McNeil was given the collateral duty of conducting cause-and-origin investigations for a handful of fires. He soon came under the suspicion of his supervisors, as he neglected to perform some of his assigned duties and again began "finding" suspicious fires before they were reported and "finding" incendiary delay devices when no one else was able to. The incendiary devices McNeil reported finding were designed by attaching wooden matches around cigarettes using tape or rubber bands. This was similar in design to a device used a decade earlier by John Orr. There was no record available to determine if any of these devices were sent to crime labs for forensic testing.

At some point, USFS Investigator Huxman realized that McNeil was back in the area and began his investigation into his activities anew. There were reports that McNeil had acted suspiciously at the scenes of a few arson fires. Some coworkers, who described him as "super gung ho", noted on at least two occasions that McNeil was parked near an arson fire when they arrived but did not participate in the suppression. When they confronted him about this odd fact, he denied being in the area, despite being seen by witnesses. On other occasions, they watched him as he attempted to conduct his assigned cause-and-origin investigation. Soon they realized that he did not appear to know how to conduct one. His supervisors realized that his reports were poorly written, grossly misspelled, and were not consistent with the work of other cause-and-origin experts. Investigator Huxman approached his supervisors and declared that he believed McNeil was starting fires and was not the arson investigator he proclaimed to be. After this, Huxman was surprised to receive an e-mail from McNeil containing the photos of several burned delay incendiary devices that McNeil claimed to have located at arson scenes. McNeil never produced the actual devices for forensic testing, and Huxman was well aware that the chances of an investigator finding one such device was extremely rare. The odds of McNeil finding several devices over a short period of time were beyond astronomical.

At this point, Huxman and his colleagues took the dramatic step of actually trying to follow McNeil with a mobile surveillance operation, and at some point they applied an electronic "bug" to his vehicle. The bug was in place for at least a month and positively cleared McNeil in at least nine of the suspicious Banning Pass fires. It proved that he was in another area when those fires were reported. As is the case during many fire investigations, it was impossible to keep this operation confidential, and McNeil soon realized he was being followed. He began a long game of cat and mouse with investigators and began driving and acting in a suspicious manner to see if he would be confronted. On more than one occasion, he ran into the brush as if to light a fire and was immediately confronted by investigators. He would then laugh and drive away. This game went on for weeks, with the frazzled investigators eventually giving up.

In the Banning Pass area, 2006 was an extremely active year for arson investigators. A lengthy report written by Forest Service Agent Diane Welton almost two years after the 2006 fire season, commented that the wild land arson fires in the Banning Pass area in 2006 "rocketed to levels rarely observed". The main topic of the report by Agent Welton was the forest service's belief that Mike McNeil was associated in some manner with a number of these suspicious and incendiary fires. Welton's report indicated that 90 percent of the suspicious fires occurred within Mike McNeil's designated fire patrol areas. Whether McNeil was involved or not, there was a lot of evidence pointing toward at least one and maybe two serial arsonists at work in the wild land of the area. By early spring, numerous arson fires had been found in the hills and grasslands of the area, and several delay incendiary devices had been located. At least two of these devices were processed at a crime lab months later and bore the DNA of the same offender. These two devices were cigarette/match devices known as "layover" devices. In the vernacular of the arson investigation world a layover style cigarette/match device is one where the matches are placed at a 90 degree angle to the cigarette. There are at least three variations of the layover device; one is where paper matches are pulled from a matchbook and placed at a 90 degree angle. The second is where paper matches are left in the matchbook and a cigarette is placed within the book at a 90 degree angle to the heads of the matches. A third variation is where wooden or kitchen matches are placed at a 90 degree angle over a cigarette. There are even subtle variations within these to include the covers being torn or partially torn off the matchbook, and the use of tape or rubber bands to secure the matches. The devices with measurable DNA on them appeared different than the ones previously "found" by McNeil. The McNeil devices were described as having matches placed around the cigarette as opposed to the layover style. The DNA results months later would identify Ray Oyler as at least one of the arsonists operating in the Banning Pass area.

Other fire personnel in the Banning Pass told author John Maclean several interesting details about Mike McNeil. Maclean documented the haunting specter of Mike McNeil during the intense death penalty trial of Raymond Oyler in his highly detailed book *The Esperanza Fire*. A hotshot firefighter named B.J. Scott commented that McNeil was fond of using the lights on his fire patrol vehicle to pull over and stop motorists like cops do. He also recalled that McNeil could find a small fire at times when none of the other engines in the area were able to locate it. The firefighter was quoted by author Maclean, "That kind of thing just doesn't happen. You don't find fires like that". This knack of finding a small fire or its origin when other professionals could not hearkened back to the days of John Orr and his "uncanny abilities".

By October of 2006, the McNeil arson investigation had fizzled with no results. However, Investigator Huxman did discover the shocking truth that McNeil had been a convicted felon twice over and had lied on his application when he was originally hired back in 2001. Despite this, it took several more months for the forest service to terminate his employment. Meanwhile, McNeil became connected to a catastrophic event. On a windy night in

FIRERAISERS, FREAKS, AND FIENDS

late October of 2006, a massive fast-moving brushfire erupted at the base of Mount San Jacinto in the Banning Pass area. Several hours later this fire exploded up the side of the mountain and claimed the lives of five USFS firefighters. This blaze, known as the "Esperanza Fire," resulted in the arrest and prosecution of a local mechanic named Raymond Oyler under the charges of arson and capital murder.

At the time of the fire, McNeil was not on duty. He and his wife, Yevgeniya, were living in Idyllwild, about thirty minutes from the origin of the Esperanza Fire. Oddly, this "super gung ho" firefighter/investigator would not go into work the next day. His wife later told investigators that McNeil was crying and acting very oddly that day. When they were later watching a press conference of the event together, McNeil commented that "If [he] told them what [he] knew, it would blow everybody away." She said that he acted strangely all day and appeared to feel guilty about the fire. Later that day, he told her he wanted to name their baby (who was due in four days) "Mark," after one of the deceased Esperanza firefighters. She thought it was really strange; as they both knew very well that she was due to have a baby girl. When interviewed nearly a year later by detectives about his connection to the Esperanza fire, McNeil told them he was at the hospital for the birth of his daughter when the fire was begun. His wife confirmed that this was a lie, as his daughter had been born four days after the start of the fire. From the start, USFS Investigator Ron Huxman believed that McNeil was a strong possible suspect in the Esperanza Fire.

In the months after the Esperanza Fire, McNeil's life started to unravel even further. He was transferred out of the Banning Pass area to the Lassen National Forest near the town of Susanville in Northern California. Unbelievably, while the forest service brass contemplated firing him because of the false claims on his application and his recently revealed criminal record, and with the knowledge that more than one investigator believed McNeil to be involved in a long string of arson fires, someone in the forest service decided to promote him to battalion chief. Huxman later expressed his frustration with the McNeil case to me in a personal conversation. He said he had passed on his suspicions to investigators in the Lassen National Forest. Almost immediately following his arrival in the area, the Lassen National Forest also began to experience an increase in arson fires. This went on for several months until, mercifully, someone in the forest service hierarchy decided to suspend McNeil pending dismissal. By June of 2008, steps were taken to officially fire him from the forest service.

The dates of this are a bit murky and there had been little clarification from the forest service. I learned from a couple civil attorneys in early 2013 that McNeil was still showing up at fire scenes as late as September 3, 2007, in the Susanville area. Those same attorneys are currently attempting to hold McNeil responsible for starting the large "Moonlight Fire" that took place that year and in that area during Labor Day weekend.

Over these same months, McNeil continued his pattern of marital issues. In April of 2007, McNeil's second wife, Yevgeniya, after some marital discord, returned to Kazakhstan with her new baby to visit her mother. She was gone for three months, and McNeil became convinced that she had begun hooking up with old boyfriends. When she returned to Susanville in July, the two began fighting and arguing constantly. In August of 2007, he got a restraining order against her, which he later recalled. In October, she got a restraining order against him, and he moved from Susanville back to San Gabriel to live with his parents.

On October 28 of 2007, just one year after the deaths of the five firefighters at Esperanza, an unknown suspect attacked the McNeil's home in San Gabriel with a Molotov cocktail firebomb while he and his parents slept. The device did minimal damage, and a wick was recovered. The Los Angeles Sheriff's Department's Arson unit was called in to investigate this attempted murder/

arson. McNeil identified himself as a federal firefighter who was off duty and on medical leave. He told investigators that he was going through a messy divorce and that he believed his wife and her ex-boyfriend, a Russian mobster, were trying to have him (McNeil) killed.

Two days later, in an attempt at reconciliation, McNeil moved back to Susanville to be with his wife and young daughter. Six weeks later, on December 15, he attacked his wife with a knife and was arrested for domestic abuse and assault with a deadly weapon. He again obtained bail and returned back to San Gabriel to live with his parents, while criminal charges were pending in Susanville.

Yet another odd occurrence in McNeil's life was that he attempted to get a restraining order or "Request to Stop Harassment" against a forest service supervisor named Dave Ramirez. This document was submitted by McNeil on November 13, 2007, in the Lassen Superior Court. The magistrate soundly denied the order the same day and cited insufficient evidence. This surely irritated McNeil even further, and his downward spiral continued.

In January of 2008, an ever-increasing series of bizarre events surrounding Michael McNeil began. On January 17, vandals attacked his parent's car, which was parked in front of their home, and scratched the words "Boom U Dead" on it. Five days later in an identical attack on the same vehicle, vandals scratched the words "Die Crazy Family" across the hood. Two days after that, unknown suspects attacked a different car owned by McNeil's father and attempted to destroy it through arson. The suspects placed a cloth wick into the gas tank of the Ford Mustang and poured gas over the trunk and fender. This fire caused only moderate damage to the car. Forensics would show that the wick in that attack was near identical to the wick of the Molotov cocktail used in the October attack. It was identified as a medical bandage frequently carried by paramedics. McNeil became insistent that these attacks were related to Russian mobsters who were sleeping with his ex-wife. LASD detectives found no evidence of Russian mob activity and found the whole series of events quite unbelievable. Detectives began to suspect that McNeil was nuts but were unable to conclusively rule out his wife and her friends in these incidents.

At some point the detectives from LASD conferred with investigators from the USFS and the ATF and realized that McNeil had a lengthy criminal past. They also came to believe that he was forging documents and qualifications. On March 22, 2008, ATF agents raided McNeil's parent's home and seized, among other things, his desktop computer. During a search of that item, they recovered templates and evidence that McNeil had forged dozens of certificates from federal schools. On May 21, the ATF served a second search warrant on McNeil's home, and they recovered a large number of phony badges, identification cards, and certificates for various schools. The certificates were extremely well-made forgeries that proclaimed McNeil to be a graduate of several highly specialized law-enforcement and fire-investigation courses. These included various ATF arson investigation courses, FBI bomb and explosion schools, FEMA arson training, and dozens more. A follow-up investigation would reveal that McNeil had never attended any of these schools. It became clear after the search that McNeil had significant computer skills, as he was able to make very authentic-looking forgeries.

During this ATF raid, agents also found a slew of phony letters from various government agencies to judges, McNeil's wife, and to the Los Angeles Sheriff's Department. All of these letters would later prove to be forged documents crafted on McNeil's computer. During this raid, ATF agents confronted McNeil, who in turn gave them a written admission that he was forging official documents. He was not arrested at that time.

Despite being under the scrutiny of both local and federal agencies in three different criminal investigations, McNeil stepped his activity up to new, unprecedented levels that would baffle investigators for weeks. He somehow obtained another computer and purchased an online service that would hide his computer address. With this he was able to route his computer offshore and he then began composing bizarre and threatening e-mail messages to numerous public officials. These e-mails appeared to come from a Russian web server and appeared to come directly from McNeil's Russian wife and her former boyfriend's computers. For several weeks in the summer of 2008, extremely threatening e-mails were sent from these two people to the LASD investigators. The e-mails contained confessions to the two arson crimes and vandalisms at McNeil's parent's home and dared the investigators to arrest them. There were also admissions by the pair that they were both illegal immigrants and dared the government to arrest and deport them.

When the LASD detectives failed to act on these, the messages turned violent. They began claiming that they were going to kill McNeil, his parents, his kids, the investigators, and various public officials, including the judge overseeing the Susanville assault by McNeil, Congresswoman Mary Bono of Palm Springs, and Los Angeles County Sheriff Lee Baca. The pair threatened murder, arson, bombings, and the detonation of a nuclear "dirty bomb" in the Los Angeles area. Over the several-week period that these e-mails were being sent to officials, McNeil sent e-mails from his own computer to various officials at various agencies, all complaining that his wife and her boyfriend were threatening him and declaring that the ATF and Los Angeles Sheriff's Department were ignoring him.

Although the threatening e-mails and web service looked legitimate, the rants and threats in them bore a familiar tone. When LASD and federal investigators compared them to other documents they knew to be written by McNeil, a notoriously poor speller and writer, they recognized the same words and phrases being routinely misspelled. A visit to his Russian wife confirmed that she did not even own a computer. She also advised investigators that Michael was an expert with computers and fancied himself a spy or secret agent.

Tiring of McNeil and his bizarre games, the LASD took a proactive approach with him. On July 31, 2008, they served yet another search warrant on his parent's home. They seized another computer from him and found an entire book full of forged federal documents and certificates. They also found body armor bearing phony federal agent patches and wording. McNeil had a large amount of other suspicious police paraphernalia. One interesting item was a very expensive-looking badge with McNeil's full name inscribed on it along with the title of fire warden. This badge also bore the name and insignia of the 2002 Olympic Games that had taken place in Salt Lake City. Several LASD investigators (including this author) had in fact been assigned as special bomb technicians at that event and had received nearly identical badges from the Olympic Committee. It appeared to us that McNeil had seen one of these real badges and somehow (no doubt through fake documentation) had one made for himself. This item was seized by investigators. McNeil also possessed a folder containing dozens of business cards from area fire officials. This folder also included various business cards, all bearing the name of Mike McNeil and presenting him as holding a variety of titles within several agencies. Many of these appeared to be fraudulent as well.

Another bit of information was gained via that search warrant. Detectives found a stack of letters of recommendation made out by various fire chiefs and officials on behalf of Michael McNeil. These letters stated that McNeil had worked for several very small fire agencies and that the chief was recommending McNeil as a model employee. A review of these letters showed that most appeared to have been written by the same person (probably McNeil). All appeared to be faked and written to give McNeil the appearance of a legitimate work history.

Another interesting item found did appear legitimate. Mike McNeil did receive basic law-enforcement training in 1990 while studying as a member of the San Gabriel Law Enforcement Explorer Academy. It was clear that from a very young age he had desired to work in law enforcement.

In an open first aid kit in his truck, detectives located bandages that were identical to the two "wicks" found at the arsons that had taken place the previous year at the McNeil's' home. Investigators concluded that McNeil, in an attempt to vilify his wife during a child-custody dispute, had staged these two incendiary attacks. Lastly, detectives found documentation and credit-card receipts showing that McNeil had purchased (with his own credit card) the unique computer program designed to hide his computer address. It was clear that he was sending all of the phony messages from his own computer. A later forensic inspection of his computer would confirm this fact. One last interesting item was found at the scene, and it provided great insight into McNeil's psyche. Despite being dismissed from his job, McNeil still possessed a federal government citation (ticket/infraction) book. On McNeil's kitchen table the lead detective found the cite book open, and in it was a brand new citation that had been written out that day by McNeil. The citation charged the lead detective with falsifying evidence and making false statements. McNeil had a habit of attacking the investigators who were after him.

This final warrant served at McNeil's home had two purposes. First, it recovered specific computer information investigators had not been aware of during the previous warrants. Secondly, it enabled the LASD, under the guise of searching McNeil's car, to secretly install a tracking device. This device was hidden and monitored in accordance with a court order. The officers noted that McNeil's personal license plate on his truck referred to the fire service: FDK9.

Within days, McNeil was at it again, and more threatening e-mails appeared at the sheriff's office and at the offices of some members of congress. This time, the LASD used computer forensics to trace back the web addresses. They found that these e-mails had come from a computer at a Kinkos within a couple miles of McNeil's home. They checked the tracker on his car and found that it had been at the same Kinkos when the e-mails were sent. The LASD, using a covert surveillance team and some undercover detectives, set up an elaborate "sting" operation on McNeil. The lead detective told McNeil via phone that the e-mails had ceased and that there was no evidence to link his wife to the threats. The detective knew this would infuriate McNeil, who desperately wanted someone to arrest his wife. The very next day, the surveillance team followed McNeil as he drove to the Kinkos and sat at a computer. Hidden cameras and several undercover detectives seated next to McNeil watched as he logged into a Russian website and began immediately sending a series of threatening e-mails to public officials. The entire incident was caught on camera and sheriff's detectives literally yanked McNeil out of his chair before he could erase or shutdown the website. On August 6, 2008, Michael McNeil was arrested by detectives from the Los Angeles Sheriff's Department. He was subsequently charged with making over thirty-five terrorist threats to public officials. His bail was set at $2.8 million. For the first time in his life, he was not able to make bail.

That same day two things occurred. First, directly after his arrest McNeil was brought to a polygraph examination, which he had agreed to undergo. Once inside the room and with the polygraph examiner, McNeil became extremely nervous and gave a videotaped confession, admitting to sending all of the threatening messages over the Internet. He denied, however, that he committed the staged arson attacks. He also did not take the polygraph exam. This was at least the third documented case in which McNeil confessed to police about his criminal activity. The second thing that happened that day was that, immediately after his arrest, McNeil began complaining of stress and chest pains. He was rushed to an emergency room by deputies, but the doctors advised that nothing was wrong with him and that he appeared to be faking his ailment. The last bit of interesting information that McNeil yielded that day was the password for the computer he had used to access the Russian server; he told investigators that is was "451451," which is the California penal code section for arson.

While McNeil languished in jail awaiting the results of three different cases against him (the Susanville assault against his wife, LASD arsons and terrorist threats, and the ATF forgery cases), other larger incidents were occurring. The Esperanza Fire suspect, Raymond Oyler, was on trial for his life. His attorneys, while admitting that Oyler was a serial arsonist, tried to prove that the Esperanza Fire was lit by the other suspected serial arsonist in the area. They had gotten wind of the Michael McNeil case.

In January, 2009, defense attorneys for Raymond Oyler tried to introduce evidence into the trial that a second serial arsonist (McNeil) had been at work in the very same area where the Esperanza Fire had occurred. The prosecution contested this evidence being presented to the Oyler jury, and a hearing was conducted by the trial judge to determine if this "evidence" was relevant to the case. Of course, this hearing was held out of the presence of the Oyler jury, but it was open to the public and heavily reported in the local media.

Defense attorneys called to the stand a formidable witness, recently retired United States Forest Service Investigator Ronald Huxman. During a lengthy hearing, Huxman related that he had been conducting a several-year-long investigation into a man named Michael McNeil. McNeil had been employed for several years by the forest service as a fire prevention technician. He had even been promoted to the rank of battalion chief. His duties included driving around in patrol vehicles looking for fires and looking for areas overgrown and ripe for massive fires.

Investigator Huxman related to the court that McNeil had a history of odd and bizarre behavior and had been moved to three different forests in the state of California over a several-year period. In each area that he moved into, a rash of arson fires had erupted. Delay incendiary devices were found at some of these sites. The delay incendiary devices were similar to the device found at the Esperanza Fire origin; a bundle of wooden matches held around a cigarette with a rubber band. This device was somewhat different from the "layover device" that Oyler's attorneys admitted that he favored.

Huxman told the court that he first noticed McNeil when he worked in the Angeles National Forest in the Los Angeles region. McNeil seemed to have a gift for "discovering" fires. Later, McNeil was transferred to the Banning Pass area near the origin of the Esperanza Fire. Shortly after his arrival, that area seemed to have a spate of suspicious and arson fires. At that time Huxman spoke to many supervisors, outlining his suspicions about McNeil. Huxman told of the botched surveillance operations, McNeil's cat-and-mouse games with investigators, the fact that McNeil seemed to find fires where others couldn't and his knack for finding delay incendiary devices. He admitted that he strongly suspected McNeil as a serial arsonist but also admitted that he had no tangible proof of that assertion. He also admitted that the tracking device on McNeil's vehicle excluded him as a suspect in at least nine fires and Oyler's DNA on devices excluded him as the suspect on at least two more. Despite all of this Huxman was firm in his belief that McNeil was a viable serial arson suspect, and was unaccounted for at the start of the Esperanza fire. At the end of a long day of testimony at the Oyler trial, Investigator Huxman and defense attorneys were stunned to hear the judge announce that he believed the state had proven that McNeil was not a suspect in the Oyler case. The judge would not let Huxman tell his story about McNeil to the Oyler jury citing the fact that McNeil had never been linked by evidence to any of the Banning Pass fires. While issuing his ruling, the judge acknowledged this about McNeil, "He was a bad seed everywhere he has been".

A few weeks later, Raymond Oyler was convicted of five counts of first-degree murder and nearly twenty counts of arson. He was sentenced to death. He was the first person in the United States to be sentenced to death for lighting a wildland arson fire.

McNeil closely monitored this trial from his jail cell in downtown Los Angeles. Despite his incarceration, Michael McNeil still would not go away quietly. In September of 2009, the largest brushfire in Los Angeles County's history raged for several weeks across the Angeles National Forest, destroying over 100,000 acres, hundreds of structures and homes, and killing two Los Angeles County firefighters. This fire, known as the "Station Fire," was determined to be an arson event by forest service investigators, and the murder/arson investigation was turned over to the Los Angeles Sheriff's Department. Several weeks into this massive manhunt for the arsonist, sheriff's homicide investigators received a letter and numerous phone calls from Mike McNeil, who was still being held at the county jail. McNeil demanded to speak to investigators, as he claimed to have "intimate knowledge" about who set the massive Station Fire.

This author, as part of the investigative task force into the Station Fire, accompanied Homicide Detective Todd Anderson to interview Michael McNeil. We listened to McNeil speak for almost two hours and concluded that he did not have any personal knowledge of the Station Fire. However, we were struck by how clever and sly he was, as he reiterated many events that had already been covered in the local media and was able to tell them in such a manner that would lead a person to believe that he in fact did have personal knowledge of the fire. McNeil came off as a very skilled con man, and he placed the blame for the Station Fire on the very investigator, Ron Huxman, who had been dogging him for years. Listening to him tell his story, it became evident that McNeil was an aficionado of John Orr, as he had intimate details and knowledge of Orr's fire-setting activities. During the interview, he made the outrageous claim that the series of suspicious fires surrounding him (McNeil) was in fact a cunning conspiracy concocted by the forest service to frame him, thereby covering up the fact that forest service arson investigators were in fact the serial arsonists. McNeil claimed that he was "on to the true arsonist" and that federal officials wanted to silence him. He also claimed to be a leading expert on arsonists and to have formed a Riverside arson task force. Both claims proved to be complete fabrications.

In the weeks following this interview, Michael McNeil sent letters to me and the homicide investigator asking to be used as an undercover informant in any number of operations inside the massive Los Angeles County Jail. He had been passing himself off as an Aryan white supremacist gang leader and had even conned jail officials into believing he was influential in the group. After having read his letters and listened to him in person, I am convinced that Michael McNeil is the ultimate poser or wannabe. He believes he is a secret agent or spy and has been playing con games with authorities for most of his adult life. He is an extremely skilled storyteller and comes off as very genuine and sincere. He is highly intelligent and manipulative. It completely explains how he was able to talk his way out of at least two firearms arrests over the years and probably talk his way out of going to prison. There is no doubt that McNeil produced some sort of forged badge or credentials and convinced authorities that he was on an undercover mission of some sort.

McNeil's assertions about the forest service and Inv. Ron Huxman were soon discredited. To me, McNeil seemed to display the traits and knowledge of a serial fire-setter, and it will be difficult for the courts to determine McNeil's involvement in any of the Oyler fires. On a final (and satisfying) note in this bizarre story, Michael McNeil pled guilty in early 2011 to numerous counts of making terrorist threats against public officials. He was sentenced to over nineteen years in state prison. He has adamantly denied involvement in any wildfire arsons or the two staged arsons at his home.

Despite his guilty pleas, McNeil would not just go away. Two months after he pled guilty, he attempted to withdraw his pleas. The courts, finally tired of him, reviewed his guilty pleas and concluded that they were legitimate and factual. He was finally ushered off to state prison in the summer of 2011. On his way out the door though, McNeil revealed yet another trick up his sleeve. He solicited and got permission from the courts to be assigned to the California Department of Corrections Inmate Fire Camps, where he wanted to work as an inmate firefighter. The judge who heard his request obviously was not familiar with his case history. She naively granted his request and advised the California Department of Corrections (CDC) to assign him per his wishes. LASD investigators finally got wind of this latest twist and went back to court to block this ludicrous assignment. The last thing any of us wanted to see was a suspected serial arsonist working in the wild land on an inmate fire crew. As of September, 2011, the issue was still up in the air.

As this book was going to print, I was contacted by a civil attorney in Sacramento who was leading a case to hold Mike McNeil responsible for a massive wildland fire in the Lassen National Forest on September 3, 2007. There is confusion over whether McNeil was actually employed or suspended from duties at the time, but what is clear is that he did respond to another fire in the same area that same day, which was well out of his patrol district. The attorney, Mr. Richard Linkert, informed me of another suspicious event that occurred that same day; McNeil's own landlord had a fire on his property. McNeil volunteered to investigate it and told the landlord that it was probably caused by an ember from the "Moonlight Fire," even though it was still many miles away and there were no other "spot" fires attributed to it. Mr. Linkert suspects that this fire may also have been set by McNeil. While I have no knowledge to support this, I cannot find any fault with the attorney's suspicions. Every incident surrounding Mike McNeil has an air of suspicion; they all seem staged. On that same day, McNeil was at or near four different wildland fires; three of these were considered suspicious in nature.

> **Author's note:* I am aware that Kazakhstan is a country separate and independent from Russia (both former Soviet republics) and that Yevgeniya is in fact ethnic Kazakh and not Russian. However, she is referred to as "Russian" by police reports, investigators and sometimes McNeil. According to some investigators, she has occasionally referred to herself in this manner for brevity's sake. It is not uncommon for people from the Ukraine, Latvia and sometimes Armenia who have immigrated to the Los Angeles area to refer to themselves generically as "Russian" as they are acutely aware that few Americans know of and understand the difference. With all apologies to the protocol officers at the State Department and to Yevgeniya, I have kept the phrase "Russian wife" in the story.

Investigator's Analysis:

This investigator's final assessment of Mike McNeil is that his life had been one large exaggeration, if not an out-and-out fraud. He desperately wanted to become a law enforcement official, but with his early criminal history, he was unable to penetrate those ranks. Like John Orr before him, he then entered the fire service and almost immediately began working in the field of fire investigation as a way to step toward the law-enforcement career he had always desired. The various detectives from the LASD, ATF, Cal Fire and the forest service who have had dealings with Michael McNeil all strongly believe him to have staged the arson and vandalism attacks at his home and to probably be a serial arsonist who may have lit dozens of wildland fires. He is a true spawn of John Orr.

Another aspect of McNeil that needs explanation is his fake persona. He and a few others I have run across in my career have convinced their loved ones, friends, families, and peers that they are secret agents, undercover cops, arson investigators, bomb technicians, or a member of an elite military group. At some point, the lies have become so ingrained and so elaborate that the liar starts to believe them himself. Such is the case with McNeil. I spoke to him for two hours, during which time he claimed to be one of the most gifted arson investigators in the country (much like John Orr), and I was quickly able to prove to myself that he knew virtually nothing about modern arson investigation. He was instead only spouting decades-old firemen's lore that he no doubt read in an old manual or bad novel. What fascinated me most about him was his chameleon personality. He was a small and not particularly physically able, but in jail he carried himself like a hardened convict. He had convinced jail staff that he was a high-level Aryan affiliate and had mimicked and copied the intense and intimidating mannerisms of many of these truly bad guys. He was housed in a section reserved for only the most dangerous of criminals and seemed to be getting along just fine. We were stunned because we were all well aware that this guy was a complete fraud. However, he was able to carry off this macabre masquerade in even the harshest of environments. He is truly gifted as a con man.

McNeil is extremely clever and intelligent. He was able to produce and manufacture the documentation necessary to back his lies and land employment at more than one federal agency. His danger level is off the spectrum and there is no doubt that, even while he sits in prison, he has convinced himself that he is on yet another "secret mission."

STEVE ROBLES, AKA "SPARKY THE FIRE DOG" SAN DIEGO COUNTY, 1997

Author's Note: Information on this case came from a Los Angeles Times *story by Timothy Hughes published on September 25, 2002; a* San Diego Union-Tribune *story written by Kristina Davis and pub-*

lished on November 17, 2007; and conversations and war stories shared by several Cal Fire investigators in 2010 and 2011.

Steve Robles lived in the inland Southern California town of Escondido. Escondido is about thirty miles east of the coastal town of Oceanside. A working class town, Escondido is nestled in the dry hills that run north and south along the 15 Freeway. The closest big city is San Diego, which is about thirty miles south along the freeway.

Growing up, Robles was the youngest of three brothers in a Mexican-American family. Although he was always a husky kid and able to defend himself, Robles was often the victim of merciless teasing and harassment at the hands of his classmates. This was mostly due to an undiagnosed learning disability, which in those days landed Robles in special classes for slow learners. He was later described by his mother as a very sensitive and shy boy who avoided confrontations. It was obvious that this disability and the relentless teasing had a profound effect on Robles, as his mother described that he began cutting himself with a razor blade during his teen years.

Robles started high school and began trying to attach himself to something, anything, that would give him purpose and status. He enrolled in police explorer and junior firefighter programs with local agencies. He was unable to finish either of these programs, but he did gain a lifelong fascination with the fire service. He also enrolled in a similar program at the nearby sprawling Camp Pendleton Marine Corps Base called the "Junior Pups." Robles completed this two-week introductory program into the United States Marine Corps.

After he graduated from high school, Robles wanted to follow his dream of becoming a wild land firefighter for the California Department of Forestry (now known as Cal Fire). Too young and inexperienced to gain full-time employment, Robles was able to sign on as a volunteer with a smaller local fire department known as the San Pasqual Volunteer Fire Department. Almost immediately he became enthralled with the job. He threw his entire being into the lifestyle of the fire house. Later, observers would point to him as an obvious hero wannabe.

Among his part-time duties with the fire agency was one somewhat less-than-desirable task. Robles was picked to tag along with Cal Fire firefighters at community events and schools dressed as the mascot "Sparky the Fire Dog." Robles went from school to school with the real firefighters, dressed in the costume, and handed out Smokey the Bear key chains. Despite this somewhat humiliating task, Robles loved the company of firefighters and soon began going along with the crew to fight the annual brushfires that plague the foothill areas of east San Diego County.

Family, friends, and coworkers would later tell investigators that Robles loved being a firefighter. He always carried photos of the fires he had been involved in fighting. Like a typical over-eager rookie, his uniform became his persona. He even had his 1996 state driver's license photo taken while he was wearing his firefighter work uniform. Robles worked, volunteered, studied, and sweated, all with every fiber of his being focused on becoming a full-time, paid, professional firefighter.

This dream would just not materialize for the eager young man. His struggles with learning came back to haunt him. No matter how hard he worked, he was unable to achieve adequate scores on the numerous tests assigned to him. After a period of failed tests, even the volunteer company had to let Robles go. He simply could not cut it as a firefighter. At twenty one years old, Steve Robles' only goal in life had come up short.

Completely heartbroken, Robles took a menial job as a shuttle driver for an Escondido car company. He still did not want to let go of his dream. He kept wondering if there was a way he could prove himself and convince Cal Fire, or even the forest service, that he would make an excellent wild land firefighter. As he sat in his shuttle van during his lunch breaks, eating and staring at the brush-covered hillsides surrounding his town, he thought of a way he could prove to people that he could help them. He'd remembered a scene from one of his favorite local television shows, a brief reality series called *LA Firefighters*. Robles knew what to do.

In early August of 1997, several fires broke out in San Diego County. On Friday, August 2, a fire started at one in the afternoon at the base of a steep, brush-covered slope in the Lake Wohlford area. Whipping winds and high temperatures pushed the fire, and it soon destroyed twenty-six structures and thirty vehicles while consuming over 1,100 acres. Among the losses were eleven homes. Nearly 530 firefighters arrived to fight this blaze. Among them were investigators from Cal Fire, who quickly descended upon the area of origin. Through hard work and a lot of luck, the investigators were able to locate a delay incendiary device known as a "layover device." This is most often created using a cigarette placed within a book of matches.

This fire nearly cost at least a couple of lives, as a forest-service water bomber, scooping water near Ramona, crashed into the San Vicente reservoir. Luckily, both crew members escaped with only minor injuries. The fire season was just getting under way, and soon San Diego County had many similar fires.

A fire in the hills immediately around Escondido soon followed. This 450-acre blaze was also classified as arson, as were seven other fires which occurred that summer in the same area of the county. During one of these events, a professional firefighter in the middle of a blaze came upon a young, husky man dressed in full firefighter brush gear trapped by flames in a neighborhood. The young man had been knocking on doors and trying to help people flee their homes. The pair hunkered down and barely survived the fire. After the danger passed, the two spoke, and the professional realized that the young man was not actually a firefighter. He got his name and noted that the man had left the area in a white Ford Bronco with the word "FIRE" drawn on it.

Fireraisers, Freaks, And Fiends

Cal Fire investigators would note that this was the same description given to them at an earlier arson fire in the area in which two citizens had noticed a man acting oddly by himself in the wildland area minutes before a brushfire broke out. They soon identified this man as former volunteer firefighter Steve Robles.

Southern California in late September of 1997 was disastrous as far as firefighters were concerned. It was a Santa Ana wind condition and blazes were raging simultaneously in several areas around the Los Angeles basin, sixty miles to the east in Banning, and again in San Diego County. At a quarter to one on a Wednesday afternoon, a fire broke out in the Del Rios area of San Diego County. Aided by the gale-force winds to the west, the fire quickly spread over 1,200 acres and was threatening many homes and structures. Soon 700 firefighters were battling the blaze

The same Cal Fire investigators from the previous month's fire arrived, and again they were lucky enough to locate the charred remains of another layover incendiary delay device. They were now convinced that they had a serial arsonist on their hands. A few very experienced arson investigators know that there is a significant difference between wild land serial arsonists and other serial arsonists. For one, most wildland serial arsonists use vehicles and set their fires during daylight hours, whereas urban serial offenders usually walk or ride bikes and caper in the darkness. Another trait of wildland arsonists, particularly those with any sort of firefighting or forest service in their backgrounds, is that they are more likely to use an incendiary delay device than any other type of arsonist. Investigators soon recognized this dangerous series as most likely having been committed by a firefighter arsonist.

The Cal Fire investigators immediately began a serious surveillance operation using mobile assets, fixed cameras, and tracking equipment. They focused their attention on likely areas of ignition and on the particular travels of Steve Robles.

Within just a month they had their man. A fire broke out in a rural canyon, and within minutes numerous agents and investigators stopped a surprised Robles nearby. He was arrested on the spot and driven to the Escondido Police Station for a detailed interview. Like many serial arson offenders, Robles quickly confessed to his deeds and gave investigators a meticulous account of his life, failures, disappointments, and arson activity.

Robles, a fairly pathetic criminal, told the investigators about being harassed as a child and about his numerous failures at the various organizations he so desperately wanted to be a part of. He seemed angry and distraught when he discussed finally making it onto a volunteer fire squad, only to be kicked off of it several months later. Robles described this as the lowest moment of his life, and he assured the investigator that his only goal in life was to be a firefighter so that he could serve his community and help people.

Robles went on to tell them that he had learned to build an incendiary delay device from the television show *LA Firefighters*. He had thought that if he started a few fires—and was seen warning people, helping them, and fighting the fire—that Cal Fire officials would recognize his value and give him another chance as a firefighter. Robles then admitted to setting his incendiary delay device and starting seven brushfires in the late summer and fall of 1997.

The investigators noted that he seemed to grow very excited as he told them the story of being trapped in one of his own fires. Even though he admitted that it was a very scary moment, he seemed to revel in all the excitement and danger. He said that in that moment, he finally felt like a hero.

Although officials believed Robles had lit several more large brushfires during his 1997 spree, they only charged him with the seven he admitted to. He was soon convicted by a jury, and a sentencing hearing was run in order to determine his danger level and risk of reoffending. His lawyer had a unique take on Robles. He argued that Robles was not a serious danger to society, because he was not in love with fire-setting but in love with firefighting. He argued for mental-health treatment and a lenient sentence. The court, noting the tremendous damage caused by these wildfires, imposed a fairly harsh sentence, giving Robles eighteen years in state prison.

The Steve Robles case did not end there. Like many arson cases before and since this one, the offender seldom serves any length of prison time for his offenses. This was true in Robles' case. Despite having been convicted on seven counts of arson, each one being considered a serious and violent felony in California, Robles was paroled after having served just half of that time. In May of 2007, Steve Robles walked out of prison a free man, with only an overworked parole officer to monitor him. Six months later, in the midst of yet another busy fire season in San Diego County, Robles asked to join the very rural and tiny Ranchita Volunteer Fire Department. His application, like many across the nation for volunteer firefighters, asked no questions about his criminal background. He simply told them he had no firefighting experience and wished to help. The Ranchita volunteer chief, Gary Loyd, was happy to receive any help at all and accepted his application that very day.

Two weeks later, the Ranchita crew was assisting numerous agencies in fighting the massive Witch Creek fire. After thirty straight hours on the fire line, the exhausted Ranchita crew, along with Steve Robles, was finally relieved. Later, Cal Fire investigators in the area stopped by their fire house, and one of them immediately recognized Robles. They informed the shocked chief that his newest volunteer was in fact a convicted serial arsonist. The news for the poor chief only got worse; days later he was informed that a volunteer in the medical services section in his area had also lied about her credentials. She had falsely claimed to be a registered nurse. The battered chief would lament to a local reporter, "All I can do is the best I can do…as a volunteer fire chief, I take who I can get to fight fires and protect the community."

Steve Robles did not come up as a suspect in any of the 2007 San Diego County fires, but due to a technical violation of his parole—not informing his parole officer of his volunteer work—he was sent back to prison on a violation.

Investigator's Analysis:

Arson investigators will note that Robles manifested many signature traits of the hero or recognition subtype of serial arsonist. He was mostly a loner, had a poor work and educational history, had a mental or emotional disability, was extremely passive and non confrontational, had been teased and bullied as a child, had made several (ineffectual) attempts at suicide, and had a deep fascination with the fire service, even though he was unable to pass the requirements of even their explorer or volunteer programs. He dreamed of being a hero, and he put thousands of people's lives in danger to fulfill those dreams. His fire-setting was a learned behavior, as it is with most serial arsonists, and he remained in the area after he lit the fire to revel in the excitement and place himself in a position to appear as a hero.

One of the most tragic aspects of this case is that from the onset it was clear that this troubled and challenged young man would never be a firefighter. I find it disturbing that a fire chief would hire him at all, or string him along as a volunteer, when it was clear that he could never pass the tests. Added to this were the humiliating circumstances they placed him in by having him dress up as a cartoon character, all with the intimation that it might help him make it as a real firefighter. This sort of behavior is nothing short of mental torture. More professional leadership would prevent people like Robles from hanging out at fire stations and fostering the false hope that they may someday make it in the profession. Fire chiefs have the responsibility of maintaining their fire stations as professional places of work and not club houses. Allowing non-members of an agency to hang out and loiter at fire stations just to be "in on the action" is an ongoing problem.

WILLIAM BROCK, PHONY FIREFIGHTER
SAN DIEGO COUNTY, 2007

Author's note: The following story comes from the case files of LASD Arson Sgt. Craig Anderson and this author's personal involvement in the case.

San Diego County area fire officials were very busy in the fall of 2007. The massive fires that devastated a large portion of the county caused widespread chaos. Thousands of people were forced from their upscale homes and sought refuge at Jack Murphy Stadium just east of downtown San Diego. Officials went into full panic mode in an attempt to avoid a repeat of the 2005 debacle at the Super Dome in New Orleans following Hurricane Katrina.

In the midst of dealing with several large and active brushfires and the evacuation of thousands of homeowners, fire and law enforcement officials were further plagued by at least two suspicious characters. The previous case of firefighter/serial arsonist Steve Robles took place that year. A second, similar event was the discovery of a man named William Brock.

On Wednesday, October 24, 2007, San Diego County sheriff's detectives were patrolling a residential area in the town of Fallbrook that had been evacuated as a brushfire swept through. The fire had passed, destroying or damaging dozens of homes, and hundreds of firefighters were actively involved in the "mopping up" operations of persistent hot spots. To prevent much feared looting and injuries to citizens, all fire areas had been ordered closed by law enforcement officials. This Fallbrook neighborhood was one of those closed areas.

As the detectives entered the area near Gumtree Lane and Live Oak Park, they found a solitary firefighter using a hose to extinguish a hot spot. The detectives immediately noted a few odd things about this event. There were no other firefighters or fire trucks in this neighborhood, and all firefighters work in teams, not alone. They also noted that the man was driving an old, beat-up, personal pickup truck, and his firefighting uniform appeared to be a hodgepodge of gear. They watched him for a few minutes and then decided to make contact with him.

The man identified himself as William Brock, a forty-four-year-old white male from the Los Angeles area. The cops saw that Brock had a personalized firefighter license plate on his vehicle, and the bed was half-filled with lengths of fire hose. He had on yellow brush pants and a blue tee shirt with the word "firefighter" printed on it. He had several other items of firefighting equipment, including a uniform shirt in his truck with his name on it and patches from the Morongo Valley Fire Department. His uniform also bore a metal firefighter badge. They also noticed that Brock had a side-handled police baton in his vehicle. Additionally, Brock was using a nearby hydrant to supply water to his hose and had even come to the scene equipped with a hydrant wrench.

The detectives began talking to him and realized quickly that he was giving very vague answers to their questions of where he worked and what strike team he was on. They made a call and were able to confirm that this man did not work at the small Morongo Valley Fire Department. They confronted him, and he changed his story about being a firefighter. He finally told them that he had been a reserve firefighter several years ago. The detectives ran his name in their computer and found that he was a convicted felon and was currently on probation for a narcotics violation. He had been convicted earlier in 2007 for transporting cocaine in the Los Angeles area.

The detectives arrested Brock for several charges, including possessing a dangerous weapon (police baton), impersonating a firefighter, unauthorized entry into a disaster area, and making false statements to a police officer. Shortly after his arrest, and after a detective drove to the Morongo Valley Fire Department, they confirmed that Brock had indeed been a volunteer with that department from 1995 until 2000. There was no record detailing why his service was terminated.

As part of the following investigation, San Diego detectives and arson investigators learned that Brock still possessed several items of firefighter gear at his home in the Los Angeles suburb of Rolling Hills Estates. They contacted arson investigator Sergeant Craig Anderson from the Los Angeles County Sheriff's to conduct an investigation into the activities of Brock. Sergeant Anderson developed information that led him to believe that Brock had stolen gear in his home and in a rented storage locker.

On November 2, 2007, Los Angeles area arson investigators led by Sergeant Anderson served a search warrant on the home and storage locker of William Brock. Brock was still in custody in San Diego at this time. In the bedroom of his home, investigators located three rifles and a shotgun, all of which are illegal for a convicted felon to possess. They also found firefighter's paraphernalia in the room, including calendars, firefighter identification cards, badges, and numerous newspaper articles concerning the recent large brushfires that had occurred throughout Southern California. The garage held several sections of fire hose. The investigators also discovered a makeshift laboratory used to grind, mix, sift, measure, weigh, and "cut" cocaine. Two bags containing cocaine were found within this room.

The investigators then drove to Brock's nearby storage locker. Within it they found several additional lengths of fire hose, numerous fake firefighter badges and identification cards, and an amount of other firefighter paraphernalia.

Within six weeks of his arrest, Brock admitted that he was not a firefighter and pled guilty to reduced weapon charges in this case. He was placed back on felony probation for five years.

John Alfred Piller III, aka "Johnny on the Spot"; aka "118 Freeway Arsonist"
Los Angeles and Ventura Counties, 2000

Author's Note: This case comes from the author's personal files and is written from a first person perspective. Additional information comes from case files of the LA City FD, LA County FD and the Ventura County FD. The names of many of the witnesses and victims are purposely omitted.

Captain John Haberek felt uneasy. The fifteen-year veteran of the Los Angeles County Fire Department never fancied himself a cop. He was a professional firefighter and a captain at one of the largest agencies in the world. He knew almost everything there was to know about firefighting, a teeny bit about arson and arsonists, and almost nothing about police work. However, for the past two days he couldn't help feeling a nagging in the back of his head that he needed to tell someone about his suspicions. On May 25, 2000, he picked up the phone at Fire Station 75 in the county area of Chatsworth and called the local sheriff's, who then referred him to the sheriff's arson and explosive detail. Yours truly (me) answered the phone that day and spoke to Captain Haberek.

Haberek immediately made excuses for bothering us with this minor matter and proceeded to tell me he felt silly for even calling us, as he was probably wrong about his suspicions. But he couldn't get over the feeling that he was on to a possible serial arsonist operating in his area. Captain Haberek told me that he and his crew had responded to four different brushfires in a very small area along the 118 Freeway in the Chatsworth area over the past week. He said that all the fires occurred along the north side of the roadway (westbound) and all were very minor in nature. Haberek said that none of the fires were related to a broken-down vehicle, and because it was still springtime, it seemed an odd time of year for these fires, which were much more common in the very dry and hot later summer and fall. Most suspiciously,

Fireraisers, Freaks, And Fiends

Captain Haberek wanted me to know that the same tow-truck driver was on scene at nearly every fire. The driver worked for the Freeway Service Patrol.

The Freeway Service Patrol is a service operated by the California transportation agency, known as Cal Trans, which is the state entity in charge of all California freeways. This service is a free towing service that routinely patrols sections of the freeway and renders immediate assistance to stranded motorists. This service is designed to keep the freeways clear of stalled vehicles and vulnerable citizens, trying to repair flats, push their cars off the roadway, or refill empty tanks in lanes of traffic. The tow trucks in this service are employed by private companies contracted by the state to patrol certain assigned sections of the freeway during the peak traffic hours during work days. The trucks are all painted a uniform white color, are clearly marked "FSP" for Freeway Service Patrol, and the drivers all wear distinctive blue uniforms. The driver's must adhere to strict standards and are not allowed at all to solicit or take payment or tips in any form. Their job is just to get stranded motorists off the freeway and to the nearest gas station or garage as soon as possible. The contract for the FSP is monitored and controlled by each local California Highway Patrol (CHP) main station.

I would later learn that a small company from a nearby town held the FSP contract for the 118 Freeway in Los Angeles County. The company was contracted to provide four tow trucks along the fifteen-mile route from the Interstate 5 freeway on the east to the Ventura County line in Chatsworth/Simi Valley on the west. The four trucks were to be in the patrol area from about six in the morning to ten in the morning and return again from two in the afternoon until about seven in the evening. This would cover the two main rush hours that occur each business day. The FSP did not work on the weekends.

The 118 Freeway passes mostly through the San Fernando Valley area of Los Angeles. It starts on the eastern end of the

San Fernando Valley and leaves the western end of the Valley at the Santa Susana Pass. The 118 continues westward over the pass into rural Ventura County and goes another twenty miles until it ends somewhere near the Reagan Presidential Library, hence its formal name, The Ronald Reagan Freeway. Due to some odd quirk in regulations, the police and fire responsibilities for that stretch of road are varied. The roadway itself is the responsibility of the CHP, who handle everything short of assault and murder. For most of its length in the valley, the LAPD patrols either side of the freeway, and its partner, the LA City Fire Department (LAFD) handles the firefighting. At the western end of the valley, however, is a very small stretch of unincorporated land policed by the Los Angeles County Sheriff's Department (LASD), with its sister agency the Los Angeles County Fire Department (LACoFD) handling the firefighting. To make things more confusing, this small piece of county land also borders on Ventura County on its west side, which is patrolled by the Ventura County Sheriff's Department (VCSD) and the Ventura County Fire Department (VCFD).

Captain Haberek's LACoFD Station 75 sits in that very small stretch of unincorporated land between the city of Los Angeles and Ventura County. It was within this small area that he noticed the four suspicious fires. This area, known as Box Canyon or Topanga, has a very colorful history. It is a rough and rugged canyon in the foothills of the Santa Susana Mountains, and it is partly city of Los Angeles, with homes and strip malls, and partly county, with small ranches and dark canyons. This is the same area notorious for being home to various cult groups over the past five or so decades. The odd "Fountain of the World" religious cult members were denizens of this canyon in the 1950s. They were led by a self-proclaimed relative of Christ and were often seen barefoot and wearing flowing white robes as they volunteered as firefighters at numerous brushfires and at a famous plane crash. Their group came to a quick end when two disgruntled members, agitated that the leader was having sex with their wives, blew up the leader, themselves, and half the cult, along with its headquarters, using a suicide vest made out of thirty sticks of dynamite. Ten years later, the notorious Manson Family would take up residence in the same area and terrorize the neighbors for years.

After speaking to Captain Haberek, I drove to Station 75 the next day to retrieve the information and interview the other captains. It didn't take long for me to get lost in the foothills and winding canyons. I was unable to find Station 75, but soon spotted a fire engine pulling into another station. As I got there, I realized that the engine and station were from the city of Los Angeles. Figuring that these guys would know where County Station 75 was located, I walked in to find a captain. As soon as I inquired, I learned that all the captains were in the briefing room being debriefed by a battalion chief about a possible serial arsonist in the area. I invited myself into the briefing and found the chief handing out a flyer entitled, "Confidential: Grass Fires along the 118 Freeway." I read the flyer and was stunned. The flyer described a series of thirteen suspicious grass fires in almost the exact area as the four I was investigating. I noted that this LA City fire area abutted the County 75 area.

I had a contact in LA City's arson unit and later met with senior investigators Dave Liske and John Little. They told me that they had recently had an unusually high number of fires directly alongside the freeway and that they were occurring during very specific time periods. The bulk of the fires were occurring at the peak of the evening rush hour, at about four thirty in the afternoon. Nobody had found any incendiary delay devices, and no witnesses had come forward. All of the fires were fairly small in size, and there had been almost no property damage. I asked them how the fires had been reported. They told me that at least half of the fires had been reported by one or the other of two drivers from the FSP. I showed them my information from

Captain Haberek, and we realized that it was the same two tow truck drivers in most of these fires.

We immediately formed an informal task force between the three of us. I also had close connections to investigators at the neighboring Ventura County Fire Department. I met with Arson Chief Mashburn, Investigator Hall, and Investigator Saqui of the VCFD. They too had suffered a recent unexplained spate of suspicious fires along the 118 Freeway in their county. They had documented ten fires in the past few months, nearly all occurring between the hours of two in the afternoon and six in the evening. Chief Mashburn checked his notes and found that at least one of the fires had been spotted and reported by an FSP driver by the name of John Piller. This surprised me, as the fire that Chief Mashburn was referring to was several miles into Ventura County and out of the patrolling area for the FSP. How did it happen that this driver was able to find and report the fire? We asked VCFD to join our informal task force on this case.

The first thing we did was to reexamine all of the fires. After several days of looking at the records and response reports, we found that one or two of the fires on our lists were duplicated. We also found that one or two were directly related to a broken-down vehicle. In the end we whittled down the list of suspicious fires to twenty-seven—all of which occurred along the 118 Freeway and between the driving hours of two and six thirty in the afternoon on week days. Almost half a dozen of these fires were reported by a FSP driver to the highway patrol. This driver's name was John Piller, and was known to the firefighters and CHP officers as "Johnny on the spot". All of the fires occurred in short dry grass and brush, and no incendiary devices of any sort were located.

While the other investigators were reinvestigating the fires, I took on the job of looking at potential suspects. The first group I decided to examine was the four tow-truck drivers assigned to this section of the freeway. All were easy to examine, as the CHP had their personal identifications written into the contract. I contacted the CHP Cal Trans coordinator in the region and learned some very interesting things. First, I was able to get the drivers' schedules for the past several months. From this I was able to tell who worked which days. I would later match this schedule up to the list of fires. Secondly, I learned that the tow trucks used for this service already had tracking devices installed within them, so that the CHP could ensure the drivers were in their assigned patrol districts at the assigned hours. Each truck had a transponder device wired into the battery of the vehicle. These were set to register every few minutes and give the locations of the tow trucks. The final item I learned from the CHP was that more than one of their officers had already picked out one of the FSP drivers as an oddball. His name was John Alfred Piller. This was the same person that VCFD Chief Mashburn had documented weeks earlier as having reported an arson fire deep into Ventura County and several miles out of his tow-truck beat. He also discovered and reported a large number of the fires.

Three different CHP officers who worked the area reported several bizarre things about Piller to me. All reported him as a typical wannabe cop. They said he responded everywhere, even to nonemergency events, with the rotating lights of his tow truck on. They said he presented himself as extremely neat, tidy, and meticulous in appearance and that they were all amazed to see a tow-truck driver who habitually spit-polished his boots, wore a military-crisp uniform, and constantly cleaned and polished his tow truck. They said Piller was also extremely officious in his duties and was a bit overzealous when called to direct traffic or place cones around an accident scene.

One CHP officer told me that he had threatened Piller with arrest several weeks before when he saw Piller fake getting hit by a car at an accident scene. The officer explained that Piller had assisted him at a traffic collision scene and that Piller was putting out traffic cones and directing the jammed traffic around the cones. This CHP officer had heard Piller yell at citizens several times before for driving too fast at accident scenes, and on this particular day, he was doing it again. At one point the officer heard Piller yelling at a citizen who was passing the scene at about three miles per hour. As the citizen passed, he saw Piller get brushed by the driver's side mirror. The officer watched as Piller threw himself violently to the pavement and began screaming as if severely injured. The driver, who was an elderly gentleman, exited the car, and Piller began screaming that he had run him over. The CHP officer, a very large and intimidating guy, stormed over to a writhing Piller and told him to get his ass off the street and leave the scene or he would arrest him for staging an accident. He reported that Piller leapt to his feet, sprinted to his tow truck, and sped off without so much as a limp. That officer described Piller as a weirdo but all-in-all a fairly harmless geek whom everyone made fun of. The CHP did not have a written record of that staged fall, but they did have a complaint on file about Piller from one of their dispatchers. What the CHP was not aware of was that shortly after this staged accident, Piller had driven himself over to LAFD paramedics to report being hit by a car. During a search of his home a year later, we found the original medical assessment written by paramedics on January 25, 2000, for this incident. This was among dozens of similar documents linking Piller to a myriad of accidents, emergency room visits, and civil litigation.

I later contacted the female CHP dispatcher and interviewed her at her home. She said she was married to a CHP officer and that she had known John Piller for nearly a year. She said that he saw her at work one day and had come to flirt with her over the months, despite the fact that both he and she were married. She reported that he started out fairly nice and would bring her a drink or treat at the end of his shift. When he began to get a little more flirtatious, she told him she was married and he needed to stop. Piller persisted with this unwanted behavior for weeks until she made an official complaint and he was ordered to stay away from her. She said that when she did talk to Piller, he frequently told her what she thought were really exaggerated stories about his duties and the calls he went on in his truck. She said that he always fancied himself to be on a dangerous assignment, as if he were a cop. At first he was just a harmless flirt, but after a while she sensed an odd danger about him and was afraid of him. She thought he was a stalker of sorts.

These first inquiries about Piller brought his name to the forefront of the case. I conducted a background check on him and noted that he had applied to both the California Highway Patrol and the Los Angeles Sheriff's Department for employment. He was turned down for both jobs. He also had held a job as a security guard at a local college. Turning to additional law enforcement networks, I found a bizarre item. John Piller had been involved in a very large number of car accidents within the past few years. Additionally, he and his wife, Tina, reported that they had been the victims of several crimes, including some very serious offenses. I knew from past training in the serial arson field that many serial arsonists are notoriously poor drivers and that many are also witnesses or victims of crimes much more frequently than the average citizen.

Through this joint investigation, our task force had soon eliminated the other three tow-truck drivers as suspects in the arson series. We compared Piller's work records with the dates of the fires and found him to be on duty on the dates of all but two of these fires. He actually was the reporting person on no fewer than five of the fires, and he was one of the two suspects the firefighters had reported as acting bizarre. We started to focus on John Piller as a serious suspect in our case.

Based on the story told to me about Piller faking an injury and the large number of car accidents on his record, I believed he may have a history of insurance fraud. I contacted agents from the National Insurance Crime Bureau (NICB) and inquired about their records of John Piller. They soon gave me a ream of reports on Piller and his wife. After I reviewed these documents, I found some really bizarre incidents. John Piller had been in at least two-dozen reported vehicle accidents within the past three years. Astoundingly, he was never found at fault in any of these collisions. This was an extraordinary number of car accidents for a person who drove a truck as their profession. Other interesting tidbits in the insurance files showed that Piller and his wife were reported as victims of a few industrial injuries. They both reported numerous slip-and-fall injuries and had often sought emergency-room treatment. Piller's own insurance carrier, State Farm, had even tagged a few minor claims by him as somewhat suspicious. Based on the inordinate number of insurance claims for such a young couple, along with the large number of car accidents and police reports associated with the pair, I believed that they were possibly involved in some sort of staged accident or fraud scheme. I ordered copies of all the reports to review. This took several weeks to accomplish, but I was soon able to put together a bit of a profile on the life of John Piller.

As part of my investigation, I drove out to the Pillers' home with my partner. We saw that it was in a small neighborhood of similar tract homes in a rural enclave called Lake Elizabeth. This small neighborhood was twenty miles from the nearest sizable town (Palmdale), and practically everyone in the town knew each other. The Lake Elizabeth area was in the foothills fifty miles north of Los Angeles. The area was surrounded by steep hills covered in dry grass and ten-foot-high brush. In the year 2000, this area was also in the midst of a several-years-long spree of suspicious brushfires.

The Piller home, which was very ordinary in appearance, stood out immediately to me for two reasons. The first was that the wood fence which shielded the entire west side of the home had fire damage along its entirety. It bordered on a dirt field with no brush, so I was surprised to see that a fire had occurred along it at some point. The second fact that made the home stand out so much was that someone had filled the section of the street directly in front of the Piller's home with "Cal dots" and reflective highway markers. Cal dots are the circular raised markers placed on the highways in California to mark lanes. When you drift in your traffic lane, you are forced to drive over the Cal dots, and they are loud, bumpy, and tend to alert a drowsy or drifting driver that they need to pay attention. I had never seen these items on a residential street. I also saw that someone had erected two yellow signs stating "Slow" and "Children at Play" on the street on either side of Pillers' home. This was the only home in the area with such safety devices on the street in front of it.

A neighbor behind Piller's home was in his garage. We spoke to the burly mechanic and inquired about his neighbor (Piller). He immediately said, "Oh, the firefighter?" He then told us that he had known the Piller family as neighbors for a few years and found them to be friendly but very reclusive. He knew that Piller was a firefighter/paramedic because he always wore a hat and windbreaker resembling the Los Angeles County Fire Department's paramedic uniform. He usually wore dark blue uniform pants and highly polished black boots. The neighbor did mention that it was odd that on some days he noticed the hat said "LAFD" for the Los Angeles City Fire Department, while on other occasions it said "LACoFD" for the Los Angeles County Fire Department. He said that Piller frequently carried what looked like a paramedic rescue bag as he got into his truck. The neighbor also knew that Piller's small Mazda pickup was painted red, had emergency-style lights on it, and bore a "Los Angeles City" fire sticker on its rear bumper. He also said that the license plate frame indicated he was a firefighter. When we told him that Piller was not a firefighter but was in fact a tow-truck driver, the neighbor believed that we were mistaken.

We then asked the neighbor about the burned fence. He told us that it was a weird story, but that the fire had happened over a year before in March of 1999. He then called over another neighbor, and the two of them told us the story. They said that one very cold and windy night, someone noticed a large fire burning around midnight. The fire was in the very back corner of Piller's yard, where the fence abutted his northern neighbor. All of the neighbors began yelling and rushed outside of their homes to fight the fire. The only ones not in view were the Pillers, even though the fire started in their yard. Ever fearful of wildfires in their rural neighborhood, the three neighbors aggressively attacked the fire. They noticed that the fire was in a large pile of dry tumbleweeds surrounding a 500-gallon propane tank in the Pillers' yard.

After the fire was mostly controlled, one of the neighbors ran to the front of the Piller home to see if he could arouse them. He was shocked to see the entire family in the car in the driveway, with the wife, Tina Piller, holding a stack of photo albums and what looked like her wedding dress. The neighbor saw John Piller putting packed suitcases into the car. He told the neighbor he wanted to leave before the propane tank blew. The neighbors were stunned that this "firefighter" had done nothing to stop the fire and appeared to have his car fully packed in the middle of the night. They reported these odd actions to the fire captain and a sheriff's deputy.

Soon Engine #78 of the Los Angeles County Fire Department arrived along with the local area sheriff's deputy, Bill Axelrod. I later interviewed both Deputy Axelrod and Fire Captain Bill Glancy. Captain Glancy said the fire was suspicious in nature, but he had neglected to call his arson investigators due to the rural location and lack of serious damage. He said it was suspicious because the large amount of tumbleweeds that had burned appeared to have been placed into the area directly around the propane tank and ignited on purpose. He said the winds in the area normally stacked tumbleweeds along the west side of fences. In this case he believed that someone had taken the tumbleweeds from the west side of Piller's fence and thrown them over the fence and onto the propane tank. He said there was no accidental source of ignition in the area, and he believed that someone had lit the weeds on fire with a lighter. Glancy said he questioned Piller, who told him that someone must have been trying to get him. He said that Piller seemed evasive and didn't want to fully cooperate. He also said he knew who Piller was as he occasionally stopped by the fire station to complain about some small thing or another.

Deputy Axelrod was the resident deputy living in that neighborhood. He said he knew Piller well and regarding him as a real oddball. Axelrod said that Piller always called him to complain about small, insignificant things. He said that Piller's biggest complaint was the constant speeding of vehicles up and down his street. Axelrod said that he thought Piller was a nut, as no more than twenty cars a day ever traveled up and down the street. He said he was aware that Piller personally glued the reflectors and Cal dots onto the street in front of his home to deter speeders. He was also aware that Piller had erected the caution signs in front of his home. At one point, Piller had tried to get the county to erect speed bumps on either side of his property in order to slow down cars in the area. Deputy Axelrod said that the entire thing was weird, because there were never any speeders in the area, and Piller and his wife never let their kids play outside anyway. He said they were also obsessed about their kids being kidnapped, and they frequently reported suspicious strangers lurking about their street.

Deputy Axelrod said that he had confronted Piller after the fence fire. He told Piller that the neighbors suspected him of having set the fire in an attempt to make a propane explosion. He said that he was going to keep an eye on Piller for a while. Axelrod said that Piller seemed to act very guilty after the fire and didn't bother the deputy for several months. Both Deputy Axelrod and Captain Glancy believed that Piller had probably lit the fire on purpose, but neither one of them found incriminating evidence, and neither one of them forwarded this information to investigators. Based on the statements of the neighbors, the firefighters, and the sheriff's deputy, I reopened this incident and classified it as arson. This was another arson fire now associated with John Piller.

By now the task force was beginning to plan a detailed surveillance operation against John Piller. Meanwhile, the police and insurance reports related to him started to pour into my office. By reviewing these reports, I found that John Piller had made over a dozen insurance claims in the past year for vehicle breakdowns. Each time his vehicle broke down, he would make out a claim to his State Farm agent for roadside assistance reimbursement. The totals were always between eighty and two-hundred dollars. I noted that he always used a tow company that he was currently employed with to provide the tow. I couldn't believe a tow company would actually charge one of its own employees for a tow. I drove to one of Piller's former employers and asked about several tows that John had asked for. The tow operator immediately told me that Piller was a troublemaker and a real weirdo. The owner said he would never charge his employees to tow their own cars. He reviewed the towing bills Piller had submitted to State Farm and proclaimed nearly all of them to be fraudulent. He said that Piller appeared to have greatly enhanced the dollar amount on the tows to make more money from State Farm. Additionally, Piller never paid any money on those tows because he was never charged for them. The boss believed that none of these tows had really occurred. Piller's boss went on to say that Piller had worked for him and nearly every other tow company in northern Los Angeles County. He said Piller was extremely litigious and sued or threatened to sue most of his past employers. He said he had fired Piller after Piller was routinely late for work or unavailable to take calls. In turn, Piller scoured the state manual for tow trucks and found several obscure codes with which to sue his employers.

I told the tow company owner that I was investigating fires related to Piller, and he started laughing. He said it was an ongoing rumor that John Piller had bragged about setting an arson fire at his home for insurance money. Further, the owner was aware that Piller had had more than one fire in rental cars he had driven. Lastly, the owner was aware that Piller was on duty one night alone in a nearby tow yard when a suspicious fire broke out in a car that had been in the yard for over a month. All the other drivers believed that Piller had set that fire for some unknown reason. After speaking to the owner of the tow yard, and a few more people he referred to me, I realized that the number of fires associated with John Piller was growing.

However, the fires were not the only disturbing trend emerging around Piller; his former boss also told me that Piller was found to behave inappropriately toward female motorists. This owner reported that, on more than one occasion, female customers had called him to report that Piller had been acting odd toward them. When they first met Piller, he was extremely kind, helpful, and pleasant, and he went beyond the call of duty to assist them with their vehicle problem. However, some of the women said that Piller practically begged them to write a letter of commendation to his boss for his actions. Additionally, on more than one occasion, he showed up at the woman's home days or weeks after the towing incident to "check on them." These women said that Piller had never threatened them, but his behavior seemed strange at the very least. On more than one occasion, the women had to tell him bluntly to leave them alone. This owner then referred me to no fewer than three other companies, all of whom had similar anecdotes about John Piller.

As of this point, I had a provable case of insurance fraud against John Piller. I was able to confirm that he had indeed filed numerous small insurance claims and had submitted fraudulent towing bills as part of that process. These alone were worth several felonies, but all-in-all they didn't amount to more than a couple thousand dollars in losses; they really weren't much of a case in California. Still, it was enough to prove that John Piller was engaged in ongoing criminal activity.

When I looked deeper into his insurance claims, I saw that the vast majority were for car accidents. Each time he got into an accident, Piller would lease a rental car while his vehicle was being repaired. Sure enough, there was a record of two suspicious fires occurring in the rental cars that John Piller had driven. A check of the rental companies showed that they had not referred these cases for investigation but did consider them highly suspicious. In both cases, in the days prior to the fires, Piller had come to the rental company and asked for a free upgrade on his rental, as he believed the brakes were wearing out. Since this is a somewhat common scam used by people to get freebies from rental companies, the company checked out the cars and found them to be working fine. They refused to give the visibly angry Piller a free upgrade as he demanded. In both cases, John Piller drove the cars away. Later, these same cars had mysteriously started on fire on remote canyon roads—of course, there were no witnesses. Piller was the only occupant and reported that he had barely escaped the burning car.

Suspecting that Piller was staging incidents, I began examining all of his car accidents. Several occurred on rural roadways with just one other witness. Piller claimed to have gotten into the accidents by swerving to evade both deer and coyotes, while the other drivers who stood witness to these incidents didn't see these alleged animals. Many more accidents occurred in which people rear-ended Piller as he was driving in a tow truck or personal car. I read the reports and noticed some peculiar patterns. I began contacting some of the other drivers who had been involved in the accidents. All of them had vaguely similar stories. The most common story was they were driving alone when a vehicle stopped quickly in front of them, causing them to collide into the back of it. The driver (Piller) always jumped out carrying some sort of medical bag and immediately began to inquire about their welfare. He often began minor treatment for any injuries. He usually told the other party that he had to brake for some unseen animal or other motorist. In none of the cases was there a witness that could describe an animal or other offending motorist. Most of these victims described Piller as either an off-duty firefighter or possibly a police detective working undercover. On more than one occasion, he showed the other driver some form of badge and seemed to speak in a police vernacular. He seemed to know or be friendly with all of the arriving highway patrol or sheriff's deputies. Most importantly, all of the motorists had the same feeling that the accidents were not their fault, but that Piller had convinced them and the responding police officers that it was. Even after all this, most of the motorists described Piller as extremely friendly, helpful, and concerned about their welfare.

    I showed many of these reports to both a local highway patrol and a sheriff's traffic collision investigator. Both of these men actually knew Piller and knew him to be a geek. They said he was an overly officious tow-truck driver who regarded himself to be a self-taught expert on traffic collisions and driving. Both investigators were shocked to learn that Piller had been involved in so many collisions and never found at fault. They agreed that he appeared to be somehow staging or manipulating the incidents. They did admit that what Piller appeared to be doing was so out of the norm and weird that it would be difficult to prove that he purposely staged these collisions.

    As all this odd evidence kept piling up, the arson investigation against John Piller was continuing. Within a few weeks the task force had come up with a surveillance plan. I wanted to place a full-time surveillance team on Piller and monitor his activities for a few weeks during the hottest part of the summer. To do this I wrote a grant to get federal funding and decided to bring in a special undercover team who normally followed Mexican and Columbian drug lords. These guys were the best in the business. I also arranged for the CHP mechanics to adjust the tracking system on Piller's tow truck so that it would show the truck's location at one-minute intervals. We knew we had only one shot at this guy, and we wanted to do it right. Lastly, I briefed several of my co-investigators on the case. This was to cause me many problems.

By early summer of 2000, we decided to implement our surveillance operation. The final briefing was given to the five members of my small task force. We kept the number of people on a need-to-know basis very small, as we required a great deal of secrecy on this case. One of my cohorts, after our briefing, gave a courtesy briefing to the area's battalion chiefs within his fire department. That group was told about the surveillance operation beginning the next day. Among that group was a thirty-year veteran of the fire department. Enraged that a suspected arsonist was running loose in his area, he left the meeting and got into his chief's car with his driver. They drove immediately to the 118 Freeway and stopped the first white FSP tow truck they saw. The angry chief confronted the driver and told him to tell all his fellow drivers to stop lighting fires in his area, because the sheriffs were following them.

I learned of this buffoonery when my phone rang that night and the owner of the tow-truck company asked me why I was following his drivers. He said that the fire chief had told him all about our investigation and the surveillance operation that was starting the next day. Shocked by this confrontation, I sat back and watched five weeks of work go down the drain. I called my peer at the fire department, who sheepishly admitted that one of his battalion chiefs had in fact spilled the beans. When I asked why, he said only that the chief, a very crusty sixty-something-year-old, was not a big fan of cops and had unashamedly proclaimed that it wasn't his job to catch arsonists but to prevent fires. He firmly believed that he had just prevented further fires. As pissed as I was, I gave serious consideration to actually arresting the fire chief. However, I eventually talked myself out of it. Because of this incident, and one other nearly identical incident, I have never again allowed such sensitive information out to investigators who felt compelled to brief their chiefs.

Over the next week, I sat around disgusted and trying to figure out how to restart this serial arson investigation. I was soon called by a driver from the FSP who wanted to give me some information. This driver, who was the son of the owner of that particular company, wanted to talk about Piller. This driver was one of the original suspects in this case but was soon cleared because his work schedule wasn't a match for the fires. I eventually met with this kid and his father, the owner of the company. They told me that within days of learning that the drivers of the company were being followed, John Piller had abruptly quit the company. The owner felt that this was odd, since Piller absolutely loved his job as a tow-truck driver.

The owner and his son gave me some more insight into Piller. They described him as a complete loner who did not get along with the other drivers at all; they said that he was the total opposite of what anyone would describe as the usual tow-truck driver. They described him as overly neat and fastidiousness, bordering on obsessive/compulsive about neatness. He was routinely late for work and for calls, as he spent hours each day obsessively cleaning and polishing the interior and exterior of his truck. He wore a perfectly crisp uniform each day and spit polished his boots every morning. He wore his hair neat and trimmed short in a military fashion. They said he usually carried a cooler of drinks in his truck so that he could provide them to the motorists he serviced. He often went many miles out of his area to give motorists rides home, even though the rules dictate that they are not to do these things. The other drivers for that company described Piller as a loner and somewhat effeminate, who always wore a small earring.

There were also more stories from women motorists. The owner of this company had similar stories to those of the other towing-company owners. One woman motorist had called to tell him that Piller stopped to get her groceries when she just wanted a ride home. She thought that it was very nice, but when they got to her home, Piller overstayed his welcome to the point where the woman had to tell him to leave. Another complaint the owner frequently received was that John Piller frequently asked the stranded motorists he serviced to write him a commendation. The owner acknowledged that the FSP contract was very important to him, and he did not disclose all these odd things about Piller to the highway patrol for fear of losing the contract.

Another driver from the company referred us to another female customer. We interviewed her, and she related yet another odd story about Piller. She was a tow customer whose car had broken down on a rural roadway. Piller picked her and her vehicle up on a large, flatbed tow truck and drove her toward her home. Coincidentally, she lived within a few blocks of Piller's rural home. She said Piller became quite excited when she told him her husband was a firefighter. As she and Piller drove out of the narrow canyon and crested a large hill overlooking their valley, they both saw a wildfire burning in the distant hills. They also saw several fire engines and at least five helicopters fighting the fire. The woman said Piller practically screamed in glee and sped up the large tow truck. According to the woman, he drove like a maniac, passing several stopped cars and a roadblock by moving down the wrong side of the road. As soon as he got to the area with the most firefighting activity, Piller leaped from the tow truck and pulled out a camera. She said he was excitedly running around and shooting pictures of the helicopters and fire engines. He soon ran out of film, and he ran back to the truck and begged her to check her purse for film or a camera. He promised to pay her back. The woman thought he had lost his mind, as he was completely enthralled with all the firefighting activity. Eventually she persuaded him to drive her and her vehicle home.

The tow-company owner's son, another driver like Piller, then told me that he had long suspected Piller of lighting fires. He asked Piller about it once, and Piller had just laughed and said, "I know you're doing it too." The son had never actually witnessed Piller lighting fires, but he knew him to have reported at least ten brushfires. He described John Piller as wanting to be either a highway patrolman or a firefighter.

The tow-truck owner told me that he thought Piller had taken a job as a tow-truck driver in the Palmdale area, about forty miles up the road from the 118 Freeway beat. They also knew Piller to have been fired as both an ambulance driver and a security guard.

In the remaining six weeks of summer in 2000, two remarkable things happened. The first was that, after Piller quit his job, there was not another suspicious fire along the 118 Freeway. This continued for the ensuing several years. The second thing that happened was directly related to the first thing. A wave of suspicious grass and brushfires erupted along the 14 Freeway in the areas south of Palmdale. We later determined that John Piller was driving a tow truck through that area during that time frame. We could never tie this latest series of fires to Piller, but we now saw that wherever he went, suspicious fires occurred.

Despite him leaving the 118 Freeway, the investigation of Piller continued, albeit without the help of the task force. By late 2000, we recognized that we had several provable counts of insurance fraud against John Piller. We also had the old fence arson that had never been resolved. On January 17, 2001, I went with several other detectives to Piller's home in Lake Elizabeth to serve a search warrant. We were looking for any evidence linking him to the insurance fraud schemes and to any arson fires. We were not disappointed.

At the home we met Piller's wife, Tina. She can only be described as a meek, mild, stay-at-home wife who wore more makeup than Dolly Parton. She home-schooled their two children and was an avid collector of photo albums. She tearfully defended her husband and described their family as long being victimized by the authorities and pretty much everyone else in the world. She said that they were strong Christians, and she felt that we were sent by Satan to test them. When we asked Tina Piller about the night of the fire to her fence, she said John couldn't have started it as he was in bed with her when the flames were first noticed. She did admit that she had placed her photo albums in the car because they were so precious to her—despite the fact that her children were still in the home. Piller's wife admitted that she and her husband had been in at least thirty car accidents that she could recall, but she thought that was a normal number for any family. She admitted that three additional accidents had occurred since the investigation began seven months prior. Her only explanation was that her life has been plagued with "bad luck." Piller's wife was arrested for several counts of insurance fraud, as she had fraudulently endorsed fake documents and cashed the checks. Because she was a stay-at-home mom and played a minor role in the scheme, we opted to release her on the spot with her promise to appear in court.

We found many things in the home that piqued our interest. Piller had a collection of police and fire-related regalia. He carried a very expensive paramedic trauma kit that he had purchased. He had an application for a state firefighter license plate for his car. A check of his personal truck, which was red, showed that it had hidden custom lights installed that mimicked "wig-wag" lights on police and fire vehicles and a scanner with all the local fire department channels programmed into it.

One of the more interesting things in the house was a photo album entitled "John's Book of Blunders." It was filled with car accident photos, and Piller had made comments beneath the pictures, similar to the comments made by traffic investigators. Near the end of the book were photos of Piller posing with firearms and several photos of fire scenes. We saw that some of the fire scenes were fires in their incipient or beginning stages. I later showed these photos to my colleagues at work, and we were able to identify two of the fires as unsolved arsons. Again, John Piller was linked to a couple more suspicious fires.

Lastly, the search warrant produced dozens of documents linking John and Tina Piller to a large number of lawsuits, accidents, injuries, and emergency-room visits. There were several letters written by the pair to creditors, businesses, and insurance companies telling of their ongoing misfortune. Many of these letters were written by John and showed he had a flair for the dramatics. One such letter was to a car company who he was refusing to pay. In it he cites that among the reasons he refused to pay was the fact that he had recently been "broadsided by an 18-wheeler." His own insurance papers and a police report indicated that this accident caused less than a thousand dollars in damage to his truck and only minor bumps to Piller. The true incident was hardly as impressive as being broadsided by a mammoth truck.

When we were done, I arrested John Piller for insurance fraud. My partner and I drove him to the nearest sheriff's station, which was forty-five minutes away. We had planned and contemplated how best to get him to talk to us, and we were dying to interview him about the arson fires. We read him his Miranda rights, and he soon waived them. Throughout the forty-five-minute trip, and over the next three or more hours, John Piller barely took a breath; he just wouldn't stop talking. It was one of the few times in my career that I terminated an interview simply because I was so tired of listening to the suspect talk!

Not only was John Piller not upset by his arrest and the search of his home, he was practically giddy. He seemed excited and pleased that we suspected him of this wave of crimes. He was more than happy to chat about anything and everything. During the interview, Piller went through no fewer than a dozen mood swings. He started out nervous and jittery. He then cried, laughed, moaned, cried, laughed, giggled, and finally broke down and cried out a confession. In the end he was extremely upbeat and proud.

Piller told us that he suffered panic and anxiety attacks. Because of this he also suffered from migraines and insomnia. We recognized all of these maladies as quite common among serial-arson suspects. He was a frequent user of prescription medications and an excessive cigarette smoker. He claimed not to drink alcohol. His mannerisms and speech were very effeminate, and he admitted to being obsessed with neatness and tidiness. When he talked he whined and mostly depicted himself as a tragic victim of circumstances.

We knew we had very little physical evidence in regards to the freeway brushfires. We needed Piller to admit his role and describe how he had set the fires. It was decided prior to the interview that we would "salt the scene" a bit. I spent a couple hours amassing oversized photos of footprint casts, satellite imagery, tire impressions, and a stack of videotapes, all labeled "Brushfire Arsons, Subject Piller, tape #33" etc. All of these items were strategically placed in the interview room, giving the appearance that we had hours and hours of surveillance footage and lots of physical evidence (which of course we didn't). Upon his booking at the jail, we removed his boots and made a big show of examining their treads. This investigative ruse worked well in this case.

As soon as John Piller walked into the interview room and saw all the footprint photos and satellite images on the wall, he began intently staring at them and making numerous spontaneous statements. First and foremost he blurted, "I know you've been following me." He then gave detailed descriptions of half a dozen undercover detectives, their vehicles, and where they liked to eat. I found his descriptions of counter surveillance over the past few months fascinating. I didn't have the heart to tell him that we hadn't followed him for a single minute. Obviously paranoia was another of his mental health issues.

When we brought his boots into the room, we also brought a slip of paper from the crime lab that stated the boots were a positive match. Of course all of this was staged as well. As soon as it was mentioned, Piller admitted to being at about fifteen of the fire scenes. He then said, "Check the other drivers; we all wear the same brand." He saw an enlarged photo of a cigarette on the ground and the words "DNA-positive" on it. He shook his head and admitted that it had been pretty careless of him to leave his cigarette at a fire scene.

Despite the ruses, we still had to get down to the nitty-gritty with Piller. We began intently questioning him about all the fires he had reported along the freeway. After a couple hours of tearful denials and accusations toward other drivers from his company, he finally said, "Okay, I may have accidentally lit a couple of the fires by carelessly discarding my cigarettes." We recognized this as a partial admission, which is common among some offenders who want to acknowledge what they did but minimize their actions. Oddly, when we pressed Piller for specific details, he began admitting to a couple of fires that we were unaware of. The dates of his fires differed from the dates of any of the fires on the list. Piller was insistent that he believed he had accidentally started fires on two days we did not have any reported fires!

We then addressed the subject of the fire at his home the previous year. After several denials, he finally broke down and admitted that he had lit the fire with the intent of setting the propane tank on fire. He believed that he could make some money off the insurance claim if there were a large fire. Piller told us that he was in deep financial troubles and had tried to sell his home for several months. When that had failed, he came up with the idea of starting a fire to destroy the house. When we asked him how he had lit the fire, he surprised us. He told us that he had used a delay incendiary device. He seemed surprised that we were surprised and asked, "Don't all arsonists use them?" He then described a cigarette/match delay device. He asked me to go find some materials, stating that he would make one for me. I gathered his materials, and we watched as he placed a single paper match around the filter end of a cigarette and secured it with a piece of clear tape. He said that it was identical to the device he had used the night of the fire at his home. He said he built it so that he would be in bed with his wife when the fire started. He said he placed this device into the pile of tumbleweeds behind his home, and the fire started fifteen minutes later when he was in bed.

Piller said that after the fire, he was aware that the local deputy and the fire captain were suspicious of him. Early the next morning, he went outside and placed matches at the scene to make it look as if someone else had set the fire. Later, after the local deputy told him that he thought Piller was acting suspicious, Piller decided not to file an insurance claim and actually replaced his neighbors burned boards himself so that no one would complain.

At the same time that he admitted to this staged arson, Piller also admitted that he had committed fraud several times by faking or exaggerating the vehicle break-downs and tows he had claimed. Piller also admitted to having several emotional problems. He said he was a very rash and angry driver, and he hated people who drove carelessly, recklessly or used excessive speed. He admitted that on several past occasions he had actually chased down and confronted numerous speeders and other drivers he deemed to be driving carelessly. He denied staging accidents and said every one he had been in was related to someone else's bad driving.

Piller also admitted a lifelong obsession with firefighting, law enforcement, and traffic investigation. He said he had always wanted to be either a highway patrolman or a firefighter.

We then addressed the subject of the freeway fires. Piller again began crying and finally stated, "Okay, I admit I have a problem." When we asked him to specify, he couldn't, and just continued to say that he had a problem.

Piller admitted that he was an overzealous employee, and that he could not stand to see a dirty or messy uniform, pair of shoes, or truck. He acknowledged that he was often late for calls as he couldn't be rushed in cleaning his truck. He proudly said that he had been forced out of several jobs for confronting and suing his bosses over violations of various state codes. He said that he had been a security guard at one point and was fired for over enthusiastically enforcing the law and for pulling a gun on a homeowner.

Another topic we discussed with Piller raised some alarms with us. When we searched his home, we found several more references to car accidents, emergency-room visits, and possible lawsuits. As we began asking about these, Piller again brightened up, seemingly proud of his dozens of legal struggles against businesses. He said that he had personally been involved in many car accidents, almost all of which had caused him some sort of soft tissue injury and a visit to the emergency room. This in turn would almost always lead to some sort of threat of legal action by Piller. He and his wife had become quite skilled at writing heart-wrenching letters to insurance companies, businesses, and attorneys. These letters always described the Pillers as victims and always demanded some form of monetary compensation. Piller proudly proclaimed that he usually got some form of settlement from each incident. At one point he alarmed us with tales of his children being injured in slip-and-falls or other odd incidents at large stores. He said that at least twice his children had been injured by the automatic doors of a business closing on them. Like his wife had earlier in the day, John Piller painted a picture of their family as poor Christians, who were frequently the victims of large businesses. To illustrate this mindset, Piller had a lawsuit pending against a car company whom he accused of pressuring him into purchasing a car that he could not afford, thereby leading to later financial troubles. It seemed that John Piller was incapable of accepting blame or personal responsibility for anything.

At about five hours into our interview, we got tired of John Piller. He, on the other hand, was quite happy to continue talking about himself for several more hours. He was later released from jail pending the outcome of our expanding investigation.

The John Piller investigation lasted for another year, but we were unable to positively link him in a legal sense to any more fires. We did find and interview over a dozen persons who had been involved in traffic collisions with John Piller. Upon reflection, nearly all said that the accident was Piller's fault and that they felt he had purposely driven into them or purposely failed to avoid a collision. However, they also said that he seemed extremely helpful and kind after the accident. Many of them believed him to be an off-duty officer or firefighter.

Another incident came to us from one of Piller's former employers. We showed him some of Piller's photos of accidents and fires. This former employer recalled an incident in which a motorist driving a motor home on a rural roadway had a breakdown. After attempting repairs, the motorist had locked and left his inoperable motor home, catching a ride to the nearest town. An hour later, as Piller made his way to work, he "found" the motor home burning. He gave his boss a breathless tale of derring-do, detailing how he had tried to fight the flames and enter the motor home to see if occupants needed rescuing. He then valiantly tried to extinguish the fire to no avail. The boss said Piller seemed extremely excited by this event. The motor-home owner was later stunned to find out that his motor home had burned, as he felt the mechanical problems were totally unrelated to the fire and he had stayed with his vehicle for over an hour after it had broken-down without it igniting. He felt the incident was highly suspicious, but the CHP did not investigate the fire.

After his arrest, Piller's life began to unravel. He started and stopped a few more towing jobs and finally put in for unemployment and disability benefits. At some point his wife began to suspect he was having affairs. She and her sister discovered at least three women John had been habitually meeting. John eventually moved out and began living with another woman. Finally, his wife realized that her "idyllic Christian husband" was a bit more flawed than she had originally thought. She began an aggressive campaign to reunite with him. Meanwhile, the criminal case was moving forward.

On January 30, 2002, I presented this case to Deputy District Attorney Bob Foltz, an expert prosecutor in arson cases. He agreed that Piller was a serial arsonist and filed four felony arson counts against him and his wife. He also filed several felony insurance fraud charges against the pair.

March 29 of 2002 became a significant date for John Piller. On that day, he took a plea deal that spared him state prison and spared his wife a criminal conviction. He pled guilty to one count of felony arson. Because arson is considered a serious and violent crime in California, from that point until the end of his life, John Piller will be a registered arsonist. He received "time served" in jail and walked out of the courtroom after the plea to start his probation. He seemed very agitated by the whole affair. I told DA Bob Foltz that day that I predicted that Piller would either get in a car accident or start a fire within a week of the plea deal.

Later that same day, I was contacted by Tina Piller's sister. She told me that the day before being sentenced, John Piller had intentionally driven his truck into his estranged wife's car. At the time, there were young children in both vehicles. John left the scene after the collision, and his wife was too afraid to report the assault to the sheriff's. She eventually reported it and accused John of assault with a deadly weapon (vehicle). It was at that point that we met with Tina Piller's sister, and she gave us John Piller's whole back-story. She said that she had told her sister for years that John was a weirdo and extremely dangerous. She said John was a chronic liar and had made up dozens of bizarre stories about his heroic deeds over the years. Tina's sister told us several stories in which John had staged attacks on his own family or faked assaults by unknown felony suspects. She said that on more than one occasion, John had damaged his own cars in an attempt to persuade his rather gullible wife that people were after him. Other family members had witnessed Piller damaging his own vehicles during these staged events, but Tina would not believe them. Tina's sister told us that John would shoot at his vehicles, damage them with a tire iron, slash the tires, and then later submit insurance claims for the damage.

She said it was well-known in the family that John often lied about his employment, claiming to be or have been a "set medic"—which she explained to be a paramedic on movie sets—a private traffic investigator, and even a secret government agent. In a recent incident, Piller (dressed in a trench coat and dark glasses) was at the scene of a family dispute, and when police arrived, he began talking into his sleeve, pretending to be a secret service agent.

Because I had already been too involved in the Piller case, I called in a major crimes detective named Todd Anderson to conduct an independent look into the antics of John Piller. He and I met with Tina Piller's sister and another male relative. Tina's sister described John Piller as being absolutely obsessed with speeders and bad drivers. She had personally witnessed several occasions on which he had chased down speeders and tried to run them off the road, even with his own family in the car. She said his road rage was so severe at times that he endangered himself and others in his attempts to apprehend the offenders.

Tina's sister then brought in another relative, who admitted that he had seen John Piller commit credit-card fraud numerous times over the past few years. He said that Piller used credit-card numbers he took from towing clients. He told us that Piller had bragged about staging dozens of car accidents and claimed to be highly skilled in constructing pipe bombs.

Tina's sister also offered that John Piller had been addicted to one medication or another for most of his life. She said that he claimed to the family that he was emotionally abused as a child, as his mother had forced him to watch her having sex with various men.

On a final note, both informants told us that Piller was concocting a plan to "get Nordskog," as he felt that I was responsible for all his woes. Part of the scheme to "get" me was to sue me and take my house.

After this interview of Piller's relatives, we began looking for his truck to see if it had physical damage matching his wife's statement about the recent assault/collision. Four days later, Tina's sister called me again and told me that John had been in another "accident" in an attempt to cover up the damage from his attack on Tina. She told me that John's truck was in a local tow yard. Detective Anderson and I examined his vehicle at the tow yard. We saw that the truck had numerous aftermarket items such as high quality music systems, radios, and custom rims, that the witnesses said Piller had acquired via credit-card theft. These items were seized. Additionally, we saw evidence on several parts of the truck that indicated that it had been involved in at least two, and possibly three, traffic collisions. All of these collisions appeared to be low-speed events, as the damage was fairly minor in scope.

We found police reports and insurance records showing that John Piller had in fact been involved in a collision with a man on April, 3, 2002, just four days after his assault/collision with his wife and three days after his arson sentencing. In retrospect I was wrong with my prediction to the DA; Piller was not involved in a single accident but two within days of his sentencing! We contacted the driver of the final accident, and he was adamant that John Piller had purposely swerved into him. He felt that because he was a gang member, the responding sheriff's deputies did not believe his version of the "accident." We came up with the opinion that Piller did indeed stage this collision in an attempt to cover up the damage from his assault/collision a few days before. The damage from the latter collision was in the exact spot on Piller's truck as the damage from his collision with his wife.

Piller's crazy week was not quite over yet. On April 4, 2002, he struck again. He called 911 via a cell phone and told them that his estranged wife, Tina, "was dying inside of her home." When the sheriff's and fire departments arrived, Piller was waiting nearby. The emergency responders had to force entry into the locked home, only to find that no one was there. An angry fire captain confronted John Piller, who only stated that he was told by an unknown party that his wife was in distress. Minutes after this incident, Tina and other family members returned home to find their doors and windows smashed. John just smirked at Tina's sister and stated, "I told you I was going to get you." He also promised to call the department of child services on Tina and her sister.

Judging by these increasingly bizarre incidents, we believed that John Piller was spinning out of control so fast that he was in great danger of hurting someone or himself. We met with Tina Piller who proved to be a very reluctant victim. She was still madly in love with John and was determined to save her marriage, even though John was living with another woman. She told us that she felt that the other woman was responsible for all of John's erratic actions. In the end, Tina Piller was a very inconsistent witness, as her stories changed each time she told them. She eventually dropped all charges on the vehicle assault.

A few weeks later, John Piller voluntarily came in for an interview. He gave us his version of all these events, and of course painted himself as the victim. He did admit that from our point of view, he could understand why we suspected him of being guilty. However, he came up with an exotic explanation for every odd incident in his life. He also told us that he was addicted to a drug called Klonopin, which he had been taking for almost fifteen years to treat frequent panic attacks. After speaking to him, we realized that John Piller was in his own little fantasy world, and he truly believed himself to be a crusader against injustice. He believed that there were forces and entities out in the world trying to ruin his life, and he waged a courageous battle against them on a daily basis. He painted himself as a dedicated public servant.

Over the next few months, we assembled evidence of these latest allegations. We contacted numerous persons regarding Piller's car accidents and interviewed them. We consulted with experts from the highway patrol and the department of motor vehicles. All of these people agreed that Piller was staging car accidents, but what he was doing was so bizarre that it would be difficult to get prosecutors to take on the case. Nonetheless, we took a case to the local district attorney in the summer of 2002, alleging several staged car accidents, credit-card fraud, and the staged arsons of a couple rental cars. There it sat for several months, as a senior prosecutor waited to decide what to do with it.

In July of 2002, I received a strange call. A senior homicide detective from my department wanted to talk to me about John Piller. The detective, Sgt. Rich Longshore, was working a high-profile case involving the murder of a former cheerleader in the Lancaster area, and he had received a tip that the murderer may have been driving a tow truck. There were also indications that the victim may have been approached by a person posing as a police officer. The pretty young girl was confronted and shot several times as she was picking up her car from a park-and-ride lot. This unsolved murder had occurred in 2000, and the park-and-ride was located alongside the 14 Freeway and within a couple miles of where Piller had worked as a tow-truck driver.

The homicide investigator had inquired with the highway patrol about John Piller and had received some interesting news. The highway patrol and one of Piller's former bosses had confirmed that Piller, in his duties as a FSP driver, had received complaints about bothering female motorists and at least one female employee. He had also received discipline or censure on three occasions, on one of which he was harassing a female employee.

I contacted Piller, and he agreed to come in for an interview with homicide Sergeant Longshore. It was a surreal experience. John Piller, instead of being shocked, outraged, or angry at being questioned in regards to a notorious murder in the area, seemed positively excited to be involved. He only became shocked in the middle of the interview, when he realized that the suspicion was directed toward him. Sergeant Longshore noted in his report that Piller showed up wearing a hidden tape recorder on his belt. He also noted that Piller had attempted to control the entire interview and wanted to discuss many things other than the murder case. Piller spent over an hour painting himself as a good guy and a victim of circumstances. He maintained that he was a dedicated public servant who always seemed to get blamed for things.

After the interview, Sgt. Rich Longshore spent a long time discussing John Piller with me. He said that Piller was indeed a strange and unique character who seemed to be suffering from Munchausen's Syndrome. This mental health issue has many forms, but in one form the subject constantly perceives himself as a victim. This type of person has an inordinate number of accidents, is the victim of crimes at an alarming rate, and always seems to be the center of bizarre and weird events. This description fit John Piller perfectly.

However, to be fair, both the homicide sergeant and I agreed that Piller had nothing to do with the girl's murder. It should be noted that this notorious murder was solved a few years later with the arrest and conviction of a security guard in the area; this security guard had also told many lies about himself, his qualifications, and his personal life.

After a year of the latest Piller case sitting on the district attorney's desk, the DA called me and said that he wasn't going to file charges over the staged car accidents, false reports of emergencies, frauds, and related incidents. He said that what Piller had done was so bizarre and beyond description that it would be difficult to present in the historical vacuum of a courtroom. He felt that Piller's wife was a terrible victim, as she had frequently vacillated between condemning John and defending him. Besides, the DA confided in me, he was retiring and just wanted to clear a bunch of old cases off his desk. With that, John Piller's legal odyssey was over—or so I thought.

With dozens of other more pressing cases on my shoulders, I moved on and forgot about John Piller, although I was fairly sure he would surface again. In the summer of 2003, John Piller filed a personnel complaint against me with my department. The complaint alleged false arrest and harassment. He did this despite the fact that I had not seen or spoken to him in over a year and had not arrested him in nearly two years. The case was investigated by internal affairs, and I was cleared of wrongdoing.

Not to be dissuaded by this setback, on February 3, 2004, John Piller followed up an earlier threat and filed a civil lawsuit against me claiming $5,000 in damages. We appeared in court in March of that year. While I was represented by my department's attorney, Piller acted as his own attorney. The hearing lasted less than thirty minutes, as the judge dismissed the lawsuit after hearing just a few words from Piller. He asked Piller the nature of the suit, and Piller said that I had illegally labeled him an arsonist. When my attorney produced the criminal court records showing that Piller himself had admitted to being an arsonist both in a written confession and in open court, the exasperated judge said, "Well, you are an arsonist." Piller said, "I know, but I don't want Nordskog telling people that." The judge also told Piller that he was two years too late to file a civil case.

Since that day, I'm surprised to admit that John Piller has not seemed to have any other significant criminal issues. His name came up again in 2009 when I was part of a team investigating the murders of two firefighters during a brushfire. We were doing a check of all known arsonists in the area. A computer check showed that Piller had stayed crime-free for the past nine years. Maybe getting a new wife and raising a family had calmed him down a bit. An analyst for my unit did find some interesting photos of Piller on the Internet. He had placed several photos and videos of himself on various social media sites. In many of the photos, Piller is seen wearing either a medic tee shirt or, more alarmingly, a badge on his belt. Additionally, he has posted several photos of his personal vehicle. This completely tricked-out, red, pickup truck is shown sporting emergency lights and a sign indicating it is a volunteer rescue vehicle. Piller has posted videos of the vehicle speeding along with red lights flashing and a siren wailing, or "code 3" in police jargon. Apparently, he still considers himself a hero. What did disturb us was his 2009 DMV report, which showed that he was continuing some of his bizarre behavior. The DMV showed that he had been involved in nine additional reported traffic "accidents" since his spree in 2002. Again he has almost never been found at fault. DMV investigators have had his information since 2002 and have never taken steps to remove his license.

John Piller has remained crime-free since about 2002…that we know of. There have been no other fires associated with him. Hopefully this continues, and Piller has freed himself from his obsessions and demons.

Author's Note: John Piller has only been convicted of starting the one fire at his home. That being said, I and the other investigators from the Los Angeles City Fire Department and Ventura County Fire Department have no doubts that he is a serial arsonist who will always remain at risk of reoffending the next time his life gets a little difficult. He has many of the recognized traits of a serial arson offender. He is a self-proclaimed firefighter and police aficionado; he has frequent issues with road rage and is obsessed with other bad drivers; he has an extremely spotty work record; he has addiction issues with prescription drugs; he has an admitted medical history of migraines, anxiety, stress, and panic attacks; he is obsessive in his neatness and effeminate in his mannerisms; he has a lengthy history of association with fires (his younger brother is also a convicted arsonist); he has "found" and reported no fewer than eight fires and has been the "victim" of no fewer than three; he has been the "victim" or "witness" to numerous odd crimes and incidents; he has a lengthy history of presenting himself in life-and-death situations or telling exotic stories to that effect; and he has always dabbled in jobs related to the fire, police, or rescue community. He has presented himself as a "hero" his entire adult life. He fits the classic definition of a serial arson offender motivated for the purpose of recognition or vanity.

Wherever John Piller has held a job, unexplained fires and odd accidents have seemed to abound. The moment he left these positions and places, the odd events ceased. The 118 Freeway fires stopped immediately after Piller resigned his position. The 14 Freeway fires stopped as soon as he stopped working in the area. When it comes down to it, this is the most compelling argument I can offer to convince people that John Piller was a danger to his community. Hopefully maturity and family stabilization has caused Piller to evolve beyond that danger level.

CHRIS IVES, THE POSER
ORANGE COUNTY, 2009

In September of 2009, the largest fire in the history of Los Angeles County raged for nearly a month in the national forest just above the Los Angeles basin. Forest service investigators proclaimed the fire to be an act of arson. Three days after the start of this fire, hereafter known as the "Station Fire," two Los Angeles County firefighters were overrun and killed by the flames while performing a backfire operation. Immediately their deaths became classified as murders, and the investigation was turned over to the Los Angeles County sheriff's homicide and arson units.

As part of this task force, I was assigned the duty of organizing old files and databases in order to assign detectives to locate and interview all known arsonists, suspicious persons in the area of the fire, and persons who were identified as "suspicious" through the tip lines that were established. Among these groups of suspicious subjects was an unofficial set of oddballs classified as wannabe firefighters. This is a small but amazing group of creeps and kooks who masquerade as firefighters and actually attempt to join in on fire-fighting activity. While what these people do is not illegal in most cases, they present a huge problem for investigators, as their activity can be distracting and highly suspicious. We were aware of at least twenty of these types of people in the Los Angeles area. Many were checked out and cleared, and others were developed through new citizen tips. One such tip came in a few weeks into this investigation from detectives in nearby Orange County.

Police Detective McMullin from the city of Orange had a case that had emerged about a year before. In November of 2008, a year before the Station Fire, McMullin and other detectives were serving a search warrant in Lomita, California. The location of their warrant was the home of a man named Christopher Paul Ives. Ives, a thirty-year-old white male, was arrested for burglary and theft charges, along with a narcotics charge for possessing methamphetamine. During the search of his home, detectives found a large amount of firefighting equipment.

Among the multitude of items found were several navy-blue tee shirts adorned with the either the words "Cal Fire" or "CDF," both referring to the present and past names of the state of California's firefighting agency. There were many other items, including Cal Fire stationary and business cards in the name of Chris Ives, Cal Fire ball caps with Ives's name and the title "Captain" imprinted on them, a Cal Fire sweatshirt, two police scanners, portable emergency lights, Cal Fire lapel pins, a rank bar with the word "Captain" imprinted on it, key rings and fobs, and finally several *Orange County Register* newspapers, all depicting recent large brushfires that had occurred in the area.

The business cards and stationary each gave Ives the title of "Fire Behavior Technical Specialist," and identified him as being a command member of the "Cal Fire Incident Command Team 6." He also had a realistic looking US government license plate. Detectives saw that the plate had Velcro straps on the back, which would allow it to be placed quickly onto any vehicle. They noted corresponding Velcro pads on Ives's personal SUV, which bore normal civilian plates.

A search of Ives's vehicles showed that each bore a small fire helmet union sticker indicating "CDF Firefighters" on the rear windows. Each vehicle also had a large "FIRE" placard on the dashboard and a corresponding card indicating a command position on "Command Team 6." The cars also contained uniforms, two-way radios, map books (with fire-scene markings in them), firefighting handbooks, and hoses in the trunk areas.

The firefighting clothing and equipment was very important to Detective McMullin and his partners. The reason they were serving the warrant was that they suspected Chris Ives of having been involved in many crimes, including burglary, fraud, forgery, and identity theft. Among his many acts leading up to the warrant, Ives had been seen committing some of these felonies while impersonating a firefighter.

Ives's capers came to the attention of Detective McMullin in September of 2008. At that time, McMullin, a burglary detective, was assigned to investigate the theft and subsequent unauthorized use of several credit cards. The items were taken from the home of Mr. Mark Saito while he was out of town. After he noticed unauthorized purchases on his account, Mr. Saito notified the

Orange police of the theft. One such purchase occurred at a Wal-Mart store in Orange. Store security cameras showed a white male wearing a blue CDF FIRE tee shirt making an unauthorized purchase with the card. The victim's adult daughter, Jamie Saito, viewed the security video at the police station to see if she recognized the suspect. She was shocked to see and identify the suspect as her own boyfriend, Christopher Ives. She told detectives that Ives had been at her home several times while her parents were out of town. She identified him as a full time firefighter. She said she knew this because he had told her and because he routinely wears firefighting shirts around her.

Mr. Saito then reviewed his cell-phone bill. He noted that over the several days his stolen credit cards were being illegally accessed, his daughter had received calls from Chris Ives's cell phone, showing him to be in the same areas as the fraudulent purchases.

A second store security video was found. This video showed Ives making a fraudulent purchase with the victim's stolen credit card at a Home Depot in Torrance. In this video Ives was again wearing a blue CDF FIRE tee shirt. The detectives developed a few more bits of evidence and finally served their search and arrest warrants on November 18, 2008.

Ives was not home at the time, but investigators conducted a search of his room. Among the firefighting clothing and associated gear, investigators also found two glass methamphetamine pipes that appeared to have been recently used. They also found a couple bindles of meth, some larger rocks of meth, and a mini digital scale that appeared to be used to weigh the narcotics. Based on what they found, the detectives believed that Ives was both using and selling methamphetamine. Hidden under Ives's mattress were eleven stolen credit cards, all reported by the victim, along with numerous other items including credit cards and forms of identification in the names of several other persons. Lastly, investigators found two boxes of loan and escrow papers in the names of thousands of other persons. It was clear to them that Chris Ives was engaged in narcotics sales, grand theft, burglary, and identity theft.

Ives returned to his home in the middle of the search warrant. Detectives noted that he was wearing a CDF FIRE sweatshirt. They questioned him about the thefts from his girlfriend's father, which he denied. Finally they told him they had already found the stolen cards. They were surprised when he just grinned and said, "Sneaky....Yeah, I did it." He eventually admitted to stealing the cards, a Rolex watch, and some cash. He also admitted to making unauthorized purchases with the stolen cards.

The detectives then began asking Ives questions about his fire service. He admitted that he did not work for a fire department but claimed to be a volunteer. When they pressed him, he finally admitted that he was not an official volunteer but just liked to help. He admitted to helping on all the recent Orange County fires in the 2008 year. He said he did not actually fight any fires but was instead at the scene to relay messages and make copies. Ives told investigators that the US Government plate, the one found in Ives's possession with Velcro on it, was in his car when he bought it. This proved to be a bit of a lie. A follow-up investigation into the plate revealed that it had been recently stolen from an Air Force recruiter's vehicle in Orange County. Ives was additionally charged with this theft.

Chris Ives said he was unemployed, received unemployment checks each month, and sold a little methamphetamine to make some money. He also sold some of the stolen credit cards to other thieves. He was basically a goofball who had too much time on his hands and had taken on a firefighter's persona.

Orange detectives called a local fire investigator to assist them in the case. Orange City Fire Department Investigator Keith Marshall interviewed Ives shortly after his arrest. Ives admitted to him that he had never been to any fire training whatsoever and had never belonged to any firefighting agency in either an official or volunteer capacity. He only stated that he did frequently go to fire scenes to assist the firemen. Cal Fire officials would later confirm that Ives had never been a part of their organization.

Ives did admit to making the business cards by copying the Cal Fire logo off the Internet. He also admitted to taking photos at fire scenes. The investigators would later find Ives's camera and numerous fire-scene photos. They found indications that he had attended numerous wildfire scenes dating back to at least 2007.

Ives said he had purchased all his firefighter clothing from online stores and that he got his fire hat decals by donating to local agencies.

Ives's girlfriend was interviewed. She told detectives that she had known Chris Ives since April of 2008. She had often seen him wearing firefighter uniforms and driving his jeep, which was outfitted with firefighter radios and stickers. She believed he worked for Cal Fire. He had told her that he was a supervisor in charge of a truck. She had received several phone calls and text messages from him in which he described being at a fire scene with his unit. He often gave her vivid descriptions of the fire and the activity. She said she could hear sounds in the background consistent with his stories. Among these events, she had received several calls from him from the recent massive Yorba Linda fire. He again described in detail all the activity and his role in fighting the blaze. She said that one night during that fire, Ives arrived at her home in full uniform driving his white jeep. She believed he had just come from the fire. He was carrying a portable radio on his belt. Chris Ives was arrested and later convicted for multiple felonies. To date, Chris Ives has never been positively linked to any arson events. His interest in the fire service goes far beyond the normal aficionado. He seems to have an obsessive personality and to have taken on the alter ego of not just a firefighter but a supervisor on a firefighting command staff all to impress a young girl. He was fulfilling his own fantasies and no doubt fooled many professionals involved in the hectic and chaotic world of wildfire firefighting. It would not take a stretch of the imagination to see Ives making the next small step and becoming an arsonist.

Alien Head Guy
Los Angeles and Ventura Counties, 2000

In 1997 I joined the Los Angeles Sheriff's Arson/Explosives Detail (Arson/Bomb Squad). We had twenty-two full-time arson and bomb investigators who, besides staffing the bomb squad, responded to over 2,500 fires per year. Los Angeles County has over six-million residents and encompasses over sixty cities, beaches, harbors, rail systems, deserts, mountains, forests, and areas of brush land. On any given day, we investigate eight to ten fires that occur in boats, vehicles, factories, residences, trailer parks, schools, wildlands, forests, and just about any other setting imaginable. About half of these fires are accidental—the others are incendiary or intentional acts. Because of the very heavy traffic congestion and great distances we travel, our boss frequently assigns us fires in the general geographic vicinity of our homes. Since I lived in northern Los Angeles County in those years, the bulk of my fire investigations took place in the northern suburbs, deserts, and Los Angeles National Forest. As such I became very familiar with the other fire-investigation entities in these areas, and we formed loose alliances and ad hoc task forces as the need arose.

Typically a wildland fire in the fall months was our greatest concern. When one occurred, it triggered a massive response from numerous suppression agencies, and quite often several investigative agencies had to meet to figure out who would lead the investigation of each event. Normally the location of the fire's origin determined who the lead agency was. In many of these events, the origin seemed to start near the jurisdictional borders of multiple agencies. This meant that we frequently worked with our partners from Cal Fire, LA County Fire, LA City Fire, Ventura County Fire Department, ATF, and the United States Forest Service.

From 1997 until about 2002, there were an extraordinary number of brushfires in the northern Los Angeles County foothill areas. Many of these were considered highly suspicious in nature. Looking back with a decade's worth of hindsight, I now know why. We had no fewer than three serial arsonists living in the hills in this area at the same time. The arrests and convictions in the early 2000s of John Piller, tow-truck driver and suspected arsonist in at least thirty brushfires, Rickey Jimenez, serial arsonist convicted of over twenty-five arsons and suspect in about fifty more, and Fire Captain Mike McNeil, a suspect in several dozen wildland fires, led to a dramatic decrease in the number of wildland fires in the area for the rest of the decade. All three of these people lived or worked in the heart of all of the suspect brushfires from that era. A fourth individual, a "stringer" who was suspected of several brushfires, left the area after his arrest for multiple arsons. He was acquitted of the arsons in jury trial but has since left this part of the county.

During our lengthy investigations into these fires, we began to form a series of informal task-force meetings with arson investigators from all of the above mentioned entities. Starting in 2001, we began openly discussing among ourselves potential suspects and others who had come to our attention during the last several brushfire seasons. At one point we all began to talk about someone we soon dubbed, "Alien Head Guy."

On May 11, 2002, a large suspicious brushfire broke out in the forest service area just north of the Santa Clarita Valley. This fire was later classified as incendiary and considered to be associated with a couple of similar fires that had occurred in the area during over a one-month period. This fire grew to over one-thousand acres before it was "knocked down."

During the follow-up investigation into this fire, forest service investigators were contacted by a citizen who had observed something odd during the fire. The citizen, who was out riding a mountain bike in a remote canyon, came across a massive white male sitting in a Mitsubishi Montero on a dirt road. This was on the first day of the fire. The biker stopped and talked to the man, noticing that he had a life-size blow-up green alien doll sitting in the passenger's seat next to him. The man seemed overly excited about the fire and told the biker he was a US Forest Service "fire spotter." When the biker said he had never heard of such a job, the man stated that he was "spotting" for air tankers in the area. The biker did note that there were fire scanners and radios within the man's vehicle and that he spoke using a firefighter's vernacular. However, the two men soon got into a heated argument as to which airfield the air tankers were deployed from, and the biker noted that the large man seemed very irrational.

This encounter was discussed by task-force officers at our meeting, and soon several of us were relating stories about "Alien Head Guy." I had seen or heard of this guy on at least two or three previous fire investigations in the area. He stood out because he was massive in size (about six foot five and over three-hundred pounds) and he always had this large green alien doll in the passenger's seat of his truck with him. Many of the firefighters knew him and believed him to be an eccentric millionaire and the ultimate wannabe firefighter. He was routinely seen mingling in the command posts at massive brushfire scenes.

Soon another partner of mine, Detective Mike Cofield, chimed in that he had purposefully investigated this man as a potential brush arson suspect in 2000. Several persons had told Cofield that "Alien Head Guy" was sitting with his alien doll at the scene of a massive brushfire in the mountains above Los Angeles prior to the fire department's arrival. Cofield began following leads and eventually identified the vehicle and the owner. The man's true name was Steve Brokaw, and he did live at a wealthy mansion in Beverly Hills. Cofield was unable to link Brokaw (or his alien buddy) to the cause of the brushfire in 2000.

USFS investigators, Ventura County, and LA City investigators all reported Brokaw as having been seen in fire command posts in their areas along with his ubiquitous green partner. His behavior was described as overzealous, bizarre, and weird, but never criminal. He befriended any firefighter who would talk to him and gave varying accounts of his background, profession, and motive for being at the fire scenes. The fire suppression bosses just accepted him as a part of the fire-ground landscape and seldom kicked him out of their area.

Because we were trying to get a handle on every potential arsonist in the brush land areas, we decided to take a really good look at this guy. Investigators backtracked him to Beverly Hills and found that, while he did reside on occasion with a wealthy family, he was a guest and not the owner of the large mansion. He had held a multitude of jobs and worked as a security guard, event promoter, bodyguard, chef, and makeup artist. He had no record of ever being a firefighter or even an applicant. A criminal background check showed that he had arrests for some odd offenses, including trespassing, defrauding an innkeeper, and grand theft. These minor things dated back about twenty years. More recently, Brokaw had arrests that were much more sinister and alarming to the investigators. Starting in 1985, Brokaw received a felony conviction for falsely reporting a bomb and an emergency. For this bizarre stunt, he received his first state prison sentence. He was paroled in 1987 and was arrested again shortly after that for theft. A couple months later, he was again arrested for falsely reporting an emergency. Despite being on parole for a somewhat similar offense, Brokaw received only a misdemeanor conviction the second time around and spent about fifty days in jail. Shortly after his release from jail, he was sent back to state prison for violating his parole. This pattern of release, parole violation, and return to prison continued for another three years. In 1989 Brokaw was convicted of grand theft auto and sent again to state prison. Paroled a year later, he immediately violated his parole and was sent back yet again.

In 1991 the strange behavior continued, and Brokaw was again arrested for falsely reporting an emergency. In 1992 he had moved up to the Lake Tahoe area and was arrested for stealing another car. This sent him back to prison yet again. By 1993 he was out again, and this time he was arrested and convicted for burglary. He got another two years in state prison for this serious crime. He was released back to the Los Angeles area in 1994 and promptly rearrested for stealing cars again. Now the courts were really irritated and gave Brokaw a five-year stretch in the state pen. This may have calmed him somewhat, as he wasn't heard from again until 2001 when he was arrested for fraud in West Hollywood.

In 2009 we were involved in a heavy-duty task force trying to solve the massive Station Fire in the Angeles National Forest. During that year I ran Brokaw on the police computers to see where he had been during this fatal fire. I was pleased to see that he was not involved in the Station Fire, as he had been incarcerated in a federal prison in the Midwest during this event. He was evidently let out shortly after my inquiry; because he was rearrested in Pasadena in 2010 for yet another auto theft. Unbelievably, despite his lengthy prison record, he received only a misdemeanor conviction for this latest offense and was released after only twenty-two days in jail.

To date, Steve Brokaw has never been legally linked to arson activity. He is just another of those people we can't quite get a grip on but who seem to gravitate toward major fire events.

Investigator's Analysis:

Steve Brokaw is one of those really weird guys you come across in my business. Treated as just a friendly and colorful oddball by the firefighters, he was somehow allowed into many major-fire incident command centers over the years. When we began looking at him in connection to a few arson fires, a local fire chief chided us for picking on a guy who was just another fan of firemen. The chief was very irritated with us (investigators) when we advised him and his colleagues to keep all of these wannabes and fake firefighters out of their command posts. This chief believed that firefighter aficionados were complimentary to the fire service and should be treated as friends. That same chief was shocked to learn that Brokaw had a significant and ongoing criminal record.

We were most concerned about Brokaw's fascination with the fire service and his affinity for calling in false emergencies. Although we could never prove it, we were under the impression that Brokaw had most likely caused more than one wildfire in an attempt to be part of the action.

In my seventeen years in the arson business, I have been to dozens of large fire-department command posts set up during massive fires and events. In over 75 percent of those incidents, I have seen Brokaw or guys like him posing as firefighters by driving retired fire-department or police-department vehicles, wearing some semblance of a firefighter's uniform, and immersing themselves in the excitement and action that swirls around these events. Professionally, I am shocked that major agencies continue to allow such suspicious people inside active command centers.

CHAPTER FIVE:
Mad Men

Every arson investigator who has been on the job for more than a month will tell you that the primary motive for arson has historically been one of spite, revenge, and rage. This motive is manifested through the disintegration of personal relationships, and in the field of arson, it often results in a poorly planned but ruthlessly carried out act of arson. In these cases, there are often predictable events leading up to the act of absolute rage. An ongoing bit of "dark comedy" that investigators joke about in the arson world is the fact that one of the major "triggering events" of many arson attacks is the issuance of a court protection order by a judge, more commonly called a "restraining order." We can all recall dozens of attacks that were perpetrated by an offender within hours or even minutes of him having been served such a court order. The arson attacks are the culmination of a festering feud and are often committed in the direct presence of witnesses or the victims themselves. Following are a few of the revenge-spite-rage arsons from the foothill regions.

WOODWARDIA FIRE, ANGELES NATIONAL FOREST, 1959

Author's Note: This case was told to me during a face-to-face interview with retired chief John Graham in August of 2010. These are his recollections of a fifty-year-old case. Many of these facts were verified using online research of the history of the Angeles National Forest.

On October 13, 1959, a schedule change would end up becoming the root cause of one of the more devastating fires in the Angeles National Forest's history. The Santa Ana winds, always the bane of firefighters in the coastal California mountain regions, had begun to stir the night before. Most Santa Ana events last from three-to-five days and cause the flare-up of dozens of fires that quickly rage out of control in these situations.

On the night of the twelfth, the tanker boss at the United States Forest Service fire station, just six miles above affluent La Canada, would make a command decision. He would need all of his available firefighters on duty the next day. As part of this decision, he cancelled the scheduled days off of several crew members, including Crewman William Grader. This decision did not make Grader happy, not in the least.

On the morning of the thirteenth, the Santa Anas were beginning to build and would reach their optimum levels in the late afternoon. That morning, a visibly disgruntled William Grader was assigned to a painting operation while standing by for a wildfire call. At some point, Grader found a reason to take a truck, leave the station, and head up the hill toward the Angeles Crest Highway. He returned within a half hour. Just after Grader returned to quarters, panicked motorists drove into the station lot and reported a fast-moving brushfire just a half mile above the ranger station, alongside the highway.

The fire started just as the winds were really beginning to howl near Woodwardia Bridge, and would thusly be dubbed the "Woodwardia Fire." The winds quickly drove the fire across Highway 2 and into a heavily wooded area that was totally inaccessible to firefighting crews. Before nightfall, the fire started down slope in a two-pronged advance toward the cities of Pasadena on the south and La Canada on the west. A massive fire response from all sectors began as the blaze threatened the Jet Propulsion Lab and hundreds of expensive homes.

All through the morning and afternoon of the fourteenth, the flames pushed down hill into the populated areas above the two cities. As the winds pushed the flames right to the edge of La Canada, the local fire chiefs conceded that they were going to lose many homes that night. However, for some reason, the winds abated late into that second evening and the area was blessed with a dramatic rise in humidity. These natural effects enabled the fire crews to beat back the flames with only the loss of one home. A backfiring event the next morning and a shift in winds caused the fire to leap eastward, where it completely burned out several large drainage systems and canyons.

This mega fire resulted in many "firsts" for the Los Angeles area firefighting profession. While fixed-wing water bombers had been deployed during many past fire events, this was the advent of the first "helitack" deployment, with two specially outfitted helicopters dropping retardant in specific locations. Another first in this fire was the fact that Los Angeles County authorities, sensing impending disaster on the second day, appointed County Fire Chief Klinger as the first "fire czar," giving him unlimited authority to take any measures necessary and order any equipment and manpower he saw fit to fight the fire, no questions asked. The successful defense of the urban areas justified this decision and lay the groundwork for the vast power that future fire incident commanders would be granted.

While major disaster was eventually averted, this fire was not without its tragedies. A water-bomber pilot was killed during an accident. Later in the fire, two Zuni Indian firefighters, brought in from Arizona, were killed as they were literally blown off of a ridge by a 600-gallon air drop of borate fire retardant.

The Woodwardia Fire burned for three full days and consumed 14,000 acres of wildland. Numerous structures were damaged or destroyed and at least two firefighters were killed. Eerily, the Woodwardia Fire would start at and burn in almost the exact areas as the fatal Station Fire of 2009—exactly fifty years later. Both fires would also claim the lives of two firefighters.

In 2010 I had the pleasure of interviewing John Graham on an unrelated matter. It came up at the time that the eighty-something Graham was a retired Los Angeles County Sheriff's chief. Before climbing the ladder of promotion, he had spent an exciting tour of duty as a detective sergeant in the department's arson and explosive squad (my own unit) between the years of 1958 and 1962. As such, he helped investigate several hundred fires. He was the lead investigator for LASD on the Woodwardia Fire.

Chief Graham related to me that immediately after this event began, he, as was the custom in those days, was teamed up with United States Forest Service Investigator Elwood Stone. The pair was tasked with conducting both the cause-and-origin investigation and the follow-up criminal investigation on the Woodwardia Fire. Graham recalled that they immediately drove to the ranger station just above La Canada to receive a briefing on the event. They drove to the first area the flames had been seen, just under the Woodwardia Bridge, and began searching for an ignition source. At the base of a burned tree, in the area where the fire indicators showed the blaze to have initially erupted, they found the burned remains of a paintbrush. Stamped on the metal side of the paintbrush were the initials "USFS." This item was the cause of the fire.

Sergeant Graham and Investigator Stone drove back to the ranger station and began their inquiry. Their interviews quickly revealed the fact that Crewman Grader had been highly upset at being forced to work and had been in possession of a paintbrush earlier that day. He had also left the fire/ranger station by himself for a half hour only to return just minutes prior to the fire being noticed. Eventually, Graham and Stone confronted Grader with the brush and the statements of his fellow firefighters. He subsequently confessed to the event. He admitted that he had been upset and had left the station to cool off. When he got to the Woodwardia Canyon area just above the station, he had ignited a forest service paintbrush from his truck and tossed it over the side and into the canyon. Immediately feeling guilty, he returned to quarters.

In those days, investigators were hampered by the penal codes in effect. This massive event could only be charged as a wildland fire, despite having cost the lives of two firefighters. The arsonist, an on-duty firefighter whose criminal act caused the death of two comrades, could not be charged with murder. He was convicted of setting a wildland fire and was sentenced to the maximum amount of time, exactly one year in jail. He also paid a $1,000 fine. Making matters even more painful for then-Sergeant Graham, William Grader was the son of a retired Los Angeles sheriff's lieutenant.

In recent years, major events have led to changes in this law. Starting with the 2006 Esperanza Fire, arsonists can now be charged with murder if their acts lead to the death of firefighters. There is no doubt that William Grader would have been charged with these two deaths had this event occurred fifty years later.

Chang Chinglan
Rowland Heights, 1998

Author's Note: This case comes from the case files of retired LASD arson investigator, Sergeant John Ament.

Chang Chinglan was a Taiwanese immigrant of Chinese descent. Like many of his countrymen, he settled into the San Gabriel Valley, east of Los Angeles. This valley and its surrounding foothills have an extremely high population of Asian-Americans. In the hillside town of Rowland Heights, with its close proximity to a large Buddhist temple, the area in 1998 was almost 80 percent ethnic Chinese. The vast majority of the business signs in this area are in an Asian language, and it is easy to pretend you are in the Far East when you drive through this town. The area is patrolled by the Los Angeles Sheriff's Department.

Just after eleven at night on March 28, 1998, a violent traffic accident occurred just south of the major intersection of Colima Road and Nogales Street in the Puente foothills. At least all of the responding patrol personnel believed it to be an accident. Sheriff's deputies soon arrived and saw a small, white Ford sedan smashed into an overturned, red Honda Passport SUV. The impact had crumpled the nose of the white Ford and caused the red Honda to spin around at least once and flip over. Deputies could see that a hysterical Asian female had been removed from the upside down Honda and was being assisted by several citizens. The driver of the white Ford, on the other hand, was in a bit more dire circumstances. His car was engulfed in flames, and the driver was slumped over in his seat, completely on fire. Despite a fast response from both the police and fire agencies, there would be no saving this victim. Firefighters eventually extinguished the car fire with some foam.

Original patrol deputies attempted to talk to the female who had been driving the red Honda, but she was too excited and was speaking only in Mandarin Chinese at this point, which none of the patrolmen understood very well. They ran the license plates of both cars and were a little surprised to see that they both were registered to the same person, Lydia Ngo. Looking into the still-smoking white car, deputies saw what they believed to be a primary causal factor in this accident. They saw at least two wine bottles on the front seat of the car and guessed that this might be yet another tragic drunk-driving case.

Soon a sheriff's fatal accident investigator arrived at the scene, and along with the coroner, he supervised the fire department's use of equipment to remove the doors and extricate the deceased driver from the car. Due to the severity of the fire damage to the victim's head, the investigators were unable to determine the race or gender of the victim. The clothing suggested a slightly built male adult. Even after the fire had been extinguished, the investigators and firemen were somewhat alarmed by the strong smell of gasoline emanating from within the car. They assumed it had come from the overturned red Honda. An examination of that vehicle showed that the gas tank was intact, along with the rest of the fuel delivery system, and that no fluids were leaking. They then took a closer look at the red Honda and could see that its gas tank was also intact and had therefore not added to the fire.

The traffic and coroner investigators soon became very alarmed as the doors of the car were pried off by the hydraulic "jaws of life." The driver, who had sustained heavy fire damage to his head area, was slumped over onto the passenger's seat. Next to his head was a fully intact wine bottle that had a white, cloth "wick" protruding from its neck. This item smelled of gasoline. The firemen and investigators recognized this as a Molotov cocktail firebomb. This device had not ignited and was in fact full of a substance that smelled like gasoline. Even more alarming, the responders at the scene could see a couple more of these items in the front and backseats. They evacuated the scene and called the sheriff's arson/explosives detail (bomb squad) to come and render the scene safe.

Senior Investigator Sergeant John Ament and his new trainee, Detective Gary Spencer, arrived and processed the scene along with the coroner's investigator. Among their observations, they noted that the car itself was not the cause of the fire. The engine area was pristine, although damaged by the collision, and the rest of the car was undamaged except for the interior of the passenger compartment. Sergeant Ament looked at the car and determined that there was a "live" Molotov cocktail on the seat directly next to the deceased driver. However, Ament was well aware that this type of device does not in fact explode and is fairly innocuous if it is not subjected to flame. Since the fire was out and the interior of the car somewhat soaked in firefighting foam, there was little chance of this device igniting. Ament consulted with the coroner's investigator and said it was possible there was another device under the body. The two agreed that it was probably a better idea to remove the burned body from the car prior to dealing with any suspected hazardous devices. They did just that.

When he was removed, they could see that the driver was male and clad in a heavily burned pair of blue jeans, a flannel type shirt, and a tee shirt. Black loafers and white socks completed the ensemble. The green-and-white flannel shirt was heavily burned by fire and smelled of gasoline. The driver's head and face were the most severely damaged portions of his entire body. In the grand scheme of burned bodies, the detectives noted that this one did not have significant deep-tissue damage. The hair, head, and face were destroyed by fire, but the skin was present and there was no long-term burning of the tissue. This was a result of the body having been on fire for a relatively short period of time.

Once the male was removed, the detectives could clearly see that the Molotov on the front seat was in fact "live" and still full of gasoline. There was a second Molotov on the rear seat, and this one was broken. The fire from this item was significant and had caused the rear seats to ignite. The most severe damage to this car had been to the rear seat area. There was a third empty wine bottle in the car and an unburned white cloth wick nearby.

Detectives further scoured the car and found a green butane lighter on the floor at the driver's feet. This appeared to be the item that had ignited the fire. There were no other sources of fuel or ignition in the small car.

Investigators began interviewing witnesses to the "accident." Several reported seeing the red Honda driving normally on the roadway and the small white Ford speeding out of a nearby parking lot, striking the Honda on the driver's side door. The Honda spun around once and eventually rolled over. The female driver of the Honda was able to climb out of her overturned car, but the male driver of the Ford appeared to be trapped in his vehicle. Several witnesses reported the male to be violently thrashing his arms around, and eventually a spark was seen in the driver's seat area. Then a sort of fireball exploded out of the passenger compartment. Several people saw this, but like all witnesses they each had a slightly varied version of the event in their mind. One witness even reported that the male driver appeared to be pouring a liquid over himself just prior to the fire.

The investigators were still having difficulties communicating with the female victim. This problem was eventually solved when a citizen, who spoke both Mandarin and English fluently, stopped by to assist the detectives. After much discussion and excited gesturing, the true story turned out to be even more strange than imagined. The driver of the red Honda was forty-year-old Miss Lydia Ngo (the registered owner of both vehicles). She told investigators her story. Ngo said that she was a fairly recent immigrant to the United States from Taiwan and was on her way from work to her nearby home. She shocked investigators when she identified the badly burned driver of the white Ford as her former husband, fifty-one-year-old Chang Chinglan.

Lydia said that she and Chang had been married in Taiwan many years ago. They remained husband and wife for about seven years total and had a fourteen-year-old daughter together. Several years ago, while still in Taiwan, Chang began beating Lydia. Lydia's family had already immigrated to the United States and owned a restaurant in the Rowland Heights area. As the physical abuse continued from Chang, Lydia decided to flee Taiwan to join her family. In 1989 she and her daughter fled Taiwan and arrived in the Los Angeles area. Chang followed her six months later. The two maintained a tenuous relationship, as Chang kept asking to be reunited and to spend more time with their daughter, while Lydia wanted him to stop being abusive and get a real job. Lydia said Chang had an explosive temper and continued his physical attacks on her as recently as a couple years ago. He was eventually arrested for assaulting her, and she filed for divorce shortly after. Lydia was later awarded full custody of their daughter by the courts.

A year ago Lydia remarried, and Chang became really upset when he heard the news. He started calling her home at all hours of the day and showed up at her family's restaurant on numerous occasions to confront her. He would create a loud scene, refuse to pay for his meals, and then refuse to leave the restaurant. Eventually he had to be escorted out by sheriff's deputies, which further inflamed his anger. Chang continued his harassing phone calls and eventually hired a shady attorney to send bogus paperwork to Lydia. Eventually the harassment became more sinister. Three days before this "accident," Lydia's car had been parked at her family's restaurant. She came out to find that all four tires had been slashed by a knife.

In describing the events of this evening, Lydia Ngo said that she had been driving from her work toward her nearby home when she saw her ex-husband's car speeding out of a Pic-and-Save parking lot toward her. He rammed into her driver's side door, spinning her car around and flipping it over. She was upside down, and her head was sticking out of the sun roof. She could see that Chang was still in his driver's seat, waving his arms wildly and yelling. She saw him reach for something in the car, saw a spark of flame, and then she saw and felt an explosion that produced a fireball. Lydia, with the help of some citizens, was able to crawl out of her car and was not seriously injured. She could clearly see that Chang was dead in his car.

What started out as a suspected drunk-driving traffic accident was later classified as the attempted murder of Lydia Ngo by Chang. Investigators believed he planned to run Ngo off the road and then throw the Molotov cocktails into her vehicle in an attempt to murder her. Investigators theorized that when

Chang became trapped in his disabled car, he decided to commit suicide by pouring gasoline on himself and igniting at least one of the Molotov cocktails. The physical damage at the scene indicated that the second Molotov in the rear seat may have been broken during the collision. This extra fuel added a serious amount of explosive and flammable vapors to an already volatile scene. The witnesses reported feeling and seeing an explosion, which is consistent with the rapid ignition of gasoline vapors.

Homicide investigators and later coroner's investigators eventually classified the bizarre incident as a botched attempted murder followed by a suicide.

Investigator's Analysis:

Readers of this section will recognize that tire-slashing attacks, broken windows, and other nuisance vandalisms are described in most of these case histories, as they often precede spite/revenge arson attacks. The entire incident is consistent with the typical disputes that precede spite/revenge arsons. One party begins harassing and annoying the other. Quite often this is manifested through phone calls or, more recently, via online taunts, posts, and the display of very private images. If these are ignored, the harasser steps up his campaign to more physical attacks such as tire slashing, keying cars, minor theft and vandalism, and window breaking. At some point this crosses over into the very dangerous behavior of stalking, burglarizing, prowling, and eventually following or "lying in wait" for the victim, as in this case. A review of this event clearly reveals that there had been some significant planning involved in the gathering of materials and stalking of the victim. Along with this, there was very little chance that the suspect would be able to get away with this crime, and he may not have been planning to survive the event himself.

Gary Gene Glazier, aka The Cat Killer of el Caminito La Crescenta, 2001-2004

Author's Note: This case derives from the author's own case files. Due to the continuing and very real threat that this man presents, several last names were omitted, as were the entire names and identification of some witnesses.

Evil personified:

Gary Glazier is the most evil man I have ever met. Our personal relationship started at 11:00 a.m. on May 13, 2004. Thirty minutes later, Glazier was handcuffed for the first time in his life. This was very strange, since Glazier was sixty-two years old at the time, and I later became absolutely convinced that, among other things, he was a serial arsonist who had attempted to kill seven people and had burned or attempted to burn three homes in his neighborhood over a three-year period. Additionally, other witnesses and relatives would later testify to his thirty-plus-year reign of terror that included probable ritualistic child molestations, abuse, dozens of alleged instances of animal torture and killings, dog poisonings, the ongoing stalking of women, voyeurism, peeping and prowling, dozens of suspected felony vandalisms, and just generally terrorizing an entire neighborhood. I was actually quite surprised later to learn that I was the first cop to ever put handcuffs on this fiend.

My very first perception of Glazier was that he was not very physically imposing and presented himself as a prick of an old man. He whined when he talked and invoked the United States Constitution as a threat to get us off his property (which we weren't even on at the time). When his original bluster failed to rattle or deter us, he became somewhat quiet. He continued to be uncooperative and refused to assist our investigation in any way. Minutes later, when he forced our hand and we handcuffed him, his mood changed nearly instantaneously. He became a befuddled old man who, for the first time in his life, really didn't know what to do. At that point he uttered words that we would soon know to be prophetic..."You got me!" We really didn't understand what he meant at that moment, but it was to be made clear to us several years later. But I'm getting way ahead of myself at this point. Let me set up how Gary Glazier and I first met.

Gary Gene Glazier:

Gary Glazier's history has always been murky and secretive. We were able to cobble together a meager synopsis of his life based on interviews with a former wife, stepdaughter, neighbors, current girlfriend, and a woman he paid to have sex with him, along with a psychiatric report prepared at the time of his sentencing. Gary Glazier was extremely private and secretive and would never have divulged a single shred of this information himself.

Gary Glazier moved into his home at 3031 El Caminito, La Crescenta, in the 1960s. It appears that he had lived most of his life with his mother prior to that. At the time he was a single man who worked as a technical writer for the defense contractor Litton Industries. He worked at the site in nearby Pasadena, which would later become known as the Jet Propulsion Lab (JPL). Gary's mother and father lived within just a mile or two of him in a similar home. Gary obviously had a high intellect, and he possessed an engineering degree. Very little is known about his youth other than the fact that he was an avid collector of high-quality antiques. He and his mother had been involved in collecting and restoring antiques for over fifty years.

Glazier's known history:

In the early 1970s, Glazier met and married a divorced mother named Janet. She had a young ten-year-old daughter named Jeanette, and the three lived for less than ten years at the El Caminito address. At the time, the neighborhood was a classic Southern California foothill community. It sat several hundred feet higher in elevation than the nearby valleys, and the neat streets were lined with tall shade trees and pines. The area was cooler, quieter, and less smoggy than nearby Pasadena, Glendale, Burbank, and the San Fernando Valley. The area was almost 95 percent white and was comprised mostly of families. The area then and today is virtually free of violent crimes and gang activity.

Janet gave me some insight into her decade-long relationship with Gary Glazier during some very colorful conversations in the months following his arrest. Janet revealed that she lived a wild and risqué life prior to meeting Gary Glazier. She found him to be neat, polite, and very old-world in his style and mannerisms. He owned his own home and made a very comfortable living. He drove perfectly restored antique cars, always dressed neatly, and was very romantic. She said that this side of him changed literally the day after they were married. Her first indication that he was less than romantic was when he insisted on having their wedding the last day of the year in order to get a significant tax break. Janet was later to learn that Gary had several odd obsessions. One was that he was obsessed with "beating the government" in all tax matters. She said he literally planned their entire life and purchases around tax breaks. She said he seldom kept money in banks, made most of his purchases "under the table," and stockpiled and hoarded large amounts of cash.

Janet knew Gary to hide large sums of cash in the home. She believed he may have built unique hidden drawers and cubbies into furniture or possibly one of his cars. He never let her into certain areas of his garage or basement and he would stay locked in a room in the basement for hours.

Another odd obsession that Gary had was his fascination with the silent screen era. He collected hundreds of classic silent movies and maintained an extensive photo collection of actresses from that period. Once, he confided in Janet that he had been arrested by the LAPD for making lewd phone calls and stalking an old silent screen actress. Janet was never able to confirm that story. I later researched that information and found that there was no record of such an arrest in any active police computer.

The most sinister of Gary Glazier's obsessions, as described by his wife Janet, was his absolute hatred of anyone touching, molesting, or trespassing on his property. She said that he would become enraged if anyone parked in front of his home, parked too close to his cars in a parking lot, or entered his property. She knew him to frequently vandalize cars on the street in front of his home with an ice pick. She knew him to pour sugar in gas tanks, "key" the paint on vehicles, flatten tires, puncture radiators and tires with an icepick, poison neighbors' trees, and conduct other forms of vandalism in retribution for these supposed trespasses.

Janet said that Gary became livid when kids, dogs, or cats entered his property. During several interviews (and later grand jury testimony) with Janet and her daughter, Jeanette, detectives and prosecutors learned that both had been witness to several episodes fueled by Gary Glazier's cruelty and obsessions. Both reported seeing him build animal traps and lures. They saw him on several occasions trap neighborhood cats and dogs and then torture them in various ways. Jeanette (daughter) was a favorite play thing for Gary Glazier. Several times during her young teen years, Gary would announce to her that he had captured a cat or dog. He would then make her watch as he tortured, strangled, and drowned the helpless animal. She described him gutting the animals and even electrocuting some of them. Later, Jeanette would learn that the neighbors would find dead animals in their pools, boats, or in their front yards. One time, she saw Gary actually mail a piece of a dead cat back to the neighbors across the street.

Janet (mother) knew Gary was killing cats and dogs. She never actually saw him kill an animal, but in front of the grand jury she had shouted, "I saw frozen cats in my fucking freezer... that's how I know he killed them." She said he kept them frozen until he either threw them away on trash day or put them in someone else's yard.

Nocturnal activities:

Janet and Jeanette both described Gary Glazier as keeping a ritualistic schedule to his life. He always napped in the afternoon, so that he could go out at night. They said he frequently spent many late-night hours in his yard or walking through the neighborhood. He was often outside after midnight until about three in the morning. They said he frequently studied the neighbor's nighttime activities and would occasionally remark on personal events that happened inside of neighbor's homes. They both would later realize that he stalked, or at least spied upon, several women in the neighborhood on a routine basis.

Fetishes:

Janet reported that Gary Glazier was very sexually active and was obsessed with "dirty sex." She described him as being very interested in feces, anal sex, and integrating other bodily functions into intercourse. She said Gary liked to have Janet powder his bottom and put a diaper on him. Late in their relationship, she learned that Glazier, who had assumed the role of stepfather to Jeanette, was overly concerned about Jeanette's physical habits. He frequently smelled and checked her panties for signs of her period and "sexual activity." On a nightly basis, he would lock the young girl in a room in the basement and force her to stay there until she defecated into a coffee can. At which point he would sit with the young girl and sort through her fecal matter with her as if it was some sort of a science experiment. He always insisted on tucking the girl into bed alone and would lay on the bed with her. Janet would later come to believe that Gary must have been molesting her daughter on a regular basis. After hearing of this bizarre and abusive behavior toward the teenage girl, it came as no surprise to me to learn that Jeanette would endure years of therapy, psychiatric treatment, and medication in the years after Glazier. I spoke to her at length on these matters, but Jeanette now has no recollection of whether she was molested or not. She feels that she must have been but can't recall. Her various psychiatrists and psychologists are convinced that she was ritually molested on a nightly basis by Glazier.

Neighborhood incidents:

A young neighbor girl, a friend of Jeanette's, later told investigators that a childhood pet dog of hers went missing one day and was never seen again. Years later, after Jeanette had run away from home, she called that friend and tearfully told her that she had been forced to watch Gary Glazier kill the pet.

Still another neighbor (now a large man in his mid-forties), testified tearfully to the grand jury that as an eleven-year-old he had seen his dog returning home from Glazier's property, whimpering and whining. The boy was horrified to see that the dog had its stomach sliced open and its entrails dragging on the ground. When the boy entered Glazier's property at a later date to retrieve something, he was grabbed by Glazier and menaced with a butcher knife. Glazier told him he would cut his guts out like he had done to his dog. The boy ran home and reported the event to his parents, who then summoned the sheriff's. The case was referred in the late 1970s to the district attorney for an "office resolution hearing." No criminal charges were ever recorded. Glazier denied the events and said that the dog must have been injured by coyotes.

A long list of other neighbors reported to detectives and the grand jury that they had been terrorized by Glazier over a period of thirty years. Many reported vandalism damage to their cars or guests' cars if they had ever parked in front of Glazier's home. One neighbor, who'd had a minor dispute with Glazier twenty years earlier, reported that his home had been flooded via a garden hose twice while he was on vacation. On yet another vacation, he returned to find his power had been cut, causing all the food to spoil in his freezers. Still other neighbors reported their trees being poisoned, as someone had drilled into them and placed some sort of chemicals into the trunks of the trees. These events were preceded by Glazier complaining about the leaves from their trees falling on his property. Still other neighbors complained of smoke bombs being placed under their homes in the middle of the night and numerous acts of vandalism perpetrated against their homes around holiday seasons—Christmas, Halloween, the Fourth of July—immediately following parties.

Many neighbors had actually left the state and even the country as a direct result of the suspected activities of Gary Glazier. A woman from England learned of the current investigation and established contact with the detectives and prosecutors. She stated that twenty years ago, Gary Glazier had been a Peeping Tom who frequently spied on her while she showered. She claimed to have received numerous stenciled letters from someone accurately describing her bathing habits. At one point she or her husband confronted Glazier, but he only ran back into his home. She strongly believed he had spied on her for years. She even believed that he had actually crept into their home at night on more than one occasion.

The most interesting part of all of these reported incidents is that Gary Glazier was never observed or implicated in any of them. He either was innocent (no fucking way) or was so adept and skillful that he eluded detection for over thirty years. Past and present neighbors told me that they had contacted the local sheriff's station regarding Gary Glazier on numerous occasions, but the responding deputies were unable to speak to him and could not link him to any crimes. I personally tried to verify these incidents. I ran Glazier's name through every law enforcement and public records database I could think of and got no results other than the reports he had filed on more than one occasion complaining of neighbors' pets to the animal control agency. I went into the local station and hand-searched old files dating back two decades and could still find no report with Gary Gene Glazier listed as a suspect. There were several dispatch records of reported vandalisms on the street in front of his home and an old burglary report that listed him as a "person of interest" in the burglary of a vacant home. However, all of these reports ended the same way. A neighbor or witness told responding deputies that they *believed* Glazier had something to do with the crime, but the deputies were just never able to make contact with the man, and the case was made inactive. The man was a true enigma.

THE MCCARTHY INCIDENT:

In May of 2004, as three seasoned arson investigators stood face-to-face with Glazier, we knew none of this. As he stood there in front of us, we were not at all impressed; he looked weak and wimpy and did not appear to be a serious threat. We would later become very impressed. The information found in this case study slowly revealed itself over the next four years through exhaustive interviews and painstaking fact-checking. But again, we're getting a bit ahead of the story.

In the early morning hours of February 13, 2001, the McCarthy family was asleep in their home at 3032 El Caminito. Ed, Deb, and their teenage son, Kel, were a self-admitted dysfunctional family. All three struggled with long-term alcohol problems, and Kel added some weed and bad behavior at school to the mix. While they were inwardly mixed up, from the outside they appeared to be normal, hardworking people with a neat home and yard. They were fairly well-liked in the neighborhood, with only Kel's wild teen activities being somewhat of a distraction to the neighbors. That night, typical of many others, all three were sleeping off the effects of heavy drinking. Ed and Kel were in their upstairs beds while Deb was sleeping in front of a burning fireplace in the downstairs living room. The night was cold and rainy. The family dog, Waldo, was sleeping downstairs near Deb.

At around a quarter past three in the morning, Ed was awakened by Waldo whimpering and climbing on the bed. Waldo's feet were wet and he smelled strongly of gasoline. Ed bolted awake and ran downstairs to an overpowering odor of gasoline throughout the bottom floor. He yelled for Kel to wake up, and he shook Deb awake on the sofa. They went into their kitchen and saw a one-inch-deep pool of gasoline spread over the entire floor. They saw two five-gallon, red, plastic gas cans standing near the closed exterior kitchen door. Most alarmingly, they saw the burners of the gas stove turned on "full." They fled the home into the rainy, cold night and ran to their next-door neighbors, still barefoot and wearing pajamas and underwear. Firefighters, sheriff's deputies, and eventually sheriff's arson investigators arrived. After the home was vented and washed out, they determined that someone had entered the home via the side kitchen door, or possibly through a large "doggy door" on that same kitchen door, and poured about ten gallons of gasoline on the floor. The suspect then turned on the open burners to the stove and fled the scene, leaving the plastic gas cans to burn up in the ensuing fire. Due to the vagaries of fuel-to-air mixtures, the lower and upper explosive limits of volatile gasses, a whole bunch of luck, and the sheer grace of God, the gasoline vapors never reached the height of the open burners or pilot lights to ignite. Nor, for some unknown reason, did Waldo's movements, and the fact that he was stirring up more vapors and carrying them throughout the home, cause an ignition of the gasoline vapors. Most amazing of all, the vapors did not, for some unknown reason (probably divine intervention), migrate twenty feet across the living room floor to the open burning fireplace and ignite in a massive fireball. The scientific explanations for all of these things might include the heavy atmospheric conditions and high humidity caused by the rain and cold weather—or maybe it was just a *goddamn miracle!*

Either way, this was a really unique event. Someone had attempted to kill a family of three with fire while they slept. Even in the arson business, a murder-by-fire scenario is the rarest of all events.

The Los Angeles sheriff's arson investigators handle about 2,500 fires a year. That equals about a hundred-and-fifteen cases, give or take a dozen, per investigator on the twenty-man squad. This is probably one of the busiest arson squads in the nation. During a given year, the arson investigators handle fires in every area of the county of Los Angeles where the sheriff's department patrols or contracts for services. This encompasses over sixty communities and over six-million people.

Each year, we handle roughly a dozen or so arson murders. Almost every one of those cases involves the use of arson as a tool to hide evidence after a murder has been committed. Fire is such a finicky weapon and is not very reliable as a mechanism of murder. While fire kills dozens of people in LA County each year, they are mostly accidental events. In the dozens of cases each year where a suspect attempts to murder someone with fire, he almost invariably fails, as the victim is able to successfully flee the scene. Additionally, attempted-murder-by-fire scenarios are most often related to gang or narcotics activities, and usually an extremely crude and juvenile device or technique is employed, such as a Molotov cocktail. These devices have an extremely high (upward of 90 percent) failure rate, as they usually bounce off soft-skinned cars or wood and stucco homes. A Molotov cocktail doesn't blow up like in the movies and is most likely to be found burning like a candle in the yard. Lastly, the vast majority of attempted-murder-arson cases are perpetrated by suspects from outside of the targeted structure, as even the most intrepid criminal lacks the guts to enter a residence to commit their crime.

All in all, on that February day in 2001, the investigators were extremely surprised by the complexity of the event. They had to weigh the theory that a suspect from outside of the home had soundlessly entered it in the dead of night, (with a large dog present) poured several gallons of gasoline on the floor with an open fire burning several feet away, and then ignited the open burners on the stove, all in an attempt to murder an entire family. And all of this while the mother lay sleeping fewer than fifteen feet away. Investigators could only conclude that this act was perpetrated by someone driven by either sheer madness or thoughts of suicide.

That being said, investigators looked at the suicidal aspect of this event and sized up the immediate family as potential suspects. Deb, a very pretty woman in her midfifties and an executive secretary, was dismissed fairly soon by the detectives. Ed was in his midsixties and, while obviously a functioning alcoholic, was also dismissed after some lengthy questioning. Both Ed and Deb said that they had lived for years in the neighborhood and were friends with most of their neighbors. They didn't gamble, owe anyone a large amount of money, or live high-risk lifestyles. They had no recent disputes with anyone. They readily admitted that they had alcohol issues and had begun having severe discipline problems with their son, but they had no idea why anyone would want to kill them.

And then there was Kel; now, he posed a problem to the investigators. An obviously troubled teenager with anger issues, he was scrutinized much closer than either parent. He freely admitted to often fighting with his parents and going out late at night against their wishes. He left the home via an upstairs window and climbed over the roof to get down. He also admitted to having reentered the home on occasion via the doggy door in the kitchen. The detectives saw that Kel's room was strewn with beer bottles and cigarettes, while the rest of the home was neat and orderly. He said he was having recent girlfriend issues and was in a dispute with another high-school friend over the girl. A background check revealed that he had recently been arrested for alcohol, marijuana, and an illegal knife. The neighbors confided that Kel frequently fought with his parents, drove his car like a maniac, and was probably using drugs. He was your basic sullen, sarcastic, angry teen and seemed like a decent suspect to the detectives.

The detectives focused on Kel and his rival at school for the next few months. The gas cans did not have any fingerprints on them, and there was no other forensic evidence to test. They went to Kel's school and interviewed some of his friends. During this time, the family received a letter in the mailbox. Kel retrieved it and carried it to the home. The letter was written in block letters similar to stencil. Several words were misspelled and the tone was very threatening. It said that the previous incident was just a warning for "Kel to pay us." The letter alluded to Kel owing someone a large sum of money, and on the last line it said that the next time they would "get Waldo too." Kel showed it to his parents, and they turned it over to detectives a few days later. The family found it very odd that anyone would refer to Waldo, since few of Kel's friends knew about the dog. More importantly, no one ever called him Kel except his mother. All of his friends knew him as Kellen. The letter was tested but would yield no usable forensics.

Thinking outside the box, the detectives tried a more exotic investigative technique. They utilized a scent dog and "scented" the letter. The dog gave a positive alert and led them to Kellen, which solved absolutely nothing since he had handled the letter several times.

The detectives then got a warrant and searched Kel's and another boy's school locker. This met with negative results. Lacking any further leads, the detectives urged Kel to come to the sheriff's crime lab to take a polygraph exam. During that lengthy process, Kel gave several statements that were determined to be partially deceptive. The detectives confronted Kel with this information and began a very intense interview. About an hour into this, Kel finally blurted out that he had tried to kill himself and his family. Luckily, the detective handling this interview, Mike Cofield, was very experienced and recognized that an upset teenager may be giving them a false confession. When he further pressed Kel for details, none were forthcoming. Kel eventually admitted that he had confessed falsely only to "get out of there and go home." The detectives let a very upset Kel go home and then gave a polygraph to his father, Ed. Ed passed with flying colors, and the detectives were back to square one.

By the summer of 2001, there were absolutely no workable leads in the McCarthy attempted murder and arson case. Kel was never fully eliminated as a suspect, but the detectives were skeptical that he had done this. They never filed charges, and eventually they made the case "inactive pending new workable leads." In other words, it was tossed into the archives with the hundreds of other unsolved arsons from that year.

In retrospect, the arson investigator running this McCarthy incident was probably not the best guy to have out there. While he put in a lot of credible work, he made several glaring mistakes that would come back years later to damage the entire investigation. He failed to properly handle and forensically examine the gas cans left at the scene. He failed to look at the fire scene and profile a probable offender from the scene alone. The scene would have told him that this was no deed committed by a teenager or a drunk. The scene would have told them that this was a highly organized and extremely intelligent offender with nerves of steel and close knowledge of the family. A proper reading of the scene should have eliminated Kel and any of his stoner friends. Another mistake was a noted lack of neighborhood canvassing. Brief statements were taken from one set of neighbors, but they were pointedly directed at Kel and his behavior. A more open approach would have immediately led investigators to a much more suitable suspect, as several neighbors had for years voiced strong suspicions about a neighborhood man whose alleged activities and personal profile would have fit this fire scene. Lastly, there was some poor follow-up by the lead investigator on the forensics in this case, leading to the destruction of extremely important evidence, which would haunt and undermine this investigation for years. While all this activity was happening at the McCarthy's home in the spring of 2001, Gary Glazier stood in his dark and overgrown front yard directly across the street, taking it all in, no doubt with glee.

THE ARTSVELYAN FAMILY:

Albert and Anahit (Ana) Artsvelyan were Russian Armenian immigrants. Not your typical dirt-poor, third-world peasants that wash ashore on this land, but educated professionals with legitimate jobs and careers. Albert and Ana had long felt the sting of oppression as minority Armenians in Russia. They had fled that country several years before to make their way in Los Angeles. Albert has an engineering degree and worked for an engineering firm in Sylmar. Ana has two master's degrees in education and is employed as a teacher in the Pasadena school district. They made a very handsome living and invested all of their time and money into their home and two young daughters. The Artsvelyans were extremely family-oriented and loved to attend and host family parties. Ana was always fashionably dressed and doted on her husband and daughters. A pretty woman, she had a Russian accent but spoke fluent English. Albert had a much thicker accent and looked like a Russian Armenian out of central casting. He was fond of wearing nice clothes, but the clothes looked like those worn in every movie I have ever seen featuring Russian or Armenian gangsters. He frequently wore smoked glasses, dark pants, dark turtleneck shirts, and those nice thin leather jackets you only see in Europe or on the East Coast. Both Ana and Albert are very emotional and excitable and both chain-smoke cigarettes. Both always look perpetually worried. As it turned out, they had a good reason to be worried.

By the mid-1990s, the lily-white neighborhoods of La Crescenta were in transition. It was a desirable area in terms of real estate because of its low crime rates and excellent schools. During the real estate boom of the '90s, the large Korean and Armenian populations of nearby Glendale began to migrate up the hill into La Crescenta where the older homes with large yards beckoned. By the late '90s, the nearby busy Foothill Blvd was beginning to transform into trendier restaurants and many of the signs began showing Korean-language subheadings. Real-estate agents specializing in Armenian and Korean clientele began to aggressively prowl the quiet neighborhoods of La Crescenta, approaching long-term homeowners. As the market prices began to explode in 2000, the ethnic realtors began to be real pests; they were aggressively approaching homeowners and offering outrageously high prices for really old tract homes. Many of the long-term residents who were approaching retirement could not resist the dollar signs and sold out. They then took their lucrative earnings out to the retirement communities of the Colorado River area, Utah, and Arizona. The influx of Korean and Armenian families was easily visible. Almost as soon as the escrow was closed on these fifty-year-old homes, the new owners began massive renovation projects. The constant remodeling and major construction projects filled the quiet streets and neighborhoods with noise and activity. Later interviews would show that this invasive, noisy, and dusty activity was probably the sole mechanism which elevated Gary Glazier's nocturnal activities from irritating to near-deadly.

Into this environment moved the Artsvelyan family. When they purchased their forty-year-old home in 1999, they had no idea of the history of the neighborhood. Their home was on a quadrangle-shaped elevated property with a detached garage. They immediately began saving and planning for a major renovation of the home. Included in those plans was a lavish pool and hard-scape for the barren backyard. The backyard was rather interesting. La Crescenta, an unincorporated area of the county of Los Angeles, was not subject to the strict zoning guidelines that rule the incorporated cities. The Artsvelyans learned that the property line on their north side was comprised of a stone fence and a garage. The rear wall of the garage, built about fifty years before, was acting as part of the property line. In effect, the Artsvelyan's north fence was in fact the rear wall of their neighbor's garage. That garage, they were to find out later, belonged to none other than Gary Glazier. At the time, the Artsvelyan's only knew that the garage was a colossal eyesore. It had old, faded light-green paint that looked about as old as the garage. The paint was peeling badly. Also faded and peeling were large block letters that appeared to have painted several years before. The letters were mostly faded away but appeared to say "stop putting dirt against the wall." Because the Artsvelyans were two-to-three years away from starting their project, and did not even use their backyard, they ignored this garage for the time being.

As is the custom of their heritage, the Artsvelyans made it a point to knock on doors and meet all of their neighbors. They also brought the gift of a bottle of wine to their neighbors after they introduced themselves. While they didn't realize at the time that they were in a country where neighbors were slightly uncomfortable with that "old world" sort of neighborliness, they were nonetheless accepted by all in the neighborhood. Most of the neighbors would come to find out that Ana and Albert Artsvelyan were genuinely nice and friendly people. They got a warm reception from just about everybody. That is until they knocked on Gary Glazier's door. They had seen him in his yard and knew him to be home. He greeted their knocks by shouting, "Get out of here and stay off my property." He never opened his door and never faced them. He continued to yell at them until they actually left his yard. That is the only contact the family had with Glazier for the next four years or so.

Rio:

Albert had two young daughters, Ani and Lilit. He wanted to buy the girls a pet, and he liked the idea of having security at his home. With that in mind, he purchased a German shepherd puppy named Rio in 1999. The family fell in love with Rio, and he grew large quite quickly. He freely roamed the barren backyard and driveway at night. The entire Artsvelyan property was fenced, and Rio was unable to escape. Sometime in early 2000, Rio was heard barking vigorously at four in the morning. Albert and Ana looked out to see what the dog was barking at. Stunned, they saw their reclusive neighbor, Gary Glazier, frantically digging with a shovel in his front yard. They turned on their light and watched as Glazier scampered back into his home. That was the first of many times they noticed Glazier out in his yard in the very early morning hours.

The problem with Glazier's property was that it was extremely overgrown with high hedges, cluttered with large untrimmed trees, and raised above the street. It was impossible to look into his yard from the street, and very difficult to look into it from any neighbor's yard. Glazier had no lighting in his yard, and it was extremely dark. The only people who could see in directly were the neighbors on the sides and to the rear.

Within a week of this late night sighting, the Artsvelyans found that Rio appeared very sick. He was whining, lethargic, and unable to control his bowels. They took him to a local vet, who diagnosed that the dog appeared to have been poisoned. He told the Artsvelyans that the dog may have gotten into a household chemical like antifreeze and made himself sick. They took Rio home, and he began to recover. A little over one year later, they noticed similar symptoms from Rio. They went outside and found a pile of Hershey's chocolate bars soaked in antifreeze in their driveway. They called the sheriff's deputies, who photographed the evidence. The deputies and the Artsvelyans concluded that only someone from Glazier's property could have reached over the fence and placed the items in that location. A sheriff detective began to conduct a follow-up investigation on the two alleged poisonings. He questioned the Artsvelyans thoroughly and found them to have no enemies and no family disputes; there was no one with a motive for the crime. There had been no complaints to the sheriff's or animal control about the dog and no way for the dog to get out of the yard. Lacking any further leads, the sheriff's detective knocked on Gary Glazier's door on at least five occasions. Glazier never answered, even though it was obvious to the investigator that he was home. The dog poisoning event went into the usual "inactive investigations" file. Several months later, Rio again became sickened and was taken to the vet. The vet again said that he appeared to have been poisoned, and this time his internal organs were failing. Within a week, Rio died from organ failure, despite Albert and

Ana pouring several thousand dollars into treatment. The family was heartsick over the death and bewildered at what might have caused this. The Artsvelyans often wondered if Glazier had anything to do with these events.

THE TRIGGERING EVENT:

In 2002 the Artsvelyans were finally able to start their long awaited home remodel. Besides customizing the detached garage into a working office and temporary kitchen (while their new kitchen was being built), the family added a room at the rear and customized the entire home. This included the installation of high-quality kitchen appliances, new wood floors, and (in the Armenian tradition) liberal amounts of high-quality granite, tile, and mirrors in every room of the home. By early 2004, the family had moved back into the main house. At this point they had put close to $200,000 into the project. They had yet to finish their driveway and landscaping and were in the process of building a very large custom pool. The home was livable, but they had not yet purchased many pieces of furniture for the family and dining rooms.

Other than the sad incidents with Rio, they had had no further interaction with their neighbor. Anytime the Artsvelyans spotted Gary Glazier in his yard or at the curb, he quickly scurried back into the darkness of his yard or home. He was a true enigma to the family, but since he hadn't bothered them, they just ignored his oddities.

In late 2003, Albert had his contractor break ground on the custom pool and pool deck in the backyard. During the first week of that busy, dusty enterprise, Albert spotted Glazier out in his yard glaring menacingly at the contractors. Albert later testified that Glazier appeared to feel a significant amount of anger toward the workers. Albert rushed out to contact Glazier for the first time since they moved in. Albert apologized for the noise and dust and told Glazier that he would pay for a cleaning of his home after the contractors were finished. Glazier, for the first time since they moved in, said his first and last words to a member of the Artsvelyan family. He said simply, "You think you are a good neighbor? No, you are a bad neighbor." With that statement, Glazier turned and retreated back inside his home.

For the next few weeks, the pool contractor's Hispanic employees reported to their boss that the "old white guy" next door was throwing rocks and dirt at them while they worked. They never actually saw him throw anything, but they felt and saw numerous items come flying toward them from his densely foliaged yard. When the contractor went to speak to Glazier, he refused to answer the door and instead yelled through it, "Get off my property."

By early February, the pool was in and the hardscape and landscape process was set to begin. Throughout this entire time, the peeling paint and words on Glazier's garage remained in full view of the new pool. Albert wrote a note asking for permission to paint Glazier's entire garage for free. He placed the note on Glazier's door. The next day,

Albert found the crumpled note in his driveway next to Glazier's fence. A few days later, Albert saw Glazier get into his truck and leave the neighborhood. Albert, tired of dealing with Glazier, quickly got a sander and sanded down the side of the garage that was facing his pool. He then primed and painted the side of the garage. He thought that Glazier, who couldn't see that side of the garage from his property, would never even notice this. Albert couldn't have been more wrong.

That night, the Artsvelyans were planning a birthday party for one of their daughters. The party would be small, with only about twelve relatives attending. The day before the party, the Artsvelyans lost their home telephone service. They went outside and found the service line cut, as if by a knife or pair of scissors.

They decided to contact the phone company and possibly the sheriff's the next day. The phone company responded, saying that it couldn't make it out for a couple of days, and asked the family to use their cell phones in the meantime.

That evening they held the party as planned. The last relatives left just after midnight. As usual, the adults drank wine and alcoholic drinks, while the kids played in the new, virtually-empty common rooms. Albert and Ana took many photos of the happy family enjoying their first party in their "new" home. This would be the last worry-free night of their lives. It was February 21, 2004. Ana and Albert went to their bedroom at about 12:30 a.m.

First Artsvelyan fire:

Sometime after three thirty in the morning on February 22, Albert awoke with a start. He was restless and felt that something was wrong. A heavy smoker, he decided to go outside for a cigarette. He left his wife sleeping on her side of the bed and walked toward the kitchen. He noticed a strange bright glow coming from the kitchen area. As he entered the kitchen, he smelled smoke and saw that a fire was burning outside his kitchen window. He ran outside and saw a large fire burning under and up the side of his home in the driveway area. He immediately started to do several things. Panicked, he ran back into the home and awoke Ana and the girls, who were all still asleep in their beds. He yelled for them to grab their phones, purses, and jackets. He grabbed his cell and wallet. He then ran to the kitchen and found a fire extinguisher. Albert expended the entire contents of the extinguisher on the fire and saw no results. In shock, he stood in his driveway and watched the fire increasing in size and intensity and spreading completely under his home. Sheriff's deputies would arrive in four minutes, followed about three minutes later by the first fire engine. They would find the entire Artsvelyan family yelling, crying and screaming on the street in front of their home. Luckily, the family was completely unharmed—at least physically.

From the time the first deputies arrived until the investigators left the scene nearly eight hours later, almost every neighbor on the street would come out to stand in front of the Artsvelyan home, watching and talking to the authorities. There was, however, one notable exception. Not one person ever saw Gary Glazier ever come out of his home to watch, even though he was the neighbor closest to the fire. At about seven that morning, he did emerge from his driveway in a truck and disappear for about an hour. When he returned, he drove past the several fire trucks and sheriff's cars on the street, but he didn't stop, slow down, or even appear to notice them. He went directly into his driveway and then into his home.

The responding fire captain, who had extinguished the fire, determined that it had started in the open crawl space directly under the kitchen. The captain found no source of ignition in that area, but he could smell a strong odor of gasoline. In accordance with the law, he immediately summoned sheriff's arson investigators to the scene. This time, a different investigator, named Rick Velazquez, arrived. Throughout his investigation, he was completely unaware of the event that had occurred at the McCarthy's home directly across the street three years prior. There had been over five-thousand fire investigations conducted by the sheriff's arson unit since the McCarthy arson attempt, and it would have been impossible for investigators to remember every one. The McCarthy investigator and Detective Velazquez seldom worked together, so each was not aware of the other's investigation.

What Detective Velazquez did find was an extremely upset Albert Artsvelyan. Albert and his family were very upset by the fire. They did not originally point to any particular sinister source that could have caused the fire, but instead they kept asking Velazquez how the fire could have happened. Right next to the origin of the fire was the natural-gas meter for the home. This device was torn open by the fire and had vented some of its contents. However, the majority of the gas system was intact and did not add to the fire. Velazquez and a partner investigated and saw that the fire had started about five feet inside of the crawl space under the home. They also found a large amount of gasoline in the area of origin and no accidental source of ignition. Rick and his partner also recognized that the fire had done major damage to the underside of the home, and that it had just started to breach through the floor when the firemen arrived. Later estimates would indicate that the family got out of the home within about three minutes of this becoming a fatal event. Had the fire successfully breached the kitchen floor it would have quickly spread through the open house filling it with heat, flame, and lethal levels of smoke and carbon monoxide. Clearly, this was an attempt to kill the family as they slept.

There was one large oddity in this case. The Artsvelyan home was completely secured by a fence that was fairly difficult to climb. The arsonist, if entering the scene from outside of the property, would have to scale the fence carrying some sort of large accelerant container. Rick Velazquez and his partner believed that the arsonist had to have used anywhere between two and five gallons of gasoline at this scene. Further, the arsonist had to have some way to place, pour, or spray the gasoline under the raised foundation of the home where four people were sleeping. The suspect would have to light the gasoline and then somehow scale the fence again, all the while in the dark. This act alone would take some incredible nerve and would most likely leave a large amount of physical evidence at the scene. There were no footprints in the dirt, no drag marks left from a gasoline container, no container left at or near the scene, and no indication that the lock on the gate had been opened.

When Rick advised Albert of his findings, Albert was visibly shocked. For several minutes he could not understand it could be a criminal fire and had no idea who would have done this to him. If the truth were known, Albert would have been really upset if Rick had told him that he (Albert) was considered the primary suspect at this time. As is well-known in the arson community, many cases of arson are motivated by insurance fraud. A home under construction also raises many red flags to the investigators. Contracting disputes, failure to pay bills, failed city inspections, and cost overruns are very common reasons for either the contractor or the homeowner to commit this crime. Like in a murder, the person closest to the victim is always considered the first suspect until they can be eliminated. Unofficially (and way beyond the scope of political correctness), the ethnicity of the homeowner is always considered as a possible factor in fraud cases. The fact that Albert was both Russian and Armenian, both ethnic groups with a healthy reputation for fraud in the Los Angeles area, gave him two immediate strikes against him. After several hours of questioning over the next few days, Albert began to realize that Rick and his partners suspected him of involvement in the fire. Rick later admitted that the focus of the investigation was immediately pointed toward Albert and his Armenian contractor. Albert began to bristle at the increasingly inflammatory questions centered on whether or not he was a gambler, used narcotics, was having an affair, or owed money to gangsters. Eventually, he became downright pissed off. For the remainder of the investigation, Albert remained on very cool personal terms with Rick.

Rick and his partner conducted a much more diligent investigation than the detective on the McCarthy incident. However, the results were much the same. Within a few short weeks, Rick had interviewed insurance company reps, contractors, family members, and some neighbors. Rick finally concluded that Albert and his family were most likely not responsible for this event. One of the main factors was that the home was woefully underinsured. While Albert had put about $250,000 into his remodel, and thereby adjusted the value of his home to nearly $700,000, he had neglected to change his insurance policy from its original $250,000 amount. This home was tragically underinsured and the fire caused catastrophic financial loss to the family. Rick, after his detailed look at the Artsvelyans also just didn't think Albert was the kind of guy to commit this kind of crime. His lifestyle suggested the normal family life of a hard-working, law-abiding citizen.

About a week into the case, Albert did approach Rick with a possible suspect. He said that after thinking long and hard on the subject, he had come to the opinion that the only person he knew who may have set fire to his home was the weird guy next door, Gary Glazier. Albert gave the brief history of the family's interactions with the man and included the dog poisonings and Glazier's odd nighttime activities. Albert even brought over a neighbor named Ann Lewis, who said she was aware of a number of evil acts committed by Gary Glazier as far back as thirty years. When Rick interviewed her, she admitted that she had no personal knowledge of these acts but had heard the stories from neighbors who had long since moved away. Rick found the allegations somewhat far-fetched, and he continued with his normal investigation.

When Rick ran out of active leads and had positively cleared the Artsvelyans as suspects, he turned back to the prospect of Gary Glazier. He conducted a criminal work-up on the man and found no history whatsoever. He found no witnesses in the neighborhood that could say they had ever actually seen Glazier do anything illegal. They did, however, reiterate the same story as Ann Lewis, saying that Glazier was really weird and had been terrorizing the neighborhood for over thirty years. Rick could find no one who had personally witnessed these acts of alleged terror. Rick then began looking at the facts of the case. Glazier was the closest neighbor to the spot where the fire had occurred. However, the Artsvelyan property was completely surrounded by fences that showed no signs of having been climbed or circumvented. Rick, a fairly young and very strong person, realized that he would have a lot of difficulty climbing the fences between the properties, even without carrying gallons of gas with him. He could not conceive of how a sixty-two-year-old man, who by all descriptions was not athletic and quite pudgy, could accomplish this feat in the dark, without making a lot of noise, and without leaving a large amount of forensic evidence. Rick seriously doubted that the man could have physically committed this act.

Nevertheless, Rick and his partner tried on several occasions to contact Glazier at his home. Each time they visited, they saw his gate open and his vehicle present. They also heard music and movements coming from within his home. Each time, their very loud knocks and shouts went unanswered, and each time Rick left his business card at the front door. Three weeks went by with no results, and Rick finally reached into his detective bag of tricks and found a way to locate Glazier's unlisted phone number. Using a pretext number, he called Glazier's home one night when he knew Gary was home. Glazier answered, and Rick identified himself. Glazier became very upset that the police knew his number and demanded to know how they had gotten it. He was upset that he was being "intruded on by the government" and wanted Rick's full name and badge number. When Rick failed to be intimidated by the man's tactics, Glazier began to meekly answer questions. He said that he knew nothing about a fire and nothing about his neighbors. He refused to meet with detectives in person and told them not to call him again. He then hung up the phone.

A few weeks after this, all workable leads in the case dried up, and Rick eventually reported to a very unhappy Albert Artsvelyan that he had no clues as to who had committed this act. When Albert insisted that he was convinced Glazier was responsible,

Rick explained Glazier's lack of cooperation, and his own doubts that Glazier could have physically entered the property. Albert was very upset by this news and told Rick that he was going to hire a private detective to look into his neighbor. Rick advised him not to waste his money but that if he was going to spend money anyway, to spend it on a video system to see if in fact his neighbor was the suspect. He advised Albert that if he was going to get a video camera, to get a good one.

By April of 2004, a lot of things were happening. Albert and his family had relocated to an apartment and started the tedious insurance claim process. They continued their pool project since they had already paid for the job. Their home remained a construction site, and the builders were forced to bring in temporary power because the main electricity had been lost in the fire.

Albert had consulted a private investigator, who of course asked for a lot of money. Albert then went to a "spy shop" and hired a man to install a $10,000 video system. This state-of-the-art system utilized fourteen pinhole cameras, all connected to a central computer that was installed in Albert's detached garage. These cameras were low-light operable and motion sensitive. They recorded every time there was movement. They did not record if there was no movement. The technician who installed the system looked and acted like an Eastern European spy. He arrived dressed as an electrician and wired the entire system in broad daylight (probably while being watched by Glazier). He also disguised each camera in phony pieces of wood, gate posts, and even a hollowed-out rock. It was really an expert job; it was done in such a way that he appeared to be just another contractor on the property.

Other things were happening in the neighborhood at this time. Ann Lewis, the "nosy housewife" across the street, began to rally the neighborhood in an effort to help the Artsvelyans. Her activism, like something out of the 1950s, brought together every single family on the street. She organized a community meeting at the local sheriff's station in early May, where she gave a stunned deputy sheriff a list of over forty current and past neighbors who all had something bad to say about Gary Glazier. Some of these past neighbors were now residing out of state and out of the country. They all provided a quantity of stories—some witnessed, some only heard about—detailing dozens of acts of vandalism, animal abuse, animal torture, poisonings, stalking, burglary, and possibly even murder, stretching back to the mid-1970s. These people encompassed nearly every race and ethnic group in the area, and their stories spanned almost a thirty-year period. The one thing these people did have in common was an adamant belief that Gary Glazier had been covertly committing evil acts for as long as they could remember. The station community service deputy did not know what to do with this seemingly outlandish accumulation of stories, so he just forwarded them on to the detective handling the current case, Rick Velazquez.

Second Artsvelyan fire:

The Artsvelyans finally completed work on their pool, and in the first week of May, 2004, they brought their kids from their temporary apartment over to the house to swim in it. Albert and Ana took a single dip into their $80,000 pool. They last visited the scene at 11:00 p.m. on May 12. When they left the property that night to return to their apartment, they checked and locked all gates. All of this was captured on the hidden cameras.

On May 13, 2004, at 4:10 a.m., a neighbor who had been outside with his dog reported a large fire burning at the vacant Artsvelyan home. A sheriff's deputy arrived within two minutes and found the driveway gate locked and a fire freely burning under the home and in the kitchen area next to the driveway. The deputy saw no one around, and a neighbor told him the family had moved out three months earlier after the first fire.

When the fire department arrived, they cut open the gate lock and extinguished the fire. The captain reported that he smelled gasoline throughout the driveway area and requested the immediate response of a sheriff's arson investigator.

THE INVESTIGATION:

I was just the guy to get assigned this tricky case. Just a few weeks prior, I had received a prestigious award from the International Association of Arson Investigators as their "2004 Investigator of the Year." A week later I received similar recognition from the International Association of Special Investigators, an insurance industry group. These awards were for my casework on a five-year investigation into the largest arson-for-profit ring ever investigated in California. That case resulted in the arrests of over forty people for the torching of fifty-five homes, businesses, and vehicles for insurance fraud. I even went undercover and paid the group to burn a rental property for me for the purpose of insurance fraud. As the arsonists broke into the vacant rental property at midnight armed with bottles of gasoline and lighters, they were arrested by detectives. Since my assignment to the arson unit, I had investigated over 700 fires and had arrested over 180 people for arson or insurance fraud related to arson. I had over fourteen years as a detective, eight of which were spent in an undercover role, with most of my work occurring in heavily-gang controlled areas. I had investigated every conceivable crime and had met, arrested, and interviewed the most dangerous people in Los Angeles. But I had never met anyone like Gary Glazier.

I got called by my desk, and they told me they had a high-priority arson fire in La Crescenta. While I was rolling to the scene, I was updated that the local sheriff's captain, a real paper-pushing jerk who I had had problems with in the past, was on scene awaiting my arrival. I was impressed by that alone, as I knew it would take something serious to get that guy out from behind his desk. Furthermore, my desk informed me that another of my colleagues, Det. Rick Velazquez, had investigated an arson fire at the same residence about three months before and that he was on his way to assist me.

I arrived at eight in the morning and saw the most amazing scene I have ever witnessed in my career. The quiet residential street in a crime-free city was filled with sheriff's cars and several fire trucks. A fairly good-sized crowd of neighbors had gathered across the street directly in front of the burned home. Neither of these two facts was out of the norm for a fire scene. What was odd to me was the fact that the neighbors, who spanned several ethnic and racial groups, were really upset and behaving hostilely toward anyone in a position of authority. There were several very animated discussions going on between the sheriff's deputies and several middle-aged citizens. The citizens, who all appeared, to be normal, law-abiding people, were yelling and confronting the uniformed deputies. Part of me enjoyed watching the local sheriff's captain (who commands the local station and is basically the police chief of the local area) take a verbal beating from some really pissed-off people. This guy, who was a career chair warmer and "hatchet man" for other administrators, deserved every bit of this verbal abuse for his past sins alone. However, I couldn't figure out what everyone was so upset about at this scene. I later commented to my boss that they looked like the angry mob outside of Frankenstein's castle, just without the torches and pitchforks.

When the sheriff's captain saw me, he rushed over with his lieutenant and gave me the run down. He was extremely happy to turn the scene over to me and head back to his comfortable office. He did tell me that everyone on the street was really upset that the sheriff's had failed to prevent this fire by not arresting the neighborhood creep, a man who lived next door to the burned home. He pointed at 3031 El Caminito. He told me that there had been a citizen's meeting at the sheriff station within the past two weeks concerning the owner of that home, Mr. Gary Glazier, whom the group of thirty or so neighbors blamed for every sin, crime, and trespass over the past thirty years. The captain, ever the adroit administrator, then blamed the failure of the sheriff's to act on the previous arson investigator, Rick. The captain led me to an Armenian man named Albert, whom he introduced as the owner of the burned home. Much to my dismay, he told Albert that I was "the best arson investigator in the department" and that I "would solve this crime for him." With that added onus placed on my shoulders, the career bureaucrat jumped back into his car, yelled out, "keep me up to date," and sped off, leaving me with a fire crew, a harried sheriff's deputy, and a street full of agitated people, all staring at me.

    I spoke briefly to Albert and immediately sensed a distrust and hostility toward me. Standing nearby was a tall, white male, who appeared to be an attorney or something. Albert was visibly upset and trembling, but he kept his voice low and in control. He demanded that I arrest the next-door neighbor, as he was sure this man had set both fires. Albert also voiced his deep displeasure with the previous investigative efforts by the sheriff's arson unit.

    I got a brief statement from Albert and his immediate family, which included his wife and her brother. All were very upset, highly agitated, and speaking in heavy Russian accents. They gave me reams of information about their neighbor that seemed to have nothing to do with this fire. Within a few minutes, I had a vague outline of the previous incident and this latest fire. I infuriated Albert by telling him to stay off his own property until I had completed my scene investigation.

    I knew this was going to be an important case and immediately called for two more arson investigators, an arson criminalist, and a photographer from our crime lab. I began my scene investigation. About this time, I was contacted by my desk, which just happened to be manned by the lead investigator on the McCarthy incident of 2001. When he gave me the address of the McCarthys, I could see that it was directly across the street from my incident. He told me briefly about that unsolved attempted murder and arson, and he said that there had now been three major arson incidents within about one-hundred feet of each other. He handed one of the responding arson investigators a copy of his three-year-old investigative report to bring to me. He said that these cases all appeared to be related. While I didn't have a high opinion of this particular investigator's skill level, I agreed with him on this point. The possibility of these three unique events being related was very high.

A fire investigation has two major phases. The first phase includes the forensic analysis of the fire scene itself, and it is called a cause-and-origin investigation. The ultimate goal of this phase is to locate the origin of the fire, and then attempt to find the exact cause of the fire within that area of origin. There are many factors that make this an extremely difficult task. The fire and the subsequent firefighting operations are extremely destructive in nature, and evidence is often destroyed, moved, altered, or trampled on. Once this cause-and-origin part has been established, the investigator must make a determination as to whether the event is accidental or incendiary. Incendiary fires are intentionally set fires. If a fire is ruled incendiary, the second phase of the fire investigation begins. This second phase revolves around determining who is responsible for the criminal act. While the cause-and-origin phase is highly technical and takes a specially trained fire-scene investigator, the second phase is basic criminal investigation. Some agencies use two different investigators, one for each phase. My agency uses one detective who is equally trained in both phases.

The scene investigation involves a large number of photographs, notes, sketches, collections of soil, and wood samples as well as the analysis and recording of fire patterns. We the scene as a well-coordinated crew, as I had personally selected the investigators I wanted to assist me. I had called the very experienced Detectives Rick Velazquez and Mike Digby to my scene, along with Senior Arson Criminalist Phil Teramoto from the crime lab. We quickly determined that the fire was set using gasoline poured, placed, or sprayed under the home in the open crawl space under the kitchen. Rick, who had been at both fires, said this was an exact clone of the event three months earlier. We could not find the source of the gasoline; there were no containers or forensics in the form of footprints, drag marks, or scuff marks on fences. We additionally could not find an ignition source. This is not uncommon, as gasoline is most often lighted by an open flame, usually a match or lighter. We would have some difficulty finding a match in heavy fire debris, and of course a lighter would most likely be carried away by the arsonist. However, we were mystified as to how a suspect could circumvent the high fences on the property, commit this act, and flee without leaving any visible evidence.

This second fire at the Artsvelyan home burned fairly deeply into the heavy wood timbers supporting the home. It breached the kitchen floor from underneath and completely gutted the entire kitchen. The rest of the home received heavy smoke and heat damage. This fire did an estimated $300,000 in damage, or about as much as Albert had poured into the remodel. It was really a catastrophic event for the family.

We finally determined that an unknown suspect had somehow entered the yard and placed, poured, or sprayed gasoline under the home via the open crawl space; the gasoline was then ignited with some sort of open flame. Rick pointed out that the time of day, use of gasoline, and area of origin were identical to his fire from three months before. We absolutely believed that the same suspect had committed both crimes.

We saw that the stone wall in Glazier's heavily shrouded front yard was about fifteen feet away from the crawl space hole. We spent a long time examining that area but could not find any way that he or anyone could have climbed the fence between the properties. Based on the physical description provided to us by the neighbors, we were doubtful that a portly, sedentary, sixty-two-year-old man could have accomplished this act. With no other leads at this point, we decided to walk next door and talk to him. I knocked on his door and could hear music and someone moving about in the home. We knocked very loudly and yelled to Glazier, but he refused to answer the door. A neighbor pointed out that Glazier was a creature of habit, but that for some reason, he was violating his habit today by putting his trash out early. The neighbors said that Glazier always put his trash out just minutes prior to the truck arriving on the street, and then always quickly removed his cans after the truck had passed. We saw that he had three trash cans out on the edge of the street, and the trash truck was not due for a few hours.

I decided on a little proactive investigation and began systematically dumping each trash can into a pile on the street and going through them for evidence. By this time we had already searched several neighbors' yards and other trash receptacles on the street for an accelerant container. It was our experience that arsonists quite often throw an accelerant can either into the fire or into the nearest hiding space for fear of being caught with the evidence. The search showed no accelerant containers. However, there were some other interesting items in the trash. Glazier had torn all of his junk mail and other correspondence into hundreds of tiny pieces. He had removed his name from all magazines and other items. He was obviously someone who was very careful about his personal information and security. We also found a large number of completed crossword puzzles, all in ink, all with few to no mistakes. This led us to believe that Glazier was a very intelligent person. Lastly, and most interestingly, we found several television schedule pages from either the Sunday newspaper or *TV Guide*. On each of these pages, certain shows were circled in ink. Every single show circled was some kind of crime and investigation drama, such as *CSI* and *Forensic Files*. It was clear that Gary Glazier was a student of criminal investigation. Finally, we found that one of his trash cans was half full of trimmings from the large bushes that lined Glazier's front yard. This seemed odd; since the yard was really overgrown and looked like it hadn't been groomed or trimmed in months.

In the midst of all of this investigative activity, Albert Artsvelyan stood quietly nearby, watching me as I was involved in all of these tasks. The whole time he was talking to the tall white male. At one point I heard the two discussing a video recording system. I walked over and asked Albert if he had such a system on his property. He said that he did and that it was run by a computer that was located in his detached garage. He explained that he had had a specialist install the system and that it had fourteen pinhole cameras hidden throughout the property. As Albert went with me to unlock his garage and show me the system, the white male began to follow us into the crime scene. I finally stopped him, and he identified himself as a former FBI agent and Albert's private investigator. My many dealings with private investigators had left me with the opinion that they were by and large incompetent morons who could not make it in the law enforcement field and were experts only at the excessive billing of gullible clients. Added to this opinion was the fact that this guy was ex-FBI agent, a group known to have precious little experience in street matters and no experience whatsoever in arson investigation. I was not impressed with this guy, and I ordered him out of my crime scene under threat of arrest. That was the last Albert or I ever saw of the PI.

There was no power at Albert's property because of the fire, so we carried the computer to a neighbor and used their keyboard and monitor to view the images. I was impressed! The cameras were very high quality and worked decently in low light. It took some figuring out, but we were able to back up the digital images to about three that morning, where we saw the first suspicious activity. What the images showed was a flashlight beam being played onto the Artsvelyan's kitchen wall from the dark Glazier front yard. You could see no persons on the Glazier side of the fence, only the actions taken by a hidden suspect. What happened next was nothing short of astounding to me. For several seconds, an unseen person standing in Glazier's front yard began pumping a quantity of liquid in a steady stream over the fence, over the twelve-foot gap of Artsvelyan's driveway, and into the open doorway of the crawl space under the home. I estimated that one or two gallons of liquid were streamed in. The camera then deactivated until about a half past three in the morning. This time the cameras showed a long pole with a glowing tip being extended through the fence from Glazier's front yard into the crawl space. It was retracted for a minute or two back to Glazier's side, and then a burst of flame ignited in Glazier's front yard. The pole then came back into view with a ball of flame burning from the end. When it got under the Artsvelyan's home, the flame ignited the gasoline vapors that had been sprayed into the area, and the entire under side and side of the home burst into flames. The pole, which appeared on camera to be two eight-to-ten-foot lengths of PVC pipe taped together with something resembling electrical tape, was last seen being withdrawn back into Glazier's darkened front yard.

Unbelievable! As an arson investigator, I had never seen anyone go to these lengths to commit a crime. I called Rick over to view it a few times with me, and he was equally stunned. However, we now had the answers to the questions that had been bothering Rick for over three months. How was no forensic evidence left at the scene, and how did a sixty-two-year-old, pudgy guy get over the fence to commit these arsons? It was clear as a bell now that he had never set foot on the property but had instead relied on some sort of pumping device to propel the gasoline. He had then used an extended pole to light the fire from almost twenty feet away. Like I said, unbelievable! We were also ecstatic, because we knew we could just look over the common fence to find some sort of forensics in the yard on that side. We had never yet been to an arson scene where the suspect did not leave evidence of any kind.

We secured our video evidence and went to the Artsvelyans' driveway and the exact spot where we knew the pole had crossed the fence. We looked into Glazier's front yard at the exact area where we knew the arsonist had to have stood to commit this crime. We were happy to see no grass in the yard, but soft dirt. We knew we should be seeing footprints, burned plastic or rags, or the imprint of the poles or pumping device in the very soft dirt. We saw nothing but rake marks in the dirt. Oddly, this was the only spot in the entire, unkempt yard where someone had recently raked. We now knew that we had an arsonist on our hands that had spent over twenty minutes in the dead of night committing his crime; he had then had the nerve and wherewithal to carefully disassemble his two poles and the pumping device and carry them away. Then to top it all off, he had come back to rake the area where he had committed the crime. This took a very sinister and deliberate mind and nerves of steel. It also hearkened back to the bizarre and nervy events at the McCarthy home three years prior. There was only one person who would have a reason to hide the evidence in Glazier's front yard—Glazier himself. Any other arsonist would look very suspicious running down the street or attempting to speed away in view of many neighbors while carrying twenty feet of pipe and a pumping device, all while a house was burning nearby. Only Gary Glazier had the means to commit all of these acts undetected, shrouded in the heavily shadowed and obscured front yard of his home.

At this point we knew we had to legally get into Glazier's front yard to closely check for evidence. I was certain no one was canny enough to be able to hide all the evidence while a large fire was burning just twenty feet away. I then remembered that we still had Glazier's trash can half on the street in front of his home. I directed my partners Mike Digby and Rick to finish sorting through the trash. Apparently, as things came to pass, this was the straw that broke the camel's back. We later learned that Glazier just hated anyone touching his property, and we believe it was this hatred coupled with the painting of his garage that was the final driving motive behind his murderous behavior. In this case, he had been watching us for some time but had yet to come out of his home. His anger at seeing the two detectives rummaging through his trash got the better of him, and he came out to confront them. He stomped down the driveway like an older version of Elmer Fudd, and I saw him approach Mike, who stands about six foot three and weighs over 230 pounds. Glazier demanded to know on whose authority we were able to go through his trash. He then began invoking the Constitution of the United States and other rights he believed he possessed.

That's when I walked over to meet this guy for the first time; and this is where this story originally began. As I said earlier, despite his fuming, whining, and bluster, once confronted by a person who was not afraid to look him in the eye, Gary Glazier reverted back to the coward he had been all his life. I eventually told Gary that he was not free to go and that I was going to get a warrant to search his home for the evidence I knew must certainly be there. He became even meeker and told me that he didn't want me going into his home or on his property. Too bad, we did it anyway!

Five hours or so after cuffing Glazier, I had written and secured a search warrant for his property. The judge told me that I was on a wing and a prayer with this one and wished me luck. Two hours later my search team entered his weather-beaten old home on his unkempt property. We were expecting the worse. Oddly (and I know I keep using that word in this case but it is so applicable), Glazier had turned on an alarm as he had exited his home to confront us and had also turned off the water supply to the home. We later learned that this was his ritual every time he walked out the door. What a freak!

The home threw us for a loop. Despite being an eyesore on the outside, it was the neatest, cleanest home any of us had ever searched. Every room was filled with museum-quality antiques. The shabby exterior hid an interior as nice as any showroom I had ever been in. He had an antique radio collection that filled every room of the house and was later found to be worth in excess of $250,000. He had antique beaded purses (yeah, purses) hung on nails in every room. He had antique toys and games, an antique motorcycle in mint condition, and half a dozen antique and collectible cars in the rear garages. We later estimated his collection of antiques at over $800,000. Weirdly (for California where few homes have them), he had a basement in his home. Its entrance was hidden, and we found it by accidentally hitting a foot lever in his bedroom. The basement stairs were hidden behind a sliding pantry wall in the kitchen. The basement gave us the most reason to pause, as the more we searched this guy's house, the more we believed that he was an extremely sinister person. To this day I can't explain why, but all of us expected to find something terrible—a dismembered hooker, animals hanging from traps, or even a mummified ex-wife. This guy and his house just had that feel about them.

However, the basement had more antique toys and games. It also had a very large collection of videotapes numbering in the hundreds or thousands. They were all neatly arranged on specially made shelves. A random check showed them to be mostly copies of silent movies from the twenties and some sound films from the thirties. He had framed photos of many starlets from that era in several areas of the home. Even though he was probably only a boy during that period in history, it was clear that the man was fascinated with it, as at least two of his touring cars were from the late twenties or early thirties. We found several small stashes of cash but didn't know what to make of them.

The good stuff was mostly upstairs. He had a porno collection that made me blush. Most of his porn was recorded on low-budget videotapes that were obviously mail order. A brief perusal showed that he was enamored with anal sex, enemas, possibly some bestiality, and very fat older women. His magazine porn collection was found hidden in his bedroom. This again was filled with fetish porn, and it was almost entirely made up of two British publications, *Plumpers over 50* and *Plumpers over 60*. It was obvious that Glazier enjoyed older fat women. I found nothing mainstream and nothing that we had found that would interest normal guys.

His room yielded a couple things of interest. We found a Glock 9mm and a cut down .12 gauge shotgun in his closet. He did not seem the type to own these items. I also found what I originally believed to be the mother lode. I had searched lots of bad guys' homes in the past and knew that they always had super-secret caches. If you were clever and looked hard enough, you could find them, and that's where the best stuff is hidden. Taped to the back of a bureau drawer, and obviously not meant for anyone else's eyes, was a set of folders. Each folder had the name of a woman and within each was similar information. He had met several women in past years via newspaper personal ads. Like he did with everything else in his life, he kept detailed notes of those encounters, including their vital statistics, conversation content, employment, family, pets, and sexual history. He appeared to actually go on these dates and interview these women. He included such mundane things as the number of miles to their work and home and what the names of their kids and pets were. He mostly had files on Asian and white women in their mid to late fifties. He made comments about their reactions to particular sexual questions, such as whether or not they enjoyed anal sex. Glazier then kept detailed notes on each of these women until the relationship ended, which quite often was after the first meeting. Some folders were fairly extensive and some were one-time events. The most extensive folder was for a woman named "Dora." Glazier kept detailed notes of all his many sexual adventures with Dora, including anal sex, blowjobs, and enemas, and he detailed such things as where they were when all of these events occurred. He had Polaroids of Dora posing in some weird clothing or in the nude. She was much younger than all of the other women, and her photos were extremely racy. The photos included several shots of her receiving an enema or exposing her vagina while seated in Glazier's car. I wanted to talk to her, as I believed her to be a prostitute and likely to be able to tell me the really dark stuff about Glazier. The more I looked at this stuff, the weirder Glazier seemed to me.

I later found and interviewed Dora. She was sickened by what Glazier had documented about her and vomited and cried during the interview. She said she was looking for a rich man but was not a hooker. She said he was bizarre sexually to say the least. He could not orgasm while having sex, instead having to stop intercourse and finish by masturbating over his porn. She said he made her pose for the photos and even made her dress in his "dead wife's" clothing. She said he had become physically abusive after a few months, and she left him.

Glazier not only kept meticulous notes on the women he encountered but on every facet of his life. Pinned or in the pockets of his clothing were pieces of paper outlining the date he had last worn the item, the circumstances he had been in, and who he was with. He kept lengthy notes on each antique radio and car he had purchased, including what work or expense he had exerted on the item. He appeared to spend mostly cash on his purchases. His clothing was older in style, but it was neat and clean.

The search warrant ended up being a dramatic success, as we eventually found everything we thought we would find. We found a gasoline receipt showing that

Glazier had used his credit card to purchase gasoline from a nearby Shell just hours prior to the fire. Locked in his truck was the really good stuff. We found a two-and-a-half-gallon commercial paint sprayer from Sears that was empty but smelled of gasoline. It had a homemade wand, hose, and fitting that allowed it to stream a liquid as opposed to spray or mist. Each of these items later tested positive for gasoline residue on them. Adding to our delight, we saw that all of these items were wet and appeared to have been rinsed out with water. Inside the truck we found wet paper towels and surgical gloves. The wet paper towels were an exact match to a roll above his sink in his garage. It was clear to us that Glazier had used the sink in his garage in an attempt to clean out the gasoline from this device. He had then hid and locked all of these items in the back of his truck and placed bags and blankets over them. We later learned through interviews that our ability to find these items still on his property was due to the fire department being parked across Glazier's driveway; he had been unable to leave. In his garage, we found two long PVC pipes that fit within each other and appeared to be the ones used on the video.

The crime lab would later tell us that all the items found in Glazier's truck were positive for gasoline. Furthermore, Glazier's DNA was on several of these items, and his prints were on the trash bags covering them. Short of an eyewitness, we had every single thing we needed for a successful prosecution on this case. We had a video showing how the event had occurred, albeit with no suspect visible. We found the exact pumping and incendiary device we had hoped to find when asking the judge for the search warrant, and we knew that Glazier lived alone and only he had access to his property, his truck, and his home. The only thing we were missing was the motive. Most crimes have a suspect with motive, means, and opportunity. Glazier clearly had the means and opportunity, but what about the motive? Only he knew what his was, and my next task was to get it out of him.

Before I left Glazier's home, I took one last look around. I knew I needed about a week and twenty detectives to properly search the place. However, we had found within just a short time everything we had asked for on the warrant, and we had no legal reason to look further or to dig up the yard as the neighbors were begging us to do. They insisted that he had dozens of tortured and murdered animals, and possibly a murdered ex-wife, buried in an ominous pit in his front yard.

As we were locking up and leaving, Albert Artsvelyan and his wife came over, both literally in tears with the news that we had locked up Glazier. Albert embraced me and told me I was his hero and savior. Other neighbors, who had stayed around to watch for hours, gave us a standing ovation as we left the street. Ann Lewis, the neighborhood activist and organizer was finally vindicated, and she proclaimed that the reign of terror was over. Because of our extreme exhaustion (we had been on scene for over sixteen hours), Digby, Velazquez, and I were a bit embarrassed by all the gratitude. We still had not grasped what this man had done to an entire neighborhood.

I wanted to break Glazier in an interview. I knew just by having gone through his home that if I approached him correctly he would talk—they always did. I knew it would not be easy and would take hours, but I knew he would break. My experience is that people with deep, dark secrets want somebody to tell. Amazingly, they frequently confide in the very detectives who are trying to lock them away. At the station I met Glazier's current girlfriend, a very obese woman of about sixty-five years but who looked at least ten years older. She was very congenial and did not seem at all surprised that Gary had been booked for arson. She asked only if he had used a spray device. When we questioned her about that, she could only say that she thinks they saw one once on a crime drama. She confirmed that he lived alone but that the two of them watched crime dramas on a nightly basis. She said he was a brilliant man who planned everything in life and was obsessive about people touching his property. She said that even she could not go to his home without his permission and that he shut off the water to stop vandals who might want to flood his home. She said that she had witnessed Gary vandalize cars on one or two occasions but that other than that, "he was a good man." I found this woman's IQ to be slightly above imbecile, and it was clear that she was kept around for sex only. To our discomfort, this elderly, overweight woman was quite happy to describe her very colorful sex life with Glazier, which included enemas, an anal fixation, and Glazier's curiosity with "poopy sex."

When I walked in to interview Glazier, I could see that being in jail for several hours had him completely docile. I knew immediately he was out of his element and wanted to talk. He kept asking me for legal advice and wanted to know if he should talk to me or not. Just as I believed he was going to speak to me, a moron of a sergeant walked in and began insulting Glazier, calling him a "sick, evil fuck." Glazier became upset and immediately asked for an attorney. I was pissed at the idiot sergeant for wasting the one opportunity we had to talk to this maniac. However, I knew I had more than enough evidence to convict Glazier of his crimes. I just wanted to discover his reason and gain his admission for the McCarthy event. This was never to be. Glazier never said a word to anyone, including his attorney, for almost six months after this meeting.

The court odyssey

The case was bizarre enough that the following week it hit the papers. The judge who signed the warrant had read the paper and congratulated me on getting the guy. I filed the case, and the next step would be a bail hearing. I began to realize by this time that Glazier had most likely attempted to murder seven people (the McCarthys and the Artsvelyans) by fire as they slept. I charged him with four counts of attempted murder and two of arson of an inhabited structure. At this point I was still trying to revive the botched McCarthy investigation. I realized that by owning two homes (according to his girlfriend he owned both his mother's house and his own house outright) Glazier could probably accumulate a million dollars in bail. Going out on a limb, the DA asked the court for a "no bail" hold, usually reserved for murderers. A bail hearing was set. These affairs are usually five-minute events with no witnesses in the courtroom. I had already briefed the Artsvelyans that it was entirely possible that a bail would be set that Glazier could meet that day. They were hysterical and showed up to court in a highly agitated state. They were not alone. The judge handling the bail hearing watched as his courtroom filled up to capacity with a half dozen reporters and over fifty visibly upset neighbors, all demanding to speak at the bail hearing. This sort of calamity is usually only seen in street gang or celebrity trials. The judge was noticeably alarmed and summoned extra bailiffs. He questioned me about the people in the court and asked why they were at this bail hearing. He was quite impressed by the response and addressed the group. He then heard my testimony followed by both side's arguments, and for the first time in recent Los Angeles County memory, he held a man who had not committed murder and was not considered a flight risk "without bail". When Glazier's attorney protested, stating that Glazier had never murdered anyone, the judge wryly replied, "Well counselor, he may not have murdered anyone to our knowledge, but it appears he has certainly tried to murder several people—bail denied!"

This was the first of dozens of court hearings over the next four-and-a-half years for Gary Glazier. Only one of them went well for him. He retained private counsel for about eight months. That attorney tried a second bail hearing, only to be denied, and lost a preliminary hearing on the matter. He spent several months after that asking Glazier to take a deal and spare himself a life sentence. This attorney later confided that Glazier seldom acknowledged him and refused to talk at all about the case. The first attorney was fired later that year after Glazier became upset that I was able to get a warrant for his DNA. My only real satisfaction in the case up to this point was getting that DNA. In all our court appearances, I had not seen Glazier look at anyone, speak to anyone, or react to anything whatsoever during the proceedings. I wrote a court order to take a DNA sample from him at the jail. When I used a swab to take a DNA sample from his mouth, I fully expected him to rebel because of his hatred for having his privacy invaded. However, he was docile and submissive and gave the sample without a word. I was actually a bit disappointed by this lack of reaction. However, as soon as I left the jail facility, the deputy who had brought Glazier to me called. He said that after I left, he put Glazier into a room by himself and soon saw Glazier yelling and smashing his head against the wall. Maybe my instincts were correct, and his DNA would come back linking him to a murdered hooker or raped girl somewhere. Whatever it was, Glazier finally lost his composure, and it gave me a degree of satisfaction.

A few months later, Glazier realized that he was in a lot of trouble and hired the biggest name he knew from watching TV. He hired OJ Simpson's attorney, Robert Shapiro, to defend him. Over the next three years, Shapiro became a bit of an irritant. Not because of his courtroom brilliance—he was actually a very mediocre trial attorney—but because of the dozens of personal attacks he aimed toward the Artsvelyans and me. Although he was pretty weak on the law and in court, he was an absolute master at the art of hyperbole, deception, and deceit, and he was really able to fill his pockets on this case. Reports from inside his defense team stated that Shapiro was able to pull a $2 million fee out of Glazier. He then was successfully able to block the Artsvelyans from pursuing a civil case against Glazier that would tie up Glazier's assets. Glazier signed all his properties over to Shapiro, who immediately sold them via his law firm. Shapiro, after getting his handsome fee, then set about trying to do what he does best—deal the case away as quickly as possible. He didn't understand the ego and mindset of his client at that point, and Glazier refused to budge and would not plea to anything, ever.

The court cases went on *ad naseum*, and Shapiro got a partial acquittal from a jury trial in 2005. This was mostly because of the very poor case preparation conducted by the deputy district attorney. This man, who was more focused on an upcoming promotional exam, declared the case a "slam dunk" on the eve of trial and did nothing to prepare exhibits, photos, or experts. Shapiro, realizing that the DA wasn't ready, lied to us and stated that he was going to ask for a three-month continuance in the case as he was dealing with his son's recent death. This caused the ill-prepared DA to leave on vacation. The next court day, Shapiro reneged on his request for a three-month delay and announced that he was ready for trial. He demanded to start the case that day, knowing full well the handling DA was out of town. The case was given to another DA, who had less than twenty-four hours to prepare for a two-week long trial. The new DA and I spent the next two weeks working twenty-hour days to try to get exhibits ready for the trial. We still weren't that concerned, as we felt that we had more evidence than most criminal investigators ever get. We had a video, fingerprints, DNA, and the fact that the entire incendiary device had been found locked in Gary Glazier's truck.

Unfortunately, the prosecution's case was disjointed at best and poor photos were shown to the jury to illustrate the events. The judge, who was obviously enamored by Robert Shapiro's celebrity status, allowed him to do things in the courtroom that almost no other judge would ever allow. My observance of Shapiro led me to believe that he had probably not even read the case file and had instead relied on reports handed to him by a very skilled assistant. He knew nothing of the case, and his defense was strictly theater at its best. However, he apparently earned his money and somehow confused the jury to the point that they gave a partial acquittal on the attempted murder charges but hung on the arsons. This of course is bizarre, seeing as the charges were one and the same crime.

I was very embarrassed by this courtroom farce. In fact, I was too embarrassed to face the Artsvelyans, who had put their faith in the American justice system. After yet another tough hearing, we were able to keep Glazier in jail pending a new trial. Of course Shapiro wanted to plea him to a very minor charge. However, I knew that if we had a more prepared district attorney, we could easily win the case. So I went shopping for one.

A month later, the DA's office, still reeling from a letter-writing campaign started by the Artsvelyans and their friends, came through. They assigned a new deputy district attorney to the case, Susan Schwartz. This tiny woman was the most tenacious prosecutor I had ever met, and together we pulled the case out of the ashes. Within a month we took the case to the grand jury and indicted Glazier on several new counts, including the McCarthys' attempted murder. It wasn't a perfect case, but I was able to use criminal and arson profiling techniques to link all three events. A full year later, after more attempts by Shapiro to get Glazier to plea, we re-indicted him on the same charges plus a few additional charges of animal cruelty/poisoning and stalking thrown in. We now had dozens of witnesses from out of state and out of country willing to fly in to testify against the "Cat Killer Arsonist of La Crescenta" as an internet site glossed him. This second grand jury really exposed Glazier for the evil little man that he was. We were able to find even more witnesses to tell their stories of pet mutilations, poisonings, and stalking. After this, Glazier made the Internet, as an animal rights website listed him as an animal torturer.

What was divulged later was that I had been covertly listening to all of Gary Glazier's phone calls since he had been incarcerated. His only calls were his weekly conversations with his girlfriend, Linda Rea, whom he had conveniently married in jail just days after his first bail hearing. He had no other family or friends. Through Linda he had taken great steps to hide his assets. Immediately after his preliminary hearing, Linda, acting as Gary's agent, took steps to sell his houses (to attorney Robert Shapiro), move all of his property out of state, and "gift" his extraordinary car collection to a man in Washington. All of this was done to prevent the Artsvelyans from seizing his assets in a civil action.

Listening to Gary Glazier's phone conversations gave me further insight into how despicable he really was. By late 2007, Linda Rea announced to him on the phone that she had terminal cancer. This lady was his only friend and only outside contact. She had assumed an active role in his defense and was spending dozens of hours each week attempting to do detective work on his behalf. This woman had dedicated the last three years to Gary Glazier. Upon hearing the news of her terminal cancer, Glazier's callous reply to her was, "That's too bad, but did you get my legal work done this week?"

More than anything else in the case, this was a very clear indication of Glazier's character. Linda Rea was his only friend and relative in the world and his only contact outside of the jail. We were pretty sure that Glazier still had over $500,000 in cash hidden somewhere, and yet this gullible and pathetic woman was living at just above the poverty line in Washington. Gary's only response to her plight was that she needed to tighten her belt and put more money on his jail account so that he could make phone calls and buy potato chips and soda. More than anything else, these phone calls gave me a complete insight into the cold callousness of Gary Glazier.

Glazier was also highly disciplined and cunning. He spoke constantly in code for fear of eavesdropping and never discussed his case without using code words. He was frequently espousing a myriad of conspiracy theories as to how he had been "set up" on this case and speculating as to who was really behind it. He also admitted to adapting well to life in jail and to have been running scams with other inmates. In retrospect, Gary Glazier appeared to me to treat his time in jail and court as just another experiment he was observing. He was not suffering nearly enough for my tastes.

Gary Glazier, after reviewing all the facts and adding in the stories that were most likely true, was a very difficult man to describe. He had no friends and no living relatives, and his work colleagues had all disappeared decades ago. There was really no way to trace his background, and he certainly wasn't talking about it. Criminally, he was also a bit difficult to classify. Based on the three fire incidents, he fit the category of serial arsonist. We believed that his motive was pure hatred and that he may have gravitated to fires later in life. Based on his activities with his step-daughter, he could also be classified as a serial sexual predator/child molester. Based on his crimes against other neighbors, he could be classified as a serial stalker, Peeping Tom, vandal, voyeur, and prowler.

Personally, I believe that he has committed even more serious crimes that we are simply unaware of. A true sociopath like him doesn't just develop these patterns at the age of sixty-two. What we really thought best described him was "serial asshole." He treated women like shit, most likely sexually abused his stepdaughter, was obsessed with feces and rectums, and killed and tortured animals. I found that he fit into the unique category of offenders who are constantly committing nuisance crimes, though he is clearly the most extreme example of this category. Men in this category usually screw with their neighbors unmercifully for years without being noticed, and they are seldom suspected. They are the assholes who let the air out of your tires, steal your lawn sprinklers, put dog shit in your mailbox, steal your mail, and throw bleach on your lawn. There seems to be quite a few of them in this world, as I have encountered several during my investigations. They are difficult to identify and catch using law enforcement, and they are nearly impossible to prosecute. They are all loners and cowards and, frankly, just plain pricks. That's what Glazier is—a good old-fashioned prick. Not exactly a criminological term, but it seems to fit.

Finally in late 2008, Gary Glazier's world came crashing down on him. His wife of convenience had died several months before, and he had no one to communicate with. Deputy DA Susan Schwartz, who had resurrected and intensified the case against him, had moved on through a promotion in the office. Listening to his phone calls, I found out how much Glazier had feared Susan Schwartz; he was practically ecstatic when she was taken off the case. He soon resumed his glum ways when he found out that the case was being given to two male prosecutors. Deputy DAs Phil Stirling and Darren Levine were also considered to be superstars within the offices of the district attorney. They, along with their assistant Emily Chang, were specially assigned to this high-profile case by their boss, who was a legend in the office himself, Supervising Deputy District Attorney Bill Hodgman. They all took a special interest in Gary Glazier and began building an incredible case to present at jury trial.

Glazier's famed attorney, Robert Shapiro (who was ordered to stay on the case by the judge despite his pleas to be released from it), could not get him out of the inevitable, and Glazier was finally convicted of arson and some other charges. Glazier received a ten-year sentence. However, he was also forced to undergo a court-ordered psychiatric exam, against his strenuous objections. The psychiatrist, after eighty lengthy pages of babble, concluded that Glazier was not at all remorseful for his actions and would not be a suitable candidate for any sort of rehabilitation. He called him cold, callous, narcissistic, and manipulative. He said that Glazier often took minor infractions or trespasses against him and magnified them in his mind for months while he plotted and schemed murderous responses. The probation officer advised me that Glazier had a special hatred for both me and DDA Susan Schwartz. He said that Glazier felt that we were responsible for him being in prison, not the crimes he committed.

Because he confided in no one, we never learned Glazier's true motivation. Our best guess is that he was the sort of person who obsessed over his privacy and developed an intense hatred for anyone who trespassed in the slightest way against him. He was obviously a coward, as most of his victims were helpless pets, small children, and women. He avoided confrontations of any sort with adult males. The McCarthy trespass against Glazier had been that their teenage son, Kel, had rolled a ball onto Glazier's property six months prior to his attempting to murder them. The Artsvelyans' crimes were that they had apparently made too much noise during construction, their dog had barked at Glazier, and they had had the gall to paint a garage that was actually on their own property

Although the length of his jail time was not what we had originally hoped for, we knew that the two worst things that could happen to Glazier were being exposed to the public as the evil monster he was and suffering financially. Bob Shapiro and another attorney had already relieved him of about $2 million, and the judge ordered an additional $400,000 in restitution to the victims and the insurance company. Glazier lost his homes, his cars, and his precious antiques.

In the end, Glazier will get out of prison when he is about seventy-one years old, and at which point he will hopefully be friendless and penniless. We're sure his burning hatred will still be smoldering. Sadly, the McCarthy and Artsvelyan families will never have a restful night of sleep for the rest of their lives, as the unthinkable happened to them—the boogeyman attacked them in their homes as they slept, in the dead of night and without any provocation. For the rest of their lives, they will wonder, "Is he coming back?"

Author's Note: During the writing of this book in the summer of 2011, Gary Glazier was released from prison. Despite a deal at sentencing in which he agreed to be paroled to the state of Washington, Gary Glazier was in fact paroled to a halfway house in Sylmar, California, or about ten miles from the scene of all his crimes. I learned of his release and contacted his parole officer, who blurted out, "Who the hell is this guy?" The officer told me that he had received nearly a dozen frantic calls over the past week about Glazier and had expected him to by a six-foot-four, 280-pound, muscle-bound gang member. When he saw his prison photo, he was not impressed by the seventy-something, paunchy, wimp of a man. I told the parole officer the case background and that I had arrested over one-thousand people in my career, including hundreds of gang members, murderers, rapists and arsonists; regardless, Glazier remains the most evil and fiendish man I have ever met. In short, he's evil personified; the true boogeyman.

Investigator's Analysis:

I was consumed and haunted by the Glazier case for years. I knew that we had missed a lot of stuff on this guy and that he had a whole trove of secrets out there that we were never able to locate. Of course the only time I was able to search his property was on the day of his arrest, and it would be months before I knew the true scope of his evil. My partners and I have huge regrets about this case, and knowing what we now know about him, we would obviously love another crack at searching his property.

Shortly after Glazier's case, I began heavily researching serial arsonists and serial offenders in general. I read many documents, studies, and books written by persons involved in behavior analysis and the profiling of crimes and criminals. The more I read, the more I was struck by the unbelievable similarities in lifestyle, mannerisms, and actions between Gary Glazier and some of the more notorious serial murderers ever identified. One only has to look at the case history of a highly organized serial offender like Dennis Rader, the notorious "BTK" killer of Wichita, to see *how similar he and Gary Glazier seem—without the body count, of course. Both were extremely intelligent, paunchy, overly fastidious, white males who obsessed over minor trivial issues in their daily lives. They planned, waited, and schemed out their attacks and were patient enough to carry them out weeks or months after conception. Both appeared obsessed with the fields of investigative science and criminal justice, as both expressed a lot of interest in either TV forensic crime dramas or detective magazines (depending on the era). Another person who comes to mind is the notorious serial arsonist John Orr, who was operating in the same area as Glazier during roughly the same time period. Orr and Glazier were physically similar and each carried out their crimes against preselected and scouted targets, only after intense planning and the arrangement of specific, unique ignition devices. Each had massive egos and considered themselves much smarter than the persons investigating them. Each, to this day, despite mountains of evidence against them, still feels that they were "railroaded" or given a "bum rap" by the system. Neither will ever admit that they did anything wrong in their lives or that they were caught fair and square. Their swollen egos just won't allow it.*

I learned a very interesting fact from this case that has proven itself true on other weird cases. Modern law enforcement, with all its training, equipment and analysis systems, is extremely skilled at dealing with traditional crimes such as burglary, assaults, murders, and fraud. These crimes are straightforward and easy to comprehend by even the most unskilled of patrol officers. However, even the most seasoned and skilled patrolmen—and quite a few experienced investigators—can't seem to wrap their minds around certain types of crimes or criminals. Robert Ressler is literally the father of the FBI's Behavior Analysis Unit, which practically invented profiling and the term "serial killer." He was the first person to begin interviewing serial killers in prison and compiling data on them for use in these profiles. He co wrote a book in 1992 called, Whoever Fights Monsters, which I read after the Glazier case ended. I have read several books by other profilers, but Ressler appears to have written the most down-to-earth account of this field of study. He remarks in the book that "One of the greatest problems in law enforcement today is that the police don't know how to deal with unusual cases." He goes on to say that, when confronted by an unusual case or crime scene, the typical officer or detective doesn't know what to look for, and that they often miss things that may be of extreme importance later when trying to track the motives or movements of a serial offender.

After having been personally involved in about three-dozen cases of various types involving serial offenders of one type or another, I can attest to the fact that Robert Ressler is absolutely right. In every one of these cases, when we looked back at it after the court proceedings were over, we said to ourselves, "Damn, I wish we had looked at this," or "I wish we had taken that evidence," or "Now I know what this meant." In our minds, the vast majority of criminals are fairly straightforward and easy to figure out. The evidence at the typical gang shooting scene is obvious and easily dealt with. However, when we find a serial rapist, arsonist, stalker, murderer, fetish burglar, or someone similar, the evidence we want from them is completely different and not at all obvious. In cases like this, we would be seeking notes, drawings, diaries, pictures, trophies, stalking dossiers, fetish photos, and anything else that would give us a clue to past or future victims and the suspect's bizarre obsessions.

In 1995, Dr. Dian Williams, a nationally recognized arson profiler, contacted me in a state of alarm after I had given her a short synopsis of the Glazier case. She was concerned about my safety and the safety of any females involved with the investigation of Glazier, and she felt sure that he would obsess about someone on the prosecution's team. She warned me to take personal precautions as she found Glazier to be clearly on the high end of the danger scale. She stated, "This is the kind of guy they make movies about." I thought she was being a bit dramatic at the time. Five years later, Dr. Williams proved extremely prescient, as Glazier had clearly begun obsessing over me and a female prosecutor. To this date, he is the most dangerous and evil person I have ever been involved in a case with.

Grail and Madiha
Altadena, 1999

Author's Note: This case is from author's own case files.
Nothing brings out unmitigated rage as much as a woman scorned, or in this case a man flimflammed by a cagey bride.

At 3:29 p.m. on the afternoon of August 20, 1999, the Altadena substation of the Los Angeles Sheriff's Department received a frantic 911 call from a woman named Madiha Fields. The abridged version of that 911 call went like this:

Dispatch: 911, what is your emergency?
Caller: I have a restraining order on my husband, and he's on the property...please hurry up and come fast.

Author's Note: Nothing causes violence and rage faster than the issuance of a restraining order by a judge. Readers, take note of how many of the arson events in this book are preceded by restraining orders.

Dispatch: Ma'am, ma'am, ma'am, just stay on the line...
Caller: Danielle, come here. (Talking to her seven-year-old daughter) Please hurry! (Talking to the dispatcher)
Dispatch: Okay. What's he doing, ma'am?
Caller: He's evidently trying to break in. He's breaking in! (A man's voice and loud crashing is heard in the background)
Caller: Get away from the door! Get away from the door, baby. Get away from the door. Danielle, come here. (Talking to her daughter)
(Loud crashing noise and a man yelling)
Caller: He broke the door. He's trying to start my place on fire!
(The phone drops; there is screaming, yelling in background)
Dispatch: Ma'am? Ma'am? Hello? (frantic) Come on, come on, come on, get my emergency call going.

Fireraisers, Freaks, And Fiends

The Altadena substation is nestled in the foothills of the Angeles National Forest, just above the city of Pasadena. For decades, the small city of Altadena had been a blue-collar town with mainly African American residents. The town was filled with older Craftsman homes built in the 1920s on huge lots. By the 1990s, the older homes were being purchased by upwardly mobile persons who sought to renovate the properties. It was becoming a hotbed for real estate speculators and for younger, upscale Black families. The crime that had plagued the area in earlier decades had greatly diminished, and Altadena was becoming a quiet, pleasant community. The local sheriff's station was quite small in regards to the other twenty-five stations within the massive department, and there was not a lot of violent crime anymore.

Nonetheless, sheriff's deputies were quite familiar with the home located at 797 Ventura Street, as they had been there more than once in the past week. Just two days prior to this 911 call, the station had taken a similarly frantic call from the same woman, Madiha Fields. In that call, she had expressed fears that her husband, Grail Wayne Perkins, was drunk and going to kill her and her daughter. When deputies arrived, Grail was gone, and Madiha gave them her version of the story. She said the pair had been married for about two years and that they had purchased the home as an investment about a year before. She said that she held a job at a bank, but Grail had not worked much over their entire marriage. He was currently working at her bank in a part-time capacity. She said that she had put a lot of money into renovating the home, while Grail sat around and began drinking a lot. He had become moodier and had recently started threatening violence, as she constantly harped on him to get a better job. Finally, she said he had threatened to harm her and her child, (his step-daughter), Danielle. The patrolmen advised her to get a restraining order on Grail if she felt her safety was in danger.

The next day, on August 19, as soon as the courts opened, Madiha applied for and received a temporary restraining order (TRO) from Pasadena Court. In the application, she claimed to be a victim of domestic violence. The TRO was issued by a judge, and it mandated that Grail Perkins was to immediately move out of his home until a proper hearing could be conducted. At four that afternoon, sheriff's deputies served the TRO to a shocked Grail Perkins at his home. The deputies later told me that Grail appeared genuinely surprised and shocked by this legal service. Nonetheless, after a few minutes, he begrudgingly packed several items into a couple suitcases and left the property in his Jeep. Madiha and her daughter came back to the property shortly after they saw Grail leave in his Jeep.

The next day, August 20, Madiha called a local locksmith to her home to change all the locks. At about 11:20 a.m., this man was working on an exterior gate when he saw a large black male (Grail) drive up in a Jeep. Grail appeared visibly angry and confronted the locksmith, who told him that he had been hired by Madiha to change all the locks. Grail then went inside the home and began a loud argument with Madiha. He told her that "someone is going to get hurt if you don't put an end to this." As Madiha picked up the phone to call the sheriff's, Grail stormed out of the home. As he walked past the locksmith, he yelled, "Don't change my fucking locks." He then left the home driving his gray Jeep. Patrol deputies soon arrived to take a report on the violation of the restraining order. They then went to his work to look for Grail Perkins.

Grail did not go to his workplace. Instead he drove three miles to Pasadena's courthouse, and just before noon he entered the courtroom of Judge Louise Halevy, the judge who had signed the TRO. The large and visibly agitated Grail immediately drew the attention of the bailiffs, who asked him his business. He demanded to see the judge about the TRO. Since the judge was already involved in other matters, the bailiffs told

Fireraisers, Freaks, And Fiends

Grail to come back after the noon break. Sure enough, Grail returned promptly when the court opened again in the afternoon. By about two in the afternoon, the judge found time to hear Grail's argument about the TRO. She sympathized with him, but said that absent a true hearing and without Madiha in court to present her side of things, she was unable to remove her TRO. Grail became even more agitated, and additional bailiffs were summoned to the courtroom. The judge spent a few more minutes attempting to calm and reason with Grail, and she advised him to get some legal help. He finally left the courtroom. After the hearing, bailiffs escorted Grail out of the courthouse. He left the building at about a quarter to three in the afternoon.

Forty-five minutes later, Madiha was in her home when she heard Grail's jeep enter through the gate to their property. She ran to get her daughter, and the pair looked out their kitchen door to see Grail approaching the home with a red plastic gas can in one hand and a green, butane lighter in the other. She then called 911 for the third time in three days. Because of the changed locks, he was unable to open the door. He began pounding on the living-room door and yelling for Madiha to open it. Madiha saw her seven-year-old daughter run to the door to let Grail in, but she stopped her before she could open it. They both saw and heard Grail kicking the living-room door, and soon it broke open. They saw him enter the living room and bedroom area with the gas can. He was yelling, "I'm gonna kill you, Madiha!" They saw him walk down a bedroom hallway pouring liquid from the red gas can. Both Madiha and her daughter, Danielle, took this opportunity to escape the home through the kitchen door. They ran out of the driveway and saw Grail's gray Jeep in the yard. As Danielle ran to a next-door neighbor, Madiha took the time to close and lock the exterior metal gate, effectively locking Grail's Jeep in the yard. She was hoping that he wouldn't set the house on fire if he was trapped in the yard.

A minute or so later, Madiha and Danielle were standing in front of a neighbor's home when they heard Grail's Jeep start up and begin to rev its engine. They then heard a loud crash and saw the Jeep knock down and drive over the heavy metal gate of the driveway. The Jeep sped off out of sight. Within seconds, they saw a large volume of smoke pouring from their home.

There is a Los Angeles County fire station (Engine 12) just six blocks from the Perkins/Fields home. As luck would have it, the crew of that station was out on another matter at the time, so there was a ten-minute delay until neighboring Engine 11 could respond and begin its suppression activities. By this time, the entire middle section of the home was fully engulfed in fire, with a large volume of flame blowing out of the living-room area. It took three engines and a dozen firefighters about twenty minutes to extinguish the fire. During the height of this operation, the fire severed power lines over the property, dropping them onto the home and a nearby chain-link fence. This charged the fence with electricity. At some point, Firefighter Robert Nowaczyk came into contact with the charged fence and was electrocuted. As happens when a person is electrocuted, he was unable to free himself from the electrified fence, and it was only after a few minutes that he collapsed and was able to free himself. He was rushed to a nearby hospital for treatment. He later recovered from his moderate injuries.

As soon as the fire was out, Fire Captain Dana Provost recognized the strong smell of gasoline in the living room and bedrooms of the home. He then spoke to Madiha, who told him the story of Grail Perkins. Captain Provost prudently secured the home and turned it over to responding sheriff's deputies for an arson investigation. They called me.

I arrived at the scene at about five in the afternoon. Seeing that I would need some expert help, I called for a photographer, an arson criminalist from the crime lab, and an accelerant K-9 from my office. After interviewing Captain Provost and the local sheriff's deputies, I spoke with Madiha. From the outset, I got a strange feeling from her. She was unemotional, which is not on its own uncommon after a tragic loss, but she also seemed to be not very forthcoming when I questioned her. She told me the story of her and Grail and the restraining order. When I began to question her about the root of their problems, she provided only vague answers. She gave no real reason for why Grail would have done this. When I began inquiring about financial and insurance issues, she became extremely evasive. She would only tell me that, despite the two of them being married and both of them purchasing the home together, the property was somehow in her name only. She explained vaguely that it had been Grail's decision to put the title in only her name.

From the start of this case until it finished a year or two later, I never felt comfortable around Madiha Fields. She seldom gave direct answers to questions and she was always vague about her past. I realized that this case was going to be a he-said-she-said problem, as there were no other adult witnesses to the event. I needed to work hard on the physical evidence to make this case.

I found two bright spots that day. The first was when I interviewed seven-year-old Danielle. Despite her youth and the traumatic circumstances, she relayed a detailed story of how Grail approached the home with a gas can, demanded entry, kicked in the door, and then went down the hallway pouring gas. Her mother had told the same story, but coming from the little girl, it seemed more truthful.

The second bright spot occurred when I conducted a neighborhood canvass for witnesses as I waited for my helpers to arrive. The neighbor to the east was a throwback to the 1950s. She was a very elderly eighty-year-old black woman who called me and everybody else "child." While she was not very mobile, and she didn't have the best vision, she had great hearing. She said she had heard screaming from the couple next door, a door breaking, and then later the sound of a car's engine revving. She then heard a very large, metallic crash followed by tires squealing. By the time she was able to get to the front door of her home, Madiha and Danielle were standing in front of their house on the street. She did not see the vehicle she had heard, but she recognized its sound as the Jeep driven by Grail. She also saw the heavy, white metal gate of the Perkins' property lying on the ground. While the case seemed fairly straight forward at this point, this woman would become a very important witness in the future.

Eventually, Det. Sylvia Faris and her accelerant K-9, Billy, arrived. I monitored while the pair worked the fire scene. Billy showed positive alerts in both of the back bedrooms and at the base of the living-room door, where Grail had been seen kicking. The investigation would reveal that the back bedrooms belonged to Madiha and Danielle. Grail actually slept in his own separate bedroom. There were no accelerant alerts in his room.

After the K-9 left the scene, I entered the structure with a photographer and Senior Criminalist Phil Teramoto, an expert on fire-scene forensics. He began processing the fire scene for physical traces of accelerants. After several hours of processing, and later a laboratory analysis, we would find that gasoline had been poured at the base of and completely around Madiha's bed. There was also gasoline at the base of her closet. The gasoline had also been poured in the room occupied by seven-year-old Danielle. The gasoline had been poured along the entire hallway leading into the bedrooms and was also found at the doorway where Grail had entered. Finally, we located a partially scorched, red gasoline can in one of the bedrooms. It appeared that it had been thrown into the room after it had been emptied.

Other evidence we wanted to examine was the doorway that Grail was alleged to have kicked in. It had sustained heavy fire damage, but we were able to piece it back together to show that it had in fact been kicked in, as it was clear the wood had been broken and splintered at the lock before the fire had damaged it. So far the physical evidence at the scene was backing up the statements made by Madiha and Danielle.

The fire damage to the house was quite severe. The entire living room and dining room were destroyed by flame. The fire appeared to originate in those areas and expand to both ends of the home. The entire home was impacted by either heavy fire damage or heavy smoke damage. Despite there being gasoline throughout the hallway and both bedrooms, the fire damage in those areas was fairly minor. We attributed this to the fact that all the windows of the home were closed, leaving insufficient oxygen in those back rooms to sustain a fire. The fires in both bedrooms had extinguished naturally. Insurance adjusters for this fire would later estimate the damage to exceed $200,000.

The one room in the home where there was no damage at all was Grail's bedroom. His door had been closed, and there was no evidence of gasoline in his room. The room suffered minor smoke damage only. A large amount of his personal property was still in this room.

The last significant piece of physical evidence at the home was the metal front gate. The family had recently installed a 250-pound, solid metal gate across their driveway. This gate was new and painted bright white. We closely examined this and saw that there were deep impact marks on the gate. One of them was consistent with the bumper of a vehicle. The others bore the circular shape and color of tire marks. It appeared that a vehicle had in fact rammed this gate and then driven over it when it was partially down. Both paint and tire rubber had been transferred onto the gate. This large gate was seized as evidence and held for analysis.

After we spent about five hours processing the scene, I sat down and looked at my evidence. The case appeared to be a domestic disturbance incident; however, the wife still gave me the creeps, and in the back of my mind I couldn't quite eliminate the possibility of an insurance job. At this time in my career

I had conducted over three-hundred arson investigations. My experience told me that the time of day for this fire was inconsistent with an insurance fraud scheme. The physical evidence at the scene also seemed to support the wife's statement. My profile of the scene made me suspect the husband. When I say "profile" I am referring to the process I used to look at a scene and ask, "Who would benefit from this fire?" In this case, all of the wife's personal property had been in the home at the time of the fire, including her jewelry, clothing, and personal papers. The gasoline was poured directly onto her personal items and into the room of her daughter. There was no gasoline poured into the room of Grail Perkins. This told me that the targets of the arson attack were both Madiha and her daughter. Finally, the boldness of the attack told me this was a crime of extreme rage and poor planning. Traditionally, most "insurance jobs" are fairly well-planned, occur late at night, and the owner usually has a thought out alibi. In the end, I determined that Grail Perkins was the most likely suspect in this fire.

That night I arranged for a "BOLO" (Be On the Look Out) on Grail Wayne Perkins and his gray Jeep. This also went to area emergency rooms, as I theorized that it was possible he may have injured himself when he ignited the explosive gasoline vapors.

What didn't come out for several days was that, immediately after starting the fire, Grail Perkins drove directly back to the Pasadena courthouse and reentered the courtroom of Judge Halevy. He entered just after four in the afternoon. A bailiff would later testify that he had asked Grail, "Why are you back? The judge has already made her decision on your case. Grail replied, "Back? I never left. I've been here the whole time." Because he still appeared highly agitated, several bailiffs were summoned to speak to him. Eventually, the judge took the bench and addressed Grail again. She too asked him why he was back in her court. He just stated, "You might as well lock me up.

I have nowhere else to go." He was eventually persuaded to leave the building.

By August 23, we still had not been able to locate Grail or his gray Jeep. That morning he made a phone call to his boss at the Bank of American in Brea. He told his boss that he would be coming in a little late for work that day. The boss, who also employed Madiha, was well aware of the fire. He called Madiha, who then called me. Worried about a workplace violence episode, and knowing that Grail owned a handgun, Madiha was ordered home, and Brea PD officers were dispatched to the bank. As the officers were meeting with the bank manager, Grail Perkins walked in as if he were reporting to work as usual. The Brea officers arrested him and found his gray Jeep in the parking lot.

I responded immediately to interview Grail at a local sheriff's station. The interview was going to be crucial to me. If Grail admitted that he was home and having a fight with Madiha but that she was the one who lit the fire, I would have some serious difficulties dealing with the information. It would be a typical he-said-she-said event. In this case, I already knew that Madiha owned the home and the insurance money would go to her, so she might have a motive to burn it. Then the entire case would hinge on the testimony of a seven-year-old girl who might be swayed to side with her mother against her step-father. This was not a clear-cut case at all.

Luckily, Grail waived his Miranda rights and demanded to tell his side of the story. First and foremost, he expressed shock and disbelief that his home had been burned. He made the huge error of claiming that he had never been there that day and didn't know anything about the event. In fact he claimed that he couldn't have been there because he was in court all afternoon. He even provided the names of the judge and bailiff as alibi witnesses.

Next, Grail went on the offensive. When he was arrested a few hours earlier, he demanded that the arresting officers bring a briefcase from his Jeep. He begged me to get the briefcase out of his jail property. I obliged him, and we went through the contents of the briefcase for about a half hour. It was some very compelling evidence. He showed me dozens of documents from welfare agencies and assistance/aid agencies in two states. He said that Madiha was committing welfare fraud, credit-card fraud, and social security fraud in various names throughout both Michigan and California. He gave me a list of the eight or more names she used. Indeed, the documents showed indications of alterations, forgery, and the use of several names similar to Madiha's. He even stated that she was somehow behind the mysterious death of a former husband and that she was illegally using his name to get more benefits. He said she was a skilled con artist and had gotten both of them master's degrees from a bogus college in Los Angeles, despite the fact that neither of them even had bachelor degrees.

Grail told me that he and Madiha had been married for two years. During that time they had agreed that he would not work but instead spend his time completing a massive renovation of the home the two had purchased. Over the past few months, she had grown more distant from him, and the two seldom engaged in sex. She began getting "preachy" and told him she didn't like his drinking and watching sports. He noticed that she kept buying items they had absolutely no use for, like snow skis, snowboards, and other sports gear that neither of them would use. He said that she was using fraudulent means to buy these items. At some point within the past two months, she came to him and told him that the home needed to be in her name only, so that she could get some sort of government loan. With this new loan, they could finish the large renovation project. Grail was worried but knew that she was very clever with money, so at some recent point in the past he had put the home solely into her name.

He said that on the eighteenth of this month they had had a very minor argument. The next day he was shocked and stunned when she filed a restraining order. He admitted to being extremely upset and felt that he was "put on the street like a dog." He soon realized that she now had full ownership of the home, as he had foolishly signed it over to her. He admitted that he felt completely duped by this woman. He admitted to me that he violated the restraining order and came back to the home on the morning of the twentieth. He wanted more of his property, and he wanted to find her briefcase that he knew contained the fraud-related documents. He then threatened to go to the police on her. Grail said that Madiha knew he had found some of her documents and that she had burned the home in an effort to destroy the remaining evidence of fraud.

The more he talked, the more I agreed that she did have a good motive to burn the home. Crime concealment has always been a motive for arson. Grail was starting to make a bit of sense. I then asked him about his second visit to the home that day, when the fire occurred. He still maintained that he had not returned to the home after the morning visit. Based on the physical evidence I had with me, I knew that Grail had been to the home. I offered a polygraph exam, and he refused and became enraged. He jumped up as if to fight me. It was at this point that his explosive temper manifested itself. Grail Perkins was obviously a man who could not control his temper. He calmed down and then immediately invoked his right to counsel. Grail Perkins would never speak to me about this case again.

I now began checking into Perkin's alibi. I went to the Pasadena court and interviewed the bailiff, Deputy Alvarado, and the clerk of court. They both clearly remembered Grail Perkins and the day in question. They said that Grail had written out a restraining order against Madiha Fields that day, which the judge denied. They said he was quite agitated and left the courthouse around two thirty in the afternoon. He returned again just before four. I drove the distance from the court to the residence and determined that Grail Perkins could easily have done this crime and returned to court by four.

I contacted the locksmith, who reiterated his story about how angry Grail had been that morning. He added that Madiha Fields had bounced the check she had given him for the work and had since refused to make good on it.

I then examined Grail's Jeep in the tow yard. The vehicle was stuffed full of suitcases and duffels with Grail's clothing and personal property. I noted that the black bumper did have impact marks and white paint on it that identically matched the marks on the white gate. I noticed that the passenger's side front tire was slightly torn and had an abrasion mark and white paint transfer on it, again consistent with the damage to the gate. Both of these items were removed from the Jeep and sent to the crime lab to be forensically compared with the gate. The Jeep was compelling evidence. It clearly showed that Grail had removed the bulk of his personal items from the home. It also showed that, without a doubt, his Jeep had been in the yard that day and had caused the damage to the gate that both Madiha and her elderly neighbor had described. There was no doubt in my mind that Grail Perkins had lied to me about being at the location.

I went to a special district attorney to file this case. This DA later interviewed both Madiha and Danielle. The DA agreed that Madiha was a less-than-credible witness, but her daughter was fine. We compared their statements with the 911 tapes and the physical evidence found at the scene: the forced door, gas in the hallway, fires in every room but Grail's, the neighbor's statement, the paint transfers on the gate and the Jeep, and Grail's very agitated state (as described by the locksmith, bailiffs, court reporter, judge, and court clerk). The DA filed seven felony counts against Grail Perkins, including two counts of both attempted murder and domestic violence, burglary, arson of an occupied structure, and terrorist threats. He was looking at about eighteen years in state prison.

The preliminary hearing was short and sweet, featuring only my testimony and young Danielle's. She stole the show when she pointed at Grail and said, "Grail, you know you burned my house." Grail was held to answer on most of the charges.

After several delays, a private defense attorney was retained by Grail Perkins, and the case finally made it to a jury trial in early 2002, over two-and-a-half years after the incident. Grail, who had gone to jail fairly youthful looking, had not done well. He had been in a few altercations with other inmates and some deputies. His black hair had turned completely gray, and he was growing angrier by the minute.

His attorney did him a huge favor. She was sort of a ditsy blonde who didn't seem organized or prepared at all. Her defense arson expert showed up to court without having read the majority of the case file, and his expertise was severely called into question by the judge. He was not allowed to testify as an arson expert, and this was a guy with over forty years of experience in the field! The defense spent a large amount of time trying to get Madiha's obvious fraud-related activities into court, but the judge ruled against them over and over again, as they had nothing to do with the fire. Finally, because the judge was so irritated with the lack of preparation and organization of the defense counsel, he (the judge) began doing the defense attorney's job and asking what should have been the defense's questions. While this was all a bit amusing, we recognized this as a serious problem. We didn't want Grail to be able to appeal the case based on poor representation.

In the end, Grail Perkins was convicted by the jury. He was sentenced to prison for a fifteen-year term for the fire. Two years later our fears came true, and an appellate court found that the judge had interceded too much in the trial. They gave Grail a new trial because of judicial misconduct. In the end, Perkins's ill-prepared defense attorney actually saved him from years in prison. A new deputy district attorney was assigned, and he couldn't have cared less about the case. He was being promoted and did not want to go through another trial. He offered Perkins (who had by now spent about five years in jail or prison) a plea deal for one felony count and a sentence of "time served." Perkins took the deal, despite continuing to proclaim his innocence, and was released from custody on the spot.

Investigator's Analysis:
Madiha Fields-Perkins, or whatever her name is at the moment, was not a sympathetic victim. She clearly was involved in a large number of scams in her life and appears to have victimized more than one man in her life. When Madiha heard that Perkins was released from jail, she was petrified and called me in a panic. She told me that she was with another man, and they had moved out of state when she heard about Grail's release from prison. By this time I knew for sure that the fraud claims against her were pretty accurate and that she had probably helped cause the fire by scamming Grail. I also found out that she had had her home repaired after the fire using the insurance proceeds. The contractor she hired to do the $100,000 plus job later told me that she had refused to pay him a large chunk of that money. It seems that she scammed a lot of men in her time and running from an angry Grail Perkins was just one of her problems.

PATRICK WILSON
LA CRESCENTA, 2000

Many people in the arson world think that arsonists are special criminals that are investigated using different methods than those used on any other crook. The reality is that there are just a few simple motives for arson, with spite/revenge being the most prevalent. Knowing this, any decent detective can investigate an arson case if they just follow time-tested police methods and stay on the trail. Arson suspects are no cleverer than any other criminal. This case will demonstrate how successful one can be when simply following the basic rules of investigation and never stopping the chase.

If you've committed a serious crime, there are just some guys you don't want chasing you. I can think of guys like Cal Fire Captain Tom Oldag or Investigator Chris Vallerga as examples. Seattle Lt. Randy Litchfield is another guy I'd hate to see in my rear view mirror after lighting a fire. There are plenty more. Detective Mike Digby is one of those guys. In early August of 2000, Detective Digby of the Los Angeles Sheriff's Department sat in a booth at the restaurant Salty's on the Columbia inside the Portland, Oregon airport. The man across from Digby was slumped over in his seat with his head buried in his arms, and he was crying softly and moaning over and over, "Why are you chasing me so hard? Why are you making this such a big deal?" While this meeting took place in Portland, Oregon, the incident that caused this meeting between detective and fleeing felon occurred three months prior and seven-hundred miles away in the foothills above Los Angeles.

The Los Angeles Sheriff's Department patrols over fifty contract cities throughout the Los Angeles basin. As the world's largest sheriff's department, it has over six million people within its policing areas. The department has over twenty-five separate patrol stations (precincts) which each have anywhere from one-hundred to three-hundred patrol deputies. Some of these stations are in the sprawling deserts and mountains above Los Angeles. Others are in more glamorous areas, such as Malibu, West Hollywood, and Marina Del Rey. Several patrol the gritty inner-city neighborhoods of South Central Los Angeles, Compton, and East Los Angeles. Many of these "fast" stations respond to a lot of in-progress shootings, assaults, murders, and robberies. The Crescenta Valley (CV) station, in the foothill area above Glendale and Burbank, is not one of these "fast" stations.

The CV station has very little violent crime, and the area is known for its excellent, placid neighborhoods and award-winning schools. Practically nothing happens in the areas patrolled by CV station sheriff's deputies. But, for some reason, at least five of the strange and bizarre stories in this book can be attributed to that very small and quiet policing area.

This case occurred very close to the area of the Gary Glazier cases in 2004. Incredibly the same businesses Gary Glazier used to purchase his arson equipment were also visited four years earlier by Patrick Wilson, and they bought the much of the same supplies.

In 1985 Sharon Bunce married Patrick Dale Wilson. They moved into a three-bedroom, two-bath home with a detached garage in the foothill community of La Crescenta. For the next fifteen years, the couple raised three children. The pair jointly ran a business out of their home called "Wilson Mechanical," for which Sharon assumed the title of president. Patrick listed himself as CEO, and the business was listed as a plumbing contractor.

Over the years the marriage began to deteriorate, with Sharon complaining that Patrick was violent and had an explosive temper. Despite the slowly deteriorating marriage, the pair made an agreement in 1995 for Patrick to "quit claim" the home over to Sharon as part of a financial gambit. With this maneuver, Sharon became the sole owner of the property. As time went on, the marriage started to dissolve further, and in February of 2000, Sharon called it quits and asked Patrick for a divorce. Patrick agreed and moved into the office behind the home. They both informally agreed to a tentative divorce settlement.

A few days later, Patrick approached Sharon with new, revised divorce terms and told her that if she didn't agree to them he would "make sure that all the money burn[ed] up." That threat caused a heated argument, and Sharon and the kids immediately moved out. She then purchased a nearby townhome in the city of Glendale, pending the divorce. For the next two months, the pair conducted a typical "cold war" through their respective attorneys. A critical point arose on April 19, 2000, when a court-appointed psychologist determined that Patrick needed some psychological counseling before he could be granted any form of child visitation rights. Just as a restraining order often has an incendiary effect on events, a child custody ruling often has similar traumatic consequences. Sharon reported that the judge had agreed with the court psychologist and ordered the suspension of Patrick's visitation rights. Sharon said she recognized that Patrick was incensed by this ruling.

Shortly after this ruling, Patrick filed a police report with the sheriff's stating that Sharon had illegally written herself a check for $12,000 out of the business account. He wanted to press charges of grand theft against her.

By mid-May Sharon, through her attorney, offered Patrick a deal in which they would sell the home. She would keep the proceeds from the home sale and let him have the business assets. She considered this a fair offer, since both items were roughly equal in value. Sharon also asked her attorney to help her obtain a restraining order against Patrick. (Uh-oh—I think we all realize by now that rage and violence soon follow the issuance of a restraining order.)

On May 25, Sharon's white Ford Aerostar was stolen from her parking spot at her townhome. She immediately suspected Patrick, as she knew he still had a key for the van. She reported this theft to the Glendale police, who immediately drove to Patrick's home. They did not find the van, nor did they locate Patrick. What they did find at Patrick's home (remember it was actually owned by Sharon, but Patrick was staying there pending the finalization of the divorce) was that massive vandalism had been done to the structure of the home. The Glendale cops immediately notified Sharon and then called Crescenta Valley sheriff's deputies to take a report of the incident.

The vandalism report taken by Deputy Michael Koch that day was quite impressive. In ten pages of written description, he noted the massive damage done to the home, which he estimated totaled at least $150,000 in losses. Among the damage listed was damage to walls, ceilings, and floors in nearly every room; major damage to the plumbing and electrical systems; and most alarmingly, damage to the main support beams in the ceiling, load-bearing walls, and basement of the home. The deputy believed these items had been cut with a chainsaw. The deputy noted that an unknown person had posted handwritten warnings stating, "Danger do not enter building," near at least two of the beams that had been cut through with a saw.

Interviews with the neighbors placed Patrick Wilson at the home just the day prior and uncovered that he had been removing major appliances from the property and driving away in his pickup. Other neighbors reported loud construction noises of within the home over the previous few weeks. Many reported that Patrick Wilson was the only person staying at the home during that period. Another neighbor would also report that she had spoken to Patrick Wilson during this time period. He told her that since his wife had left him, life hadn't been "worth it" and the he had "nothing to live for."

The next day Sharon put the home on the real-estate market. While the market was really hot for homes in the area, she knew she would not make nearly as much off of it because of the considerable damage to the home. Amazingly, her realtor had a hard offer for the home within a day. She sold the home to a buyer on May 27. The buyer immediately took possession and over the next two days the buyer began shoring up the support beams. That buyer finally left the property around sundown on May 28.

At about nine thirty in the evening on Sunday, May 28, a mother and daughter in the neighborhood were driving toward the old Wilson house. They saw a white minivan speeding away from the street. The van passed them driving erratically and sped through a stop sign. After the van had passed, they turned onto the street and saw a large amount of smoke belching from the Wilson home. They called 911. The two women would later tell detectives that the white van resembled the Wilson family's van.

Two neighbors, one of which was an off-duty firefighter, heard a muffled explosion and then saw flames coming from the garage of the home. As soon as they got closer, they saw heavy smoke coming from all areas of the home, including the area under the home. Responding county firefighters also noted flames from nearly every portion of the home and a strong smell of gasoline throughout. They requested mutual-aid support from the nearby Glendale FD. The first two firefighters on the scene were paramedics. They immediately entered the structure to determine if anyone needed rescue. The two men crawled low under a thick layer of smoke and did not notice a drawn sign that said, "Danger: unsafe." They crawled into a living room and found a pile of books laid out in a row. These books smelled of gasoline and were on fire. Had they been able to see, they would have noted that the books were various fire-protection handbooks and catalogs. The paramedics soon found a red plastic gas can on the living-room floor. At the same time, they observed with some trepidation that the home seemed to be swaying and shifting. Not finding any victims, the pair quickly exited the building. They reported the swaying structure to the on-scene chief, who had just heard the same thing from a second squad he had sent into the other side of the home. At that point, fearing an imminent collapse of the home, the battalion chief ordered all firefighters out of the home. He ruled the fire as a probable arson and called the Los Angeles Sheriff's Arson and Explosives Detail to respond.

LASD Arson Detectives Larry Lewis and Mike Digby arrived, with Digby assuming the role of lead investigator. During his initial walk-through of the scene, Digby smelled gasoline throughout the structure. He also found a bag containing fifty books of matches lying on the living room floor next to the gasoline can.

He recognized this as very common in arson cases—excessive amounts of both fuel and ignition sources. Additionally, Digby noticed the massive damage that had been done by a chainsaw on the many support beams, ceiling joists, load-bearing walls, and wall studs of the home. At one point, Digby entered a crawlspace under the home and found that someone had laid out a large amount of combustible material in a linear fashion under the home. This material included clothing, books, magazines, and cardboard boxes. This combustible "trailer" was soaked in gasoline. The stacking and arranging of combustible materials and gasoline was duplicated in all three bedrooms, the living room, the kitchen, the bathrooms, and the garage. Digby and his partners realized that not only did someone want to start a fire in the home; they in fact wanted to burn it to the ground or at the very least cause a catastrophic collapse of the structure. They recognized that this sort of arranging of the scene took significant time to complete. This overkill of preparation and planning is very consistent with a spite/revenge arson attack in which the arsonist is absolutely consumed with anger. Another peculiarity of this scene was the fact that many of the books and magazines that were part of the "trailers" were in fact publications related to a field known as fire protection engineering. The irony is that fire protection engineering is actually the science dedicated to making materials and structures in a manner that prevents the spread of fire.

In the back of the investigators' minds were the reports of some type of explosion at the scene. Based on the large amount of gasoline at the scene, the detectives were of the opinion that the witnesses heard a gasoline vapor explosion. This type of explosion occurs occasionally when arsonists are distributing large amounts of gasoline to an arson scene. As the gasoline is poured, a large volume of explosive vapors are created, and when they come into contact with an ignition source, it is not uncommon to experience a vapor explosion. The sheriff's detectives thought it possible that the arsonist in this case may well have injured himself when setting this fire. It is something that is seen every other month on the arson squad.

The detectives and their crime scene specialists spent hours processing the scene. Just to make sure, Detective Digby called in the services of the unit's accelerant K-9, Billy, and his handler, Detective Sylvia Faris. In the end all of the results were the same. The lab tests came back positive for gasoline in nearly every room of the home.

After processing the scene, Detectives Digby and Lewis spent some time interviewing Sharon Wilson. It was at this point that they got the full history of the events leading up to the fire. They noted with interest that Sharon's stolen van matched the description of the white van seen speeding away just prior to the fire. They also learned that Patrick Wilson had friends in Oregon. Lastly, Sharon viewed the handwritten warning signs found in the home and told the detectives that she recognized the writing as her husband's.

About a week after the fire, Digby returned to the burned home for further investigation. At that time he found a second red plastic five-gallon gasoline container. This one was barely recognizable, as it was heavily burned and in the debris under the home. From this the detectives concluded that at least ten gallons of gasoline had been used to set the fire. Digby also noted that both gas cans were identical and were manufactured by Rubbermaid.

At this point, Detective Digby strongly suspected Patrick Wilson of setting the fire. However, no one knew where Patrick was, and they still hadn't found Sharon's stolen white van. Digby began a lot of foot slogging to track down leads. He canvassed the entire neighborhood. He discovered that Patrick had a rental unit at a local storage facility. When he checked it out, he learned that Patrick Wilson had vacated his unit two months prior to the fire. Digby continued his footwork. Another neighbor reported that she had seen a white van pull quickly away from the curb in front of the Wilson home just moments after hearing the explosion. This witness also believed the van resembled the Wilson family's van.

The footwork continued. Detectives Digby and Rich Edwards began checking area businesses for recent sales of gas cans. They scored big when they discovered that the only store in the area that sold this brand was Orchard Supply Hardware (OSH) nearby. The manager of OSH confirmed the sale of two of the cans at 6:41 p.m. on the evening of May 28 (four hours before the fire). That same customer also purchased some other items, including a package of teriyaki beef jerky.

By mid-June, Digby had learned Patrick Wilson's credit-card numbers and written a search warrant for the purchase records of the card. Among the items of interest on these records was the purchase of a United Airlines ticket for May 28, the day of the fire. This ticket was for a one-way flight from Portland, Oregon, to Burbank.

Digby went to the airlines and found that Patrick Wilson was on the passenger manifest from Portland on May, 28. He arrived at the Burbank airport at 1:45 p.m. that day, just seven hours prior to the fire.

Additionally, the credit card showed purchases at a Jiffy Lube in the immediate area of La Crescenta. The credit-card records showed that Patrick Wilson brought his Ford truck to Jiffy Lube in La Canada on May, 25. Three days later, on May 28, he had brought in a white Ford Aerostar with the license plate 3HYK-218 to the exact same Jiffy Lube.

The credit-card purchases showed that Patrick had been using the card in Oregon in the days prior to and following the fire. He had stayed at motels and rented a storage unit in Clackamas, Oregon.

Based on this follow-up investigation, Digby determined that Patrick Wilson had established himself in Clackamas, Oregon. On

May 28, he had flown from Oregon on a one-way ticket to Burbank, only ten miles from the scene of the fire. On that same day, he had driven a stolen white van into a Jiffy Lube just a mile or two from the fire scene. On that same day, a person had made a cash purchase of two five-gallon gas cans at the OSH, just a mile from the fire scene. On the same night, three witnesses reported seeing a white van similar to the stolen van, leaving the scene of the fire. This was shaping up to be a fantastic circumstantial case.

Detective Digby also found evidence showing that Patrick Wilson had purchased a Craftsman chainsaw from OSH on May 12, 2000—two weeks prior to the fire.

By early July, a judge had reviewed the evidence and issued a warrant for the arrest of Patrick Wilson for arson and the theft of the van.

Now began the hard work. Detective Digby established a relationship with local detectives in Clackamas, Oregon. Detective Tom Dryden and Detective Kim Klusmann of the Clackamas County Sheriff's Department tracked down Patrick Wilson at his new place of employment, Interface Engineering. They arrested him on the outstanding California warrant on July 20, 2000. They learned an interesting fact from the human resources manager at the firm. She told them that Wilson had been hired in early June as a fire protection engineer for the company. On the day he first showed up to get his work identification photo taken, everybody had noticed that he had burns to his entire face that resembled very bad sunburn. He had split lips, difficulty speaking and turning his head, and his entire face had a thick coating of ointment. He would not tell other employees how he had obtained the burns. When questioned by the human resources manager, he only stated, "I did something stupid." Sadly, because of the burns, they did not take his employee photograph that day. A friend later told investigators that Wilson had told him that a catalytic converter had exploded when he was repairing it. Digby's hunch about the suspect possibly burning himself had been spot-on!

Following the arrest, the two Clackamas detectives drafted and served a search warrant at Wilson's residence in Milwaukee, Oregon. Again, dogged detective work paid off and the pair located a Craftsman chainsaw and a gun at that location. They also found a lease agreement to a local storage facility. Additionally they found a letter from Patrick to the divorce judge. This letter mentioned that his wife could "have the lot," indicating that he was giving her the property on which the house stood but not the house. He also chastised the judge for being "reckless" and "ignorant." In a letter to the judge regarding money for child support, he stated, "I will burn it before I give it to you." At the end of the letter, he gave the judge an ultimatum and signed off with a rakishly flippant, "Your choice, stranger. My best, Patrick Wilson."

On July 21, Wilson had an extradition hearing in Oregon during which he refused to be returned to California. He was incarcerated in Oregon pending a full hearing. At some point within the next few days, a local judge granted bail to Patrick Wilson, and he was free for the time being.

Meanwhile, Digby kept building his case. He went to Burbank airport and contacted the parking enforcement unit. He knew that regular patrols noted the license plates of cars at the airport on a daily basis. A computer check quickly showed that the airport parking enforcement had noted the stolen Aerostar van's plate in their lot at around two in the morning on May 27, the day after it was reported stolen to Glendale police. Because it was not a suspicious vehicle to them, they did not run its license plate but only noted it in their daily computer log. Twenty-four hours later, early on May 28, the van was still in the same spot. Later that day, the vehicle checked out of the lot, and because the driver claimed to have lost his ticket, he had to pay full fare and provide his identification. Incredibly, the airport's parking enforcement unit had Patrick Wilson's name, driver's license number, and description and license of the stolen van, all recorded as he left the airport on the afternoon of the twenty-eighth, just hours before the fire.

Digby drove to the Jiffy Lube, and while the workers did not recognize a picture of Wilson, they knew by reviewing their invoices that they had serviced the white Aerostar van at 5:00 p.m. on the twenty-eighth, just four hours before the fire.

With the Los Angeles area leads wrapping up, Digby headed north. He flew to Oregon and met with local detectives. On August 2, 2000, he and Detective Dryden drove to Wilson's storage facility where they learned he had a stored a white van. They found and inspected the white Aerostar van which had been reported stolen by Sharon Wilson. In it they found the torn remnants of a teriyaki beef jerky wrapper. It was the same brand of item that was purchased by an individual at OSH on May 28, along with the two gas cans.

On that same day, they received a phone call from Wilson. He had heard that Digby was asking about him in Oregon. He wanted to meet with the detective from Los Angeles. Wilson drove to meet with Detective Mike Digby at the Salty's restaurant in the Portland airport. Wilson showed up without an attorney and angrily confronted Digby, asking why he was taking the case so seriously and why he was he "handling it like a homicide." He couldn't understand why anyone would go to such great investigative lengths for a dispute over property. He was extremely upset that Digby referred to the home as Sharon's and not his. He also expressed his great anger about the judge's rulings on child visitation. He lamented that he was not being treated as a man and that the judge did not take him seriously. He accused his wife of having an affair and poisoning the kids' minds against him. Finally, after crying, whining, and complaining for an hour, he begrudgingly admitted that he did steal the van. He felt it was owed to him after the way the courts had treated him. Eventually, after more crying, Patrick Wilson admitted that he torched the house. He said that he felt he was being screwed by his lawyer, Sharon's lawyer, and the judge and he believed that he would not get anything after the sale of the home. He had then decided that if he wasn't going to get anything, neither was Sharon nor their lawyers. And it was with that motive that he had destroyed the home.

Every detective waits for that one satisfying moment in their case. Not the moment where the suspect says, "I did it," but the moments after when he tells you why and how he did it. These moments come in the minutes following the suspect's admission, when he finally divulges all the particular details of the crime. This is especially important during arson cases, as there is often so much damage at a fire scene that the investigators can only take their best guess as to what the exact sequence of events was. Most arson and homicide investigators crave this moment because they need that closure. They want to see how well they processed the crime scene, followed leads, and formulated an accurate theory on the crime. In this case, because of his patient interviewing skills, Digby got his closure. Patrick Wilson began to describe the entire incident in detail.

Wilson said that he took the white van from Sharon by using an old key he had. He parked it at Burbank airport, so that after he was established in Oregon, he could fly back, pick it up, and drive it north. He flew in on the twenty-eighth and drove over to his home. He saw a contractor there working on the property. He realized that Sharon had probably sold the home, and this was the final straw that sent him into a rage. He decided at that point to wait until dark and then burn the property. He went to Jiffy Lube to service the van, and then drove to the nearby OSH, where he bought the two gas cans and beef jerky. He went next door to the Shell station and purchased ten gallons of gasoline. He went to a Save-on drugstore and purchased a carton of matches and a flashlight. He then went to a nearby theater to watch the movie *Gladiator* until it got dark.

Patrick arrived at the home in the dark and parked just east of it. He entered the property with the flashlight, matches, and gas cans. He set one can outside the house and took the other to the detached garage. He poured gas all over the garage floor and walls, stepped back, and struck a match. He said there was a loud "whoosh" and the garage exploded into flame. He realized that he was way too close to the fire. Despite some injuries, Patrick picked up the other can and carried it into the home. He poured gasoline in the kitchen. He then entered the bedrooms and knocked over books and other combustibles onto the floor as kindling. He poured gasoline over these items and finally lit the house on fire with matches. By this time the fire in the garage had begun to grow large, so Patrick ran to the white van and sped off into the night. He said he drove straight through the night until he made it back to Oregon. He stopped a few times to refuel on the way.

During this admission, Patrick offered his own legal justification for the fire. He found out that the lot and the home were of equal value, which was the community property to be divided during the divorce. He rationalized, "I burned my half, the house...she got her half, the lot." He also maintained that he had been, "temporarily out of [his] mind."

Digby asked Patrick if he was now sorry that he had done this. Patrick began crying again and moaned, "You don't understand. I had no choice. I was left with no other way. Yes, I'm sorry it caused all these problems, but I had no choice." He added that he was embarrassed but not sorry. After this, Patrick broke down into some extended crying and then just got up and walked away.

Most detectives would be happy with this type of admission. Digby was not most detectives. He took the information that Patrick had given him and attempted to corroborate it. He got a copy of Patrick Wilson's Shell credit card bill for that time period. The bill, by tracking gasoline purchases, shows Patrick driving north on Interstate 5 from California to Oregon on May 26. Then on May 28 (the day of the fire), it shows a purchase of about ten gallons of gasoline from the La Crescenta Shell station across the street from the OSH. This clearly puts Patrick back in the area just prior to the fire. The next few purchases for gas were on the night of the twenty-eighth and continuing through the twenty-ninth, again at locations heading north out of Los Angeles toward the Oregon border five-hundred miles away.

Within days of the confession in Oregon, Patrick Wilson sent a bizarre letter to Detective Digby. The lengthy letter, which showed signs of being written by an intelligent and well-read (if not delusional) man, was a rambling lambasting of the justice system, police force as a whole, the prison system, and what Patrick described as his abandonment by his own family. He blamed everyone but himself for the incident and termed the fire a "nuisance," nothing more than the consequence of a man freely "start[ing] a fire that burned [his] own belongings." It was a curious attempt to make Digby feel guilty about chasing him down and filing charges against him. In the letter, he openly wondered about Digby's personal life and what he did when he was off duty to keep himself sane after spending his days in his "dogmatic pursuit of justice." In this letter, and a second letter a week later, he implored Digby to "examine" himself, as if to say that the detective and his pursuit of the case made him a mere pawn of the courts and justice system. His letter was somewhat mocking to police, and he asserted that he was not scared of them.

His letter-writing campaign did not cease there. Later in August, he sent a letter containing a lengthy quote from Shakespeare to the judge in this case. In this extremely entertaining and colorful correspondence, he expressed regret that the only severe damage to the property had been to the garage, as he had found out that the home was not completely destroyed. He said, "I see no great crime as having been committed by my actions." He described the arson attack as merely an "unlicensed fire; a community nuisance." He did express regret that there were costs associated with fighting the fire, and he offered financial restitution to settle the matter. He reminded the court that amidst the "fervor to condemn" him, officials had failed to mention that he (Patrick) had left warning signs on the property to protect people. He accused his wife of having "shameless greed," and of committing "cold treachery." He maintained that the true crimes in the case were those felonies committed by his wife. He described her acts of "hatred, disloyalty, malice, envy, stealth, and profit" as the true crimes in this matter. In this letter he boldly demanded to be charged with the more appropriate crimes of having committed an unlicensed fire or nuisance. With unmitigated gall, he attempted to set the terms of his own punishment by offering to accept probation and pay a fine.

Patrick Wilson's wife later described that Patrick had a violent side. Years ago, while in a hospital for treatment, he had suddenly reached out and begun choking a doctor. His criminal record showed an assault several years before and an additional assault on a police officer. Sharon also said that, as their marriage began to unravel, he had become somewhat of a stalker, and she frequently caught him following her as if he suspected her of seeing a boyfriend. After his arrest, he began sending their daughters letters in which he blamed her for the problems. Sharon believed that if Patrick got out of jail, her life would be in danger.

On September 28, 2000, Detective Digby took his entire case to the district attorney's office in Los Angeles. The DA filed felony counts of arson to a structure, felony vandalism, and stalking against Patrick Wilson. He was looking at about eight years in state prison if convicted.

Despite his rambling letters that attempted to legally and morally justify the arson attack, Patrick Wilson was arraigned and assigned a preliminary hearing date on October 18, 2000. On that day he showed up in court having decided for the first time to accept responsibility for his actions. He agreed to a plea deal which would give him a five-year state prison sentence. He was sentenced on November 17.

Investigator's Analysis:

Patrick Wilson's case is one of the most familiar in the arson field, and you can see that it closely mirrors a couple of other cases highlighted in this chapter. During the dissolution of a marriage or other close relationship, the suspects engaged in overt and rage-driven activity; their crimes were completely obvious and were committed with very little expectation that they would get away with it. The offenders in cases like this are so emotional and irrational at the time of the fires that they simply don't care if they are caught. In many similar cases, female offenders burn the property of a cheating spouse in direct view of many eyewitnesses, and then began taunting or bragging about the event on telephones, computers, and social media. It is not difficult at all to adjudicate these cases, as there are plenty of witnesses and a large amount of physical evidence.

Wilson took his anger to an entirely new level when he took great steps to completely obliterate the home. His actions were reckless, dangerous, and could easily have led to the deaths of one or more firefighters.

KEVIN MICHAEL PATTEN, AKA EMPEROR SCHOOL ARSONIST
SAN GABRIEL, 2006

The number one reason for arson has historically been revenge. This continues to be the trend. The most obvious cases have been highlighted so far in this chapter. They are the relationship disputes gone sideways. Failed business relationships, cheating spouses, or disgruntled former lovers are all classic preludes to spectacular fires—or at least attempts at spectacular fires. In these cases, the suspects are readily identifiable and quite often the act is committed with very little planning and very little expectation of getting away with it. In many of these fires, the act is in direct response to a recent interaction between the suspect and the victim. Since these arson attacks are very personal in nature, it is fairly easy to identify a potential suspect.

Ask the victim. They will likely know immediately who did this to them.

Revenge motivated fires have frequently been set at schools. Most of these fires occur after hours and are vandalism-related fires set in vacant classrooms, storage areas, playground, and on athletic equipment. These fires are mostly small in scale and are often accompanied by graffiti and other acts of vandalism. Typically, the fires are set using crude materials found within the target areas and include posters on the wall, spray paint cans, and books. Trashcan fires at schools are also common and are usually set during the day as a means of disrupting school. An associated prank is pulling a fire alarm when there is no actual fire. In all of these cases, the suspects are fairly easy to identify, and school officials often can point investigators to likely suspects quickly.

All of the profiles and arson wisdom in the above three paragraphs were totally useless bits of information in the Emperor School fire of 2006.

At ten minutes after eleven on the night of January 11, 2006, a large fire broke out in a classroom at the Emperor Elementary School in unincorporated San Gabriel, California. This fire burned for nearly an hour and totally destroyed three large classrooms and the building that held them. The fire department pumped over 10,000 gallons of water into the massive fire. When it was finally extinguished, the damage to the many-decades-old building was over $1million. LA Sheriff's Department Arson-Bomb Sergeant Craig Anderson was the lead investigator on the case. Several of us assisted him at various times over the next few months as the case took many twists and turns.

During the initial fire scene investigation, Sergeant Anderson summoned four other sheriff's arson investigators and an arson K-9 to help him. He also brought along three arson criminalists from the sheriff's crime lab.

The most damaged room was known as "Classroom 12." The investigators identified the tell-tale pour patterns indicative of the use of a flammable liquid as an accelerant in the classroom. This room was so badly damaged that the ceiling had mostly collapsed. The team found no fewer than three separate areas of origin within the classroom. There was no source of ignition found at the scene. Based on the scene investigation, Anderson determined that unknown suspects had forcibly entered the building, poured a liquid accelerant in several locations, and then ignited the vapors of that liquid with an open flame source, most likely a butane lighter.

A check of the campus revealed no other physical evidence, such as accelerant containers or video cameras. However, there was one particular clue that caught the eye of investigators. On another building on campus that faced the fire scene, they found fresh graffiti that was derogatory to the school principal, Ms. Kathy Perini. The phrase painted on the wall was "Perini suck my dick." While this phrase may have been expected at a junior high or high-school campus, it seemed completely out of character for an elementary school. Sensing that this graffiti may hold the clue to whomever had set the fire; Sergeant Anderson interviewed the distraught principal.

Principal Perini did in fact have a suspicion about who may have painted the graffiti and started the fire. She told investigators that she had recently been approached by a former student and his father. The former student was facing expulsion from a local high school for his role in a suspected drug deal. The school board was set to meet on this student's expulsion within a few days. The evening prior to the fire, the student and his father had approached Ms. Perini to ask her to intercede with the board on their behalf, as the son had been a good student of Perini's years before. Due to her position in the school's administration, Perini told the pair that she couldn't get involved, and both left the school visibly upset with her. Later that same evening, the board met and the student was expelled. Board members reported that the student, his friends, and his family were extremely upset by the ruling. The fire occurred less than four hours after this board meeting.

This information seemed a perfect fit to our crime scene. The fire was definitely related to a personal attack on the principal, and it appeared to be motivated by revenge. Also, the graffiti and type of arson were consistent with the behavior of a junior-high or high-school offender.

We learned through our investigation that several students had been expelled over the same drug incident. Over the next few weeks, we located and interviewed each of these expelled students to find out what they knew of the fire. The first six students denied involvement and appeared to have airtight alibis for the time of the fire. A seventh student, the one Principal Perini had originally suspected, did not have a clear-cut alibi. Worse, he had pictures of the school on fire on his cell phone! On January 24, Sergeant Anderson and I met this student and interviewed him at length. He claimed that he and his father had been upset with the principal after their meeting and that they were further upset after the boy was expelled later that same day. The male said that he and his father then left the expulsion hearing and driven several miles away to visit relatives. Later that night, around eleven, they returned to their home and happened to see smoke and flames coming from the school as they passed by. The student said that he and his father had stopped and that he had taken a picture of the flames with his cell phone. I took his phone and examined the photos. It clearly showed the Emperor School on fire just as the fire trucks were arriving. To us this was clear evidence that the student had been at the school early in the fire event. With his recent expulsion and dispute with the principal, along with this cell-phone photo of the fire in progress, we quickly zeroed in on this kid as the likely suspect in this fire. We pressed our interview for another hour, but the boy would not admit involvement in the fire. We eventually took his cell-phone information to work on further. He was released after an hour and a half of tough questioning. When we were done, we felt a little uneasy about the kid. Both of us agreed that he seemed like the suspect for this fire, but we had met a lot of people in our lives, and our guts were telling us that he was actually telling us the truth.

We continued with our investigation for several more weeks. Using cell-phone records, Sergeant Anderson was able to positively eliminate this boy and his father as suspects in this fire. Their phones showed them to be several miles away when the fire was actually first reported. We were still unsure if another family member or one of his friends had colluded to start the fire.

Over the next several weeks, we kept knocking on doors and following leads. More than one witness had reported a lone black male on a bicycle at the time of the fire. This suspect was eliminated through interviews. Another student reported that a young Hispanic male had been bragging about starting the fire. He too was located, interviewed, and then eliminated as a possible suspect. The case wore on for a few more weeks.

A registered arsonist named Clifford was reported to be in the area. He was identified, and his picture was shown to a witness. That witness said that he had been watching the school burn. Clifford, a young male, was located, but he denied ever being at the school. Sergeant Anderson asked Clifford if he would take a polygraph exam. The young male agreed. As Clifford began the exam, it was clear the he was giving very evasive answers to the polygraph examiner. The examiner began confronting him about his deceptive answers, and eventually Clifford admitted to Sergeant Anderson that he had lit the fire. Sergeant Anderson sat down and began asking specific crime scene questions of Clifford. He soon realized that Clifford could not provide him with accurate details of the scene or the fire evidence. He confronted Clifford further, and Clifford admitted that he had given a false confession. He said that he believed he would be convicted of the crime even if he didn't admit to it, because everyone knew he was an arsonist. So he decided to give a confession to something he didn't do in hopes of receiving a lesser sentence. Sergeant Anderson eventually concluded that Clifford did not set this school fire and had in fact given a false confession. He was cleared of any crime and released.

There is an old adage in police lore that if you work hard, you will be rewarded for your efforts with good luck. While not always true, it is a theory that detectives like to cling to when they face a difficult case. By late February, Sergeant Anderson and his many partners had interviewed no fewer than a dozen potential suspects, the first of which had looked guilty as hell and another had actually confessed to a crime he didn't commit. The luck just wasn't coming in this case.

Sometimes luck needs to be prodded just a little bit. In February law enforcement and a school organization agreed to post and advertise a sizable reward for information leading to an arrest in this case. This $25,000 cash award spurred immediate results. On February 20, a caller notified Anderson that the fire had been set by a male named Kevin. The caller said that Kevin was upset with the principal for an incident that happened several years earlier and that Kevin had used a Molotov cocktail to set the building on fire. The caller said that Kevin had been with two other people, named John and Kristin, on the night of the fire. This caller only knew the first names of the people involved but gave general descriptions of them. We spent the next few weeks trying to identify these people with little luck. Principal Perini was unable to recall any persons with those names.

A month later, we still were unable to locate these people. However, on March 18, a second much more detailed tip came in. This time a caller said that the arson suspect's name was Kevin Patten. Oddly, the tipster was calling from Idaho, and he reported that Patten had been bragging in a strip club that he was wanted in California for burning a school. Patten told the tipster that he had used a Molotov cocktail on the structure because he was upset with the principal. As soon as we provided his name to the principal, she immediately recognized him as a student of hers from several years before. She found it unlikely that Patten had done this, as she had not seen or heard from him in many years.

We started a detailed investigation into Kevin Patten, and we found that he did have a local address but was currently staying in Idaho. He was currently twenty-one years old and had been arrested in the past for public drunkenness, petty theft, grand theft, and grand theft auto. He was also arrested by federal authorities in 2004 for smuggling undocumented immigrants across the Mexican border. He also had a very recent arrest in Idaho for alcohol and drug possession. We were immediately intrigued, as people who set arson fires are often drunk or under the influence of narcotics. Patten looked like an excellent suspect at that point, but we still didn't have a motive. Most arson attacks are responses to recent disputes. It appeared that Patten hadn't seen this principal in several years.

By this time a third person contacted Sergeant Anderson to tell him that a girl named Kristin had been telling her friends that she had been with Kevin Patten when he set the school on fire. This last tipster directed us to the social network MySpace, on which we located a female named Kristin Wholhueter. One of her "friends" on the site was a male named John Economou. These were the two persons we believed to have been with Patten on the night of the fire.

John and Kristin eventually came in and gave us interviews about the event. They were a couple, and John was a friend of Kevin Patten. They eventually told us that John had known Kevin Patten for a while, and they often gave Kevin rides because he did not have a car. On the evening of the fire, they picked up Kevin to drive him around, drink, and party. When they arrived to pick him up, he had already been drinking, and he showed them a glass bottle with a rag sticking out of it. He said, "Let's go firebomb some cars." They refused and then he showed them some spray cans. He told them to drive him by Emperor School, as he was going to spray-paint the buildings. He said he hated Principal Perini, because she had given him bad grades years ago when she was his third-grade teacher. John had heard Kevin Patten talk about Perini several times before, and he seemed fixated on her. Patten always got upset when talking about her, and he had once said, "She needs to die."

At about nine that night, John and Kristin parked their car near the school, and Patten left the car carrying the glass bottle and the spray-paint cans. He disappeared onto the school property. About five minutes later, he ran back to the car, jumped in, and yelled, "Go!" As John sped away, he asked Kevin what had happened. Kevin said that he had thrown half of a bottle of gasoline through the windows of the school and it had started a large fire. He said he had also painted graffiti on another building on the campus. The next day Kevin called John, and he conveyed his happiness and excitement at the fire being covered on all the news channels and in the paper. He wanted John to drive him back past the school so he could see the damage and the activity. For the next few days, Kevin called John many times proclaiming that he (Kevin) would be in the history books for causing this fire. John said that Kevin had started to collect newspaper clippings of the fire and the investigation.

After that night, John and Kristin refused to meet with Kevin Patten. Both stated that he was angry, crazy, and erratic. Both were feared him and what he may do. They said that they knew he had gone to Idaho for a while but he had returned to the area.

After this interview, Sergeant Anderson began to look for Patten. He didn't have to look long or far. Patten had been arrested a day or two earlier and was in jail for stealing his mother's car. As soon as he was released on probation for that theft,

Anderson arrested him for the arson of Emperor School. He was interviewed, and Patten gave several false statements. When the investigators pressed him on his obvious lies, he invoked his right to remain silent. The interview was terminated. Kevin named his girlfriend as an alibi witness for the night of the fire. When she was interviewed, she said that Kevin was a heavy drinker and that he had long harbored a hatred for Principal Perini, as she had replaced a more popular principal years ago.

The arrest revealed one interesting tidbit about Patten. On his right upper arm, he had a Maltese cross tattoo. Coming up from this cross were drawn large, bright-orange flames about six inches in height. He obviously had an affinity for flames and fire.

Patten was convicted of auto theft on March 28, 2006. He was placed on felony probation for this crime. His arrest for arson occurred later that same day. He was additionally charged with the use of an incendiary device (firebomb). Six months later he pled guilty to both charges and received over five years in state prison. By California law, he is now an arson registrant for life. Patten was paroled fewer than five years later and was rearrested again in 2011 for drunk driving.

Investigator's Analysis:

The Emperor School fire was a bit of an oddity. Naturally, we determined that the fire was an unsophisticated and extremely juvenile event and that the suspect was likely a current student. Two students did emerge as likely suspects but were soon eliminated. In the end, we were partially right in that Patten had been a student at the school. We were shocked to learn that, at twenty-one years old, he had not been a student there for at least ten years. He had been holding a grudge and obsessing about a teacher/principal since he was about ten years old.

Another facet of this investigation really stands out. This was a heavily publicized case in the local media, and there was a good deal of pressure to get the case solved. Two excellent suspects were developed, and either one of them could have been wrongly charged had Sergeant Anderson been less diligent in his work. While both looked potentially guilty, Anderson and his partners did the very detailed work necessary to conclude that neither of the two suspects had been involved in the fire. I bring this up because most people are unaware that it is common to have suspects falsely confess in highly publicized cases, and many past investigators have actually prosecuted people who were physically incapable of committing the crime. In this case, the truth bore out, and the correct suspect was eventually identified and prosecuted. The worst things that an investigator can do are arrest and prosecute the wrong person. It is better that a case remain unsolved than an innocent person be prosecuted.

CHAPTER 6:

Isolated Idiots

This chapter details people who became involved in criminal fires for the dumbest of reasons. These people aren't freaks or fiends—they are simply morons.

JASON'S DEAD...I BURNED HIS HOUSE!
SANTA CLARITA, 2006

The Santa Clarita area is located in the northwestern end of Los Angeles County in the vicinity of the Magic Mountain amusement park. The sprawling city of Santa Clarita sits on old acreage that used to be called the Newhall Ranch. This is a foothill area surrounding a river valley and filled with all sorts of side canyons heavily choked with dark, brooding oak trees. Some of the rural canyons in this area remain dark and ominous throughout the winter and many have a lengthy history of odd occurrences. Many were often used as havens for satanic groups in the 1960s and '70s. Historically a popular site for filmmaking, the Santa Clarita valley still has two or three small movie ranches left over from its Western films heyday.

One February evening, my partner Rob Harris and I were working the night duty. Night duty is usually a pretty quiet time; we sit in the office and get caught up on reports and follow up on old cases, but occasionally something hot comes in. This particular night the phone rang, and it was sheriff's headquarters. That usually means an immediate call out to some distant part of the county. We hoped it was something interesting this time. As it turns out, it was interesting—and very odd.

HQ said that they had gotten an out-of-state phone call asking for the e-mail address of the arson investigator for the department. After the HQ guys explained to the caller that there were nine-thousand cops in the department and twenty-two arson investigators, the caller agreed to talk to whoever was on duty at the moment. HQ then confirmed who was currently on duty and gave the caller our e-mail address. Twenty minutes later, Rob and I both received the same message. It came from a guy in South Carolina, and he claimed to be an online host for a *Friday the 13th* website and chat room. We were aware that the *Friday the 13th* movie was a low-budget slasher film originally screened in 1980. Since that time, there have been at least ten sequels to the original film, and the movie and its main character have obtained cult status. The e-mailer said he knew something about an arson committed on the movie set of the *Friday the 13th* films.

Neither Rob nor I was a particularly dedicated fan of the series, and we had no idea where the movie had been filmed or what the chat-room host was referring to. The host said that he was going to forward a copy of a few chat-room boasts along with a still photo taken of what he believed to be the torching of the original structure used as the set of Jason's house in the film. Jason Voorhees is the maniac slasher featured throughout the series. Within minutes we received a chat-room thread that appeared to have come from a male. In this thread the man proclaimed, "Jason's Dead! ...We torched his house." The chatter also stated that he and some friends had burned down the set house on the original *Friday the 13th* film lot. When others in the chat room refused to believe him, he posted a digital photo of a couple of guys and a girl standing in front of a burning structure that looked like an old house. I didn't recognize the house but did see that it was raining and near dark when the photo was taken.

We ended up calling the web host and talking to him for about forty-five minutes. He assured us that he was a real expert on anything related to *Friday the 13th* (sort of like a trekkie) and that he was 100 percent sure that the house on fire was in fact the original movie set house. The host then educated us on his site, the chat room, and how many devotees contributed to the site on a weekly basis from throughout the world. We told him that we didn't even know which film studio the Voorhees home belonged to. We also speculated that the home could have been burned by the film company as part of another movie.

The site host was quick to assure us that the home had obtained cult status and was considered nearly priceless, meaning that the film company would never burn it. Within fifteen minutes he was also able to find the exact location of the Voorhees set. We were pretty impressed by his knowledge of the film. The host said that the movie set was located on a movie ranch in a dry canyon just north-east of the northern suburb of Santa Clarita. I recognized the area, as I had frequently hunted in that spot and knew there was an old western town in the vicinity. We checked all the recent fires in that area of the county and found nothing in that canyon area. We then called the local county fire station that sat near the mouth of the canyon. They had responded to no fires in the canyon in recent months. They did say that the first heavy rains of the season had passed through the area the preceding weekend.

We contacted the site host and told him our news. He insisted that more than one person was now claiming to have knowledge about the fire. He also gave us the first and last name of the chat-room poster who had made the original claim. He followed the poster's name through several other related chat rooms and nicknames to lock down a true name. Surprisingly, the poster's last name was the same as that of a fairly wealthy family in the

Santa Clarita area. We quickly ran the full name in the police computer. We found no criminal record but did find that he had just reported his pickup truck stolen that very morning at the Santa Clarita sheriff's substation. The case was starting to get a little interesting.

Rob called the local sheriff's station and spoke to a deputy who worked the more rural areas. Rob asked him to go into the canyon the next day and contact someone at the movie ranch site. The next evening we got a call from the deputy, who reported that he had driven to the remote site and spoke to the site's caretaker. The caretaker was a Mexican rancher who lived with his family in a home at the base of the movie ranch. He was not aware of any fires but went with the deputy to check the sprawling ranch property. The two passed through the various lots and went further and further up the remote canyon. The ranch was inactive during this winter and no persons had been through the lots for several weeks. When they got to the furthest remote lot, a small village, they were surprised to see the Voorhees home—or what was left of it. It was burned to the ground; very little remained over six-inches high.

Even more interesting was the fact that within about one-hundred yards of this burned structure was a Toyota four-by-four pickup mired in the mud on a trail. The deputy checked the plates on this vehicle, and lo and behold, it was registered to the same chatter who had been bragging about torching Jason's house. It was also the same truck that had been reported "stolen" by its owner within the past two days. Rob and I sped to the scene. We also had the local deputies contact the ranch's owner to ask him to meet us at the scene.

When we got to the ranch house where the caretaker lived, we could see how the arson had played out. His home was more than two miles from the movie sets, and a four-wheel drive vehicle could easily gain access to the area without the caretaker ever noticing. We entered the property in the early afternoon of a winter day. It was a pretty eerie piece of land that contained three different movie sets. The first was a small town set in the 1930s. This was followed by a very detailed Mexican/Western town of about twenty-five buildings. And finally, at the extreme end of the property and under a dense grove of large oak trees, there was the small, unpainted *Friday the 13*th set, which contained no more than four or five buildings, one of which was burned almost to its foundation.

The fire scene was simple enough to process. There was no power to the structure, and it was clear that it was nothing more than a two-story, empty façade, with heavy beams for supporting props and cameras. All of the walls and beams were collapsed into a jumble on the floor and heavily burned. The fireplace was the truth teller. It was the only thing which survived the fire. We could see several partially burned logs in the grate of the fireplace. While the fireplace was made of heavy rock and brick, we quickly saw that it was only the bottom three to four feet that were made of these materials. The rest was a façade and made of light wood. It was easy to see that someone had lit a fire in the fireplace, which was not really a functioning fireplace. The top half of the chimney had then caught fire, and it had spread to the roof of the structure. Since no fire-protection materials are used in movie sets, the fire rapidly spread, quickly burning the structure to the ground. Based on the still-smoldering ruins, the mud in the area, and other factors, we determined that this fire had occurred within the past three or four days.

The owner showed up while we were at the scene. He shook his head, stating that it was extremely common for people to trespass on this set. He said the house had obtained cult status worldwide, and he had caught people from twenty-five different countries sneaking aboard the ranch to film, take photos, or steal set pieces. He said he had chased away people performing satanic rituals, midnight weddings, and porno shoots at this site. He said the structure could be replace for under $50,000 but that the nostalgic value of the original set made it worth over $2 million.

Within the next twenty-four hours, we learned via our technical investigators which brand and model of camera had taken the photos posted on the website by the arsonists. We also learned where the owner of the truck resided. It was our opinion that this owner (a twenty-three-year-old kid) was probably a fan and an off-roader who had trespassed onto the site during a rainstorm. He had bogged down his truck in mud and had entered the set house to seek shelter. We guessed that he had probably started the fire by accident, since an arsonist would have placed the wood in some other part of the home or used an accelerant. Our belief was that this was an illegal but ultimately accidental fire and not a malicious arson. We wrote a warrant for the kid's home looking for stolen set pieces, the camera he used to take photos of the fire, his computer hard drive (from which he uploaded the photos and chatted), and finally his cell phone. His cell phone would tell us where he had been when he made calls the day of the fire.

Two days later, we served a very low-key warrant on a two-million-dollar home in Santa Clarita. The boy's mother answered the door and said that her son was not home. She seemed to be a typical wealthy suburban housewife, and we believed her—that is until we found her son hiding in his closet. When we entered his room, we found that he had "Jason" masks and a *Friday the 13th* poster hanging on the wall, as well as other paraphernalia from the film scattered throughout the room. On his desk and next to his computer, we found a digital camera of the same brand and model as the one we knew to have sent the photos to the website. By later searching his computer and cell phone, we determined that he had made several phone calls on a rainy Saturday afternoon the day before the chatter had bragged about the fire. The cell records placed him at the mouth of the canyon, within about a mile of the burned house. His computer confirmed the upload of photos and chat-room access. There were additional photos of the burning house and kids dancing in front of it on the digital camera.

The interview was a pretty one-sided affair. It took about thirteen seconds to get the kid to admit to pretty much our exact theory. He had been off-roading in the canyon and had trespassed onto the site to see the movie set. He had been drinking with a couple of friends, and they had gotten stuck in the mud. They got wet and muddy trying to push the truck out of the mire and soon entered the set house shivering and cold. Their cell phones would not work in the remote canyon, so they resolved to wait out the night in the set house. The evening chill and rain spurred them to light a fire in the fireplace, and soon the chimney caught fire and burned the house to the ground as they watched.

They knew they were in a lot of trouble, so they just "lost it" and started to laugh and dance in front of the burning house. As a lark, he snapped a few photos. Although his friends warned him to destroy the photos, our suspect, who claimed to like the movie but hate all the *Friday the 13th* geeks, put it on the website to screw with the nerds. He said he had no intention of burning the set house down. However, he said he felt like a real ass for the entire incident. Of course, filing a false report on the theft of his vehicle was yet another charge against him. The kid sheepishly admitted that once he had gotten in deep, he had tried to lie his way out, inevitably getting himself in even deeper.

We believed him and told this to the district attorney. The last we heard, the DA was pressing "negligent fire" charges against the three kids and urging their families to work out some sort of settlement prior to trial. Bottom line, the kids got probation and had to pay a pretty stiff bill.

Not exactly the most heinous arson case of the month but an interesting one nonetheless.

An Easy Out
Carrie and Big Ray, 2009

Carrie was in a lot of trouble. Everything she did only seemed to make it worse. It had seemed like such an easy way out, and now everything was getting really crazy. Carrie worried that if the cops found out what she had done, she would be living where she was now working. A few months ago it had all seemed so easy.

Carrie wasn't the sharpest tool in the shed, but her life had somehow worked itself out. She had finally landed the stable job she had always been looking for; she was now a state prison guard. Prison guards make a very handsome income, and with overtime they can easily make over $100,000 per year. Added onto this was the famously generous benefits package her union had negotiated; one way or the other, Carrie had it made!

However, in early 2009 Carrie made the same mistake as thousands of other people in California had; she made the mistake of impulsively buying a car she really didn't need. That 2009 Toyota Corolla she had purchased less than a year before had seemed like a good idea at the time. Now, however, she wished she didn't have the $500 monthly payments so she could instead invest the money into a home with her girlfriend. She also wanted to buy a Harley, so the two could cruise together. Carrie had thought about turning her Toyota back in to the dealership, but she knew that doing so would screw up her credit and ability to finance a home loan. Carrie knew from listening to coworkers talk that there was a way out of this conundrum. She knew it was illegal, but who really cared if she screwed-over an insurance company or a credit company? God knows they had screwed her over many times before. Besides, her coworkers assured her that it was easy and that several of them had already gotten away with it.

Carrie thought carefully about how she would pull it off. She needed help and knew just the guy to help her—for a small fee, of course. Carrie figured that a few hundred bucks would be money well spent if it could get her out of this mess. Carrie then made the first two of a seemingly endless number of mistakes. She got on her cell and called Big Ray to help her.

Ray was a unique guy. At six foot ten and weighing over 360 pounds, Ray was the biggest Mexican Carrie had ever seen. He was also a biker like her. Well, at least they both liked Harleys; Carrie was still saving up for one. Lastly, Ray was a gay man whom she trusted. She met him when he was bouncing at the Oasis, a gay bar in the foothills near Pomona. Carrie frequented the place a few times with her girlfriend, Christy, and she and Ray had struck up a friendship.

Ray agreed to help Carrie for the small fee of $200. The job seemed pretty easy and simple. Carrie was going to give her car keys to Ray, and he was going to drive her car out into the desert and torch it. All the while Carrie would claim that it had been stolen from in front of her home while she had been on vacation. It seemed simple enough, but Carrie was not very skilled at being a criminal. By contacting the biker, she had broken two critical rules of being a crook. One, never caper with someone else, always caper alone. As the pirates used to say, "Two people can keep a secret—if one of them is dead." Carrie's second major mistake was using her cell phone, which established a permanent electronic link between her and her co conspirator. From that point on, the mistakes seemed to crash in like a tidal wave.

On the afternoon of July 13, 2009, Carrie and her girlfriend Christy drove the Toyota and her truck from their home in Lancaster over to the Pomona area where they met up with Big Ray. He took her key for the Toyota, put a red gas can in the trunk, got in, and drove north toward the foothills. Carrie and Christy followed in Carrie's truck. Carrie started to really worry that this was a bad idea. She had never committed a crime in her life, and now that she was in law enforcement, it didn't seem like a good idea at all. Christy was even more out of her element as she was a pretty, pleasant, and innocent-looking kindergarten teacher. Neither of these two had as much as a traffic ticket on their records. Carrie's worry soon turned to a bit of panic as Ray turned up a secluded highway leading into the Lytle Creek forest area. Carrie had been in the area at a wedding just a few weeks ago, and she did not want her burned car found anywhere connected to her. She tried to call Ray on her phone, but the cell service dropped as they entered the canyon. She controlled her panic and just decided to finish this job.

It was now approaching midnight, and it was pitch dark in the canyon. She followed Big Ray about three miles before he entered a winding section of the canyon and stopped near a dry riverbed. She saw him back her car into the rocks of the river bed and get out. Ray seemed to be having lots of problems. He was struggling with the car door, and couldn't get his lighter to work. He came to her and she finally gave him some matches. He trotted back to the car to complete the task. About this time she saw another car coming down the canyon toward them, and she panicked. Carrie turned the getaway car around and parked off the road. She turned to warn Ray when she saw him pouring gasoline from the gas can. She then heard a loud boom, and within seconds, Ray came running up to her in a panic and partly on fire, and jumped into the truck. He threw the gas can into the rear, and they sped off, just in front of the approaching car. The last thing Carrie saw in her rear-view mirror was the large fire in her car start to fade and then quickly went out. She later would say that she knew at that very instant that she had made a terrible mistake and would most likely get caught.

Carrie and her girlfriend were really mad at Big Ray. The entire job had been screwed up the moment they had met up in the canyon. First, they had asked Ray to bring the car key with him. He told them it had broken in the lock. Then he couldn't get into the trunk where he had placed the gas can. Then they watched the big moron try to light a butane lighter, but it broke in his meaty hands. Finally, Carrie had to give him some matches she had in her get away truck. When he lit the fire, it exploded all over him and then almost immediately started to go out. They couldn't relight the fire because a car was coming.

    Carrie was already scared as she sped through the canyon and drove Big Ray home. She noticed that Ray was in a lot of pain after having burned himself in the explosion of gasoline vapors. Then as they got to the mouth of the canyon, she heard Ray talking on his cell phone to the Highway Patrol. He told her that he didn't want to start a wildfire in the hills so he reported the fire. When they got to his home, they found that he had moderate burn injuries and that his shirt had burned off. Finally, Carrie paid Big Ray, and she and Christy drove home to Lancaster. Carrie had a long drive home to contemplate the mistakes she had made. She just knew she wasn't going to get away with it.

    The next day she felt a little better. Carrie called the local deputies and reported her car stolen. That went fairly smooth and they didn't seem to suspect a thing. She then called her insurance man. Carrie was not so sure after her conversation with the insurance adjuster. He had asked her many questions and had even taped the phone call. That made her nervous. She thought that she would have a check in a week or so, but this guy was telling her that they had to conduct an investigation. It got worse the next day when a guy called and introduced himself as an investigator for the insurance company. He sounded like a cop and had lots of detailed questions for her. He then told her some shocking news. Her car had been found, and the ignition key had been in it. He said that someone had tried to burn the car but that there had been very little damage, leaving lots of things to print and test. Carrie became really nervous when the investigator asked her to supply him with her cell-phone records. Carrie was not aware at this point that phone companies can map out where your phone was in use just by checking out the cell towers that had been used to make the calls. Carrie was more worried about whose fingerprints they were going to find in her car.

Now Carrie was really scared, and she probably made the most devastating mistake in this entire line of mistakes. She was a prison guard and worked in the prison's administrative area, a section in which many of the smarter convicts assist. Carrie made the fateful mistake of confiding in one of these convicts about her problems. She knew that he was very skilled with a computer and could probably alter some phone records for her. Indeed, the convict was more than helpful and agreed to alter some phone records for her. The records would show her in Lancaster at the time of the fire and not in the Lytle Creek area. She then sent these records in to her insurance man via fax. He called her back and informed her that there was something drastically wrong with the records she had sent—they appeared to have been altered. Panicked, Carrie re-contacted the convict, and he made a much more skilled and authentic copy for her. This appeared to appease the insurance investigator.

The investigator scared the hell out of Carrie when he came to visit her one day. He told her that he had found fingerprints on some items in the car and was sure they could identify the arsonist. Now she really flipped out! She did not want the investigators to find Big Ray, as he would surely lead them back to her. In extreme desperation, Carrie resorted to going back to the convict at the prison for help. She confided in him her entire story and asked for his advice and help. Like all lifetime convicts, this guy knew a break when he saw one. Sure, he'd help her out and give her advice...but for a price. He then asked her to smuggle a piece of computer hardware out of the prison. He told her that he would pick it up upon his release in a few months. They would meet at a party he was going to throw when he got out of prison. Carrie foolishly agreed and smuggled the hardware out of prison.

From this point, the story gets a little difficult to believe. The convict, like all of his type, was an extremely predatory opportunist. He saw this as a prime opportunity to screw over a guard and shave months off of his sentence. He even thought he might get a financial reward from the insurance carrier. This convict knew that all law-enforcement agencies love to go after dirty cops, and he was clever enough to have made copies of everything he had faked for Carrie. As soon as he could, he took his evidence and his story to the department of internal affairs (IA) at the prison. Like all IA types (aka the Rat Squad), the people from the prison's internal affairs department were rabid to jump on the possibility of a dirty cop. The story got really juicy at this point, as the prisoner told the IA guys that Carrie wanted to hire a hit man to kill the arsonist so that the trail would not lead back to her. The prisoner said that he had agreed to help Carrie find a hit man.

They immediately called the sheriff's major crimes detectives, as they handle murder-for-hire cases, and forwarded them the convict's story. The case ended up in the lap of my old partner, Detective Dana Duncan. Dana called me at the arson unit in August of 2009 and told me this fantastic story. He said that an inmate was alleging that an on-duty state prison guard was attempting to hire a hit man to kill the arsonist-for-hire who had burned her car. I laughed when he told me the circumstances, because I was just finishing a nearly identical case. It was bad enough that the economy had the general public getting involved in an ever-increasing number of arson-for-fraud crimes, but now we had our third case in three months involving a cop. However, like all true detectives, we weren't about to believe a damn thing the convict had to say without some serious proof to back up his claims.

We had to start this investigation from the very beginning. I ran all cars belonging to Carrie and found that one had been found torched by the highway patrol in July. A 911 caller had reported the Toyota burning in Lytle Creek Canyon around midnight. The California Highway Patrol (CHP) responded, ran the plate, and found that it was registered to a Carrie Burgess in Lancaster, which was about fifty miles away. They asked the LA sheriff's in Lancaster to contact the owner and find out what had happened to the car. In the meantime they towed it to a storage yard. True to form, the "Chippy's" (highway patrol officers) did not call a fire investigator to the scene.

The sheriff's in Lancaster did not locate Carrie until the following day, when she reported that her car must have been stolen from her home while she was on vacation with her girlfriend. She filled out a stolen vehicle report and immediately reported the theft and fire to her insurance carrier. I made a phone call to my connections at the National Insurance Crime Bureau (NICB) and they located the insurance carrier for me and told me where the car was being stored. It had been picked up from a CHP tow yard and then transferred to an insurance lot, where it had sat for the last thirty-three days. I called the lot and was pleased to hear that the car had not been crushed, as it had an insurance company investigation linked to it. Through my contacts at NICB, I found the insurance investigator, a Mr. Scott, and we sat down for a long conversation to compare notes. I also conducted my usual cause-and-origin investigation for the car fire. Not surprisingly, I found that the car had been burned by someone using a liquid accelerant. What was odd was that there was almost no visible damage to the car. The car had self-extinguished and had done less than fifty-bucks' worth of damage.

There were some peculiarities about this car. First, we were unable to open the trunk, as the lever was broken. However, we could see into the trunk, because someone had forcibly pulled down the rear seat. We presumed that it had been the towing company. We could see that there had been a fire in the trunk. We couldn't find any ignition source, and lab results showed some degraded gasoline on the seats. Finally, we found the ignition key, complete with a prison-guard key fob, in the car. This key had been broken in half, and the metal blade was still stuck in the ignition.

A few days later, Major Crimes Detective Duncan and I contacted the CHP officer who had found the burning car, and we met him at the remote canyon site. The scene yielded little evidence except for a broken blue butane lighter. The CHP did say that the 911 call had come from an excited male who didn't leave his name.

After reviewing the scene, I made a phone call to Carrie Burgess. She seemed petrified and confused on the phone. I told her that I was taking over her case and that we had some promising leads. Oddly, Carrie Burgess did not seem enthused by this information.

While all of this was happening, the major crimes guys were trying to locate the alleged arsonist, as he was the supposed target of the hit man that Carrie was trying to hire. They had a positive duty to find him and warn him of the plot, even if he was an arsonist. Simultaneously, they were attempting to introduce an undercover detective, who was a master at posing as a hit man, to Carrie. Det. Dana Duncan and his undercover hit man, Det. Mike Staley made several attempts to contact Carrie through the prisoner who was trying to set up the hit. Carrie never returned the calls, and it was soon clear that she really did not want to go through with this.

After a few weeks of putting together our case, we decided to surprise Carrie Burgess with a visit. As soon as we knocked on her door, she breathed a heavy sigh and said, "I've been waiting for this day." In about five minutes she had fully confessed and even named her co conspirator, Ray. She gave us Ray's cell number and even called him on the phone while we were sitting in her kitchen. When Ray answered, Carrie told him that she was going to tell the cops about the arson scheme. We heard Ray beg her not to. She then said, "They are sitting right here, Ray. Do you want to talk to them?" We could clearly hear a loudly screamed "Nooooooooooooooo!" on the other end of the phone. Detective Duncan took the phone from Carrie and calmed Ray down, finally convincing him to meet us.

After talking to Ray, we got into specifics with Carrie. She admitted to the entire scheme except for the murder-for-hire angle. When we brought that up, she nearly passed out. It was soon clear to us that there had never been a murder-for-hire plot, just an elaborate attempt by a prisoner to set up the guard.

A few weeks later, we met up with Big Ray. He knew that Carrie had confessed and named him, and in the meantime he had been so stressed that he had lost over fifty pounds. He was nervous, sweaty, and jittery. We met him in a restaurant near his home and had an hour-long conversation. He was still massive and looked intimidating. Our interview with him was a bit more revealing. He said he had never committed a criminal act in his entire life but that being so big and mean-looking, he had found it easy to pretend that he was a real bad-ass biker. He said that he had adopted the persona working as a bouncer at a gay bar and that it helped him pick up other guys who were into that sort of thing. In reality, Ray was about the softest big guy we had ever seen.

His story did answer some questions. He said that as soon as he had agreed to the scheme he had started to panic and try to get out of it. When Carrie and Christy showed up at his house, his mind had started racing, and he started to sabotage the plan. First, he had tried to lose her while driving to Lytle Creek. When that had failed, he resigned himself to the fact that he would have to sabotage the plan at the fire scene. He knew that Carrie wanted the car key returned to her, so he broke it off in the ignition, hoping this would cause her to cancel the plan. He said that he had been so scared as he tried to open the trunk that he had broken off the lever in his massive hands. He instead had to rip the rear seat out to access the trunk, and in doing so, he had spilled gas all over the trunk. He had then pulled out a butane lighter to start the fire but was so shaky that it shattered in his oversized fingers. He had then run to Carrie, saying that the plan wasn't going to work and that he wanted to leave. He said she handed him some matches and ordered him to fulfill his part of the deal. When he struck the match, the car exploded into a fireball, and the gas can he was still carrying burst into flames. Now in a complete panic, Ray put out the gas can and burned his bare hands in the process. His shirt and hair were on fire, and he ran around like an idiot trying to put himself out.

As soon as he got into the getaway truck, Carrie and Christy had started yelling at him. He saw that the fire had almost gone out before they had even left the scene. As they were driving away, he had begun to feel badly about setting the fire, so he called 911 on his own cell phone. He said that he had just wanted to get caught and end it all right then.

In the end, Dana and I agreed that, for the most part, we only ever catch the idiots; the clever crooks get away with their crimes. This is the ultimate example of two idiots trying to pull off a sophisticated crime. Carrie lost her job, her home, her car, and was convicted of two felonies. Big Ray, in a plea agreement, got probation, but he will carry a felony record around with him forever. At least now he can truthfully say he is a real bad-ass felon.

Stalking the Badge
Larry Bailey, 2004

In 2004 Maisha was a twenty-seven-year-old woman, a college graduate, and a sheriff's deputy with the Los Angeles Sheriff's Department. A fairly new employee, she had recently graduated from the sheriff's academy and been assigned as a bailiff in the sheriff's court services bureau. Her duty assignment was Hill Street Court in downtown Los Angeles. She lived in an upscale townhome in the foothill city of Valencia, which is about thirty miles north of Los Angeles. By all accounts Maisha was an extremely pretty, educated, responsible woman who seldom partied, lived a low-risk lifestyle, and was intent on a long career in law enforcement. Her life seemed to be in good order with no problems on the horizon.

Everything changed for her on September 14, 2004, at ten o'clock at night. Maisha was alone in her townhome as usual. The large complex she lived in did not have gates, fences, or other security systems. Traditionally there had been no need for them, as this area had almost no crime to speak of. Her particular building, number 19, sat on the edge of a hill and overlooked a fast-food area known locally as "hamburger hill."

A couple of minutes before ten, Maisha heard her neighbors yelling. Soon, there was a muffled explosion just outside of her unit. Like the other three neighbors in her building, she ran outside to see three of the four vehicles in their common carport burning. Maisha was completely shocked to see that the majority of the fire was coming from the engine area of her 2001 Honda S-2000 convertible sports car. Maisha watched in horror as the fire consumed the front half of her car, along with the cars on either side of hers and the covered car port, before the firefighters could get to the scene. All in all, the car was a total loss.

The on-scene fire captain pointed out to the responding sheriff's deputies that the fire had originated in the engine area of the Honda. He found some magazine-type paper in this area and believed that someone had possibly stuffed it under the car intentionally. The local deputies spoke to Maisha, who for some odd reason did not identify herself as a fellow sheriff's deputy. They asked her if it was possible that someone could have done this to her on purpose. After a few minutes of quiet thinking, she then told them that she believed the act had been intentional and possibly related to an ex-boyfriend.

Maisha then began telling the deputies that she had dated a man named John for several years. The two had even attended

Grambling University in Louisiana together. Both had returned to California after graduation, and they had continued their relationship. At some point, their relationship fell apart, and they went their separate ways. However, she said the two had remained friends and kept in contact periodically over the months. A while ago Maisha had learned that John had started dating another very attractive girl named Nikole. Maisha had wished her ex luck and rarely heard from him over the following months. Then, for some odd reason, Maisha began receiving e-mails from Nikole, even though the two women had never met. The e-mails were taunting and vaguely threatening, and Maisha had deleted them without responding. After that, she began receiving similar but much more sinister e-mails from some guy known to her only as Justin. These e-mails were written in the same style as the ones from Nikole, but were signed "Justin." Maisha had no idea who Justin was.

Maisha later learned that her lack of response to Nikole's e-mails had had the opposite reaction than what she had intended. At some point, her ex called her and told her that Nikole hated her and talked frequently of "getting her." He explained that Nikole was insanely jealous and believed that all of John's ex-girlfriends were trying to get back together with him. John said that he had tried but could not convince Nikole that this was untrue.

Over the last month before the fire, Maisha learned that John had broken up with Nikole. At the same time, Maisha and John had attended the same party. Almost immediately after the party, Maisha had begun receiving threatening phone messages and e-mails. The e-mails and messages conveyed the message that Nikole was convinced that John was back with Maisha, and Nikole was holding Maisha responsible for her breakup. Nikole was incensed when she learned that Maisha had been at the party with John. In truth, John had moved on to another woman altogether, and Maisha did not have any sort of romantic relationship with him.

After the deputies digested this story, they began inquiring about John and ventured the theory that perhaps he had begun the fire. In response, Maisha just stated flatly, "No, he's a sheriff, just like you. He wouldn't do that." Only at the end of about a half-hour conversation with the patrol deputies did Maisha reveal that she too was a sheriff's deputy from the same department. She only revealed this fact when the deputies asked for her work address and phone number for the police report. The deputies were caught off guard by Maisha's seeming reluctance to identify herself as a fellow law-enforcement officer to them.

The next day I was notified of the event but for some reason was not told that the victim, Maisha, was a sheriff's deputy. I examined her car at the scene and found that the fire had originated in the front grille of the vehicle. The vehicle had been parked for several hours prior to the fire, so I was sure that it was not mechanical problem. I examined the grille and found that there were several rolled-up real-estate brochures and magazines stuffed into the plastic grille. There were also fast food wrappers and a bag from Jack in the Box just one-hundred yards away at the bottom of a slope. Several ketchup packages from Jack in the Box were also stuffed into the grille. I determined that an unknown suspect had stuffed these papers and food wrappers into the grille of Maisha's car and then ignited them. I walked down to the closest Jack in the Box and its neighboring Taco Bell and found a magazine rack in front of them. The magazines in the rack were the same real-estate brochures I had seen jammed into the victim's car. It was clear to me that the unknown suspect had used these available materials as kindling for the fire. Of course, the managers of the two fast-food joints had security cameras, but they were all focused on the cash drawers to prevent employee theft. None of them showed the customers or areas outside of the businesses.

I left a note on Maisha's door asking her to contact me. As I was leaving, a neighbor advised me that Maisha was a sheriff's deputy. I soon found her in the department's e-mail system and sent her a message with my contact information. She didn't call back for three days.

After three days, I called her at her work and introduced myself. She seemed extremely guarded and did not want to tell me much. She said at one point that she didn't want to get involved and that a supervisor (a sheriff's sergeant, of all people) had advised her not to speak to any investigators. I found this extremely strange behavior for a sheriff's deputy.

Eventually Maisha began to communicate with me. She also began forwarding me the messages and e-mails she had received from Nikole. The messages were all vaguely threatening, but there was nothing illegal about them. They did appear related to some ongoing dispute between the two young women over a man. Maisha also forwarded the e-mails she had received from the mysterious Justin. These e-mails were much more sinister and intimidating. When I contacted Maisha to talk about the correspondences, she told me that she had never met Nikole and wouldn't know what she looked, though her ex-boyfriend had described her as looking just like the celebrity Beyoncé. Maisha did, however, have a new piece of information. She had told her ex about the fire, and he had said that it was probably related to an odd event that had recently happened to him.

John lived in a home in the desert town of Palmdale. On September 10, just four days prior to Maisha's fire, John had been away from home at work in the Los Angeles basin. Nikole called to tell him that she was going to drop off a check for money that she owed him. John and Nikole had been dating for a couple months, and he had loaned her a good deal of money, knowing that it was unlikely she would ever pay him back. Because the two had recently broken up, he was surprised to learn that she wanted to repay him. A short time later, Nikole called him back to tell him that she had found his house broken into and ransacked. She then called the local sheriff's to come to the scene of the burglary.

Sheriff's deputies arrived to find Nikole at the home. They entered and saw that a large number of items had been taken from the home and the screens over the back windows appeared to have been cut open. When John got home to take inventory, he reported that he was missing over $25,000 worth of clothes, shoes, jewelry, guns, tools, and electronics. He was also missing a quad-runner motorcycle. The deputies later told him that they had found his abandoned quad-runner in the desert a couple miles from the home. A local sheriff's detective investigating the scene told John that it looked very suspicious, almost as if someone had staged the break-in. John told the veteran detective that he immediately suspected Nikole of having staged the entire thing as a way to get even with him for breaking up with her. He said that she used to have a key to his place, and it was entirely possible that she had made a duplicate copy.

When Maisha told John about her fire four days later, John was convinced that Nikole was involved. He said that Nikole had been obsessed with Maisha, even before he had broken up with her. He knew that Nikole had taken steps to find out where Maisha lived and what type of car she drove. John and Maisha eventually reported all of this information to the Palmdale sheriff's detective who was handling the burglary.

The fact that both John and Maisha were active-duty Los Angeles sheriff's deputies complicated the matter. Both crimes were located in the sheriff's areas and both were being investigated by sheriff's detectives. According to LASD policy, any crime that involves a sheriff's deputy as a victim, witness, or suspect requires an internal memo to be issued informing that deputy's unit commander. That commander in turn forwards a memo up the administration tree to the chief of the region. Because of this case, a whole flurry of memos were being drafted and sent. Again complicating matters was the fact that John's father was a well-respected, retired sheriff's sergeant and one or more of the guns stolen during the burglary actually belonged to him. The internal memo flurry began developing into a bigger storm. Before the end of this case, it would progress into a full-blown blizzard.

On September 15, the day after the fire and five days after the burglary, Palmdale Sheriff's Burglary Detective Dan Gordon interviewed Nikole at the LASD Palmdale station. Gordon later told me about the strange interview. He said that Nikole had come in cool, calm, and collected. He said that she was an extremely pretty and curvy girl who did in fact look quite a bit like the singer Beyoncé. Detective Gordon mentioned this to me because he felt that Nikole had been blessed with looks that would allow her to manipulate men very easily. He said that she had attempted to control the interview and vacillated between acting cool and aloof and overly flirty and suggestive. He said that she had actually showed up wearing a clingy, low-cut top and a skirt so short that the entire staff at the station had been staring at her; he also mentioned that she seemed to revel in the attention. Feeling uncomfortable, Detective Gordon called another detective in to witness the interview.

Detective Gordon said Nikole had calmly denied being involved in the burglary of John's home and the arson of Maisha's car. When Gordon had asked her where she was the night before (at the time of the fire), Nikole had said she was at her home in Lancaster which is forty miles from the fire scene. She said that she had loaned her car to a young man named Larry Bailey that night and that he did not return it to her until about eleven that evening. She even held up a cell phone so the detective could see that Bailey had called her at about that time. The interview was terminated that day, as Detective Gordon became convinced that Nikole had been at her home during the arson attack.

On September 28, Maisha called Detective Gordon with an odd story. She said that she had been working as a bailiff in her

Los Angeles courtroom on September 24 when a strange thing happened to her. A black male had called the sheriff's office in the courthouse and asked to be transferred to her court. He actually asked for her by name. When she answered the phone, she could tell that the male was attempting to disguise his voice. The male asked her what her courtroom number was. As soon as she told him, he abruptly hung up.

Three days later, she locked her courtroom doors for the lunch break. She suddenly spotted a good-looking black male in his early twenties just standing in the empty hallway outside of her court. The male was talking on a cell phone. Ninety minutes later, when she opened her courtroom doors for the afternoon session, that same male was still there. Three hours later, when she closed and locked her court for the day, he was still in the same spot.

After Maisha changed and left the courthouse at just after five that evening, she entered the employee parking lot where her mother was waiting to give her a ride home. At this time she saw the same male loitering near the exit of the employee parking lot. By this time, because of what had happened to her car two weeks earlier, Maisha was extremely concerned about her own safety. She studied the male for a few minutes and realized that he kept looking at her and then turning away. Eventually, she ran to her mother's car, and they drove away. As they drove, they saw the male walk toward and enter a white BMW. She was able to get the license plate number as she passed. A few minutes later the white BMW was following them. After a few blocks, Nicole and her mother managed to lose the BMW.

When Maisha relayed this information to Detective Gordon, he found that the car was owned by a twenty-two-year-old black male named Larry Baily. Gordon informed Maisha that Larry Bailey was Nikole's latest boyfriend. Maisha became even more convinced of Nikole's involvement in the fire and burglary, as the only person with a connection to both Larry Bailey and John was Nikole.

Detective Gordon called Nikole and began asking her questions about Larry Bailey. She denied that Bailey knew John or Maisha and dismissed the questions. However, two weeks later on October 5, Nikole called the detective demanding to speak with him again. She again showed up at the sheriff's station wearing a micro skirt and low-cut top, both even more revealing than the previous ones. Detective Gordon and a female detective interviewed Nikole. Nikole seemed irritated that a female detective was in the room. When they finally began questioning Nikole, she told them an interesting if not peculiar story. She said that a couple of days before she had been with Larry Bailey while they were visiting another guy. During that time she had heard Larry Bailey bragging to the other guy about "blowing up a car." Bailey admitted to her and this other guy that he had used a Jack in the Box bag and an apartment rental magazine to start a fire under a car.

Nikole had more. She said that a couple weeks ago, she had been in Bailey's car and happened to look into the glove box. She said she had seen a packet of personal papers including bills and letters that had John's name on them. She said she had asked Bailey where he had gotten the items and what he was going to do with them. He refused to answer her. She seemed to be indicating that Larry Bailey had burglarized John's home and burned Maisha's car.

Detective Gordon then called me with this information. As the only person who had investigated the fire scene, I confirmed that magazines and Jack in the Box wrappers had been located at the scene of the crime and confirmed that only the arson suspects would know this information. Gordon felt that Nikole's information was way too convenient and detailed, and he had a nagging feeling that Nikole was trying to manipulate the case. After hearing about Nikole, I agreed with Detective Gordon.

Nonetheless, Gordon obtained an arrest warrant for Larry Bailey. He then drove to Bailey's home and arrested him on

October 13. He learned at that time that both of Bailey's parents also worked in law enforcement. Bailey agreed to an interview and at first strenuously denied his involvement in either of the crimes. However, he was soon told that Nikole had been the one to tell the cops about him. He seemed genuinely shocked and crestfallen.

Eventually, Larry Bailey admitted to being in the same courthouse as Maisha. He told the detective that he had been there handling a traffic ticket, which was an obvious lie that fell apart under further questioning. Soon, after he realized that the detective didn't believe anything he had told him, Bailey decided to tell the truth. He admitted to Gordon that he had indeed lit Maisha's car on fire. He surprised Gordon by telling him that he did it out of love for Nikole and because Nikole had told him that Maisha was going to have him arrested for his role in the burglary.

Detective Gordon called me, and later that night I also interviewed Larry Bailey in the Palmdale jail. He repeated his admission that he had burned Maisha's car and knew it was a stupid thing to do. I wanted to get into the specifics of the case with him, but he was somewhat reluctant to do so. Bailey eventually told me that he was Nikole's new boyfriend. He was aware of her recent breakup with the deputy named John, and Nikole had also told him about John's ex, Maisha. At some point Nikole had told Bailey that John was still upset over their breakup and that she was worried that John might conspire with Maisha (both being sheriff's deputies) to set up Nikole so that she would go to jail.

Bailey denied that he had broken into John's home. He said he had learned of the event from Nikole. After the break-in, Nikole came to Bailey and said, "I heard that Maisha is telling John that you broke into his home." Despite never having met Maisha, somehow Bailey became convinced that Maisha could have him framed for the crime because of her position in law enforcement. Bailey then began telling me the story of how he had come up with the idea of starting Maisha's car on fire as a distraction so that she would forget all about him. He said he had driven around the city of Valencia until he found Maisha's car. He said he had heard a little about it in past conversations and knew it would have a Grambling University license plate frame on it, making it identifiable. He said he had stopped to get some food at a fast-food restaurant and used some of the wrappers and the bag as kindling. He said he ignited these papers with a butane lighter. After he lit the car on fire, he drove to Nikole's home and told her about it.

Bailey's story made no sense to me at all. He had never met Maisha, didn't know what she looked like, and had no idea of her address. The city of Valencia holds over 150,000 residents and dozens of massive townhome complexes. The odds of finding her or her car were astronomical. I knew that he had been given specific directions to find the location, as it was very difficult to locate, even with a map. Based on his description of the scene, I was convinced that he had been there, but I was also convinced that he had some sort of help in finding the place. He denied that anyone had assisted him.

Bailey was held in jail for trial on an arson charge. My part of the investigation was mostly over, but there was a lot more to this case. First of all, as a victim, Maisha was very difficult to deal with. She seldom acknowledged my e-mails and was extremely cautious when speaking on the phone. When I advised her of a court hearing date she needed to attend, she told me that she couldn't make it because she worked that day. I had to remind her that she was a sheriff's deputy who actually worked in a courtroom and that she should be well aware that a subpoena was not a request, it was a demand. I told her that her unit would find someone to fill in for her that day. On another day, I became somewhat exasperated with her over the phone, reminding her that three detectives had put a lot of work into her case. She replied that her supervisor (a sheriff's sergeant) had told her to avoid us and this case if at all possible. She would not explain why, and I eventually spoke to her supervisor about his strange advice.

Eventually, a preliminary court hearing was set, and the date arrived for us all to be in court. Since I had never met Maisha, I walked through the hallways looking for a twenty-six-year-old black woman in a sheriff's uniform. Since Valencia is a fairly white community, there was only one such person in the courthouse that day. However, I was convinced that she couldn't possibly be an on-duty sheriff's deputy, because she was wearing of all things a *dashiki*, a traditional African tribal dress. I was shocked to learn that this woman was in fact Maisha, and I told her that I sort of expected to see her in her sheriff's uniform or business attire. She replied that she didn't want anyone to know she was a cop and proclaimed in a very frosty manner that her *dashiki* was in fact business attire.

Maisha proved to be a bit of a puzzle. She was an exceptionally pretty young woman, who looked a bit like the pop star Brandy. However, both the DA and I tried to make small talk with her before the hearing, and she was totally uninterested in speaking to us. She acted like she was completely irritated at being called to court and spent less than two minutes talking to us. It was a very uncomfortable situation. The hearing was not eventful, and after about twenty minutes of my testimony, Larry Bailey was held over for trial. I noted that both of his parents were in attendance. Since both were in law enforcement, it must have been a very embarrassing event. After the hearing, the defense attorney approached me and said that there was a lot more to this case than was initially believed and that Bailey wanted to cooperate in a future investigation of Nikole. I agreed that something was odd about this entire event. The defense also hinted that Bailey believed Maisha's life to be in danger.

Within days of this hearing, a defense investigator approached the sheriff's major crimes team. This investigator, hired by

Bailey's parents, gave us a different and shocking bit of news. We learned that on September 23, the day prior to him being seen in Maisha's courthouse in Los Angeles, Larry Bailey's other car, a Dodge Neon, had been repossessed in another part of Los Angeles. When it was brought to the tow yard by a repossession company, they did an inventory of the car and found a loaded semiautomatic pistol in the glove box. The repo company had turned the weapon in to the Los Angeles Police Department as "found property."

The defense investigator, after interviewing Larry Bailey, learned of another witness in this case who had a compelling story. This new witness, a girl named Dee, told the defense investigator that just before his arrest, Larry Bailey had confided in her that Nikole had solicited him to murder Maisha.

After this bombshell of a statement, this case got immediate priority. The murder or attempted murder of a deputy sheriff is a huge case! These types of cases are extremely rare, and in reality there are only a handful of cops in the world capable of bringing a case like this to justice. It just so happens that the Los Angeles Sheriff's Department has one of the few squads in the world that is devoted to murder-for-hire schemes. In this instance, the case was immediately assigned to a friend of mine who worked the murder-for-hire team, Detective Dana Duncan.

Dana and his ever-present sidekick Detective Mike Staley have handled over eighty murder-for-hire schemes over the course of their stellar careers. They are extraordinarily wise in the ways of informants, snitches, and all other denizens of the underworld. They immediately leaped onto this case and gave it their full attention.

Not wanting to rely on secondhand information, Dana went out and personally interviewed this newest informant, Dee. Dee was one of Bailey's past girlfriends, but the two had remained close friends even after they split up. Dee told the detective that Larry Bailey had started dating a very beautiful girl named Nikole a few months before and that Larry was planning to marry her. Dee said that after Larry had started dating Nikole, he learned that she was extremely jealous of all of his past girlfriends. Dee had never met Nikole but she had learned that Nikole hated her just for being linked to Larry. Nikole had accused her of trying to break up her relationship with Larry Bailey. Nikole had called Dee several times on the phone and confronted her with threats and trash-talk. Dee tried in vain to explain that she and Larry were no longer romantic but just good friends. Nikole continued her threatening phone calls to Dee. At one point, Nikole drove up to Dee in a car and accused her of trying to steal Larry back. Nikole then sped at Dee in the car and attempted to run her over. Dee was just able to escape this attack, but she spent a lot of time avoiding Larry and Nikole after this event. Detective Duncan realized that her description of Nikole's behavior was almost identical to Maisha's.

Getting to the meat of the story, Dee told Detective Duncan that in September of 2004, she had met up with Larry Bailey and that he had told her about some crazy things going on. Larry confided in Dee that he had committed some serious crimes at Nikole's behest. Larry admitted that he was crazy about Nikole and would do anything to win her approval. He told Dee that Nikole had approached him and stated that her ex-boyfriend, John, had broken up with her and that she wanted to get revenge. She knew John's work schedule, and she told Larry that she wanted to break into John's home while he was at work. She demanded that Larry help her. Larry told Dee that he and Nikole went to the home and cut the back window screens to make it appear like a burglary, while in reality Nikole had a key to the front door. They then loaded up their car with clothing and electronics. Larry also said that he had attempted to steal a motorcycle-type vehicle but hadn't been able to find the key. In anger he had just pushed it way out into the desert. Larry did not disclose to Dee what they had done with the rest of John's possessions.

After the burglary, Nikole told Larry that she had been confronted by both Maisha and John. Nikole claimed that, leveraging their positions in law enforcement, the two had vigorously interrogated her and told her that they knew Larry Bailey was involved. Nikole then warned Bailey that Maisha and John had said that they would stop at nothing, include manufacturing or planting evidence, to prove a case against Larry Bailey.

Dee confided in Detective Duncan that Bailey was not the brightest bulb and in fact should have realized that most of what Nikole had told him wasn't true, but he was just too in love with her to see the truth. He became convinced that the pair would plant evidence on him and send him to prison. He became extremely distraught and panicky. That's when Nikole pushed him over the edge. She told him that it was clear that he needed to kill Maisha in order to keep from going to prison. Bailey, who had no criminal record at all, balked at the suggestion. Nikole then gave him an ultimatum: if he did not do her bidding and kill Maisha, she would end her relationship with him. When he still hesitated, she added that she would not only cut off the relationship, but she would also tell both deputies that he had burglarized John's home.

Dee continued her story to Detective Duncan. Larry told Dee that Nikole had given him specific addresses and directions to where Maisha lived and worked as well as a description of what kind of car she drove. She then ordered him to kill Maisha. After a day or so of hesitation, Larry borrowed a handgun from a friend and began stalking Maisha. He drove to her townhome and identified her car. He followed her an entire day as she drove to the courthouse to work and then back home again at the end of the day. This was a round trip of in excess of ninety miles. He did this three days in a row. On one of those days, Nikole even accompanied him to make sure he was trying hard enough to find an opportunity to kill Maisha. Larry told Dee that he had decided to try to kill Maisha as she was opening her courtroom for the day, as no one else was usually around. However, the metal detectors at the courthouse entrance finally convinced him that this was not a possibility. He then tried to intercept her in the employee parking lot. Bailey abandoned that plan when he realized there were too many other law-enforcement personnel around the lot at that time.

Larry told Dee that he did not want to go to jail for the burglary but that he just couldn't quite bring himself to kill Maisha. He decided to compromise in order to placate Nikole. He went to Maisha's house one night and torched her car. He felt that Nikole would accept this as good enough and abandon her plan to kill Maisha. He described to Dee exactly how he had torched the car (which matched his earlier statements). He then reported the deed back to Nikole, who instead of being happy was outraged. She began screaming and yelling at him, calling him a punk. Nikole then bluntly told him that if he wanted her as a girlfriend, he had to do exactly what he was ordered to do and kill Maisha. Under this ultimatum, Bailey continued to follow Maisha for a few more days after the arson attack.

Dee told Detective Duncan that Larry had let her listen to some of the voice messages from Nikole about these events, and it was clear that Larry had been telling her the truth. Larry then stunned Dee by actually showing her the gun that he was supposed to kill Maisha with. Dee described it as a silver semiautomatic pistol (which matched the description of the gun found by the repo guys in Bailey's car a few days later).

Larry also divulged to Dee that Nikole was sending threatening e-mails to people. Larry said she used the e-mail account of a man named Justin (without his knowledge). She knew that someone might report the e-mails to the police, so she designed them in a way to implicate the unknowing Justin. Nikole had made these e-mails much more intimidating and threatening than the ones she had sent from her own account.

Detective Duncan, a man who has seen dozens of wildly outrageous crime schemes, was blown away by Dee's revelations. He called me and relayed the startling story. The idea that someone was planning to assassinate a uniformed deputy sheriff while on duty in a courthouse was nothing short of earthshaking. The secretive, internal e-mails to the sheriff's brass began flowing heavily again. This case got even higher priority, if that was possible. The original arson investigation paled in comparison and became somewhat of an afterthought.

Detectives Duncan and Staley immediately went about trying to confirm this wild tale. With the defense attorney's permission, they got an interview with Larry Bailey, who was still in jail. The defense attorney and his investigator sat in on this meeting. In the presence of two major crimes detectives and his own defense team, Bailey confirmed that he had indeed stalked Maisha at the behest of Nikole. He confirmed that Nikole demanded that he kill Maisha and that she hadn't really cared how or where he did it. Bailey said that the motive for this deadly attack was nothing more than Nikole's jealousy of Maisha's relationship with John (which no longer existed). Bailey also confirmed that he had been manipulated by Nikole into believing that Maisha and John, by virtue of being sheriff's deputies, could frame him and put him in prison for his role in the burglary.

Bailey confirmed that Nikole had ridden with him in his car as he stalked Maisha and showed him where Maisha's townhome and vehicle were. Later, when Bailey couldn't work up the courage to murder Maisha, and instead opted to burn her car, Nikole had reacted violently and threatened to tell on Bailey and to have other friends of hers kill Bailey. Despite all of this, the lovelorn Bailey was still pathetically head-over-heels infatuated with Nikole!

Bailey said that after these incidents and Nikole's threats to have him killed, he had borrowed a gun to keep in his car for protection. The rest of Bailey's admission was somewhat self-serving, and he said he really was in Maisha's courtroom to help a friend with a traffic ticket, which frankly nobody believed.

While Detectives Duncan and Staley believed most of what Bailey was telling them, they also recognized that he had lied to them at certain points to minimize his own culpability. This is pretty normal stuff in the world of bad guys. However, it called his credibility as an informant in to question, thereby hurting his chances in court. However, at the end of it all, Bailey and his attorney agreed to try to assist Duncan in getting Nikole to incriminate herself. Bailey said that Nikole had wanted to visit him in jail, and he would get her to start talking about some of the stuff they had done together. Duncan and his crew would electronically monitor all of Bailey's phone calls and jail visits. Surprisingly, even the defense attorney agreed to this arrangement.

Over the next several weeks and into a few months, Bailey attempted to contact Nikole via mail, phone, and through mutual contacts. He wanted her to come to the jail to visit him or at least call him. They did make phone contact on one or two occasions, but Nikole was a lot cagier than Bailey. She spoke very professionally and calmly, wished him well, inquired about his welfare, and asked about his parents. Every time he tried to steer the conversation to the case or the past, she deflected and pretended that they had no past. She said she would come to visit him in the future and help with his defense. Listening detectives soon realized that Nikole was ten times smarter than Bailey and appeared to realize he was trying to get her incriminate herself. She was just too street wise to fall for his clumsy attempts at getting her to talk. In the end she left him twisting in the wind and never did come to visit him or assist with his defense. His poor parents lost a large chunk of their retirement savings in his defense and still ended up losing him to state prison for several years.

Despite further effort, sheriff's investigators and the defense team were never able to produce a shred of usable evidence that would lead to criminal charges against Nikole. That is not to say that Major Crimes Detective Duncan, Palmdale Burglary Detective Gordon, and I didn't believe that the curvy Nikole had absolutely used her wits and considerable charms to compel the lovesick Larry Bailey, who had no criminal record at the start of this case, to commit residential burglary, stalking, and arson, as well as plan the assassination of an on-duty peace officer. We knew she probably did all of this.

The pathetic but dangerous Larry Bailey took a plea deal that sent him to state prison for nearly eight years on the arson/stalking charges. Nikole went along her merry way, no doubt using other men and hating other women. The attractive Maisha, with her own celebrity looks, didn't last long as a sheriff's deputy, which was really no surprise to us. She left the department a couple of years later under somewhat secretive but embarrassing speculation about her own untoward activities. By 2011 she was marketing her good looks and curvy figure as a lingerie model and on a reality TV show.

After being the lead investigator on hundreds of exotic major crimes cases—including kidnappings, murder-for-hires, arson-for-hires, major extortions, and other such high level crimes—Detective Dana Duncan joined me in the arson squad in 2011. He and I are now full-time partners and working major arson cases.

Investigator's Analysis:

Most cops are well aware that criminals are fairly easy to figure out. Most bad people are motivated by a very short list of compulsions. These include money, sex, excitement, gambling, drugs, and power. Suspects can be lured into making mistakes or compromising themselves by dangling one of these things in front of them. In this case, the tantalizing Nikole lured the lovesick Larry Bailey into contemplating committing the most heinous of all crimes, despite the fact that he had never done anything wrong in his life up until that point. After seeing Nikole, we could imagine why Bailey fell for her charms. She had all the right curves, and her attitude in life was formed by the fact that she was extremely used to getting men to do her bidding and would stop at nothing to ruin or end the life of a perceived rival.

Perception is also pretty skewed in this case. Larry Bailey believed that John and Maisha, just because they were sheriff's deputies, had an amazing amount of clout. Bailey had an unreasonable view of the pair's abilities. In truth neither of them was known for their police work or law enforcement prowess. Maisha lasted fewer than five years as a deputy, and John had a lengthy history of mediocre work performance in some real backwater jobs on the department.

Since nothing really happened in this case other than the torching of a car, very few people in our large department even recall it. However, had the assassination of a uniformed deputy sheriff actually taken place, it would have been one of the most tragic and historic events in our department's history.

Strange but True

The final story of this book is my little gift to you. It isn't a story about an arsonist but rather a peculiar tale of something that once happed to an arson investigator. It's absolutely true and nearly caused me to have a heart attack. Enjoy it at my expense.

Zombie Man

The hours involved when working on the arson squad can get a little funny, and quite often we work alone. One of these times for me was Super Bowl Sunday of 2001. I was working with a partner, and we had the weekend duty. Nothing great had come in, but it was our unit's policy to try to see to as many structure fires as possible over the weekend. Sometimes ten or fifteen fires will came in over a weekend, and we always want to investigate the structure fires as soon as possible. This particular weekend, my partner and I decided to split up, each handling three or four fires alone.

I took on a handful of fires on the west side of town. Most of that area is comprised of a black and Hispanic ghetto, and the fires in this area often occur in vacant structures. This was the case on that day. I drove to a residential neighborhood located amidst a fairly rough, gang-controlled area. I was carrying my gun, of course, and my camera and notebook. In most cases, even gang members don't bother us. They recognize us as police officers and usually show some curiosity at our unusual uniforms that say "Bomb Squad" across the back. Still, we always carry guns, because we run across some pretty crazy things once in a while.

On this day, it was as deep as winter gets in Southern California. It was about forty-five degrees outside at two in the afternoon, and the streets were nearly deserted because of the Super Bowl television lineup. For my own part, I wanted to finish up fast and get home to my own party. I drove up to the address and smiled. This would be a very simple case. The location was a long-vacant, single-story apartment building of about a dozen units. I recognized this place as having been the scene of several small arson fires in the past. These events are usually small fires associated with transients cooking, warming themselves, or on occasion using drugs. As is the case with most of these buildings, there was no local owner to deal with; almost all of these rattraps are owned by a wealthy person living in another area of the state or country. This was one of those investigations that no one truly cares about, and I knew that I would be done with the scene in about twenty minutes.

Like most of these vacant-building fires, the firefighters had arrived way too soon and had extinguished the fire before it could destroy the entire building. In reality, everyone would have been happy to see it burn to the ground; the alternative being watching the partially burned building become the office of some enterprising hooker or drug dealer. Even the nozzle heads (firemen) should have known better and delayed their response enough to let the eyesore burn. Alas, like most fire calls in the Los Angeles area, the firemen get there pretty fast (generally less than seven minutes) and put things out fairly quickly.

This building suffered severe fire damage throughout all of its attached apartments, but almost all the walls were still up and some of the roof was still in place. Still, you could see that the fire was a fairly large one. I got out of my car on the deserted street and grabbed my flashlight. I walked toward the rear of the property and entered the structure through the only open door. I could see that the building had long been deserted, as many of the rooms were stripped bare and most had a large amount of debris, foodstuffs, stolen property, and other similar items scattered throughout. Also, like in most vacant buildings, gang bangers and transients had designated certain areas the toilets; these areas almost never coinciding with the actual toilets in the building. For some reason, certain bedrooms were being used as toilets, each with a pile (or splatter) of defecation in the corner. If you've seen enough of these scenes, you can tell what kind of person has been hanging out in a building by examining the debris and the "shit piles." Gangsters leave malt liquor bottles, graffiti, bullet holes, shell casings, porn stolen from liquor stores, and the occasional condom. They also leave marijuana pipes and cocaine selling paraphernalia. Gangsters usually don't use hard drugs but are more commonly the sellers of these wares. Hookers leave dirty mattresses and various articles of disgustingly cheap lingerie, along with numerous used condoms and used cocaine pipes or heroin needles and spoons. If either of these types takes a crap in a location, it is usually fairly recognizable in texture and marked by some form of toilet paper.

On the other hand, if transients use a location, you find wine bottles, cooking items, bulk stolen or donated food items, clothing, and all the various odds and ends that transients seem to collect. They also mark their defecation areas with huge runny splatters of hideous "food" concoctions they've ingested. Despite these greasy piles of fecal matter, you seldom see anything resembling toilet paper in the area. Just one of the more disgusting side notes from the street.

Because of its many rooms and large area, this particular building held a mixture of all of the above. It had been vacant for at least a year, and every denizen of the ghetto had left their mark in some manner. I knew then and there that I wasn't spending more time than was absolutely necessary at this scene—if the owner didn't care, I cared even less.

This fire had occurred around midnight the previous night, and there was still a little residual smoke and heat rising from the scene, giving it a bit of an eerie feel. I did a quick walk around to make sure no one was prowling about and that there were no attack dogs in the area, always a concern in the ghetto. Satisfied with my scan of the area, I began my search for the origin of the fire.

I followed the fire patterns where they led me and wandered through three or four of the apartments. The maze of apartments and hallways became a little confusing as the fire had destroyed the roof and a couple of inner walls. On top of this, gangsters had punched large holes in the majority of other walls, leaving them escape routes so they could easily flee the sheriff's deputies that no doubt snuck up on the building at night hoping to catch the crooks at play. It is a never-ending game of cat and mouse between the cops and the crooks in the ghetto—but that's another story.

Eventually, I got to the center rooms of this small complex and found two or three that had been really hammered by the fire. These appeared to be where the fire started. I focused my search on locating an ignition source. Because it was winter, I was well aware that it was likely this fire had been started inadvertently by a cooking or warming fire that got out of control. I entered a room and saw that the ceiling had partially collapsed and partially been pulled down by firemen. This looked like the room where the fire started, and there was a two-foot-high pile of ceiling debris on the floor. I kicked some aside and was surprised to see a shoe. Even more surprising was that I could see that a leg was attached to the shoe, and it disappeared into a pile of debris. *Uh oh!* This wouldn't be the first time I had found a dead person at a fire scene. Seeing a half-burned broom in the corner, I used it to excavate the body. Sure enough, with each sweep I uncovered more of what appeared to be a transient. He had on shoes, pants, a heavy coat, and shirt. When I exposed the man's face, I could see that it was covered with old dried blood. The man's nose was smashed, and his entire face was swollen from a beating. After he had been completely cleaned off, I was shocked to see that his head had been bashed in and was split open like a watermelon, revealing about a half-inch-wide fissure that was oozing gray brain matter. It was very clear to me that this guy hadn't died as a result of the fire but had been murdered before the fire had occurred. The fire scene now took on a different look, as I began treating it as a murder scene that someone had attempted to cover up with a fire.

Naturally, in the middle of a half-lit, still smoky, burned-out building, I was a little unnerved to find a man horribly beaten to death. I was anxious to leave and call for patrol deputies and a homicide team to deal with the murder victim. Frankly, I didn't feel like being in the building alone any longer. I was starting to get the creeps!

I went out to my car and got on the radio, asking for a patrol unit and a field sergeant to respond. I would let them start the ball rolling with the homicide detail, and I would call a backup partner to help fully process the fire scene. It looked like I wouldn't be making it to a Super Bowl party after all. As I waited for the patrol deputies to arrive, my detective sense and curiosity got the better of me, and I decided to go back in for a little better look. Wisely, I reached into my truck and pulled out a set of vinyl gloves so that I could handle things if necessary.

Going back in, I was a bit more comfortable. You have to see a lot of awful things as an investigator, but if you know what you are about to see in advance, your mind is prepared for even the worst of it—say for instance seeing dear old granny with her face burned off down to the skull because she was smoking while an oxygen mask was blowing pure oxygen from a tank into her face. It's a pretty hideous sight any way you look at it (and I've seen more than one of those), but if you know about it before you get there, well, then it's not such a shock. However, finding a guy with his noggin split open when you weren't expecting any body at all is a bit unnerving.

This time, when I entered the room, I took a good look around to make sure I wasn't disturbing any forensics. Like I said earlier, a lot of the ceiling's drywall and blown insulation was down on the floor, and it had covered most of the body and a lot of other stuff. Since, sooner or later I was going to have to assist the homicide dicks in processing the scene, I started grabbing large pieces of drywall and tossing them into the next room. It was obvious that firemen had been inside of the room to pull part of the ceiling and walls down. I couldn't figure out how the hell they could have missed the body. Although, as I occasionally glanced at him, I saw that he had very little fire damage to him. His hair was singed and there was a lot of soot and smoke residue on him, but he was visible enough that they should have spotted him.

After I removed a few pieces of the drywall, more of the victim's body became visible. I saw that someone had really beaten the shit out of this dude. One leg was obviously broken and there was a piece of shin bone protruding through his pant leg. His left arm was impossibly twisted behind him, and it was obvious that either the arm or shoulder had been broken. He had large bruises all over his head, and now I could see that blood had been flowing from his mouth, ears, and nose. Even in this cold weather, I could see a few of the bugs that always show up at fire scenes starting to gather around the gaping crevasse in his head to feast on his brains.

Finally, I uncovered a piece of evidence. Next to this guy's left leg was a red aluminum baseball bat. My keen police mind reviewed the numerous dents in the bat and the blood splatter on it and concluded that this must have been the murder weapon. I left it where I found it for the criminalists to recover. I only used the broom to sweep away the debris around it.

As I was bending over, I spotted something of interest inside the dead guy's coat. He had a large bulge and I could see a checkbook under his jacket. Again, curiosity getting the better of me, I unzipped and opened his jacket to remove the items hidden inside. Uncomfortably, I realized as I did this that my face was mere inches away from the beaten face of the victim. "Oh, well. Better him than me," I mused. There are really very few innocent parties on the street. I saw that his jacket had been hiding a wallet, checkbook, and car stereo, complete with dangling and torn wires. This guy was obviously a car burglar, and in my brief assessment of the scene I concluded that he had obviously broken into the wrong car. As I started to remove these items from the jacket for a better look, the dead guy sat bolt upright and began to moan and howl!

Like I said earlier, I had already gotten a good case of the creeps because of the unusual circumstances that had led me to this "murder victim." Now, two things happened nearly simultaneously. First, my panic meter pegged out instantaneously at eleven on a scale of ten, and I leaped to my feet like a scalded cat and began furiously backpedaling across the room. Secondly, because of my twenty years of training in law enforcement, I did what came naturally to me in a moment of pure panic, and without a conscious thought, I whipped off my vinyl glove and swept down with my right hand to feel the comfort of the hard grip of my Beretta 9mm. I yanked it smoothly from the holster and started pulling the trigger backward to the point at which the hammer was just about to drop on this....this...this zombie! As I watched in utter horror as this thing began to try to get up from the debris, the only thing my mind could think was to start shooting and make sure all sixteen rounds landed into "its" chest and head. Somewhere in my complete moment of panic, I heard a scream like that of a little girl, and it snapped me back to my senses. It was me! I'm the one who had screamed, and luckily, it had cleared my head enough to save both this guy's life and my career.

Still, I did not stop backpedaling until I was out of the room. In the hallway, I realized that I still had my pistol up and out and the hammer resting at the hair-trigger mark. Although, through both fear and a massive adrenaline dump, my hands were shaking badly, I managed somehow to ease the hammer back down and make the pistol safe. I holstered it and slowly peered around the corner at the "dead guy." I could see that he was struggling to get up from his knees. His one arm was broken so badly that it bowed out as he tried to push up. His leg was also collapsing as it too was broken. And for the love of God this guy would not stop howling. He sounded like a wounded dog, and it was really unnerving to me. Finally, I got up the courage to speak, and I yelled at him (croaked was more like it) to lie down, assuring him that I would call the paramedics. He seemed to understand and sank back to the ground.

I couldn't get back to my car fast enough. I jogged out to the street and got back on the radio. I saw now that two young black kids were hanging around my car. "Hey, police," they said, easily identifying the only white dude in the hood as a cop. These two ten-year-olds were straddling bikes next to my car. "What's up fellas?" was about all I could muster at that point. I was really trying to cool out and regain my composure before I got back on the radio. When I did, I knew I didn't sound composed as I asked for a rescue unit to my location "Code 3" (lights and siren). That brought an immediate response from area patrol cars, who also said they would be responding "Code 3" despite my not having requested them. It's odd how the cops could sense something was wrong with my voice, even though they didn't know me. That being settled, I sat down on the curb to await the rescue team and try to stop shaking.

I knew the curious kids were still around, and I was just sort of staring at my feet when I heard one of their bikes hit the street. I looked up to see one of the kids lying on the street with eyes as big as saucers staring at the building behind me. His buddy next to him was also transfixed by something behind me, only he was staring and screaming!

Once again my adrenaline spiked as I sensed danger on the street, and I jumped up and reached for my gun again. Before I could pull it out, I turned to face the unknown threat. That's when I saw a sight which will undoubtedly scar the poor lads for the rest of their young lives. The "dead guy" had somehow managed to get to his feet and find his way out of the building. Like a cross between the Mummy and a zombie, he was hobbling down the sidewalk toward us, uttering a low moan. I say he was hobbling because that is the only way I can describe a guy dragging a broken leg and flailing a broken arm aimlessly around. To complete this walking horror show, the bright daylight did nothing to diminish the visual shock presented by the mask of dried blood on his face. The last and most disturbing aspect of this whole scene was the split head with its visible brain matter and small swarm of flies hovering around it. Yes, it would be fair to say that even in this rough ghetto, these wizened ten-year-olds hadn't seen a sight as freakish and as awful as this one!

As neighbors started to come out in response to the screams, I ran to the zombie man and urged him to sit down. He complied and sat on the curb, and for the next five minutes prior to the arrival of the paramedics, he was a source of great curiosity and disgust for the people in the neighborhood, who after being grossed out and horrified themselves, nonetheless felt compelled to bring out the wife, kids, and relatives to see the sight.

When the fire department arrived, they too were taken aback by this guy's condition. It's pretty hard to shock a paramedic in the ghetto, but this specter managed it that day. The boys on the fire truck could not contain themselves and had to get the camera out for this one. Nobody had ever actually seen the brain of a living person. As they cleaned him up a little to view the actual injuries, the two paramedics soon recognized the poor guy and said, "Hey, Rene!" This guy was an apparent regular of theirs, and they knew him as a heroin addict they had responded to several times.

The really funny part was when the fire captain, no doubt completely pissed off that he had to get out of his EZ chair to deal with this guy on Super Bowl Sunday, began to chew out Rene for going into the burned building after the fire. I had to pull the captain aside and tell him that it was pretty obvious that Rene had been in that spot *before* the fire had occurred and had somehow, as only cockroaches and drug addicts can, survived the very fires of hell. Doubtful that his guys could have missed a body in this house, I had to take him back inside and show him the evidence.

Well, Rene (aka Zombie Man) got to sleep and eat in a nice clean hospital on Super Bowl Sunday, and I made it home in time for my party. Sadly, the firefighters missed the bulk of their game, instead dealing with Rene and his medical issues. We never did find out who Rene pissed off to the point that they would try to kill him. That's just another of the millions of untold mysteries of the street.

Selected Bibliography

Aldrete, R. (1998).
Case file #198-14344-0622-261,
Los Angeles: Los Angeles County Sheriff's Department.

Aldrete, R. (1998).
Case file #498-14607-0621-053,
Los Angeles: Los Angeles County Sheriff's Department.

Anderson, C. (2006).
Case file#406-00577-0587-275,
Los Angeles: Los Angeles County Sheriff's Department.

Anderson, C. (2007).
Case file#407-00280-3310-441,
Los Angeles: Los Angeles County Sheriff's Department.

Anderson, T. (2009).
Case file #009-15531-2646-011
(selected portions only related to Michael McNeil), Los Angeles: Los Angeles County Sheriff's Department.

Bartlett, D. (1998).
Case file # 098-04613-2932-053,
Los Angeles: Los Angeles County Sheriff's Department.

Briones, P. (2008).
Case file #408-80037-0986-272,
Los Angeles: Los Angeles County Sheriff's Department.

Burklow, J. (2010).
Case file #010-04800-0986-276,
Los Angeles: Los Angeles County Sheriff's Department.

Brakebush, D. (2000).
Case file #400-05851-0536-011,
Los Angeles: Los Angeles County Sheriff's Department.

Broumley, J. (2010).
Case file #910-00010-1261-242,
Los Angeles: Los Angeles County Sheriff's Department.

Cofield, M. (2009).
Case file #409-02634-1261-279,
Los Angeles: Los Angeles County Sheriff's Department.

Car Crashes at School. April, 22, 2000.
Los Angeles Times Article Collections.
http://articles.latimes.com/print/2000/apr/22/local/me-22336.

Carter, L. (1999).
Case file #199-04317-0771-399,
Los Angeles: Los Angeles County Sheriff's Department.

CBS News. (2008).
U.S.F.S. Arson Investigator Started SoCal Fires. *Firehouse.com.*
Online forum posted on 11-24-2008,
http://forums.firehouse.com/forums/showthread.php?p=1010242.

Selected Bibliography

Chandler, R. (1938)
Red Wind. Short story from *The Black Lizard Big Book of Pulps*.
Edited by Otto Penzler. Published in 2007.
Vintage. United Kingdom.

Cordero, W. (1999).
Case file #499-04318-0771-011,
Los Angeles: Los Angeles County Sheriff's Department.

Costleigh, M. & Nordskog, E. (2009).
Case file #409-00122-3310-999,
Los Angeles: Los Angeles County Sheriff's Department

Costleigh, M. & Nordskog, E. (2009).
Case file #409-03076-1263-274,
Los Angeles: Los Angeles County Sheriff's Department

Crass, T. (2010).
Case file #2010-07-0318,
Los Angeles: Los Angeles City Fire Department.

Crass, T. (2010).
Case file #2010-08-0294,
Los Angeles: Los Angeles City Fire Department.

Crass, T. (2010).
Case file #10-11-20253,
Los Angeles: Los Angeles Police Department.

Crumrine, J.P. (2008).
Another arson suspect. *Idyllwild Town Crier*.
12-11-2008. Idyllwild, Calif.

Daily News, (2009).
Man named after Greek god of fire, arrested for arson.
Dailynews.com (staff). 5/26/2009.
http://www.dailynews.com/ci_12447055?source=rss_viewed

Daily, R. (2002).
Case file #402-05022-1192-053,
Los Angeles: Los Angeles County Sheriff's Department.

Deatley, R.K. (2008).
Another suspect was looked at in Esperanza Fire probe. Retrieved from: http://www.pe.com/reports/wildfires/esperanza/stories/PE_News_Local_S_oyler22.434cb,
on 12/12/2010

Dickard, R. (2010).
Case file #10-9052,
Burbank: Burbank Police Department

Digby, M. (2000).
Case file #400-02700-0786-270,
Los Angeles: Los Angeles County Sheriff's Department.

Duncan, D. (2009).
Case file #109-01368-3420-444,
Los Angeles: Los Angeles County Sheriff's Department.

Everett, E. (2002).
Case file #402-07716-2654-279,
Los Angeles: Los Angeles County Sheriff's Department.

Friedberg, A. (1993).
Fortune Teller's Shops Hit by Arsonists' Fires.
Sun Sentinel. December 15, 1993.
Palm Beach, FL. Retrieved from: http://articles.sun-sentinel.com/1993-12-15/news/9312150181_1_similar-fire-three-arson

Gardiner, M. (1992).
Arson and the Arsonist-The need for further research.
Thesis project. Polytechnic of Central London. London

Garrett, S. (2007).
Case file #07-CACNR000033,
Oroville: California Department of Forestry and Fire Protection.

Gregory, G. (2007).
The life and death of a serial arsonist.
Newsreview.com 11-01-07.
http://www.newsreview.com/chico/content?oid=595039.

Gordon, D. (2004).
Case file #404-16449-2619-067,
Los Angeles: Los Angeles County Sheriff's Department.

Hughes, T. (2002).
Inside the Minds of Arsonists.
Los Angeles Times. September 25th, 2002. Los Angeles.

Jones, D. (2009).
Case file #109-03086-1263-217,
Los Angeles: Los Angeles County Sheriff's Department.

Hall, D. (1999).
Case file #499-02572-0628-274,
Los Angeles: Los Angeles County Sheriff's Department.

Hinchcliff, R.F. (2009).
Media Release: Serial Arsonist Sentenced.
Office of the District Attorney, Lake County. January 11, 2009.
Lakeport, CA.

Killian, W. (2000).
Case file #400-16701-0612-277,
Los Angeles: Los Angeles County Sheriff's Department.

Koch, D. (2000).
Case file #400-02669-0786-263,
Los Angeles: Los Angeles County Sheriff's Department.

Larson, E. (2008).
Authorities arrest suspected serial arsonist.
Lake County News: Friday, 09 May 2008.
Lakeport, CA. http://lakeconews.com/index2/content&do_pdf=1&id=4144

Larson, E. (2009).
Serial arsonist sentenced to 24 years in prison.
Lake County News: Monday, 12 January 2009. Lakeport CA.
http://lakeconews.com/content/view/6931/764/

Longshore, R. (2002).
Case file supplemental report dated 9-26-2002;
from Case file #000-02442-2602-011,
Los Angeles: Los Angeles County Sheriff's Department.

Selected Bibliography

Maclean, J.N. (2013).
The Esperanza Fire-Arson, Murder and the Agony of Engine 57.
Counterpoint Press. Berkley.

Marcus, G. (2000).
Case file #100-02075-0786-444,
Los Angeles: Los Angeles County Sheriff's Department.

Masiel, P. (2009).
Incident Report #2009-0069955-000,
Ventura: Ventura City Fire Department.

McNeil, M. (2007).
Request for Orders to Stop Harassment, Case Number: 46049. 2007 Nov 13; Lassen County Superior Court. Susanville, Calif.

Nordskog, E. (2000).
Case file #400-02959-2256-279,
Los Angeles: Los Angeles County Sheriff's Department.

Nordskog, E. (2000).
Case file #400-04958-2255-444,
Los Angeles: Los Angeles County Sheriff's Department.

Nordskog, E. (2000).
Case file #400-09703-2656-444,
Los Angeles: Los Angeles County Sheriff's Department.

Nordskog, E. (2004).
Case file #404-13993-0660-277,
Los Angeles: Los Angeles County Sheriff's Department.

Nordskog, E. (2011).
Case file #911-00439-3310-999,
Los Angeles: Los Angeles County Sheriff's Department.

Nordskog, E. & Yoshino, D. (2009).
Case file #609-15407-1124-091,
Los Angeles: Los Angeles County Sheriff's Department.

Oldag, T. (2007).
Case file #CNR-44 (Cunha),
Camino, California: California Department of Forestry and Fire Protection.

Portesi, D. (2000).
Case file #100-03819-2257-444,
Los Angeles: Los Angeles County Sheriff's Department.

Ressler, R. & Shachtman, T. (1992).
Whoever Fights Monsters-My twenty years tracking serial killers for the FBI. St. Martin's Press. New York.

Sanchez, J. (2010).
Case file #2010-08-0246,
Los Angeles: Los Angeles City Fire Department.

Saqui, C. (2012).
Case file #12-13134, Camarillo:
Ventura County Fire Department.

Stone, I. (1956).
Men to Match My Mountains.
Doubleday & Company. New York.

Selected Bibliography

Twain, M. (1872).
Roughing It.
American Publishing Company. Philadelphia.

Ullrich, J. (2010).
Case file #2010-09-0116,
Los Angeles: Los Angeles City Fire Department.

Watters, E. (2010).
Case file #2010-09-0028,
Los Angeles: Los Angeles City Fire Department.

Welter, G. (2007).
Alleged arsonist's motives remain vague after death. Posted in *California Fire News, 8/28/2007.*
http://calfire.blogspot.com/2007/08/alleged-arsonists-motives-remain-vague.html

White, J. (2007).
Case file #CALMU004343,
Susanville: California Department of Forestry.

Made in the USA
San Bernardino, CA
11 August 2014